PSYCHOANALYTIC FILIATIONS

The History of Psychoanalysis Series

Professor Brett Kahr and Professor Peter L. Rudnytsky (Series Editors)
Published and distributed by Karnac Books

Other titles in the Series

PSYCHOANALYTIC FILIATIONS
Mapping the Psychoanalytic Movement

Ernst Falzeder

KARNAC

First published in 2015 by
Karnac Books Ltd
118 Finchley Road
London NW3 5HT

British Library Cataloguing in Publication Data

A C.I.P. for this book is available from the British Library

ISBN-13: 978-1-78220-014-7

Typeset by V Publishing Solutions Pvt Ltd., Chennai, India

Printed in Great Britain by TJ International Ltd, Padstow, Cornwall

www.karnacbooks.com

To Marina

CONTENTS

PART V: TWO OUTSTANDING FOLLOWERS: SÁNDOR FERENCZI AND KARL ABRAHAM

EPILOGUE

ACKNOWLEDGEMENTS

"Healing through love?" was published in *Free Associations*, 1991, 2(21): 1–20.

"My grand-patient, my chief tormentor" was published in *Psychoanalytic Quarterly*, 1994, 63: 297–331.

"Ein Nachtrag zu Freuds Analyse von Elfriede Hirschfeld" was published (in German) in *Jahrbuch der Psychoanalyse*, 2010, 61: 151–152.

"The threads of psychoanalytic filiations" was published in André Haynal and Ernst Falzeder (Eds.), *100 Years of Psychoanalysis, Contributions to the History of Psychoanalysis* (169–194). Geneva: Cahiers Psychiatriques Genevois, Special Issue, 1994.

"Family tree matters" was published in *Journal of Analytical Psychology*, 1998, 32(1): 127–154.

"Profession—psychoanalyst" was published in *Psychoanalysis and History*, 2000, 2(1): 37–60.

"Whose Freud is it?" was published in *International Forum of Psychoanalysis*, 1996, 5: 77–86.

"Is there still an unknown Freud?" was published in *Psychoanalysis and History*, 2007, *9*: 201–232.

"The story of an ambivalent relationship" was published in *Journal of Analytical Psychology*, 2007, *52*(3): 343–368.

"A perfectly staged 'concerted action'" was published in *International Journal of Psychoanalysis*, 2007, *88*(5): 1223–1244.

"Freud and Jung" was published in *Jung Journal, Culture & Psyche*, Summer, 2012, *6*(3): 24–43.

"Dreaming of Freud" was published in *International Forum of Psychoanalysis*, 1996, *5*: 265–270.

"The significance of Ferenczi's clinical contributions" was published in *International Forum of Psychoanalysis*, 2004, *13*: 26–30.

"Karl Abraham" was published (in German) in Ernst Falzeder and Ludger M. Hermanns (Eds.), *Sigmund Freud/Karl Abraham. Briefwechsel 1907–1925. Vollständige Ausgabe* (7–42). Vienna: Turia + Kant, 2009.

"Karl Abraham und Sándor Ferenczi—ihre persönlichen und wissenschaftlichen Beziehungen" was published (in German) in Ágnes Berger, Franziska Henningsen, Ludger M. Hermanns and János Can Togay (Eds.), *Der psychoanalytische Aufbruch. Budapest–Berlin 1918–1920* (115–127). Frankfurt am Main: Brandes & Apsel.

"A fat wad of dirty pieces of papers" was published in John Burnham (Ed.), *After Freud Left, Centennial Reflections on His 1909 Visit to the United States* (85–109). Chicago: Chicago University Press, 2012.

Many thanks to the copyright holders for permissions to reprint those texts, and special thanks to my co-authors John Burnham, André Haynal, and Ludger M. Hermanns for kindly agreeing to have our joint pieces published in this collection. It was a great pleasure and honour, and often much fun, to work with you.

* * *

It is impossible to list all the persons who have helped me, in the most various ways, over the course of the years. As a matter of fact, I started out with five pages of thanks, only to realise that so many names were still missing. I can only offer my sincerest apologies to those who do not find their names here. You can be sure that I treasure your help, support, and, perhaps most valuably, your criticism.

I am greatly indebted to my teachers Igor A. Caruso, Ernest Borneman, and Sepp Schindler at the University of Salzburg, now all deceased. It was an exciting time to study there in the 1970s and early 1980s, and to have such utterly different teachers, each charismatic in his own way.

The course my scientific career took after my graduation is unthinkable without two outstanding scholars and friends, André Haynal and Sonu Shamdasani. Dear André, András bácsi, you know how much I am indebted to you, and in more ways than can be mentioned here. Thank you. Dear Sonu, you are such a fine scholar, and a true friend, who was there when I needed it most. Thank you.

A quite special thanks to four quite special women who each went part of the way with me: Gerti Wolkerstorfer Falzeder, Ulli Erhart, Caroline Schwarzacher Joyce, and Marina Leitner-Dorchi Sherpa. *Tempora mutantur, nos et mutamur in illis* ... Thanks to my sisters, Eva Eckmair and Ilse Holzinger, and to Lakpa Dorchi Sherpa, a fine and unique specimen.

My children, Florian Falzeder and Eva Erhart, can and should be extremely proud of themselves. Perhaps I am permitted to share, by proxy, some of that proudness.

Thanks to Brett Kahr and Peter Rudnytsky, editors of this series, esteemed colleagues and renowned scholars in their own right, for having invited me to publish this selection of texts, and for having been always there in the sometimes difficult and delayed making of this book; to Oliver Rathbone, managing director at Karnac; to Rod Tweedy, my direct contact partner there in the initial stage; and to Kate Pearce, project manager at Karnac, who was always super-efficient and supportive.

And, finally, Marina Leitner-Dorchi Sherpa, to whom this book is dedicated. I'll do a Wittgenstein on her.

ABOUT THE AUTHOR

Ernst Falzeder, PhD, is a senior research fellow at the University College London, and editor and translator for the Philemon Foundation of the publication of the Complete Works of C. G. Jung. He is a former research fellow at the University of Geneva, as well as Cornell University Medical School (NYC), and Harvard University (Cambridge, MA). He was chief editor of the Freud/Ferenczi correspondence (3 vols., Harvard University Press), editor of the complete Freud/Abraham letters (Karnac), translator of Jung's seminar on children's dreams (Princeton University Press), and editor, with John Beebe, as well as translator of Jung's correspondence with Hans Schmid (Princeton University Press). He has also written more than two hundred publications on the history, theory, and technique of psychoanalysis and analytical psychology.

SERIES EDITOR'S FOREWORD

The field of psychoanalysis brims with some of the most riveting, the most memorable, and the most belief-defying of case histories.

Even rudimentary students cannot fail to marvel at Josef Breuer's extraordinary treatment of "Fräulein Anna O.", a young woman whose hysterical symptoms seemed to disappear simply through conversation; or at Sigmund Freud's analysis of the so-called "Rat Man", a young Viennese neurotic gripped by seemingly bizarre obsessional thoughts and rituals which crippled his life. And who could not be captivated by Melanie Klein's case history of little "Richard", whose child analysis revealed untold depths of savagery in his tiny mind; or by Donald Winnicott's work with the little girl known as "The Piggle", who struggled to welcome a baby sister into her family.

Theatrical and unforgettable as these classic clinical case reports may be, they really do pale in comparison when one studies the most dramatic, edge-of-one's-seat case history of all, namely, *the history of the psychoanalytical movement itself*.

When one considers Sigmund Freud's penchant for assassinating his one-time devoted followers such as Wilhelm Stekel and Alfred Adler; when one reads through accounts of sexual impropriety between psychoanalysts and their patients, such as Carl Gustav Jung's seduction of

Sabina Spielrein, a troubled young Russian woman who later became a medical practitioner in her own right; when one discovers the sheer number of analysts, including Freud and Klein and many others besides, who psychoanalysed their own children; when one reads the list of ostensibly well-analysed Freudian adherents who committed suicide whether by ingesting tablets, or, in the case of Viktor Tausk, by both hanging and shooting himself simultaneously, one comes to appreciate that the reports about the actual patients seem almost banal by contrast.

Of course, it would be far too easy to choose salacious moments from the lives of our psychoanalytical forefathers and foremothers and then transform them into heightened entertainment, as illustrated by the recent film about the Freud-Jung-Spielrein interrelationships, *A Dangerous Method*, directed by David Cronenberg. But the fact remains that our field does seethe with heightened proscenium-arch tragedy, approaching, at times, a Greek epic.

And few scholars have documented this often chilling, often heart-wrenching, often startling history as well as Dr. Ernst Falzeder. Although it would be easy to render this history into something journalistic or filmic, Falzeder has, over more than thirty years, succeeded in capturing and communicating these compelling stories in a sober, responsible, and professional manner, and has, moreover, done so in graceful, engaging language, which allows the reader to learn … and to want to learn more. Furthermore, Falzeder uses the compelling raw data of the early machinations of Freud and his circle not only to paint an evocative and carefully researched portrait of these chapters of clinical and intellectual history but, also, with much wisdom, he explores the origins of the drama, and expounds upon the highly pertinent implications of these events and processes for contemporary clinical psychoanalytical and psychotherapeutic practice.

Falzeder has collected some of his most engaging papers and has woven them into a tightly knit narrative which brings the history of psychoanalysis to life in a vibrant and often disturbing manner. Throughout his publications, Falzeder raises some rather crucial and oftentimes provocative questions about the nature of psychoanalysis, both ancient and modern. For instance, he challenges forcefully the notion that only the "mad" early psychoanalysts in the 1900s and 1910s engaged in technical experiments, until the invention of "classical" technique in the 1920s, demonstrating that, in point of fact, clinical practice has continued to develop again and again, so much so that even the couch—that ultimate icon of classicism—has, in recent years, become suspect in certain quarters. Indeed, nowadays, one regularly encounters modern "relational" psychoanalysts who do not use the Freudian couch at all in their clinical work with patients, as they find the divan far too distancing and hierarchical. We must wonder, therefore, as practitioners, whether our classical technique has truly "evolved", or whether many clinicians might still be engaged in wild experimentation. And who should decide whether certain furnishings—our couches and our chairs—represent good classical technique or, by contrast, retrogressive kitsch, or daring innovation?

In similar questioning vein, Falzeder invites us to review the many evident clinical failures in the early history of psychoanalysis—often quite outrageous ones, as in the multiple, disastrous, interrupted psychoanalyses of Elfriede Hirschfeld, whose case, long since buried, Falzeder had uncovered. In truly open spirit, Falzeder encourages us to regard these failures from the early days of psychoanalysis not as sources of shame to be kept hidden as Anna Freud and other early editors of Freud's letters and papers had done but, rather, as rare opportunities to learn from our ancestral mistakes.

Most disconcerting of all, Falzeder allows us to reconsider the way in which once-heretical ideas within psychoanalysis have become silently incorporated into the mainstream, as well as the way in which old shibboleths—once beyond question—have now disappeared entirely from clinical view.

Sometimes, Dr. Falzeder even dares to tackle some of the mythologies about psychoanalysis which seem so deeply entrenched in our shared consciousness that only a fool would challenge them. To cite but one memorable example from this book, Falzeder bravely questions whether Freud's break with Jung (or, indeed, Jung's break with Freud), deserves its status as the most important split of the last one hundred years or more, as most of us have long assumed. Falzeder, a specialist in restoring the marginalised to their proper place within historical discourse, has argued—quite convincingly, in my view—that Freud's falling out with Professor Eugen Bleuler, Jung's sometime "boss" at the Burghölzli asylum, has had much *more* radical, much *more* devastating institutional consequences for the history of psychoanalysis than the split with Jung. Eugen Bleuler, one of the most profoundly influential Continental psychiatrists of all time, known, *inter alia*, for coining seminal diagnostic entities such as *Schizophrenie* [schizophrenia], had once embraced Freud and psychoanalysis, but then withdrew much of his support and endorsement. In doing so, Bleuler thus left Freud and the other psychoanalysts dangling precariously outside the more conventional psychiatric establishments and universities in consequence; and to this day, the reverberations of Bleuler's decathexis still rankle as modern psychoanalysts desperately scrabble to make links with institutions of higher learning, although some might argue that any success in this arena has come rather late in the day!

Additionally, I cannot resist foregrounding another of Ernst Falzeder's many historical *aperçus*, namely, his recognition that two of the most influential figures in the history of psychoanalytical education—arguably *the* two *most* influential figures—namely Max Eitingon and Hanns Sachs, the architects of the world's first formal psychoanalytical training programme, had had *no* personal psychoanalysis of their own. Of course, Falzeder acknowledges, but refuses to count seriously, Eitingon's handful of strolls through the streets with Freud as evidence that he had undergone a training analysis. Falzeder argues that Eitingon, like Sachs, had had essentially no formal training whatsoever. Furthermore, as Falzeder has noted, the educational initiatives spearheaded in Berlin under the leadership of Eitingon and Sachs had received hearty approval from the president of the Berliner Psychoanalytische Gesellschaft [Berlin Psycho-Analytical Society], the venerable Karl Abraham, who also had never had a day of personal psychoanalysis in his life. What then, might we make of the fact that none of the principal architects of contemporary psychoanalytical training had themselves had a single taste of the curriculum itself? Can we dismiss this as a necessary evil that sometimes befalls founders, or can we dare to think through the more subversive implications of this historical information, as Falzeder encourages us to do?

Ernst Falzeder began publishing psychoanalytical papers during the mid-1980s, and since that time, he has produced a steady, coherent, body of work, and happily, shows no signs of slowing down. But Falzeder not only writes historical papers, he also possesses a great number of other skills and capacities as an archivist, as an oral history interviewer, as an editor, as a translator, as a bibliographer, as a compositor, and as a teacher. Not only has Dr. Falzeder authored a wonderful series of books and papers, but he will also be well known to psychological practitioners and to historians alike for his work as an editor of the much-lauded scholarly editions of Freud's correspondence with the German psychoanalyst Karl Abraham and with the Hungarian psycho-analyst Sándor Ferenczi, not to mention Falzeder's further work as a translator of correspondence by, and seminars with, Carl Gustav Jung. Dr. Falzeder's admirable facility as a linguist has allowed him to study the widest possible range of documents in the greatest possible detail. And his thoroughness as an historian has permitted him to correct the errors enshrined by other less scrupulous scholars in so many previous versions of these histories; hence, Falzeder has succeeded in offering us a much more reliable, much more accurate description of events.

We take great pleasure in publishing Ernst Falzeder's current col-lection of essays, *Psychoanalytic Filiations: Mapping the Psychoanalytic Movement*. The fifteen chapters contained within these covers, mostly singly-authored (with three essays co-written by John Burnham, André Haynal, and Ludger Hermanns), have all appeared in print elsewhere but not, alas, always in readily accessible periodicals, or in English lan-guage versions. It seems quite fitting that scholars of psychoanalysis should at last have one compact volume of *Falzederiana*, handsomely bound together in one spine, and written in one language. Old-timers will have the joy of re-reading these now classics essays, many of which have the added benefit of supplementary material, updating the sto-ries in certain cases; whereas newcomers will find themselves treated to a master class in the works of Freud, Jung, Abraham, Ferenczi, and so many others, and will thus receive a rich and essential education not only in the history of psychoanalysis but, also, in its theory and praxis. Being an old-timer, rather than a newcomer, I have, in fact, read all of these papers previously, but I had read them over many years between 1991 and 2012, in different books and journals, and in different languages. But now, having studied them all at the same time, one after the other, and all in English, I have had the pleasure of becoming much better informed and even more appreciative, because in this way, one can so much more readily discover the *fil conducteur* which runs seam-lessly through this *oeuvre*, allowing one to follow not only the unfolding history of psychoanalysis but also the unfolding of Falzeder's work and processes of thought.

Many talented historians have, of course, written admirable works of scholarship on Freud and his circle, on the psychoanalytical movement, and on the implications of the early schisms, heresies, rivalries, ethical blunders, as well as the great discoveries undertaken by the pioneering men and women who devoted their lives to the psychologies of Jung and Freud and Ferenczi and the others. But few historians have quite the same passion, breadth, and gravitas as Falzeder has. Further, Falzeder has the admirable capacity to write history with a fine eye for detail, checking and double-checking his facts with care, while also holding in mind the broad sweep of contextualisation. By correcting the errors of his historiographical predecessors; by unearthing new material; by translating previously inaccessible material; by restoring those figures once marginalised to centre stage, and by pushing those already down-stage back into the wings for a little bit from time to time; as well as by asking provocative questions, Ernst Falzeder has done nothing less than create a blueprint for a new, improved means of plundering, displaying, and celebrating the riches from the archives of psychoanalytical history for our edification, for our enjoyment, and for our disquiet. In these respects, he has really broken new ground.

So please find a comfortable chair or couch, sit back with an *Einspänner Kaffee* near to hand and perhaps some *Gugelhupf* or *Kipferl* as well, and treat yourself to an authentic *österreichische* immersion into the world of Freud and his followers. And prepare yourself for an extremely well written and enlightening education.

Professor Brett Kahr
Series Co-Editor
History of Psychoanalysis Series
London, February 2015

PREFACE

These are historical essays in the double meaning of the word—they are about history, and they are history themselves, in other words, they are already outdated in many respects. They cover a span of nearly a quarter century, so it goes without saying that they, especially the older ones, have gotten a bit long in the tooth, as it were. It is one paradox of historical research that the longer the object of that research dates back to the past, the more we know about it. This is especially true in Freud scholarship (and in recent years also in Jung scholarship), where the past decades and years have seen a wealth of until then unpublished materials. As I have also played my part in this endeavour, it is only natural that I drew on the sources I researched to write and publish articles of my own, so that my own editions, when they appeared, actually made at least some of the information therein obsolete. I can only hope that the light they throw on those sources, and my reflections on them, still merit some attention.

The articles are reprinted here in their original form, with only a few and minor changes: spelling and referencing were adjusted to the Karnac house style; a few, and cautious, stylistic adjustments were made; references to then unpublished materials, such as Freud correspondences, were changed to books now in print; a number of additional footnotes were inserted to update some of the information, these are marked by "[Addition]"; anything added by myself is within square brackets; translations of texts that were not published in English are my own; and I also established a comprehensive bibliography.

The texts can be read separately, and in any order. When they were written they were meant, after all, to stand for themselves, although some of them overlap, or further pursue a matter that was first dealt with in another article. A few passages were therefore cut to avoid repetitions, but naturally some topics recur.

Salzburg, July 2014

TEXTUAL ABBREVIATIONS

CL = Countway Library, Harvard University, Cambridge/Boston, MA

ETH = Archives of the Eidgenössische Technische Hochschüle, Zurich, Switzerland

FML = Freud Museum London

IPA = International Psychoanalytical Association

Jahrbuch = Jahrbuch für psychoanalytische und psychopathologische Forschungen

JH = Meyer Archives, Johns Hopkins University, Baltimore, MD

LC = Library of Congress, Manuscript Division, Washington, DC

SFC = Archives of Sigmund Freud Copyrights, formerly Wivenhoe, now at the University of Essex

Verlag = Internationaler Psychoanalytischer Verlag

Zeitschrift = Internationale Zeitschrift für (ärztliche) Psychoanalyse

ABBREVIATIONS FOR PRINCIPAL BIBLIOGRAPHICAL REFERENCES

Bausteine I–IV = Ferenczi, Sándor (1927a, 1927b, 1939a, 1939b). *Bausteine zur Psychoanalyse*. Volumes 1 and 2: Leipzig: Internationaler Psychoanalytischer Verlag, 1927. Volumes 3 and 4: Bern: Hans Huber, 1939.

Diary = Ferenczi, Sándor (1985). *Journal clinique (Janvier–Octobre 1932)*. Ed. Judith Dupont. Paris: Payot. *The Clinical Diary of Sándor Ferenczi*. Ed. Judith Dupont. Cambridge, MA: Harvard University Press, 1988.

F/Abr = Freud, Sigmund, & Abraham, Karl (2002). *The Complete Correspondence of Sigmund Freud and Karl Abraham, 1907–1925: Completed Edition*. Ed. Ernst Falzeder. London: Karnac. *Briefwechsel 1907–1925: Vollständige Ausgabe*. Ed. Ernst Falzeder and Ludger M. Hermanns. Two volumes. Vienna: Turia + Kant, 2009.

F/Adl = Bruder-Bezzel, Almuth (Ed.) (2011). "Aber lassen Sie nur keinen Spezialisten zu, machen Sie alles selbst!" (Freud, 1905). Briefe von Freud an Adler 1899–1911. *Zeitschrift für Individualpsychologie, 36*: 6–62.

F/AF = Freud, Sigmund, & Freud, Anna (2006). *Briefwechsel, 1904–1938*. Ed. Ingeborg Meyer-Palmedo. Frankfurt am Main: S. Fischer.

F/AS = The complete correspondence between Sigmund Freud and Lou Andreas-Salomé, held by the Freud Archives at the Library of Congress. For the (heavily censored) printed edition see Freud & Andreas-Salomé, 1966.

F/AZ = Freud, Sigmund, & Zweig, Arnold (1968). *Briefwechsel*. Ed. Ernst L. Freud. Frankfurt am Main: S. Fischer. *The Letters of Sigmund Freud and Arnold Zweig*. Ed. Ernst L. Freud. New York: Harcourt, Brace and World, 1970.

F/Bin = Freud, Sigmund, & Binswanger, Ludwig (1992). *Briefwechsel 1908–1938*. Ed. Gerhard Fichtner. Frankfurt am Main: S. Fischer. *The Freud-Binswanger Correspondence 1908–1938*. Ed. Gerhard Fichtner. New York: Other Press, 2003.

F/Bleu = Freud, Sigmund, & Bleuler, Eugen (2012). *"Ich bin zuversichtlich, wir erobern bald die Psychiatrie." Briefwechsel 1904–1937*. Ed. Michael Schröter. Basel: Schwabe.

F/Eit = Freud, Sigmund, & Eitingon Max (2004). *Briefwechsel, 1906–1939*. Two volumes. Ed. Michael Schröter. Tübingen: edition diskord.

F/Fer I, II, III = Freud, Sigmund, & Ferenczi, Sándor (1993, 1996, 2000). *The Correspondence of Sigmund Freud and Sándor Ferenczi*. Volume 1 ed. Eva Brabant, Ernst Falzeder and Patrizia Giampieri-Deutsch. Volumes 2 and 3 ed. Ernst Falzeder and Eva Brabant. Cambridge, MA: Belknap Press of Harvard University Press.

F/Fli = Freud, Sigmund (1985). *The Complete Letters of Sigmund Freud to Wilhelm Fliess, 1887–1904*. Ed. Jeffrey M. Masson. Cambridge, MA: Belknap Press of Harvard University Press.

F/Gro = Freud, Sigmund, & Groddeck, Georg (2008). *Briefwechsel*. Ed. Michael Giefer in collaboration with Beate Schuh. Frankfurt am Main: Stroemfeld/Roter Stern.

F/Jon = Freud, Sigmund, & Jones, Ernest (1993). *The Complete Correspondence of Sigmund Freud and Ernest Jones, 1908–1939*. Ed. R. Andrew Paskauskas. Cambridge, MA: Belknap Press of Harvard University Press.

F/Jun = Freud, Sigmund, & Jung, Carl Gustav (1974). *The Freud/Jung Letters: The Correspondence Between Sigmund Freud and C. G. Jung*.

Ed. William McGuire. Corrected edition Cambridge, MA: Harvard University Press, 1988.

F/Kinder = Freud, Sigmund (2010). *"Unterdeß halten wir zusammen": Briefe an die Kinder.* Ed. Michael Schröter, with the collaboration of Ingeborg Meyer-Palmedo and Ernst Falzeder. Berlin: Aufbau-Verlag.

F/Martha I, II = Freud, Sigmund, & Bernays, Martha (2011, 2013). *Die Brautbriefe.* Volume 1: *Sei mein, wie ich mir's denke. Juni 1882–Juli 1883.* Ed. Gerhard Fichtner, Ilse Grubrich-Simitis and Albrecht Hirschmüller. Frankfurt am Main: S. Fischer, 2011. Volume 2: *Unser "Roman in Fortsetzungen". Juli 1883–Dezember 1883.* Ed. Gerhard Fichtner †, Ilse Grubrich-Simitis and Albrecht Hirschmüller, with the collaboration of Wolfgang Kloft. Frankfurt am Main: S. Fischer, 2013.

F/MB = Freud, Sigmund, & Bernays, Minna (2005). *Briefwechsel 1882–1938.* Ed. Albrecht Hirschmüller. Tübingen: edition diskord.

F/Pfi = The extant correspondence between Sigmund Freud and Oskar Pfister, held by the Freud Archives at the Library of Congress. For the (heavily censored) printed edition see Freud & Pfister, 1963.

F/Ran = Freud, Sigmund, & Rank, Otto (2012). *The Letters of Sigmund Freud and Otto Rank. Inside Psychoanalysis.* Ed. E. James Lieberman and Robert Kramer. Baltimore, MD: Johns Hopkins University Press.

F/Sil = Freud, Sigmund (1989). *Jugendbriefe an Eduard Silberstein 1871–1881.* Ed. Walter Boehlich. Frankfurt am Main: S. Fischer. *The Letters to Eduard Silberstein 1871–1881.* Ed. Walter Boehlich. Cambridge, MA: Harvard University Press, 1990.

F/Wei = Freud, Sigmund, & Weiss, Edoardo (1970). *Sigmund Freud as a Consultant. Recollections of a Pioneer in Psychoanalysis.* New York: Intercontinental Medical Book Corporation. Reprint, with a new foreword by Emilio Weiss and a new introduction by Paul Roazen, New Brunswick, NJ: Transaction Publishers, 1991. *Briefe zur psychoanalytischen Praxis. Mit den Erinnerungen eines Pioniers der Psychoanalyse.* Frankfurt am Main: S. Fischer, 1973.

GW = Freud, Sigmund (1940–1987). *Gesammelte Werke. Chronologisch geordnet.* Volumes I–XVII: Ed. Anna Freud, Edward Bibring, Willi Hoffer, Ernst Kris and Otto Isakower. London/Frankfurt am Main: Imago Publishing/S. Fischer. Volume XVIII: *Gesamtregister.* Compiled by

Lilla Veszy-Wagner. Frankfurt am Main: S. Fischer, 1968. Unnumbered supplementary volume: *Nachtragsband. Texte aus den Jahren 1885–1938*. Ed. Angela Richards, with the collaboration of Ilse Grubrich-Simitis. Frankfurt am Main: S. Fischer, 1987.

Jones I, II, III = Jones, Ernest (1953, 1955, 1957). *The Life and Work of Sigmund Freud*. Volume 1: *The Formative Years and the Great Discoveries, 1856–1900*. Volume 2: *Years of Maturity, 1901–1919*. Volume 3: *The Last Phase, 1919–1939*. New York: Basic Books.

Minutes I, II, III, IV = Nunberg, Herman, & Federn, Ernst (Eds.) (1962, 1967, 1974, 1975). *Minutes of the Vienna Psychoanalytic Society*. Volume 1: *1906–1908*. Volume 2: *1908–1910*. Volume 3: *1910–1911*. Volume 4: *1912–1918*. New York: International Universities Press.

Rundbriefe I, II, III, IV = Wittenberger, Gerhard, & Tögel, Christfried (Eds.) (1999, 2001, 2003, 2006). *Die Rundbriefe des "Geheimen Komitees"*. Volume 1: *1913–1920*. Volume 2: *1921*. Volume 3: *1922*. Volume 4: *1923–1927*. Tübingen: edition diskord.

S.E. = Freud, Sigmund (1953–1974). *The Standard Edition of the Complete Psychological Works of Sigmund Freud*. Translated from the German under the general editorship of James Strachey. In collaboration with Anna Freud. Assisted by Alix Strachey and Alan Tyson. 24 volumes. London: The Hogarth Press and the Institute of Psycho-Analysis.

PART I

HEALING THROUGH LOVE?

CHAPTER ONE

"Healing through love?": a unique dialogue in the history of psychoanalysis

(with André Haynal)

It is true that whenever a crisis broke out Freud invariably showed himself what he really was, a truly great man, who was always accessible and tolerant to new ideas, who was always willing to stop, think anew, even if it meant re-examining even his most basic concepts, in order to find a possibility for understanding what might be valuable in any new idea. It has never been asked whether something in Freud has or has not contributed to a critical increase of tension during the period preceding a crisis. Still less has any analyst bothered to find out what happened in the minds of those who came into conflict with Freud and what in their relationship to him and to psychoanalysis led to the exacerbation. We have been content to describe them as the villains of the piece ... Maybe Rank's case is less suitable for this examination but I am quite certain in Ferenczi's case one could follow the development which, prompted by the characters of the two protagonists, led to the tragic conflict ...

—Letter from Michael Balint to Ernest Jones, 31 May 1957[1]

---

[1] Balint Archives, Geneva. [Addition] Now at the British Psychoanalytical Society.

I

Right up to the present day the relationship between Freud and Ferenczi has been a difficult one for psychoanalysis. On the one hand, this is understandable since they themselves had difficulty in coming to an agreement over important theoretical and practical questions, such as those about the nature of trauma, the relationship between inner and outer reality, the problem of granting or refusing (and how much) satisfaction in therapy, about transference and countertransference, and the nature of infantile sexuality. On the other hand, reluctance to investigate this relationship and these questions without prejudice has disturbed further developments in theory and practice and left the field open to "traveling salesmen" (F/Fer I, p. 399; see also Haynal, 1987, p. 54) and people who wanted to set up for themselves "with a cannon of their own", a reference to one of Freud's favourite stories:

> Itzig had been declared fit for service in the artillery. He was clearly an intelligent lad, but intractable and without any interest in the service. One of his superior officers, who was friendly disposed to him, took him on one side and said to him: "Itzig, you're no use to us. I'll give you a piece of advice: buy yourself a cannon and become a freelancer!" (Freud, 1905c, p. 56; trans. mod.)

Freud was attracted to intractable and intelligent people if they were interested in service in his "wild horde" (F/Gro, p. 59).

All these factors have led to a tendency to make a complete split between Freud's and Ferenczi's positions, to identify with one and declare the other wrong, dangerous, or even mad. How far from the truth the proposition of such a division is can be seen from the fact that the two protagonists themselves never took up such clearly defined positions as are often attributed to them. Even today the problems they discussed open up important, in fact basic, questions of psychoanalytic practice and theory. As is well known, there were conflicts between Freud and Ferenczi that were deep-rooted and tragic enough. It is more fruitful not to try to reconcile their attitudes prematurely—that also would not do justice to the controversial character of the dialogue.

It was a *dialogue*, it was friendship; more, it was an "intimate community of life, feeling, and interest" (F/Fer III, p. 446). In the scientific field they constantly reported their ideas and projects. Their mutual influence continued beyond estrangement and death. Ferenczi's *Clinical Diary* of 1932, the product of immersion "in a kind of scientific 'Poetry and Truth'" (F/Fer III, p. 432), may be read as a letter to Freud. A quarter of a century after Ferenczi's fragment of analysis with him, Freud was still concerned with the question of whether he, Freud, had behaved correctly (Freud, 1937c). One of Freud's last notes, concerning "The splitting of the ego in the process of defence" (1940e), in which he wrote that he did not know "whether what he wanted to say should be regarded as something long familiar and obvious or as something entirely new and puzzling" (p. 275), concerned a subject that had been central to Ferenczi's work in later years (e.g., Ferenczi, 1939[308]; *Diary*).

Freud's influence on Ferenczi's work is clear. Letters (and even Ferenczi's *Diary*) clearly show to what extent he always wrote *for* Freud (cf. F/Fer II, pp. 355–357; F/Fer III, pp. 79–80, 119–122), how he discussed content, timing, and placing of each publication with Freud, and how closely bound up with this relationship his technical experiments were. It is less well known that the ideas in his main work, *Thalassa: A Theory of Genitality* (Ferenczi, 1924[268]), were the subject of intensive discussion between him and Freud long before this was published, and that there was even a plan to write a work on "Lamarckism" together (F/Fer II, p. 170).

Freud's way of using other people's ideas was different. Although he took up other authors' ideas, he worked them over and digested them until they resurfaced as his own. "I ... am very much inclined toward plagiarism", he wrote to Ferenczi (F/Fer I, p. 133). And thus there are many of Ferenczi's ideas and concepts which reappear in Freud's work, often after a long period of latency, and integrated into his own ideas: thoughts about homosexuality, phylogenesis, trauma, transference and countertransference, ego-development, technique, parapsychology, and so on.

In addition to the scientific, there was a complicated and deep-rooted personal relationship: Freud's plan for a marriage between his daughter Mathilde and Ferenczi; the journey to America, which they undertook together with Jung; the many joint holidays with concomitant pleasures and difficulties; Ferenczi's "attempt at analysis" (F/Fer II, p. 153) with Freud; Ferenczi's relationship with his future wife Gizella and her daughter Elma, in which Freud was involved in various ways, including his 'tranche' of analysis of Elma; Ferenczi's and Freud's relationships to other analysts, which also had their role in the history of conflict within psychoanalysis: Jung, Groddeck, Abraham, Rank, Eitingon, Reich ...

Freud and Ferenczi visited one another. Ferenczi gave hospitality to Anna Freud in Hungary, supplied the Freud family with food and patients during and after the war; Freud kept Ferenczi informed about happenings in his family and the fate of his sons in the war. They wrote about cigars, flour, missing the morning shower, the political situation, mutual friends, and acquaintances, Ferenczi's military service, the lack of fuel in post-war winters, financial problems, and Freud's grandchildren. Months before their journeys they began to study Baedeker and timetables of train and boat.

There was also controversy, conflict, taking offence, and misunderstandings. In 1910, during holidays together in Palermo, Ferenczi refused to allow Freud to dictate to him notes on the Schreber case, and for the rest of the journey neither was able to speak about this incident and its emotional importance. Freud criticised, both openly and covertly, Ferenczi's behaviour towards Gizella and Elma Pálos. In 1924, he was annoyed that Ferenczi "got so deeply involved" with Rank (F/Fer III, p. 183). He then feared that his "paladin and secret Grand Vizir" wanted to take a "step toward the creation of a new oppositional analysis" (ibid., p. 373), and imagined Ferenczi going "forward in all kinds of directions" which seemed to him "to lead to no desirable end" (ibid., p. 418). He criticised with biting irony Ferenczi's "technique of maternal tenderness" (ibid., p. 422), and saw the latter's creative regression as a game with "fantasy children" on an "island of dreams" from which only violent means could tear him away (ibid., p. 433). Finally he expressed himself with considerable bitterness: "In the next sentence of your letter you accuse yourself,[2] to be sure, and in that I can only say you are right. For three years you have been systematically turning away from me, probably developed a personal hostility that goes further than it could express itself" (ibid., p. 445).

Ferenczi criticised in turn Freud's failure to "comprehend and bring to abreaction in the analysis the ... transferred, negative feelings and fantasies" in his analysis and his neglect of the healing process (ibid., p. 382). He rejected the diagnosis of his immersion in therapeutic

---

[2] In fact, Ferenczi had only written: "more courage and more open talk on my part ... would have been advantageous to me" (ibid., p. 444).

problems as an "illness" (ibid., p. 435), and wrote of "the depth of the shock" (ibid., p. 443) after their last meeting, when they had disagreed whether Ferenczi should or might be allowed to give his planned lecture on "Confusion of tongues between adults and the child" (1933[294]) at the approaching conference in Wiesbaden, and at the end of which Freud did not even shake his hand in farewell.

Shortly afterwards Ferenczi, who was already showing signs of his fatal illness, made a note "About shock", in which he said that "perhaps even the organs which secure self-preservation, give up their function or reduce it to a minimum" (1939[308], p. 253). He expressed his criticism of Freud even more in his *Diary* than in his letters (cf. also the foreword by Judith Dupont). However, we also know that when Freud was shown Ferenczi's unpublished work after the latter's death,[3] "he expressed his admiration for Ferenczi's ideas, until then unknown to him" (M. Balint, in *Diary*, p. 220).

Would it not be presumptuous to reduce this relationship to pure transference; or to give one or the other of the protagonists all the blame for their dialogue going off the rails?

II

The relationship between Freud and Ferenczi was one of friendship *and* of controversy—and psychoanalysis was always interwoven; psychoanalysis as theory, technique, and movement, but also as a *personal* experience.

On their journey to America, Freud, Ferenczi, and Jung analysed one another. We know what a deep impression it made on Jung when Freud, at a certain point, refused to be analysed any further (Jung, 1962, pp. 181–182; see Chapter Fifteen). We know about the complex relationship between Carl Gustav Jung, Sabina Spielrein, and Freud (Carotenuto, 1980).[4] Freud had given many of his disciples a short analysis, often for example while out walking (as with Eitingon; Jones II, pp. 31–32). He even analysed his own daughter Anna ("Annerl's analysis is getting very fine, otherwise the cases are uninteresting";

---

[3] [Addition] In all probability, not Ferenczi's *Clinical Diary*, as was sometimes surmised, but the posthumously published "Notes and Fragments".

[4] [Addition] Kerr's (1993) and Richebächer's (2005) books were not yet published when this was written.

F/Fer II, p. 302). On the other hand, Freud refused to analyse certain people, such as Tausk (Roazen, 1969), Federn (Roazen, 1971, p. 310), Reich (ibid., p. 493), or Otto Gross, against whose treatment "my egoism, or perhaps I should say my self-defence mechanism, rebelled" (F/Jun, p. 157). Both Groddeck (in 1924; F/Gro, p. 210) and Ferenczi (in 1926; F/Fer III, pp. 250, 253) offered to take him into analysis, but Freud refused. Ferenczi and Groddeck analysed one another (F/Gro; Ferenczi & Groddeck, 1982/2006),[5] Ferenczi analysed Jones, Freud Jones's common-law wife, Loe, and they corresponded about this (F/Fer I). Ferenczi thought that Freud should analyse Jung (ibid., p. 332), and vehemently contradicted Otto Rank who, during the controversy about him and his book, *The Trauma of Birth* (1924), had expressed the opinion that it was an advantage for him not to have been analysed (F/Fer III, p. 171).

On 14 July 1911, Ferenczi writes to Freud that he has taken Elma, the daughter of his mistress Gizella (Pálos by marriage), into analysis. Gizella had already been analysed by him too. In the course of her analysis Ferenczi falls in love with Elma Pálos, who "has won [his] heart" (F/Fer I, p. 318). He begs Freud to take over the analysis, and despite his doubts Freud agrees. Later he keeps Ferenczi informed about the details of this treatment, and in particular whether and how Elma's love for Ferenczi will 'stand up to' analysis. They commit indiscretions: Ferenczi sends Freud copies of Elma's letters, in which she "wants to know *positively* what you [Freud] have written to me about her" (ibid., p. 329). Freud writes confidentially about Ferenczi to Frau Gizella (ibid., pp. 319–321)—and, of course, Gizella shows the letter to Ferenczi. In addition, Elma's father (and still Gizella's husband), to whom she has communicated details of the analysis, wants to intervene. Ferenczi visits Freud in Vienna in order to talk to him about Elma. This meeting is kept secret from Elma, who lives in Vienna. Although Elma wishes to continue her analysis Freud breaks it off when, by his reckoning, it has reached "the narcissistic stage" (ibid., p. 357). Back in Budapest, Elma returns to analysis with Ferenczi. By this means he hopes to achieve certainty about both their feelings. He resists her "old

---

[5] [Addition] For the Ferenczi and Groddeck letters, I have deviated from the usual system of referencing, and added "2006" for the latest German edition, because this is the only reliable one. Page references also refer to that edition.

means of battle (tenderness)" (ibid., p. 374), and remains abstinent in a "somewhat brutal manner" (p. 392), but still does not achieve clarity about his own or Elma's feelings. On the other hand, "poor Elma really gets no satisfaction from it [the analysis]" (p. 397). In the end Ferenczi abandons Elma's analysis. (In "Psycho-analysis and telepathy" (1941d, pp. 191–192), Freud reports a similar triangle in which a daughter was submitted to analysis because the man concerned could not decide between her and her mother.)

Elma marries Mr. Laurvik, an American man. This marriage does not last long.[6] Years later, in 1919, Frau Gizella and Sándor Ferenczi marry. On the way to the registry office they learn about the death of Géza Pálos (a suicide?), Gizella's divorced husband. Ferenczi suffers for years in the wake of this event, complains of depression and hypochondriac symptoms, and has great difficulty in regaining his balance.

It was characteristic of his temperament that he should throw himself unreservedly and without any 'insurance' into the therapeutic situation, and that he should do so little to draw a clear and protective line between his professional and private lives. Not only Ferenczi the analyst but the whole man was involved in this relationship, and he went to the outer limits with a degree of boldness or courage that was his strength and also—in this episode—his weakness.

We see Freud pulled backwards and forwards between deep sympathy for Ferenczi's and Gizella Pálos' fate, a sympathy that drove him to intervene, and doubts about the effect of such an intervention. He was concerned "about connecting the fate of our friendship with something else, something indefinable" (F/Fer I, p. 366), and he wrote of "the danger of personal estrangement brought about by the analysis" (ibid., p. 482). He saw the danger more clearly than Ferenczi; nevertheless he analysed Elma, and later Ferenczi, too. On one occasion he described himself as someone "who has the stuff in him to be a sensitive ass … making a fool of himself, even when he has gray hair" (ibid., p. 333), and on another as "hard-hearted"—albeit "out of sympathy and softness" (ibid., p. 321).

In other relationships with followers and patients Freud varied between a "sensitive" and a "hard-hearted" approach, between a type

---

[6] [Addition] Since this was written, many more details on this marriage and Laurvik have come to light (see Berman, 2004).

of relationship that he called "unpronounced transference" (1914g, p. 151), where he allowed considerable closeness—"because I like them" (F/Fer I, p. 221)—gave presents and invited them to meals (Haynal, 1987, p. 7), which he scarcely analysed, if at all, and another type in which he was "inclined to intolerance" towards "neurotics" (F/Fer III, p. 386), in which he could keep his distance, "thwarted" their "tricks" (F/Fer I, p. 395), and was "cooling off noticeably" in the face of their transference wishes (ibid., p. 362).

His position was a difficult one. Many were disappointed not to find in him that "$\psi\alpha$ superman" that they had "constructed" (ibid., p. 221), and whatever he did there was criticism. For Freud the unverbalised area had a great deal to do with a saying of Vischer's that he liked to quote: "As to morals, that goes without saying" (Freud, 1905a, p. 267). He could not and would not take up an analytic stance towards people for whom morals were not self-evident but passed judgement on them—and who shall deny him the right?—in accordance with the morality that was self-evident to him as a man, doctor, professor, father of a family, and founder and leader of a new movement in the Vienna of his time. Thus he said, for example, that Stekel "is absolutely incorrigible, and offense to all good taste" (F/Jun, p. 418), and there were things that a "gentleman" should not do even unconsciously, as Freud remarked about Jung when the latter gave Jones an incorrect date for a meeting (two slightly different versions in Jones I, p. 145, and 1959, p. 221).

Freud's followers and patients found themselves in a dilemma when, on the one hand, he did not allow certain aspects of his role to be discussed, and, on the other, indicated that the partner should "tear [himself] away from the infantile role" (F/Fer I, p. 215).

This was Elma's dilemma, and also Ferenczi's. The latter could not accept a relationship being divided into a verbalised and an unverbalised—because 'self-evident'—part. According to him, everything can and should be said between analytically trained people: "Just think what it would mean if one *could tell everyone the truth*, one's father, teacher, neighbor, and even the king" (ibid., p. 130). And analysis seemed to Ferenczi to be the means by which even the hidden and unutterable could be brought to light and put into words.

Puzzled and uncertain in the face of the complications produced by his involvement, Sándor Ferenczi resorted over and again to analysis as a *tool*. He started with the hope of having here an objective method of clarifying human relationships. Thus he thought that every fully analysed analyst must "inevitably come to the same conclusions ... and will consequently adopt the same tactical and technical method" for any specified patient (Ferenczi, 1928[283], p. 89). He compared the process with chemical reactions, "like in a test tube" (F/Fer I, p. 53). Neither in Elma's analysis, however, nor in Ferenczi's with Freud could psychoanalysis produce that measure of chemically pure emotion, uncontaminated by conflict and ambivalence. On the contrary, the relationship did not become simpler, but more difficult.

Precisely during this episode Ferenczi had to realise painfully, both as analyst and as analysand, that psychoanalysis is not an instrument which can function independently of the person using it. Very probably these events played a major part in making him recognise the *analyst's attitude as a variable* in the therapeutic *equation*, and therefore placing this at the centre of his interest. As he suffered from not being able to distinguish between 'transference' and 'real' feelings in this web of relationships, and from the divisions between the roles of analyst, analysand, lover, friend, and disciple, in the same way he involved himself with his whole personality in this relationship and was also able to see with extreme clarity how patients suffered under the "hypocrisy" (Ferenczi, 1933[294], pp. 158–159) of phenomena of intended 'abstinence' on the part of the analyst.

A consistent line can be followed from these experiences to his technical experiments, to active therapy and relaxation methods, and further to mutual analysis and to his theoretical concept of the "Confusion of tongues between adults and the child" (ibid.), the role of adults, and the psychological atmosphere during development and as a result of trauma.

III

It is tempting to pass judgement on Ferenczi's and Freud's estrangement, their use and misuse of psychoanalysis, their indiscretions and acting out, from a supposedly superior position. As if present-day psychoanalysts with all their training, their personal analysis and supervision, and with all the theoretical and technical equipment that have since been provided, find it any easier to achieve optimal separation or optimal fusion between their professional and private lives. Some sleep with their patients, or even marry them (Chertok, 1983; Fischer, 1977), and how much must be going on between parent and child generations of analysts that can never be verbalised and worked through (see Part II).

Analysis is, in Freud's words, "actually a healing through love" (*eigentlich eine Heilung durch Liebe*) (F/Jun, pp. 12–13; trans. mod.).[7] Probably for Freud the term love means (also) transference love, and for Ferenczi (also) countertransference love.[8] In choosing this quotation from Freud for the title of this paper we intended to play on this double meaning.

Anyhow, if Freud or Ferenczi is right, the attempt to work with pictures of emotions is bound to fail, because "it is impossible to destroy anyone *in absentia* or *in effigie*" (Freud, 1912b, p. 108). Working with effigies is behaving "like that less than potent man who told his young wife after the first coitus of the wedding night: So, now you have become acquainted with that; everything else is also only always the same" (F/Fer III, p. 386).

Why do we tend to think that technique then was not so developed as it is today—as if today we had access to a definite and undoubted technique, and only the first generation of analysts was in a phase of 'experimentation', to adopt Ferenczi's expression? In fact one can just as well say that analysts then were *aware* that all this is always a matter of experimentation, and that from the moment when we spoke of 'classical' technique, we entered a phase of illusions: the illusion that there could be a technique which one needed only to learn and apply 'correctly', and about which even textbooks could be written.

We have reached the year 1932, one year before Ferenczi's sixtieth birthday. He was thirty-five when he got to know Freud; a quarter of a century of intense friendship lay between, decades of the painful and satisfying work of an analyst who wanted to go as far as possible with the means at his disposal, who tried to understand himself and his

---

[7] The translation in F/Jun reads: "the cure is effected by love". A similar idea—"Our cures are cures of love"—can also be found (in another context) in the *Minutes of the Vienna Psychoanalytic Society*, where Freud explains how much the "power" of the cure is in the (transference-) love: "The patient is compelled to give up his resistances to *please us*" (30 January 1907; *Minutes I*, p. 101).

[8] A late 'dissident' pupil of Ferenczi's, Leopold Szondi in Zurich, spoke often about the therapist as a "*Seelenspender*", a "soul donor" (a word constructed on the model of *Blutspender*, a blood donor).

"analysands" (a term Ferenczi coined; 1915[181], p. 81), with a passion that many—including Freud—considered exaggerated, because, in his desire to help, it drove him to the very bounds of possibility.

Ferenczi is no longer willing to judge himself in the mirror of his master's approval or disapproval, and decides to take his enquiries as far as possible in the form of a clinical diary. This *Diary*, covering nine months (from 7 January to 2 October 1932), is certainly a step towards self-assertion and an attempt to understand all the depths of an analyst's position, without recourse to the dialogue and interaction of correspondence. Nevertheless the transference figure of Freud, the imagined addressee of this diary, can be clearly discerned.

When an analyst considers the whole of his life and work that lies behind him with such depth of self-enquiry, this cannot be defined by the alternative of orthodoxy or heterodoxy, whatever the definitions of such terms may be. The problem is stated on the first page: the "*Insensitivity of the analyst*" (*Diary*, p. 1).[9] We are in the midst of the subject—the analyst's 'real countertransference', the need to know more about it and the idea, almost like a caricature, of "mutual" analysis. Ferenczi himself describes the connection (p. 16):

> Mutual analysis will also be less terribly demanding, will promote a more genial and helpful approach in the patient, instead of the unremittingly all-too-good, selfless demeanor, behind which exhaustion, unpleasure, even murderous intentions are hidden.

In the following passage, Ferenczi relates this atmosphere to his ideas about the *body* and *trauma*: "The end result of the analysis of transference and countertransference may be the establishment of a kind, dispassionate atmosphere, such as may well have existed in pretraumatic times" (p. 27). In mutual analysis one finds "that common feature" that is present "in every case of infantile trauma". "And is the discovery or perception of this the condition for understanding and for the flood of healing compassion?" (p. 15).

Ferenczi's concept of trauma is complementary to that of Freud. Whereas Freud concentrated on discovering the intrapsychic happenings, Ferenczi centred on the individual's relationship to the reality

---

[9] The following quotes are all from Ferenczi's *Diary*, if not noted otherwise.

around him, and investigated the different ways in which the organism responds to the changing environment—be it in phylogenetic specula- tion in *Thalassa* (1924[268]), or in his questions about the relationships between adult and child, analyst and analysand.

Ferenczi approached the traumatic event and its working through in therapy from the point of view of man as primarily a social being (Ferenczi & Groddeck, 1982/2006, p. 73). Before trauma there was an atmosphere of trust between the individual (child) and her or his social surroundings (the adults) (first phase), which is destroyed by an extreme rise in tension in the relationship (second phase). The child seeks help from *precisely* that person or those persons who were *responsible* for this rise in the emotional temperature of the relationship in the first place. If this help is not forthcoming (third phase), there will be a split within the personality, giving rise to one part which suffers under this intol- erable situation, and another which observes as from a distance and offers comfort, in fact tries to take over the assistance to ego functions that should have been carried out by the outer world. The result is a permanently disturbed relationship to social reality. The ego, the "outer layer" (Freud, 1940a, p. 145) of the psychic organisation, has withdrawn so far 'within' that it can no longer assume its function of harmonious interchange.

In therapy, Ferenczi tried to revive the traumatic sequence and find a new resolution, by offering what had previously not been offered: a trustful atmosphere, which was called by Balint later "an inno- cent, unconditional one" (Balint, 1933, p. 165). This, he hoped, would enable the analysand to heal the split in his personality. On the ana- lyst's part this requires a particular kind of listening and sensibility (pp. 169–170):

> But if the patient notices that I feel real compassion for her and that
> I am eagerly determined to search for the causes of her suffering,
> she then suddenly not only becomes capable of giving a dramatic
> account of the events but also can talk to me about them. The con-
> genial atmosphere thus enables her to project the traumata into the
> past and communicate them as memories. A contrast to the envi-
> ronment surrounding the traumatic situation—that is, sympathy,
> trust—mutual trust—must first be created before a new footing can
> be established: memory instead of repetition. Free association by
> itself, without these new foundations for an atmosphere of trust,

will thus bring no real healing. The doctor must really be involved in the case, heart and soul, or honestly admit it when he is not, in total contrast with the behavior of adults toward children.

The involvement of the analyst, the 'countertransference', becomes an important tool, the analyst's weaknesses and errors a *felix culpa* (Augustine) (p. 15):

> One could almost say that the more weaknesses an analyst has, which lead to greater or lesser mistakes and errors but which are then uncovered and treated in the course of mutual analysis, the more likely the analysis is to rest on profound and realistic foundations.

Thus the analyst's strength is defined through his way of dealing with his weakness. The light thrown on this countertransference has advantages for the analyst as well: "In one case the communication of the content of my own psyche developed into a form of mutual analysis, from which I, the analyst, derived much profit" (p. 3).

However, Ferenczi quickly recognised the "*dilemma*" of mutual analysis (p. 28), the dangers and limitations which restrict its use. Mutual analysis can be carried out "only to the extent that (a) the patient's needs require it or (b) the patient is capable of it in the given situation" (p. 34). At last: "Mutual analysis: only a last resort!" (p. 115).

Ferenczi (p. 37) sees the end of an analysis as

> a vision … which would be quite similar to the parting of two happy companions who after years of hard work together have become friends, but who must realise without any tragic scenes that life does not consist solely of school friendships, and that each must go on developing according to his own plans for the future. This is how the happy outcome of the parent–child relationship might be imagined.

"Just as Freud's strength lies in firmness of education, so mine lies in the depth of the relaxation technique" (p. 62). Ferenczi's methods led him to regard Freud's attitude—despite the latter's recognition of emotion in the transference—as intellectual and impersonal (p. 92), and to stress the importance of the analyst's own analysis. He envisaged it thus: "Proper analysis by a stranger, without any obligation, would be better. … The best analyst is a patient who has been cured. Other pupils must be first made ill, then cured and made aware" (p. 115). About supervision: "Strictly supervised by the patients! No attempts to defend oneself" (ibid.). Not: "Using analysands, instead of letting them develop" (p. 183).

Looking back, Ferenczi describes the way he has come. Freud had told him that patients were "riffraff" (*Gesindel*) and psychoanalysis was of no value as a therapy (p. 186):

> This was the point where I refused to follow him. Against his will I began to deal openly with questions of technique. I refused to abuse the patients' trust in this way, and neither did I share his idea that therapy was worthless. I believed rather that therapy was good, but we perhaps were still deficient, and I began to look for our errors.

He describes his "errors", namely, following Rank "too far", "because on one point (the transference situation) he dazzled me with his new insight" (ibid.), his "exaggeration" in relaxation technique, and he goes on to say: "In the wake of these two defeats, I am working humanely and naturally, with benevolence, and free from personal prejudices, on the acquisition of knowledge that will allow me to help" (ibid.).

This was his programme. The concepts he derived from such methods are remarkable. His notes on the sacrifice of "women's interest" read like a radical feminist critique (p. 188):

> One example: the castration theory of femininity. Fr[eud] thinks that the clitoris develops and functions earlier than the vagina, that is, girls are born with the feeling that they have a penis, and only later do they learn to renounce both this and the mother and to accept vaginal and uterine femininity. Thus he neglects the alternative possibility that instinctual heterosexual orientation (perhaps only in fantasy) is highly developed quite early on, and that masculinity only takes its place for traumatic reasons (primal scene), as a hysterical symptom.
>
> The author [i.e., Freud] may have a personal aversion to spontaneous female-orientated sexuality in women: idealization of the mother. He recoils from the task of having a sexually demanding mother, and having to satisfy her. At some point his mother's

passionate nature may have presented him with such a task. (The
primal scene may have rendered him relatively impotent.)

*Castration of the father, the potent one, as a reaction to the humiliation
he experienced, led to the construction of a theory in which the father
castrates the son* and, moreover, is then revered by the son as a god.
In his conduct Fr[eud] plays only the role of the castrating god,
he wants to ignore the traumatic moment of his own castration in
childhood; he is the only one who does not have to be analyzed.

Hard, for many perhaps shocking words, but perhaps also rousing
ones and a plea for taking up a personal *inner* psychoanalytic attitude
instead of repeating irremovable statements of 'Truths' or of unassail-
able dogma in an idealising-projective position, which certainly cannot secure the future of psychoanalysis. Psychoanalysis has to have an
attitude of re-questioning, constantly and repeatedly—or it will be in
danger of losing its functions and of ceasing to exist as such.

Ferenczi was such an enquiring "restless spirit", as he called himself (1931[292], p. 127). He would not have claimed to have resolved
the problems or to have offered an answer to the questions he raised.
His last work—the *Diary*—is a return to psychoanalysis *strictu senso*:
to self-exploration. His "experimentations", as he called them, opened
an innovative path—with many turnbacks and without definitive conclusions. Even he would not have advocated "mutual analysis" (*Diary*,
pp. 28, 34, 115) for each of his patients, and he saw clearly the shortcomings of this method, as already mentioned. But the direction he
took has proved fruitful. In a perhaps simplistic manner we may state
that, whereas Freud concentrated on theory, Ferenczi's great love was
expansion of technique and psychoanalytic practice. Freud tended to
see the patient as an object of rational study, yielding new insights for
his model of the mind, whereas Ferenczi considered his analysand as a
suffering person *interacting* with, and *affecting*, the analyst. He explored
affective communication in psychoanalysis. Freud, with his genius, constructed a "one-person psychology". Ferenczi, with intuition, opened
up the whole field of "two-person psychology" (Rickman, 1951). He
developed the 'object-related' method with high levels of transference
and countertransference work, interactive empathy (*Einfühlung* =
attunement), and the use of regression. Beginning with his interest in countertransference, the spotlight moved more and more on to
the analyst as a whole person. Every analyst who considers analysis

as an interaction, implying a high degree of personal involvement and explicit awareness of it, is heir to the pioneering work of Sándor Ferenczi. Recognising our intellectual heritage can sensitise us to important problems of psychoanalytic practice and their reflection (or absence of it) in our theoretical framework.

Various factors led to the historical fact that this pioneer's work and the subsequent discussion of greatest importance for psychoanalysis fell into oblivion.[10] These factors may in part be related to Freud, his old age and his personal limitations, but probably owe more to the relationships among analysts and their fears of and resistances to re-questioning or even giving up positions which they had thought were sure and safe. As Balint states: "the disagreement between Freud and Ferenczi acted as a trauma on the analytical world" (1968, p. 152), and it promoted a silence that suppressed all these controversial issues as disturbing and 'dangerous'.

After Ferenczi's death, analysts, impressed by the fact that even such an intimate friendship could be heavily disturbed by these problems, became extremely circumspect in their discussions of technique, even though all admitted subsequently that the analysis of transference was a central issue. But problems of regression and, above all, of countertransference seemed to disappear from discussions—until Alice and Michael Balint published their article on this latter subject in 1939. It was Michael Balint, Ferenczi's literary executor, who brought the awareness of this problem to the British Middle Group of independent spirit (Kohon, 1986) where Donald Winnicott (1949), Paula Heimann (1950), and subsequently many others took it up.

It seems essential that our recognised history should be based on the actual facts that gave this story its form. This could help analysts to free themselves from a certain sectarianism, from the unanalysed influence of local sorcerers encountered during their training. It could restore a historical perspective to the remarkable adventure of investigating inner life, that extraordinary undertaking in this century, which was started by a genius and continued by outstanding people, one of whom was distinguished not only by great charm and generosity but also by intellectual courage, independence, and uncommon honesty: Dr. Sándor Ferenczi.

---

[10] [Addition] It should be borne in mind that this was first published in 1991.

CHAPTER TWO

My grand-patient, my chief tormentor: a hitherto unnoticed case of Freud's and the consequences

I should decide to-day to send that essay into the world, and should not flinch from the scandal it would inevitably evoke. But there is the insuperable obstacle of the limitation of medical discretion ... [D]istortions are not permissible, nor would any sort of weakening help. If fate brings about the death of the two people [in question] ... before my own death, the obstacle would vanish.

—Freud, 15 February 1925; in Jones III, p. 420

Suppose that for many years Freud had treated a hitherto hardly noticed woman patient, who had meant very much to him and for whose treatment he had made the most extraordinary sacrifices; suppose he had written down her case history; suppose he had described the case in at least six articles; and suppose this woman had played a major role in the conflict between Freud and Jung—would this case not deserve our attention? But, should it really exist, why has it not, until this day, aroused the interest of psychoanalysts and Freud scholars?

Well, this case does exist. Although it has been mentioned by some authors in passing (e.g., by Grubrich-Simitis, 1993, pp. 265–268;

Krutzenbichler & Essers, 1991, p. 69; Peters, 1977, pp. 35–36), the identity of the patient has not been disclosed, nor has her case been subjected to closer study. And although Freud not only mentioned her in various writings, but also in many letters, published and unpublished, no attempt has so far been made to put together the pieces of the puzzle.

Two facts have contributed to this: (1) The editors of the various Freud correspondences did not use the same pseudonyms for the same patients; thus, the woman in question is called, in Freud's correspondence with Abraham, "Frau A.",[1] in the one with Pfister "Frau H.", in that with Jung "Frau C-", and in Freud's letters to Binswanger "Frau Gi." (2) As for the unpublished Freud letters (this case plays a central role in the unpublished part of the Freud/Pfister correspondence), it has been the policy of the Freud Archives (LC) to obliterate patients' names in the accessible copies of the original letters. The starting point of my research was the idea that these different pseudonyms and certain obliterated names in the unpublished letters might refer to the same person—and, in fact, a compilation of the passages in question has made it clear beyond any doubt that this is the case.

In what follows I will try to sketch the case history of this extraordinary woman, to show Freud's affection to her, to present his interpretation of her neurosis, and, above all, to outline the important consequences her treatment had had for the theory and technique of psychoanalysis. This is indeed one of the classical cases in the history of psychoanalysis, on a par with the cases of "Anna O.", "Cäcilie M.", "Dora", the "Rat Man", the "Wolf Man", or "R.N." (*Diary*). Like these, it significantly contributes to a better understanding of pivotal elements of a psychoanalytic history of ideas and the development of central theoretical and technical concepts. And like these, it shows Freud's capacity to advance theory in view of therapeutic failures. Apart from being a fascinating history of the past, this story might also stimulate contemporary analytic thinking. Is it not true that we, too, learn much more from our failures and blunders than from our successes? I do not

---

[1][Addition] When this was written in 1993, my 2002 edition of the complete Freud/Abraham correspondence (F/Abr), in which the full names of patients were printed, was not even planned yet. Here, as throughout this book, I have changed references to then unpublished letters to editions that have been published in the meantime.

attempt to present a full biographical account; further research will hopefully complete this part of the picture.

Stages in a life of suffering

Frau Elfriede Hirschfeld was born around 1873, and grew up in Frankfurt, Germany (28 May 1911; F/Pfi;[2] cf. 1941d, p. 185) as the eldest of five girls. Her mother "had married late—not till she was over thirty" (1933a, pp. 41–42), she "was older than her father and not an agreeable person. Her father—and it was not in years only that he was the younger—saw a lot of the little girls and impressed them by his many dexterities" (1941d, p. 185), for example, he "was an excellent draughtsman, and had often enough excited the delight and admiration of the children by exhibitions of his skill" (1913g, p. 308). "Unfortunately he was not impressive in any other way: he was incompetent at business and was unable to support the family without help from relatives. The eldest girl became at an early age the repository of all the worries that arose from his lack of earning power" (1941d, p. 185). Nevertheless—or therefore—she "had grown up with an extremely strong attachment to her father" (1933a, pp. 40–41), an "excessive fondness" for him (1913g, p. 308). This love, however, "was destined when she was grown up to wreck her happiness in life" (ibid.).

"[I]n the first years of her life, she had been a wilful and discontented child" (ibid., p. 307), but "[o]nce she had left behind the rigid and passionate character of her childhood, she grew up into a regular mirror of all the virtues" (1941d, p. 186), and became "a particularly capable, truth-loving, serious and virtuous girl ..., excessively good and conscientious" (1913g, p. 307). It is not astonishing, however, that these virtues were counterbalanced by certain "occurrences in her schooldays, which, when she fell ill, caused her deep self-reproaches, and were regarded by her as proofs of fundamental depravity. Her memory told her that in those days she had often bragged and lied" (ibid.). When she was about

---

[2]Passages quoted from Freud's correspondence were written by himself, if not indicated otherwise. [Addition] References to "F/Pfi" *without* page numbers refer to the unpublished part of the Freud/Pfister letters (LC). Translations from unpublished letters are mine, as throughout this book. References without the author's name refer to Freud's texts.

eleven years old, she dropped her youngest sibling "out of her arms when it was a baby; later she called it 'her child'" (1941d, p. 185).

> Her high moral feelings were accompanied by a narrowly limited intelligence. She became a teacher in an elementary school and was much respected. The timid homage paid to her by a young relation who was a music teacher left her unmoved. No other man had hitherto attracted her notice.
>
> One day a relative of her mother's appeared on the scene, considerably older than she was, but still (for she was only nineteen) a youngish man. He was a foreigner[3] who lived in Russia as the head of a large commercial undertaking and had grown very rich. It took nothing less than a world war and the overthrow of a great despotism to impoverish him. He fell in love with his young and severe cousin and asked her to be his wife. Her parents put no pressure on her, but she understood their wishes. Behind all her moral ideals she felt the attraction of the fulfilment of a wishful phantasy of helping her father and rescuing him from his necessitous state. She calculated that her cousin would give her father financial support so long as he carried on his business and pension him when he finally gave it up, and that he would provide her sisters with dowries and *trousseaux* so that they could get married. And she fell in love with him, married him soon afterwards and followed him to Russia.[4]
>
> Except for a few occurrences which were not entirely understandable at first sight and whose significance only became evident in retrospect, everything went very well in the marriage. She grew into an affectionate wife, sexually satisfied,[5] and a providential support to her family. Only one thing was wanting: she was childless. She was now 27 years old[6] and in the eighth year of her marriage. She lived in Germany, and after overcoming

---

[3] In the original manuscript of this paper (LC) Freud states that he was an Englishman.

[4] To Moscow (28 May 1911; F/Pfi).

[5] A "happy and almost completely satisfied wife" (1913i, p. 320). In another context, Freud even stated that she "had found entire satisfaction in her marriage" (1933a, p. 41), but he seems to have had some reservations about this, because after he had written in 1913 that she became "an affectionate and happy wife", he let drop the words "and happy" in all subsequent editions (cf. 1913g, p. 307).

[6] But "looked much younger" (1925i, p. 137).

> every kind of hesitation she went for a consultation to a German
> gynaecologist. With the usual thoughtlessness of a specialist, he
> assured her of recovery if she underwent a small operation. She
> agreed, and on the eve of the operation discussed the matter with
> her husband. It was the hour of twilight and she was about to turn
> on the lights when her husband asked her not to: he had some-
> thing to say to her and he would prefer to be in darkness. He told
> her to countermand the operation, as the blame for their childless-
> ness was his. During a medical congress two years earlier he had
> learnt that certain illnesses can deprive a man of the capacity to
> procreate children. An examination had shown that such was the
> case with him. (1941d, pp. 186–187)

"Before their marriage" (1933a, p. 42) he had been rendered sterile by
epididymitis (F/Jun, p. 183).

> After this revelation the operation was abandoned. She herself
> suffered from a temporary collapse, which she vainly sought to
> disguise. She had only been able to love him as a substitute father,
> and she had now learnt that he never could be a father. Three paths
> were open to her, all equally impassable: unfaithfulness, renuncia-
> tion of her wish for a child, or separation from her husband. The
> last of them was excluded for the best practical reasons and the
> middle one for the strongest unconscious ones, which you can eas-
> ily guess: her whole childhood had been dominated by the thrice
> disappointed wish to get a child from her father. (1941d, p. 187)

Freud did not discuss the first possibility—unfaithfulness—here, but
he stated in another context that she "clearly suffered from fears of
being tempted" into unfaithfulness to her husband (1933a, p. 41). And
although separation seemed to be excluded for the best practical—that
is, financial—reasons, "she vacillated at that time about whether she
shouldn't leave her husband" (F/Fer I, p. 263). In reality, however, there
remained only "one … way out … She fell seriously ill of a neurosis"
(1941d, p. 187).

She developed an *anxiety hysteria*[7] that "corresponded", according
to Freud, "to the repudiation of phantasies of seduction in which her

---

[7]Freud also speaks of her *Verstimmung* (ill-humour; irritation), which was translated as
"depression" (1941d, p. 187).

firmly implanted wish for a child found expression" (1913i, p. 320). One of her symptoms was "a pathological dread of pieces or splinters of glass" (1913g, p. 308). "She now did all she could to prevent her husband from guessing that she had fallen ill owing to the frustration of which he was the cause" (1913i, p. 320).

Through a second traumatic event, this anxiety neurosis changed into a severe *obsessional neurosis.* Her

> husband understood, without any admission or explanation on her part, what his wife's anxiety meant; he felt hurt, without showing it, and in his turn reacted neurotically by—for the first time—failing in sexual intercourse with her. Immediately afterwards he started on a journey. His wife believed that he had become permanently impotent, and produced her first obsessional symptoms on the day before his expected return. The content of her obsessional neurosis was a compulsion for scrupulous washing and cleanliness and extremely energetic protective measures against severe injuries which she thought other people had reason to fear from her. (Ibid.)

> Her most striking symptom was that when she was in bed she used to fasten [*anstecken* = bring in contact] her sheets to the blankets with safety-pins. In this way she was revealing the secret of her husband's contagion [*Ansteckung*], to which her childlessness was due. (1941d, p. 187; brackets in original)

From this time on, a never-ending sequence of therapies ensued, all of them failing in the end, although some of the very best psychiatrists, psychotherapists, and psychoanalysts of the time did their best to help her. "For years, she was the leading figure in the Nassau clinic (Poensgen, Muthmann)" (F/Bin, p. 132), she was treated by Pierre Janet, by Carl Gustav Jung, by Oskar Pfister, and by Ludwig Binswanger; Eugen Bleuler, too, was consulted (ibid.). But, above all, "after her illness had lasted for ten years" (1941d, p. 187), she came to Freud and was in analysis with him for nearly seven years (although there were some interruptions). To my knowledge, only very few analysands of Freud's were treated for a comparable span of time or even longer—all of them women, by the way, like Dorothy Burlingham, Ruth Mack Brunswick, or Marie Bonaparte.

"When I heard her case history, I did not want to take her at first", Freud told his closest collaborators in September 1921, "later I was sufficiently curious, ignorant, and interested in earning money, to start an analysis free of compulsion with her nevertheless"[8] (in Grubrich-Simitis, 1993, p. 265). Frau Hirschfeld and Freud started analysis in October 1908.

Freud reported to Jung on 8 November (F/Jun, pp. 175–176):

> Frau C- did actually come to me a fortnight ago; a very serious case of obsessional neurosis, improvement is bound to be very slow. The reason for her preference for me was that Thomsen[9] had advised her against me, saying that treatment by me would only make her condition much worse. But that fell in with her need for punishment.

In the following months and years, Freud kept Jung informed about the analysis (ibid., pp. 197, 310, 417). But only after two and a half years did the first manifest effects of the cure become evident: of all things, "her symptoms have grown much worse. Of course this is part of the process, but there is no certainty that I can get her any farther. I have come very close to her central conflict, as her reaction shows" (ibid., p. 423).

On 28 May 1911 (F/Pfi), Freud asked Oskar Pfister in Zurich whether he would be willing to take over the case during Freud's vacation in the summer months. It is not quite clear who had actually taken the initiative for this arrangement; Freud, for his part, attributed it to Frau Hirschfeld herself, who would "thus act out her compulsion to leave her husband for a youthful friend" (ibid.). At first, Freud asked Pfister to take charge of her only for a short time. However, when it became obvious that the two of them had begun a regular analysis, Freud would

---

[8]In late September 1921, the members of the secret Committee met in the Harz Mountains in Germany (cf. Grosskurth, 1991, pp. 19–23), for which occasion Freud had prepared a talk on "Psycho-analysis and telepathy", largely based on the case of Frau Hirschfeld. This text was published posthumously in an abbreviated form in both the *Gesammelte Werke* and the *Standard Edition* (1941d); the original manuscript that I consulted in the Library of Congress contains substantial further information about both case histories treated in the paper. Some of the pertaining passages have recently been published by Ilse Grubrich-Simitis (Grubrich-Simitis, 1993, pp. 265–266).

[9]According to William McGuire, editor of the Freud/Jung correspondence, probably Robert Thomsen (1858–1914), directing psychiatrist of the Hertz private sanatorium, Bonn.

have liked to "hand over this burden permanently (i.e., for a couple of years)" to Pfister; above all, Pfister should by no means urge her to go back to Freud (ibid.)! But this is exactly what Frau Hirschfeld did. She left Pfister on 3 December 1911, was not heard of for a few weeks, and then, around Christmas, she turned up in Vienna again. Freud, despite his objections, took her in analysis again (F/Jun, pp. 473–474). From this time on Freud kept Pfister informed about the analysis, as he had Jung before him. On 15 June 1912 (F/Pfi) he even sent a telegram to Pfister, urging him to come to Vienna for a week to help Frau Hirschfeld in her attempt "to do without custody", or, as he wrote to Ferenczi, "to help with a withdrawal process [*Entwöhnung*]" (F/Fer I, p. 406).[10] After Pfister's visit to Vienna, the prospects for an improvement in Frau Hirschfeld's condition seemed to rise.

On 10 July 1914, Freud wrote to Karl Abraham in Berlin (F/Abr, p. 255) that Frau Hirschfeld might move from Vienna to Berlin, in which case Abraham should continue her treatment. Freud would then do what he could to inform Abraham; yet, he already warned Abraham that "there would probably be little pleasure" in the treatment. Frau Hirschfeld payed only a short visit to Berlin, however, during which Abraham went to see her in her hotel (ibid. p. 262), but she did not settle there.

Instead, she went to Zurich after the outbreak of the First World War, where she lived "in a couple of very small rooms in a hotel" (F/Bin, p. 134). From there, from January 1915 onward, she spoke with Binswanger by telephone a few times, "saying that she wants to come here [to Binswanger's sanatorium, Bellevue, in Kreuzlingen on Lake Konstanz] unless I [Binswanger] will go to see her in Zurich", but: "She does not want analysis" (ibid., p. 131). Binswanger asked for further details, and Freud answered with a long letter. How and in which direction should he, Freud, give information? "There is a great deal to say about that patient", he began his account of her, and he ended it with: "In short, one could never be done with telling her story" (ibid., p. 133).

At the end of April, 1915, Binswanger went to Zurich to see Frau Hirschfeld. Their talk centered on the Freud/Jung conflict; Frau

---

[10]Probably an allusion to the fact that Frau Hirschfeld "insisted that her nurses should never let her out of their sight for a single moment: otherwise she would begin to brood about forbidden actions that she might have committed while she was not being watched" (1913a, p. 269). There are no indications she was addicted to drugs.

Hirschfeld spoke disapprovingly of Jung and wanted to know whether Binswanger were still a disciple of Freud's (ibid, p. 134). Despite her claims that she could not afford a stay in Binswanger's sanatorium, she did go there some time later. Freud included her, possibly, in his address to the "friends on Lake Konstanz" (ibid., p. 136) on the occasion of his sixtieth birthday (Fichtner, in ibid.). Gerhard Fichtner, editor of the Freud/Binswanger correspondence, also quotes a letter from Pfister to Binswanger (ibid., p. 133), in which Pfister mentions Freud's appreciative remarks about Binswanger's merits in this case.

From then on, the traces of Frau Hirschfeld in those documents that are accessible to me become scarce. Only sporadically does she reemerge in Freud's letters—for example, in letters to Pfister on 9 May 1920 and 29 July 1921 (F/Pfi). In these, Freud refused to take her again into analysis and recommended treatment as a clinic inpatient. In addition, he defended himself against the reproach that he might have used an inappropriate therapeutic technique. In any case, no later than November 1921 we find Frau Hirschfeld again in Binswanger's clinic, where she stayed at least until 1923 (interrupted by a stay in Berlin) (F/Bin, pp. 155 sqq.).

During the following summer (1924), Pfister asked Freud's advice on whether he should once again start analysis with Frau Hirschfeld. On 11 July 1924 Freud answered that he saw no reason why Pfister should not, adding that he could not comment upon Eugen Bleuler's diagnosis of imminent schizophrenia—what he had seen so far would undoubtedly have been a case of obsessional neurosis. I could not find out whether she did, in fact, return to analysis with Pfister; be that as it may, she kept in touch with him, with Binswanger, and with Freud. Freud mentioned her for the last time, as far as I know, in a letter to Pfister on 1 June 1927 (F/Pfi); she had apparently paid a visit to Freud and told him of Pfister's wish that Freud should destroy certain letters (pertaining to marital troubles and a love affair of Pfister's). Finally, Binswanger related his visit to Freud on 17 September 1927, on Semmering Mountain near Vienna, when they talked also "about the Gi. case and the reasons the treatment had failed" (in F/Bin, p. 238).

My grand-patient, my chief tormentor

Beyond any doubt, Freud had an extraordinary affection for this woman. For him, she was "extremely interesting" (F/Jun, p. 197), a "particularly fine, good and serious woman", an "impossible personality of highest standing", "more than sympathetic, rather of high principles and refined", she and her husband were "seriously noble people", her "case is surely more interesting and her person more valuable than others" (all in F/Pfi). She was "the poor thing" (F/Jun, p. 479), whom Freud sometimes called by her first name (F/Bin, p. 165), he found her "a pleasant, over-considerate, shrewd and distinguished personality", "she is also a daughter who wants to help her father, like Joan of Arc. In short, one could never be done with telling her story" (ibid., pp. 132–133). She was, indeed, Freud's *"grand-patient"* (*Großpatientin*; my ital.), as he called her at least twice (F/Fer I, p. 406; F/Abr, p. 255).

But despite Freud's efforts, Frau Hirschfeld's condition did not improve. Thus, she was not only his "grand-patient", but also his *"chief tormentor"* (*Hauptplage*; my ital.) (F/Jun, p. 417). This "very serious case" (ibid., p. 175) was "a hardly digestible morsel", and although for Freud she was "easy to see through", she did not want to or was not able to accept his interpretations: "It's so clear it makes your hair stand on end. Nevertheless the therapy is bringing meagre results. She pins herself up at night to make her genitals inaccessible; you can imagine how accessible she is intellectually" (ibid., pp. 183–184). Freud felt relieved when she interrupted her analysis for a couple of months: "I was saved shortly before the final point of exhaustion by the departure of my *main customer* [*Hauptkundin*] for Frankfurt yesterday" (F/Fer I, p. 157; my ital.). "Luckily Frau C- is [still] with her mother, who is very ill; otherwise it would be too much" (F/Jun, p. 310). "She is a grave case, perhaps incurable" (ibid., p. 423), "unfortunately, the chances are = 0", "she has no chances of getting cured" (2 January 1912; F/Pfi); she "can be entrancing until the moment when she has achieved her goal that one no longer makes any demands", and "all her magic" boils down to an effort "to gain or kill time" (F/Pfi). And she made Freud utter that heartfelt sigh: "We must never let our poor neurotics drive us crazy" (F/Jun, p. 476)![11]

Freud fought to retain his equanimity; he found it hard to be, "[o]nce again ... tolerant and patient" (ibid., p. 474). He kept "cruelly

---

[11] "The way these women manage to charm us with every conceivable psychic perfection until they have attained their purpose is one of nature's greatest spectacles", Freud wrote to Jung, referring to Sabina Spielrein (F/Jun, p. 231).

reminding her" that what she wanted most would be "an intellectual flirtation that would enable her to forget her illness for a while" (ibid., p. 479), and he was "determined to treat her very harshly" (F/Pfi).

But then Frau Hirschfeld's "completely changed behaviour" caused Freud to be "on a much better footing with her than before. So I also gain therapeutic hope again, despite the seriousness of the case" (ibid.).[12] For some time, "the prospects in the case of Frau Hirschfeld are continuously good, she finally speaks and everything falls in place" (F/Pfi). She "continues to make efforts and enthusiastically stands by me; also, she has revealed nearly the complete structure of her case. But it is still obvious that she wants to get over the stones in her path rather with the wings of transference than with the laborious steps of work. Nous verrons [We'll see]!" (F/Pfi).

Freud's hopes were to be proved deceptive. We can deduce the failure of the therapy from his letter to Binswanger, written about three years afterwards (F/Bin, p. 132):

> She is a case of obsessional neurosis of the severest kind who was *nearly* [ital. in orig.] analysed to the end, has proved incurable and has resisted all efforts because of particularly unpropitious extreme circumstances and is supposedly still dependent on me. In fact, however, she has been running away from me ever since I let her into the real secret of her illness. *Analytically useless to anyone* [my ital.]. She is pulling the wool over Pfister's eyes.

The only measure that might be of use in this severe case of obsessional neurosis would be compulsion itself (ibid., p. 133), combined with in-clinic treatment (29 July 1921; F/Pfi). Freud's final conclusion is found in a letter to Binswanger on 27 April 1922 (F/Bin, p. 158):

> Regarding Frau Gi., my opinion is that in her case it is probable that nothing will be accomplished except by a combination of analysis and prohibition (counter-compulsion). I regret very much that, at

---

[12]Cf. a similar passage in Freud's letter to Wilhelm Fließ of 16 May 1900, in which he wrote about his efforts in his then "most difficult case", also a woman patient. The turning point in the cure came only after four years, when Freud "began to get on good terms with her" (F/Fli, p. 413).

the time, I could only avail myself of the first; the second can only
be imposed in an institution.

There is a postscriptum to Frau Hirschfeld's therapy with Sigmund
Freud. In the fall of 1921 she again wanted to be analysed by him—
but Freud declined, giving no fewer than four (!) arguments, all of
them of an allegedly rational, and not of a personal nature (F/Pfi). But
his "whole plea", to quote himself (1900a, pp. 119–120; also in 1905c,
pp. 62, 205),

> remind[s] one vividly of the defence put forward by the man who
> was charged by one of his neighbours with having given him back
> a borrowed kettle in a damaged condition. The defendant asserted
> first, that he had given it back undamaged; secondly, that the kettle
> had a hole in it when he borrowed it; and thirdly, that he had never
> borrowed a kettle from his neighbour at all. So much the better: if
> only a single one of these three lines of defence were to be accepted
> as valid, the man would have to be acquitted.

Moreover, his main argument—that he would not have the time to take
her on, having a full schedule with other patients—seems to be ground-
less, particularly in this case. He had already brought this same argument forward in 1911, only to take her on nevertheless, and this even
though he had already then considered her "beyond any possibility of
therapy" (F/Jun, p. 474). One cannot help being reminded of the fact
that on a previous occasion Freud had also refused to take an important
patient of his into analysis for a second time; this patient, too, had run
away from him once he had been about to tell her "the last word of the
secret of her illness", and she, too, had been reproached by Freud with
being responsible for the failure of the cure.[13]

Learning awfully much without losing one's skin

Freud once told Max Eitingon: "*the secret of therapy is to cure through love,*
and ... with greatest personal effort one could perhaps overcome more
difficulties in treatment but one would 'lose his skin by doing so'" (in

---

[13] Dora's breaking off the treatment, "just when my hopes of a successful termination of
the treatment were at their highest, ... was an unmistakable act of vengeance on her part"
(Freud, 1905e, p. 109; cf. Decker, 1991). Freud also refused to treat the "Wolf Man" for a
third time.

Grotjahn, 1967, p. 445; my ital.). Freud, however, instead of losing his skin, finally preferred "to develop *the thick skin we need*"—the thick skin needed "to dominate 'counter-transference', which is after all a permanent problem for us"[14] (F/Jun, p. 231; my ital.).

It is not only the analyst who does not like losing his skin; a few months after his letter to Jung, Freud used the same skin-metaphor for describing the emotional situation of the patient (F/Fer I, p. 134):

> It seems to me that in influencing the sexual drives, we can bring about nothing more than exchanges, displacements; never renunciation, giving up, the resolution of a complex. (Strictest secret!) When someone delivers up his infantile complexes, then in their place he has salvaged a piece of them (the affect) and put it into a present configuration (transference). He has shed his sin and leaves the stripped-off skin for the analyst; God forbid that he is now naked, skinless! Our therapeutic gain is a substitutive gain, similar to the one that Hans im Glück makes. The last piece doesn't fall into the fountain until death.[15]

Seldom before or afterwards did Freud so strikingly describe the affective involvement of *both* partners in analysis, a situation that really goes 'underneath one's skin'. He might well have been inspired to this statement by his "grand-patient" and "chief tormentor", who was, moreover, also his "main customer" at that time. After all, it was only her departure, shortly afterwards, that saved him from the "final point of exhaustion" …

Freud's conclusion was that, in any case, one "has to remain consistent, these are the very circumstances under which one can *learn awfully much*" (F/Jun, p. 423; my ital. and trans.)—provided one displayed the "necessary roughness" (F/Pfi).

---

[14]Literally: "… into which one is, after all, always put" (*in die man doch jedesmal versetzt wird*).—Cf. also Freud's letter to his fiancée Martha Bernays: "The poor, the common people, could not exist without their thick skin and their easygoing ways" (Jones I, p. 191). That a thick skin should prevent from *sexual* arousal, can also be inferred from Freud's opinion that "the skin … is … the erotogenic zone *par excellence*" (1905d, p. 169).

[15]In the fairy tale about *Hans im Glück* (Hans in Luck) from the brothers Grimm, Hans, as a reward for his work, receives a piece of gold, which becomes a burden to him. He trades it for a horse, the horse for a cow, etc., until he is finally in possession of two stones. Because they press him, he puts them on the edge of a fountain, pushes them, and they fall in. Hans thanks God and, free of all burdens, bounds home to his mother.

This conclusion, drawn from Freud's experience with his grand-patient, can also be seen on the background of another, highly emotionally charged affair—the love affair between Carl Gustav Jung and his patient Sabina Spielrein (cf. Kerr, 1993). The two episodes overlapped to some extent, and both contributed in an important way to the conflict between Freud and Jung. Without going into much detail, let us remember that it was while alluding to Jung and Spielrein that Freud talked of "the thick skin we need", and that for the first time ever he used the term "countertransference" (F/Jun, p. 231). Given Freud's affection towards Frau Hirschfeld, it becomes plainly visible that he warned not only Jung, but so to speak also himself against the dangers inherent in too much emotional involvement. The mistakes for which he reproached Pfister in a letter of 2 January 1912 (F/Pfi) were the same he himself had made or had, at least, been tempted to make:

> Whether you made mistakes in the analysis? In my opinion: two. Firstly, that you scrambled too much for her, that you set too high a value on her staying [in analysis] (surely, you meant to be very unselfish)—otherwise she would have probably stayed longer with you; secondly, that you, in your kindness and in your ambition, yielded too much of yourself. I myself have given this up completely; in my opinion, the technique of "countertransference" advises against it.

In theory, this was to remain Freud's position; in practice, however, we witness him vacillating between sensitive and sympathetic empathy on the one hand, and a distant and sometimes harsh and crude behaviour on the other.

Abstract behaviour or a little bit of sympathy: the conflict between Freud and Jung

The question of how to react to a patient demanding sympathy and concern is also at the centre of the personal conflict between Freud and Jung—around the turn of the year 1911/1912—which was triggered to a considerable extent by Frau Hirschfeld. Although it is not easy, in the light of the material hitherto available, to reconstruct the facts and the ensuing controversy in much detail, the following can be stated.

Freud and Jung criticised each other, using the case of Frau
Hirschfeld as the ostensible motive. Unfortunately, a crucial letter from
Jung seems to be missing, so that his criticism can only be inferred indirectly from Freud's reactions. On 14 December 1911, Freud declared in
a letter to Pfister that "this time, our friend Jung ... is rather mistaken",
because Frau Hirschfeld and her husband were "seriously noble people; I have never yet looked through the appearance, and nevertheless
know much about them. I can easily explain their behaviour to myself,
if I put together your proclamation not to accept any money, and the
excessive delicacy of the other side" (F/Pfi). Two weeks later, he wrote
to Jung: "It is all settled with Pfister; your interpretation [in a missing letter of Jung's?] was unjustified; they were really at a loss, they
had to consult me" (F/Jun, p. 525). It seems that all this refers to Frau
Hirschfeld's change of therapist in December 1911, from Pfister back
again to Freud (see above). Jung, and perhaps also Pfister, had apparently criticised the circumstances under which Freud had accepted her
again as a patient.

Frau Hirschfeld, restarting her analysis with Freud, told him "all
sorts of things about you [Jung] and Pfister, if you can call the hints she
drops 'telling'" (F/Jun, p. 475). Now it was Freud's turn to reproach
Pfister and, above all, Jung; his pertinent remarks have already been
quoted many times, but they are even more revealing in the present
context (ibid., pp. 475–476; trans. mod.):

> I gather ... that neither of you [Jung and Pfister] has yet acquired
> the necessary coolness in practice, that you still engage yourselves,
> give away a good deal of yourselves in order to demand a similar
> response. Permit me, the venerable old master, to warn that one
> is invariably mistaken in applying this technique, that one should
> rather remain unapproachable, and insist upon receiving. Never let
> us be driven crazy by our poor neurotics. The article on "counter-
> transference", which I find necessary, should, however, not be pub-
> lished, it should have to circulate in copies among ourselves.

The controversy between Freud and Jung revolved around a talk Frau
Hirschfeld and Jung had had sometime in late 1911. There are mainly
two sources from which the contents of this talk can be deduced: the
Freud/Jung correspondence and Freud's account of it, ten years later.
As for the first source, Freud went on in his letter to Jung: "If you really

feel any resentment towards me, there is no need to use Frau C- as an occasion for venting it. If she asks you to tell me about your conversation with her, I beg you, don't let her influence you or browbeat you; just wait for my next misdeed and have it out with me directly" (ibid., pp. 476–477). Jung's answer is particularly interesting and is therefore quoted at some length (ibid.):

> I have waited for a long time for Frau C- to inform you, as arranged, about this awkward situation. It has been weighing on my mind. I don't know what she has told you. This is what happened: she asked me about her sister, and came to see me. Then she put the crucial question.[16] Sensing a trap, I evaded it as long as I could. It seemed to me that she was not in a fit condition to go back to Vienna. To make things easier for her I told her how disagreeable it was for me to find myself involved. I said she had given me the impression that she expected some sign of encouragement from you, and this seemed like a personal sacrifice on your part. I also told her that I did not pretend my view was right, since I didn't know what was going on. As far as I could make out, I said, all she wanted was *a little bit of sympathy* [my ital.] which you, for very good reasons best known to yourself, may have withheld. Such sympathy would ease things for the moment, but whether it would lead to good results in the end seemed to me doubtful, to say the least. I myself was unable, often very much *malgré moi* [ital. in orig.], to keep my distance,[17] because sometimes I couldn't withhold my sympathy, and, since it was there anyway, I gladly offered it to the patient, telling myself that as a human being he was entitled to as much esteem and personal concern as the doctor saw fit to grant him. I told her, further, that this was how it *seemed* [ital. in orig.] to me; I might be mistaken, since my experience could in no way be measured against yours. Afterwards I felt very much annoyed at having allowed myself to be dragged into this discussion. I would gladly have avoided it had not my pity for her wretched condition seduced me into giving her the advantage, even at the risk of sending her off with a flea in her

---

[16] *Gewissensfrage*; literally: question of conscience.

[17] *Ich persönlich verhielte mich, oft sehr malgré moi, nicht so abstrakt*: I myself would not, often very much malgré moi, behave in such an abstract way.

ear. I comforted myself with the thought that, once she was with you, she would soon be on the right track again. My chief concern was to do the right thing and get her back to Vienna, which has in fact been done. I only hope the end justifies the means.

Freud answered: "What you write about the Frau C- incident almost makes me feel sorry. You mustn't feel guilty towards me; if anything, you might modify your technique a little and show more reserve towards the patient" (ibid., p. 479).

Now to the second source. When Freud and the members of the Secret Committee met in 1921, Freud chose to talk about this case, and he spoke about its significance for his relationship with Jung (in Grubrich-Simitis, 1993, p. 266):

> She also was the first occasion when Jung revealed his doubtful character … During a holiday stay in Zurich she once let him come to make his acquaintance. On this occasion he expressed his amazement that she could endure being in an analysis with me without warmth and sympathy, and he recommended himself for a treatment in a higher temperature and with more verve. When she reminded him that she would have to report this statement to me, he was alarmed and asked her not to. The first and not yet sublimated attempt to compete with the father for the woman-object was a failure for the tender son; the next attempt followed two years later.[18]

Evidently, this discussion is about countertransference and the "little bit of sympathy" that the therapist should or must not display. Freud's criticism, however, has to be reconsidered in the light of his own feelings toward Frau Hirschfeld, which definitely involved more than just a little bit of sympathy. On the other hand, Jung's words must have reminded him of Jung's affair with his patient Sabina Spielrein, in which Jung had definitely not behaved in a very "abstract" way, and where his "little bit of sympathy" had led to a scandal. Finally, the turn of the year

---

[18] It can only be guessed what Freud had in mind when alluding to a second sublimated attempt. Grubrich-Simitis (ibid.) argues that Freud thought of Jung's venture to make psychoanalysis itself his own.

1911/1912 was also the climax of the triangular relationship between Sándor Ferenczi, his lover Gizella Pálos, and her daughter, Elma, at the same time his patient (see Chapter One).

Ferenczi knew of Jung's letter about the latter's talk with Frau Hirschfeld, and he commented on it to Freud. He suspected in Jung

> an unlimited and uncontrolled ambition, which manifests itself in petty hate and envy toward you, who are so superior to him. The case of Frau Hirschfeld is proof of that. His unsatisfied ambition makes him *dangerous* under certain conditions. He is also not very tactful in choosing his methods; the manner in which he responded to you is very significant. Even so, it would be a mistake for you to be too resentful of him on account of this *"gaminerie"*[19] [mischievousness]. The best solution would, of course, be a free discussion (with ψα. openness). For this it would also certainly be necessary that you take Jung into psychoanalytic treatment from now on. (F/Fer I, p. 351)

Freud answered (ibid., p. 353):

> It cannot be a matter of ψα openness on my part, since he is silent and hasn't been giving honest information, and I am not inclined toward "treatment". ... But I will not give rise to anything that indicates that I am taking anything amiss; I will gladly forgive, only I can't keep my feelings unchanged. The ψα habit of drawing important conclusions from small signs is also difficult to overcome. His ambition was familiar to me, but I was hoping, through the position that I had created and was still preparing for him, to force this power into my service. The prospect, as long as I live, of doing everything myself and then not leaving behind any sterling successor is not very consoling. So I admit to you that I am by no means cheerful and have a heavy burden to bear with this triviality.

The "triviality" being, as Freud later wrote to Binswanger, that Frau Hirschfeld was "one of the objects of Jung's professional laxity" (F/Bin, p. 149).

---

[19]Ferenczi is also speaking *pro domo*, given his involvement with Gizella and Elma Pálos.

So far I have summarised what her therapists said *about* Frau Hirschfeld, using her as an occasion for reciprocal reproaches. Unfortunately, we know hardly anything about her own feelings and motives. What was, for example, the "crucial question", the question of conscience, that she put to Jung? What were her motives to take Freud's part in the Freud/Jung conflict?

Freud, although finding Frau Hirschfeld "analytically useless to anyone", nevertheless considered it "her duty to sacrifice herself to science" (F/Jun, p. 474)! Although she had "no chances of getting cured … at least psychoanalysis should learn from her case and profit by her" (F/Pfi). And in fact, psychoanalysis has profited by her to a great extent, be it in the field of therapeutic technique and the theory of the analytic process, be it in that of the psychoanalytic theory of libidinal development.

Indifferent towards the incomparable fascination

The treatment of Frau Hirschfeld and its final failure mark a turning point in Freud's evaluation of the curative power of psychoanalysis. Hers was one of the cases where he made a strong personal effort to overcome the resistances and to influence the outcome. But this "substitute for love" (*Liebes-Surrogat*) (Breuer & Freud, 1895, p. 301), this "substitute for the affection she longed for" (Freud, 1905e, p. 109), did not help; evidently, for Freud she belonged to that "class of women with whom this attempt to preserve the erotic transference for the purposes of analytic work without satisfying it will not succeed. These are women of elemental passionateness who tolerate no surrogates. They are children of nature who refuse to accept the psychical in place of the material, who, in the poet's words, are accessible only to 'the logic of soup', with dumplings for arguments"[20] (1915a, pp. 166–167). In these cases it is not "always easy for the doctor to keep within the limits prescribed by ethics and technique. … Again, when a woman sues for love, to reject and refuse is a distressing part for a man to play; and, in spite of neurosis and resistance, there is *an incomparable fascination* in a woman

---

[20] Allusion to Heinrich Heine's poem *Wanderratten* (Norway rats). Freud used this same comparison also in a letter to Pfister of 10 May 1909 (Freud & Pfister, 1963, p. 24), that is, during the treatment of Frau Hirschfeld.

of high principles who confesses her passion" (ibid., pp. 169–170; my ital.). And was Frau Hirschfeld not "more than sympathetic, rather of high principles and refined" (F/Pfi)?

In any case, at the time when Freud wrote his technical papers of the years 1911–1915, in which he introduced or redefined crucial concepts of the analytic process (countertransference, distinction between positive and negative transference, the similes of the surgeon and the mirror, analysis of resistance, compulsion to repeat, transference neurosis, working through, rule of abstinence), Frau Hirschfeld was one of his most important patients, if not *the* most important.[21]

In order to evaluate the possible influence her treatment had had on Freud's technical concepts, let us briefly reconsider some aspects discussed in these papers. In general, Freud took up the lead where he had left it in the penultimate section of his chapter on "The psychotherapy of hysteria" in *Studies on Hysteria* (Breuer & Freud, 1895), and in his discussions of the "Dora" (1905e)[22] and "Rat Man" (1909d, 1955a) cases. He knew already that *transference*—"this latest creation of the disease"—is "by far the hardest part of the whole task", but at the same time "an inevitable necessity" (1905e, p. 116). He knew that this transference contained not only positive feelings, but "all the patient's tendencies, including hostile ones" (ibid., p. 117), that is, *negative* transference, whose vigorous and consistent interpretation was regarded by Freud as the "turning-point"[23] in the analysis of the "Rat Man" (1909d, p. 209; cf. ibid., pp. 199–200, and 1955a, p. 281). He knew that "personal concern for the patients" and "human sympathy" (Breuer & Freud, 1895, p. 265) are required from the analyst, but had already been warned against the danger of *countertransference love*, as experienced by some of his closest collaborators and friends: Josef Breuer, Carl Gustav Jung, and Sándor Ferenczi.

What Freud tried in the 1910s was at first an attempt to systematise his views of analytic technique in a "General Methodology of

---

[21] Among other important analysands of this period, let us mention Sergej Pankejeff (the "Wolf Man"), René A. Spitz, Elma Pálos, Eugénie Sokolnicka, and Loe Kann.

[22] Interestingly, there are some striking similarities in Freud's attitudes towards Ida Bauer and Frau Hirschfeld, and in the conclusions he drew from their cases; cf. in particular the "Postscript" to the Dora case (ibid., pp. 112–122).

[23] In the original: *Höhe der Kur*, that is, the climax of the cure.

Psychoanalysis" (F/Fer I, pp. 29–30). When this failed, he laid down his ideas in a loosely structured way in the above-mentioned papers, which he later considered as being for "beginners" (Blanton, 1971, p. 48) and "essentially negative" (F/Fer III, p. 332). He stressed the limits of the therapeutic power of analysis, he warned against the affective implication of the analyst, and attributed a strictly limited role to the analyst. In other words, he pointed out the forces that complicate and impede the cure (transference resistance, compulsion to repeat, acting out), and highlighted into what the analyst should *not* get implicated (countertransference love, emotional involvement, therapeutic ambition). The voice of reason, a certain trust in the fundamental rules of analysis, and patience should suffice as the analyst's tools. All these recommendations "have been arrived at from my own experience in the course of many years, after I had been led, to my own cost, to abandon other ways" (1912e, p. 111; trans. mod.).

While in the Dora case, for example, he had still maintained that it would have been sufficient simply to tell Dora: "it is from Herr K. that you have made a transference on to me" (1905e, p. 118), to clear everything up and obtain access to new memories, more than ten years later he declared that "in analysis transference emerges as *the most powerful resistance* to the treatment" (1912b, p. 101), particularly "in so far as it is a negative transference or a positive transference of repressed erotic impulses" (ibid., p. 105). The phenomena of transference become the battle field of a constant "struggle between the doctor and the patient, between intellect and instinctual life, between understanding and seeking to act" (ibid., p. 108). While in previous years, he "often had occasion to find that the premature communication of a solution brought the treatment to an untimely end" (ibid.), he now placed "the emphasis on the resistances which had in the past brought about the state of not knowing and which were still ready to defend that state" (1913c, p. 142). The analyst, representing intellect and understanding, should model himself on the surgeon, putting "aside *all* his feelings" (my ital.), the most dangerous of them being "the therapeutic ambition" (1912e, p. 115). "The emotional coldness in the analyst" also creates "for the doctor a desirable protection for his own emotional life" (ibid.) …

In "Remembering, repeating and working through (Further recommendations on the technique of psycho-analysis II)" (1914g), Freud dealt with at least five important concepts: compulsion to repeat, transference neurosis, acting out, negative therapeutic reaction, and working through. The *compulsion to repeat* (ibid., p. 150) would manifest itself particularly in the transference situation and help to establish a *transference neurosis* (ibid., p. 154):

> We admit it [the compulsion to repeat] into the transference as a playground in which it is allowed to expand in almost complete freedom and in which it is expected to display to us everything in the way of pathogenic instincts that is hidden in the patient's mind. ... [Thus] we regularly succeed in giving all the symptoms of the illness a new transference meaning and in replacing his ordinary neurosis by a "transference-neurosis" of which he can be cured by the therapeutic work. The transference thus creates an intermediate region between illness and real life through which the transition from the one to the other is made.

Although Freud had quite early recognised the phenomenon of *acting out* (e.g., in the "Dora" case: 1905e, p. 119), only now did he make it a central notion of his theory of therapy. He also pointed out the problem of "deterioration during treatment" (1914g, p. 152), which was later to be called "negative therapeutic reaction".[24] Finally, Freud introduced the idea of *working through the unconscious resistance*—that "part of the work which effects the greatest changes in the patient" (ibid., p. 155). And although Freud dealt with this issue in only a few sentences, it is quintessential for approaching the question of what really effects a *change* in the analysand—a question with which he was also confronted by Frau Hirschfeld. Had his first answer, in 1895, been that this change is brought about by "the 'abreacting' of the quotas of affect strangulated by repression" (ibid., p. 156), he was, in 1914, of the opinion that one "must allow the patient time to become more conversant with this resistance ..., to *work through* it, to overcome it, by continuing, in defiance of it, the analytic work according to the fundamental rule of analysis" (ibid.). "The voice of the intellect is a soft one", as he put it in another context, "but it does not rest till it has gained a hearing. Finally, after a countless succession of rebuffs, it succeeds" (1927c, p. 53).

---

[24]In this context, note Freud's statement about Frau Hirschfeld, when she had left him for Pfister, that she had "acted out" a "compulsion". He had also interpreted the exacerbation of her illness during the analysis as a sign that he had "come very close to her central conflict".

But "the voice of reason [which] should at least gain a hearing in her monastic cell" (F/Pfi), did not succeed in helping Frau Hirschfeld. The battle "between the doctor and the patient, between intellect and instinctual life, between understanding and seeking to act" (1912b, p. 108) was lost by the forces of enlightenment. This led Freud to a still more pessimistic view of the curative power of psychoanalysis in severe cases. In 1914, he was still of the rather optimistic opinion that the "doctor has nothing else to do than to wait and let things take their course, a course which cannot be avoided nor always hastened. If he holds fast to this conviction he will often be spared the illusion of having failed" (1914g, p. 155); but four years later, evidently drawing his conclusions from the failed analyses of Frau Hirschfeld and the "Wolf Man", Freud discarded this method: "In severe cases of obsessive acts a passive waiting attitude seems even less indicated. … I think there is little doubt that here the correct technique can only be to wait until the treatment itself has become a compulsion, and then with this *counter-compulsion* forcibly to suppress the compulsion of the disease" (1919a, p. 166; my ital.). "Psychic influence alone" would not help; it would have to be combined with "active therapy, i.e., prevention" (F/Pfi).

Personal concern—human sympathy—then "narrow escapes" (F/Jun, p. 230)—warning against emotional involvement and therapeutic ambition—waiting and letting things take their course—and, finally, active counter-compulsion as a last resort: a sequence of ever more pessimistic views, paralleled by a sequence of analyses with extraordinary patients, among whom Frau Hirschfeld might well be the missing link to Freud's final words on analytic technique in the 1910s. From 1918 onward, Freud seems to have preferred to leave this question to his intellectual circle—above all to Ferenczi and to Otto Rank.

Freud's warnings against the dangers of *countertransference love*, in particular, seem to be influenced by his feelings towards Frau Hirschfeld. In considering her case we can see that Freud was confronted with this phenomenon not only at the beginning of psychoanalysis (as he himself gives to understand various times), not only through experiences and reports of at least four of his closest friends and followers (Breuer, Jung, Ferenczi, and Jones), but also in his own practice, as late as in the early 1910s. Freud's notion of countertransference originated as a *defensive concept*, which should protect from being "taken in" (F/Jun, p. 230). *Each* time Freud used the word "counter-transference", he emphasised that it must be kept in check and suppressed. The analyst should "dominate" it (ibid., p. 231), "surmount" it (ibid., p. 291), "overcome it" (1910d, p. 145), even "overcome" it "completely" (*Minutes II*, p. 447), "for not till then is one free oneself" (F/Bin, p. 112). Freud used the word for the very last time in his "Observations on transference-love" (1915a), written just after Frau Hirschfeld had terminated her analysis with him: "In my opinion, therefore, one must not disavow the indifference one has developed by keeping the counter-transference in check" (p. 164; trans. mod.).[25] He stated "it as a fundamental principle that the patient's need and longing should be allowed to persist in her, ... and that we must beware of appeasing those forces by means of surrogates" (p. 165). From then on this chapter—as, indeed, the case of Frau Hirschfeld, who was "analytically useless for anyone"—seemed to be closed for Freud, and never again did he use the word "counter-transference" ...

There are a several similarities between the case of Frau Hirschfeld and those of the "Rat Man" (1909d) and the "Wolf Man" (1918b).[26] It is interesting to note that Freud developed his technical "recommendations" while, or shortly after, his most important patients were, at least according to Freud, cases of severe obsessional neurosis. Thus, they are also influenced by a struggle between a therapist who openly claimed for himself "the 'obsessional' type" (F/Jun, p. 82) and patients whom Freud considered to be of this same type—a struggle for power that could be won by neither party, and that left in Freud the conviction that, in these cases, regular analysis as such would not be of help, only "counter-compulsion". But then the method of waiting "until the treatment itself has become a compulsion, and then with this *counter-compulsion* forcibly to suppress the compulsion of the disease" (1919a, p. 166; my ital.), failed in the cases of Frau Hirschfeld and the "Wolf Man"; although the treatment did become a compulsion for them, the therapist's counter-compulsion had no lasting curative effects.

Consequently, in 1925 we find Freud even more pessimistic.[27] After having affirmed that "[o]bsessional neurosis is unquestionably the most

---

[25] Again, the published translation does not do justice to Freud's emphatic words.

[26] Like Frau Hirschfeld, the "Wolf Man" also consulted the leading therapists of his day (cf. Mahony, 1984, pp. 17–18).

[27] I am grateful for Patrick Mahony's remark "that in 1925 Freud finished his second analysis of Anna, an extraordinary factor bearing on his pessimism" (Mahony, 1993).

interesting and repaying subject of analytic research", he stated: "But as a problem it has not yet been mastered." He attributed its therapeutic resistance "to a constitutional factor", a "feeble and insufficiently resistant" genital organisation. He added, in words nearly identical to those used when describing Frau Hirschfeld (cf. 1913i, p. 320): "[W]hen the ego begins its defensive efforts the first thing it succeeds in doing is to throw back the genital organisation (of the phallic phase), in whole or part, to the earlier sadistic-anal level. This fact of regression is decisive for all that follows" (1926d, p. 113).

In a way, Frau Hirschfeld's analysis was Freud's therapeutic swan song, the legacy of which has influenced psychoanalysis up to the present day. Freud's recommendations have been taken by many as the 'last word' on psychoanalytic technique, although the problems of countertransference, of the analyst's role in general, of his "neutrality" or his emotional involvement, of "experience" or "insight" as mutative factors in therapy, are still at the core of the present discussions on psychoanalytic technique.

Psychoanalysis is indebted to her: a small new fragment of theory

"She has played a considerable part in my writings" (*literarisch ist sie viel*), wrote Freud to Binswanger on 24 April 1915 (F/Bin, p. 132), and "analysis is indebted to her" (in Grubrich-Simitis, 1993, p. 265). Unfortunately, possibly the most interesting text has been destroyed or is missing: Freud had written her "secret history for her", an "essay about her illness" (F/Pfi). In addition, Freud discussed her case in at least six texts: (1) "An evidential dream" (1913a), (2) "Two lies told by children" (1913g), (3) "The disposition to obsessional neuroses" (1913i), (4) "Psycho-analysis and telepathy" (1941d [1921]), (5) "Some additional notes on dream-interpretation as a whole" (1925i), and (6) in the thirtieth of his *New Introductory Lectures on Psycho-Analysis* (1933a) (the first part of this lecture had been prepublished in Hungarian (1932d)).[28]

---

[28]Cf. Abraham's letter of 23 July 1914: "I was surprised to learn from her that she is the disposition to obsessional neurosis" (F/Abr, p. 262); and Binswanger's from 19 April 1915: "I also know that she is 'an Evidential Dream'" (F/Bin, p. 131). Binswanger published these facts as early as 1956 (p. 74); he himself mentioned the case in "Freud und die Verfassung der klinischen Psychiatrie" (1936).

"An evidential dream" (1913a) came out in early 1913.

> [T]his paper was the first of several by various authors included under a general caption "Beiträge zur Traumdeutung" ("Contributions to Dream-Interpretation"). The paper presents the peculiarity of being a dream-analysis at second hand. Apart from this, it is noteworthy for containing a remarkably clear account of the part played by the latent dream-thoughts in the formation of dreams and for its insistence on the necessity for keeping in mind the distinction between the dream-thoughts and the dream itself. (Editor's note; in ibid., p. 268)

Even though it may not be an important paper, it is interesting to note that Frau Hirschfeld is its unnamed co-author. She tells and analyses a dream of hers that proves to her—and to Freud—that her nurse, despite her denial, had fallen asleep on guard. Freud made only a few additions, and he made it clear that he had repeatedly talked over the text with Frau Hirschfeld (p. 276) and that he "went through [the] draft" with her (p. 271).

In Section II of "Two lies told by children" (1913g, pp. 307–309), Freud dealt with Frau Hirschfeld's "hidden incestuous love" (p. 309) for her father as a schoolchild, coming into conflict with "the discovery that her beloved father was not so great a personage as she was inclined to think him. ... But she could not put up with this departure from her ideal. Since, as women do, she based all her ambition on the man she loved, she became too strongly dominated by the motive of supporting her father against the world. ... [I]n order not to have to belittle her father" (p. 308) she produced two little lies revealing her wish "to boast: 'Look at what my father can do!'" (ibid.).

One cannot help thinking that this constellation must have been conjured up again in the transference and countertransference situation of her later analyses, adding to the controversy between the 'father' Freud, his "tender son" Jung (in Grubrich-Simitis, 1993, p. 266), and her "youthful friend" (F/Pfi) Oskar Pfister. Each of them was driven to identify, in a "complementary attitude" in countertransference (Deutsch, 1926, p. 137), with certain transference *imagines*, joining in an acting-out of her nuclear neurotic structure. Succumbing to her "incomparable fascination" (Freud, 1915a, p. 170), Freud rather accepted than analysed her supporting him "against the world" and her basing "all her ambition on the man she loved" (1913g, p. 308) ...

In three papers dealing with the question of psychoanalysis and telepathy (1925i, 1933a, 1941d), Freud used an experience of Frau Hirschfeld with a fortune-teller in order to demonstrate that a strong unconscious wish can be directly transmitted to the unconscious of another person. The fortune-teller's prediction that she would "have two children before she was thirty-two" (1925i, p. 137), although it did not come true, did express "the strongest unconscious wish, in fact, of her whole emotional life and the motive force of her impending neurosis" (ibid., p. 138).

It is not without deeper significance that Frau Hirschfeld plays a central role in Freud's writings about those two unsettling and intertwined phenomena that always made him uneasy: countertransference and thought-transference. Freud's contradictory and ambivalent statements about these phenomena mirror his fluctuating moods in his relationship with Frau Hirschfeld, oscillating between a deep mutual understanding and empathic devotion—a situation in which "*Dialogues of the Unconscious*" (Ferenczi, 1915[159], p. 109) can occur, in which "the *Ucs.* of one human being can react upon that of another" (Freud, 1915e, p. 194)—and periods of time when Freud fought to keep his countertransference in check, and was determined to treat his patient harshly. Like in other cases, in whom Freud invested a strong personal interest (e.g., the case of A.B., a psychotic man treated by Freud from 1925 until 1930; see Lynn, 1993), one "can see Freud alternately experiencing a wish for attachment to A.B. and a wish to withdraw or to be withdrawn from" (ibid., p. 72). One can also observe an interdependence between ameliorations and deteriorations of the patients' conditions and Freud's *attitude* towards them. Although Freud was well aware of this, it was not him but Sándor Ferenczi who systematically investigated this connection between the analyst's emotional attitude and the patient's state as an important factor in psychoanalytic therapy.

The most important of Freud's surviving texts about Frau Hirschfeld is arguably his paper on "The disposition to obsessional neuroses (A contribution to the problem of choice of neurosis)" (1913i). It "was read by Freud before the Fourth International Psycho-Analytical Congress, held at Munich on September 7 and 8, 1913, and was published at the end of that year. Two topics of special importance are discussed in it.

First, there is the problem of 'choice of neurosis', which gives the work its sub-heading. ... [The second topic discussed is the one] of pregenital 'organisations' of the libido" (editor's note, in ibid., p. 313). The editors of the *Standard Edition* add that this "notion is now such a familiar one that we are surprised to learn that it made its first appearance here" (ibid., p. 315). This paper—and Frau Hirschfeld, on whose treatment it was based—did indeed open the door to the whole realm of developmental stages of the libido 'before' the Oedipus complex. In fact, Freud introduced in it the idea of an *anal sadistic phase*; only later, in the 1915 edition of the *Three Essays* (1905d), would he propose the existence of an oral phase, and, in 1923, of a phallic phase (1923e).

In this paper, Freud discussed the change of Frau Hirschfeld's anxiety neurosis into a severe obsessional neurosis. From the content of her obsessional neurosis (scrupulous washing and cleanliness and counter-protective measures) he drew the conclusion that these phenomena were

> reaction-formations against her own *anal-erotic* and *sadistic* impulses. Her sexual need was obliged to find expression in these shapes after her genital life had lost all its value owing to the impotence of the only man of whom there could be any question for her. This is *the starting-point of the small new fragment of theory* [my ital.] which I have formulated. It is of course only in appearance that it is based on this one observation; actually it brings together a large number of earlier impressions, though an understanding of them was only made possible by this last experience. I told myself that my schematic picture of the development of the libidinal function called for an extra insertion in it. ... And now we see the need for yet another stage [in addition to narcissism] to be inserted before the final shape is reached—a stage in which the component instincts have already come together for the choice of an object and that object is already something extraneous in contrast to the subject's own self, but in which *the primacy of the genital zones has not yet been established*. On the contrary, the component instincts which dominate this *pregenital organisation* of sexual life are the anal-erotic and sadistic ones. (1913i, pp. 320–321)

Having discussed some difficulties and complications arising from the new concept, Freud made the point that these could "be avoided by denying that there is any pregenital organisation of sexual life and by holding that sexual life coincides with the genital and reproductive function and begins with it", but that "[p]sycho-analysis stands or falls with the recognition of the sexual component instincts, of the erotogenic zones and of the extension thus made possible of the concept of a 'sexual function' in contrast to the narrower 'genital function'" (ibid., pp. 322–323).[29] It has to be borne in mind that this was the time of Freud's argument with the theories of Alfred Adler, and of his discussion with Carl Gustav Jung concerning the libido theory. Freud spoke the above-quoted words at the last psychoanalytic congress that Jung attended, he chose to speak about a patient whose treatment had been a source of serious personal conflict between him and Jung, and he used her case as an occasion to draw a line between his own views and those of Adler and Jung. Freud repudiated Jung's extended libido concept, Jung's stress on the 'here and now' in practice and theory, and, in opposition to Adler, Freud assigned aggression to a *libidinal* developmental phase.

Freud's introduction of a pregenital developmental stage was pivotal for the further development of psychoanalytic theory. It represented a breakthrough in the understanding of severe, so-called deep disturbances, in a psychoanalytic developmental theory, in opening the perspective of early object relations, and in the discussion of the role of aggression. An unfortunate woman, caught within the limits of her neurosis and society, with no real chance of being cured, greatly contributed to this. Perhaps we, too, owe her some of the affection that Freud showed towards his "grand-patient" and "chief tormentor".

Postscript

In 1994, in an article in the *Psychoanalytic Quarterly*, I first drew attention to the case history of Frau Elfriede Hirschfeld, which Freud discussed in six articles and many letters. Here I would like to add a short postscript. I recently discovered something that I had then overlooked, namely, that Freud also mentioned this case in the Vienna Psychoanalytic Society (*Minutes II*, pp. 366–368). On 22 December 1909, he used

---

[29]Cf. Freud's letter to Pfister, 9 October 1918: "Why on earth do you dispute the splitting up of the sex instinct into its component parts which analysis imposes on us every day?" (Freud & Pfister, 1963, p. 62).

the case of this "woman who has no children" and fell ill "because of her disappointment in this hope" to "call attention to the singularly disguised ways in which infantile sexual impulses can be encountered." First, he discussed her being "constantly afraid of running over a child"—a symptom not mentioned in any of his publications on her. He interpreted this as a "wish, born of envy" and as a coitus symbol: "She wishes that some man would abuse some child sexually: that man is her father, and this intentionally vaguely defined child is herself." Second, Freud mentioned her fear of glass splinters. In "Two lies told by children" (1913g) he interpreted this as follows: When she was a child, a school-fellow had boasted that they had had ice at dinner, to which she lied: Oh we have ice every day. The reason for this was that, since "her beloved father was not so great a personage as she was inclined to think him", she "boasted to her school-fellows, in order not to have to belittle her father. When, later on, she learned to translate ice for dinner by 'glace', her self-reproaches about this reminiscence led her ... into a pathological dread of pieces or splinters of glass" (ibid., p. 308). In 1909, however, he gave a different interpretation, dismissing "other motivations" as "commonplace": "as a child she had been told that the stork brings babies through the window. It so happened that actually, on the occasion of a birth, she did see a smashed window. The phobia thus conceals the wish to see splinters—in which would be proof that there is a child." On 16 March 1910, he again mentioned her case as an example of a development from anxiety neurosis to anxiety hysteria, and finally to obsessional neurosis (*Minutes II*, p. 455).

PART II

PSYCHOANALYTIC FILIATIONS

CHAPTER THREE

The threads of psychoanalytic filiations, or: psychoanalysis taking effect

The difficulties in the way of giving instruction in the practice of psychoanalysis … are quite particularly great and are responsible for much in the present dissensions …

—*Freud*, 1914d, pp. 25–26

Psychoanalysis never improves character.

—*Eva Rosenfeld*, in Heller, 1992a, p. 10

Tous un peu analysés par personne.

—*Granoff*, 1975, p. 96

Perhaps nowhere else in science are personal relationships, or, if you prefer, transference and countertransference relations, so closely intertwined with the handing over of knowledge, professional competence, and tradition as in psychoanalysis. Through the personal analysis of the analyst-to-be each psychoanalyst becomes part of a genealogy, of a family tree, that ultimately goes back to Sigmund Freud and the early pioneers of psychoanalysis.

Would it not be interesting to draw such a family tree? A close study of this genealogy and its history will certainly contribute to the historiography of psychoanalysis but, given the enormous impact of psychoanalysis, perhaps also to twentieth century history of science and culture in general. In view of this fact, it is surprising that nobody, inside or outside the psychoanalytic community, has so far established a fairly satisfying map of what Balint called "apostolic succession" (Balint, 1948, p. 170), and of what Granoff later termed "filiations" (Granoff, 1975) in psychoanalysis. Consequently, no one has, until now, considered in detail how the form and structure of these filiations have influenced the path theory and practice have taken.

My own interest is in the history of *ideas*, in tracing lines of thought back to their origins, in making visible hidden threads spun between seemingly disconnected areas; I am neither interested in Freud and psychoanalysis bashing nor in their idolatry. A history of ideas, however, cannot be separated from a study of the persons who conceived these ideas. Although we have to be well aware of the danger to equate the personal with the scientific domain, a detailed examination can often show clear and revealing connections between personal experiences and fields of interest, together with leanings towards certain theoretical and therapeutic concepts and formulations. But this investigation also compels us to reconsider the question as to whether a complete history of psychoanalysis can be written at all.

The spaghetti junction

As often happens in scientific research, I was rather naive when I began this project,[1] deeming it of secondary importance as such, but thinking it might nevertheless be useful as an informal source of reference for my editorial work on the Freud/Ferenczi correspondence. In addition, it was simply fun to see a map of psychoanalytic filiations develop on the wall in my study—I put a big sheet of paper there, and whenever I came across information in the literature, in archives, or in interviews on who analysed whom, I added an arrow to my map.

---

[1] I had already been working on such a map of psychoanalytic descent for about two years when I came across a statement of Ernest Gellner who, in an avowedly critical vein, called for such a research (1985, p. 55).

I began to grasp the significance of this leisure pursuit when I realised that:

1. In the literature this sort of information is nearly always given in passing, as if adding just a little gossip or some background information for the 'insider'. It is (again, nearly always) not treated as a material *essential* for understanding the history of psychoanalysis. But in personal letters or in private talks, quite to the contrary, this aspect is seen to be of paramount importance.
2. As the family tree grew, erratically, as it were, *clusters and patterns* became visible, centres of influence, and unexpected connections. Nodes, crossroads, bridges materialised in this 'spaghetti junction'.
3. It became increasingly clear that this network pervaded all aspects of the lives of those involved, professional or private. When I wrote to Peter Heller, himself thoroughly implicated in this network, that "blurring the borders of professional and intimate relationships" seemed to have been the rule and not the exception, he fully agreed and even added the dictum of Eva Rosenfeld: "Indiscretion—point of honor!"[2]

Back to the roots

What was the very first training analysis? This is a seemingly simple, but in fact a very difficult question. Analyses of colleagues tended to be very short (sometimes they lasted only for a couple of hours or days), rather resembling talks with a certain degree of mutuality. Can these be called analyses? Training analyses? What form must an analysis have and how long must it last to deserve this name? Moreover, from the beginning, 'training' and 'treatment' were inseparably linked. Already about his first pupil, Felix Gattel (cf. Schröter & Hermanns, 1992a, 1992b), Freud wrote to Fließ on 2 March 1899: "Pupils à la Gattel are easy to come by; in the end they regularly ask to be treated themselves" (F/Fli, p. 347). This was also the case with Wilhelm Stekel, another one of his early analysands (Stekel, 1950, pp. 107–108, 115). Or, as Jung wrote to Freud in 1909: "Dr. Seif of Munich has been here for 3 days,

---

[2] Letter to the author, 16 September 1992.

and I have put him through his ΨA paces, which he needed very much. He is a good acquisition" (F/Jun, p. 308).

Be that as it may, it seems to be undisputed that all started with Sigmund Freud, who gave over his legacy to a few pioneers. The shorter and the more direct the line can be drawn to Freud himself, the greater is one's prestige. The famous developmental psychologist, Jean Piaget, even claimed that his own analyst, Sabina Spielrein, had herself been analysed by Freud, in order to ennoble his analytic family romance: "My analysis was undertaken with a direct student of Freud's until her complete satisfaction. In the jargon of those days, I became a 'grandson' of Freud's" (in Schepeler, 1993, p. 261). It may be an irony of history that Piaget was in fact the 'grandson' of the person who might be the one to have undertaken the very first explicit 'training analysis'—but this person was not Freud, it was Carl Gustav Jung. In 1907 a young medical doctor and neurologist from Budapest had come to him to study Jung's association method, and the latter had seized the occasion to psycho-analyse him along Freudian principles, although, much to Jung's cha-grin, his analysand later got stuck with Freud himself—I am, of course, speaking of Sándor Ferenczi.[3] To be sure, this 'analysis' could not have lasted longer than a few days or, at most, weeks. However that may be, it is interesting that the first 'training' analysis along Freudian princi-ples might have been conducted not by the father of psychoanalysis himself, but by one of his then most ardent disciples while, at the same time, this disciple, too, evidently had in mind to create a following of his own.

It is also of interest, by the way, that a great number of later renowned representatives of psychoanalysis or of 'dynamic psychiatry' worked or were guests at the Burghölzli, headed by Eugen Bleuler and his chief assistant Carl Gustav Jung. Let us mention, for example, Karl Abraham, Roberto Greco Assagioli, Ludwig Binswanger, Abraham Arden Brill, Trigant Burrow, Imre Décsi, Max Eitingon, Sándor Ferenczi, Otto Gross, Johann Jakob Honegger, Smith Ely Jelliffe, Ernest Jones, Alphonse Maeder, Hans Maier, Hermann Nunberg, Johan H. W. von Ophuijsen, Nikolai J. Ossipow, Franz Riklin, Hermann Rorschach, Tatiana Rosenthal, Leonhard Seif, Eugénie Sokolnicka, Sabina Spielrein,

---

[3] I am indebted to Sonu Shamdasani for drawing my attention to this fact and to the pertaining document (a transcript of Aniela Jaffé's interviews with Jung; LC).

Fülöp Stein, Wolf Stockmayer, Johannes Irgens Stromme, Jaroslaw Stuchlík, and G. Alexander Young—and this list is certainly by no means complete. Neither Jung nor Bleuler conducted training analyses in the modern sense, although Jung did 'analyse' a couple of colleagues, thinking that a rapid summary procedure could both help them and turn them into followers, for example, Otto Gross or Leonhard Seif. There were seminars of a more general nature, and there existed, since 1907, a "Freud society", a forum for discussions where one sought to detect "Freudian mechanisms" in hospital patients (see Chapter Eight).

When we speak today about a psychoanalytic training system, we have to bear in mind that there was no such system at all in the beginnings. At first, Freud was reluctant to the idea as such, which was apparently due also to the fact that he grasped the difficulties of teaching psychoanalysis very early. It was indeed his *pupils* who broached the idea of a training analysis proper: Jung,[4] Ferenczi, Nunberg, and Hitschmann, among others. Ferenczi in particular, dissatisfied with his short *tranches* of analysis with Freud, advocated the idea of a deep and thorough analysis of the analyst (cf. Ferenczi, 1928[282]; 1928[283]), seeing in it the second "fundamental rule" of psychoanalysis (ibid., pp. 88–89).

"Apostolic succession"

It was only about half a century after the beginning of what Freud called the psychoanalytic movement that one of its important members and, at the same time, iconoclasts, Michael Balint, called our attention to the resemblance between the analytic training system and "primitive initiation ceremonies" (Balint, 1948, p. 167). "We know that the general aim of all initiation rites is to force the candidate to identify himself with his initiator, to introject the initiator and his ideals, and to build up from

---

[4] Jung seems to have been the first to advocate such a training analysis: "I count it as one of the many merits of the Zurich school of analysis that they have ... demand[ed] that everyone who wishes to carry out analyses on other people shall first himself undergo an analysis by someone with expert knowledge" (Freud, 1912e, p. 116). "[I]t was *he* [Jung] who demanded the 'analytic community' of students and treating students like patients" (Ferenczi to Freud, 26 December 1912; F/Fer I, p. 449). In this regard, it is interesting to look at Jung's advocacy of training analysis in his 1912 Fordham lectures on *The Theory of Psychoanalysis* (Jung, 1913).

these identifications a strong super-ego which will influence him all his life" (ibid.); and he added that "hardly any candidate can evade" being "subjected to this super-ego intropression"[5] (ibid.).

Initiation is aimed at turning pupils or *Lehrlinge* (apprentices) into devout followers, but what it also achieves is to make some of them rebels or *Zauberlehrlinge*. Didn't Freud compare himself, in alluding to Goethe's poem *Der Zauberlehrling* (The sorcerer's apprentice), with "the venerable old master" (*würdiger alter Meister*) (F/Jun, p. 476), and didn't he, in analogy, implicitly compare Jung with the apprentice having run havoc?[6]

A turning point in the history of analytic succession was the foundation of the so-called Secret Committee around Freud, in the beginning consisting of Freud himself, Karl Abraham,[7] Sándor Ferenczi, Ernest Jones, Otto Rank, and Hanns Sachs. In my opinion, it has not been sufficiently acknowledged that the original idea of Ferenczi was "the wish that a small group of men could be *thoroughly analyzed* by [Freud himself], so that they could represent the *pure theory unadulterated by personal complexes*, and thus build an unofficial inner circle in the Verein and serve as centres where others (beginners) could come and learn the work" (F/Jon, p. 146; my ital.). Each of the Committee's members should, in other words, undergo a purification process with the Master himself, an initiation procedure that would enable him to act as representative of 'pure' theory and 'exact' technique, and to initiate others. Here we have indeed the idea of apostolic succession, created against the background of the impending dissension of Jung.

Although Freud was fascinated by the idea of a secret council around him, he was reluctant to analyse its members. Only Ferenczi was analysed by Freud himself in a way that had some resemblance with a proper analysis (in three parts for some weeks during the First World War; cf. Dupont, 1993); Max Eitingon received a sort of peripatetical

---

[5] A term coined by Ferenczi (1939[308], p. 279).

[6] [Addition] William McGuire, editor of the Freud/Jung correspondence, notes (F/Jun, p. 476), however, that with this expression Freud alluded to what *Jung* had called him in "New paths in psychology" (1912, § 411). This raises a question of chronology: that article appeared only in 1912, whereas Freud's letter is of 31 December 1911. So either Jung had sent him a manuscript before publication (although there are no traces of this in their correspondence), or Jung himself later alluded to this letter of *Freud's* in his publication.

[7] [Addition] In fact, Abraham joined the Committee only a bit later. See Chapter Thirteen.

form of instruction during walks with Freud in Vienna (F/Fer I, p. 85).[8]
Ernest Jones was analysed by Ferenczi for two months in 1913 (F/Jon
and F/Fer I, *passim*), a fact that may have contributed to their later
tensions. The other three members of the Committee were not analysed
at all: Hanns Sachs, Karl Abraham, and Otto Rank.

There is an interesting dispute about the implications of Rank's not
having been analysed. Jones had offered to analyse Rank in 1914 (Jones
to Abraham, 1 January 1923; LC), but this did not work out. Later, in
1922, when there were serious tensions between Rank and Jones, Freud
took sides with Rank and wrote to the Committee "that during 15 years
of an ongoing and intimate working collaboration with Rank, it hardly
ever came to my mind that he, of all persons, would still need a piece
of analysis" (*Rundbriefe III*, p. 253).[9] But two years later, on the occasion of the publication of Rank's book, *The Trauma of Birth* (1924), Freud
complained to him that "you would not have written this book had you
yourself gone through an analysis" (23 July 1924).[10]

Rank rejected this reproach categorically: "In this connection I was
struck by the fact that you of all people claim that, had I been analyzed,
I'd never have supported this conception. This might well be so.[11] The
only question is, wouldn't that have been very regrettable? After everything I've seen of results with analyzed analysts I can only characterize
that as fortunate" (F/Ran, p. 210).[12]

But when even greater pressure was put on Rank by his colleagues
and Freud himself to withdraw his theory of the birth trauma, he did

---

[8] Freud also analysed van Emden during afternoon walks in Karlsbad (ibid., p. 294).

[9] [Addition] When this was originally written, the circular letters of the Committee
had not yet appeared, and I quoted them from the copies held at the Butler Library at
Columbia University. Here, the references have been changed to the (German) edition by
Wittenberger and Tögel.

[10] The hitherto unpublished Freud/Rank correspondence was kindly made available to
me by his daughter, Hélène Veltfort Rank (San Francisco), and by Judith Dupont (Paris),
whom I also thank for permission to quote. [Addition] The correspondence was published
in English in 2012, although some phrases or parts thereof are missing in it, probably by
oversight (F/Ran; the quote on p. 208). A German edition came out in August 2014 with
Psychosozial Verlag, after the completion of the manuscript of this book.

[11] This phrase is missing in F/Ran.

[12] Anna Freud commented upon this letter to Max Eitingon: "The most incomprehensible
thing about it is that even though there is so much said openly, he [Rank] is still full of
hidden, cheap malice—this becomes clear if you know that the psychoanalysed patients
[sic] he speaks of are all former patients of Papa's" (in Young-Bruehl, 1988, p. 149).

have some "analytical talks with the Professor" (*Rundbriefe IV*, p. 210), the effects of which he described in an astonishingly submissive tone (reminding one, in fact, of the self-criticisms in Stalinistic trials) (ibid.):

> Suddenly, I reemerged from a state that I can now recognise as neurotic ... I could understand my reaction [to Freud's illness] as stemming from my personal child and family history, from the Oedipus and brother complex. ... the Professor found my explanations satisfactory and he forgave me personally, too.

Here we have a striking example not only of an 'apostle' and 'prodigal son', but also of an absolution, of an *ego te absolvo* by the Master. We know, however, that Rank's conversion did not last and he later told Anaïs Nin that "Freud tried to analyze [him], but this was a failure" (Nin, 1996, p. 279).[13]

None of the closest collaborators of Freud's had what we would consider today a proper analytic training, quite in opposite to the analysts of the next generation, most of whom were either analysed by Freud himself or underwent the training at one of the institutes in Berlin, Budapest, Vienna, or London. But these institutes were headed by the members of the Committee, who thus exercised not only 'political' control over the course of the psychoanalytic movement, but also direct influence on the trainees. Naturally, they themselves analysed the most promising of the candidates, or also those who threatened to become trouble-makers. In Berlin, Sachs and Eitingon even had absolute control over the training during the first years of the institute, founded in 1920: Sachs was the only training analyst (during the first two years, he analysed twenty-five candidates, Franz Alexander being the first to complete his training along the new lines), and Eitingon was the only control analyst. When we have a look at some analysands of the members of the Committee (outlined in blue on the fold-out Chart) (see Figures 1 to 6), we see that their influence can hardly be over-estimated.[14] (Only Max Eitingon does not figure prominently here, but this may be due to

---

[13] Nin, however, is not always reliable as a historical source. She also claims (ibid.) that Freud wanted Rank to marry his daughter, although we are left uncertain which of his three daughters he had in mind. In fact, Freud wanted Ferenczi to marry his daughter Mathilde but, for instance, he strongly disapproved of Jones' efforts to court Anna ...

[14] Let us remember that these 'analyses' differed substantially in form and duration; while Medard Boss, for example, only had a few talks with Freud, the analyses of Marie Bonaparte or Ruth Mack Brunswick lasted for many years.

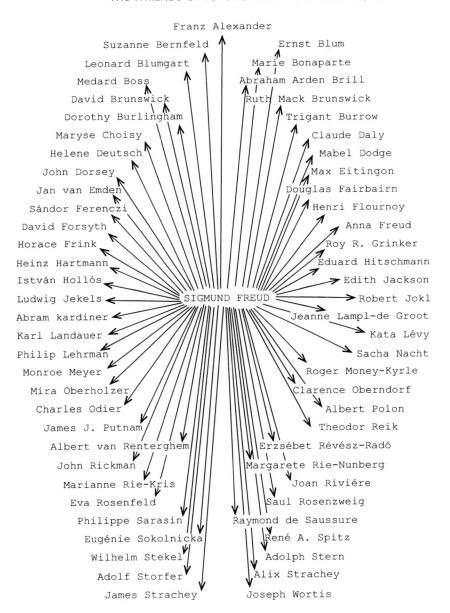

Franz Alexander
Suzanne Bernfeld   Ernst Blum
Leonard Blumgart   Marie Bonaparte
Medard Boss   Abraham Arden Brill
David Brunswick   Ruth Mack Brunswick
Dorothy Burlingham   Trigant Burrow
Maryse Choisy   Claude Daly
Helene Deutsch   Mabel Dodge
John Dorsey   Max Eitingon
Jan van Emden   Douglas Fairbairn
Sándor Ferenczi   Henri Flournoy
David Forsyth   Anna Freud
Horace Frink   Roy R. Grinker
Heinz Hartmann   Eduard Hitschmann
István Hollós   Edith Jackson
Ludwig Jekels   SIGMUND FREUD   Robert Jokl
Abram kardiner   Jeanne Lampl-de Groot
Karl Landauer   Kata Lévy
Philip Lehrman   Sacha Nacht
Monroe Meyer   Roger Money-Kyrle
Mira Oberholzer   Clarence Oberndorf
Charles Odier   Albert Polon
James J. Putnam   Theodor Reik
Albert van Renterghem   Erzsébet Révész-Radó
John Rickman   Margarete Rie-Nunberg
Marianne Rie-Kris   Joan Riviére
Eva Rosenfeld   Saul Rosenzweig
Philippe Sarasin   Raymond de Saussure
Eugénie Sokolnicka   René A. Spitz
Wilhelm Stekel   Adolph Stern
Adolf Storfer   Alix Strachey
James Strachey   Joseph Wortis

Figure 1.

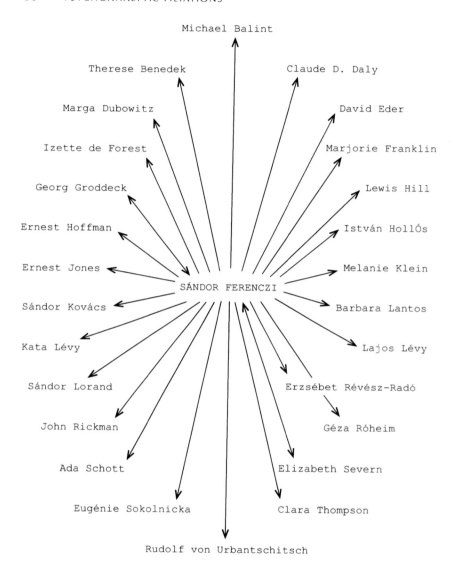

Figure 2.

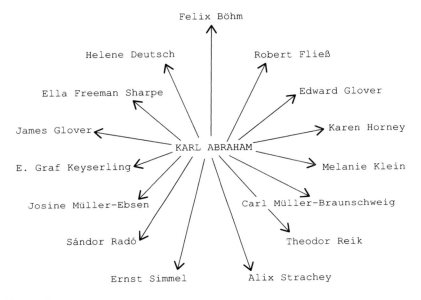

Figure 3.

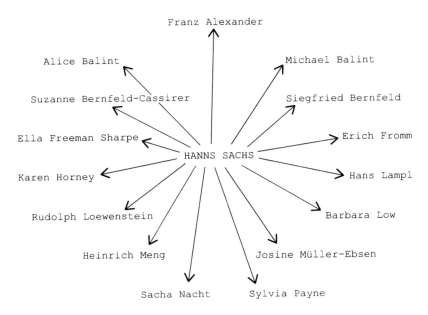

Figure 4.

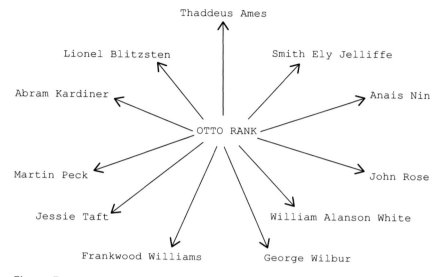

Figure 5.

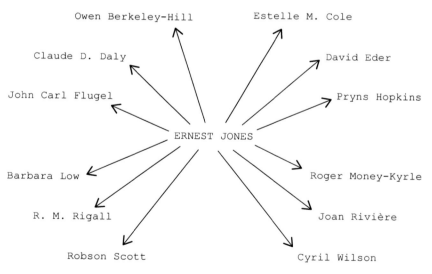

Figure 6.

the very scarce material concerning this enigmatic figure.[15]) Very early, however, there were different opinions about the impact of this influence. While Jones, who had analysed six out of the eleven members of the British Psycho-Analytical Society, found that he therefore was "in good contact" with them (F/Jon, p. 336), Abraham wrote to the Committee: "In our group a lot of difficulties arose from the fact that most of the members have been analysed by me" (*Rundbriefe I*, p. 173).

As far as Anna Freud is concerned (see Figure 7), her huge unpublished correspondence, recently made accessible in 131 containers in the Library of Congress, shows her leading position as 'grey eminence' in the psychoanalytic movement, particularly after her father's death. She exercised decisive influence on the publication of biographical works on Freud, on the form in which his correspondences were published, or not published at all, and on the publication policy of journals such as the *Psychoanalytic Study of the Child*. Her *analysand* Ernst Kris, editor of Freud's letters to Wilhelm Fließ, for example, was given orders by her of what to include in the publication of this correspondence, and what not.[16] Her most extensive and wide-ranging correspondence, by the way, is the one with Kurt Eissler (analysand of her friend August Aichhorn and of Richard Sterba), founder of the Freud Archives.

There are only very few other analysts whose importance is of comparable weight: Paul Federn or Franz Alexander, for instance, but above all Melanie Klein, herself an analysand of Ferenczi and Abraham. A look at the number and the prestige of her supervisees (green arrows on the fold-out Chart) and analysands (see Figure 8; cf. Grosskurth, 1986) does indeed make clear what was also at stake in the so-called Freud/Klein controversies (King & Steiner, 1991) within the British Society.

Apart from the number of analysands and the stature a training analyst had, several other facts can be deduced from the material I gathered, facts that complicate the picture we have of the history of psychoanalysis and that call for an explanation.

---

[15] [Addition] Meanwhile, two major works on Eitingon have been published: Schröter's introduction to the Freud/Eitingon correspondence (in F/Eit), and Wilmers' book on the Eitingons (2009).

[16] Cf. for example her letter to Kris of 11 February 1947 (LC): "should be kept"; "cut only the second part of the first paragraph"; "to be omitted!"; "cut the stories of perversions!"; "Cut by all means!"; "Cut the phrase: 'my own father not excluded'"; etc.

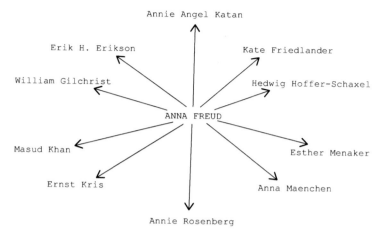

Figure 7.

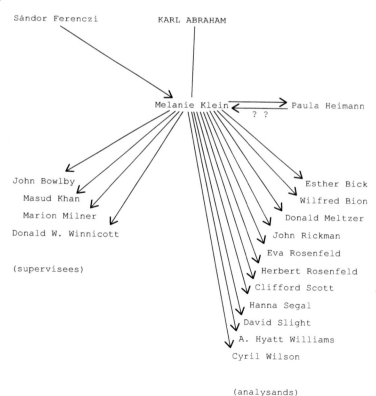

Figure 8.

Postgraduate analysis?

It was very common—indeed the rule and not the exception—that analysts had more than one analysis. But why is this so? Why do we hardly find any one, even among the most eminent analysts, who could do with just one analysis? Many, if not most of them had two, some had three, some had even four, and some were analysed by no fewer than five different analysts (e.g., Erich Fromm by Theodor Reik, Wilhelm Wittenberg, Karl Landauer, Hanns Sachs, and by his later wife Frieda Fromm-Reichmann) (Harmat, 1986; Krutzenbichler & Essers, 1991; Leupold-Löwenthal, 1986; Rattner, 1990).

There were mainly three opinions about the question of which sort of personal analysis the analyst should have. (1) Some found it sufficient to learn the profession more or less autodidactically, occasionally seeking advice from Freud when they ran into difficulties. Freud himself expressed this view a couple of times, for example, about Rank (see above) or towards Bernfeld (Bernfeld, 1952, p. 442). (2) There was the opposite argument, especially stressed by Ferenczi, that the training analysis should be a sort of 'super analysis', as long, deep, and complete as possible. (3) Finally, we have Freud's conclusion, maybe also influenced by his experiences with Rank, that analysts should periodically re-enter analysis, each of these 'tranches' lasting for not too long a time. To John Rickman he wrote on 30 June 1928 that he had "come to learn that the unconscious of the analyst stirred up by his growing analytical experience claims periodical renewals or rather continuations of his own analysis. He may deteriorate to a serious measure if he does not reply to this appeal; the more he gets mature the better the results of this continued investigation" (LC, English in original; cf. also F/Wei, p. 40). And when Ernest Jones complained, in 1933, about the poor results of psychoanalysis among analysts themselves, and promoted "what may be called post-graduate analysis", that is, the idea that analysts "must continue their analysis from time to time later on" (F/Jon, p. 729), Freud was eager to assert that this was in fact his own idea: "For years I have been advocating your idea of a 'Postgraduate Analysis', and am also trying to put it into effect. I find such supplementary analyses unexpectedly interesting and helpful. Therefore, in this instance I am stressing my priority!" (ibid., p. 731). His final conclusion is found in print in "Analysis terminable and interminable", where he first confirmed the necessity of a training analysis— although he thought that "for practical reasons this analysis can only be short and incomplete"—and secondly that "[e]very analyst should periodically—at intervals of five years or so—submit himself to analysis once more, without feeling ashamed of taking this step" (1937c, pp. 248–249).[17]

In fact, many, if not most analysts seem to have acted according to Freud's advice—but with one remarkable restriction: instead of considering this a standard part of their professional training, this whole area is treated either with shame or with pride. Are there other reasons for these postgraduate analyses?

Apart from the necessity to counteract the *déformation professionelle*, there is ample evidence that psychoanalysts seem not only to have had the same problems other human beings have—which would surprise nobody—but indeed had more of their share, and that many of them remained unhappy and not helped by their personal analyses. In fact, a great number of the early psychoanalysts committed suicide; of the 149 persons who were members of the Viennese Psychoanalytic Society between 1902 and 1938, at least nine killed themselves (Paul Federn, Max Kahane, Tatiana Rosenthal, Herbert Silberer, Eugénie Sokolnicka, Wilhelm Stekel, Victor Tausk, and Rosa Walk)—that is, six per cent or one out of seventeen (Mühlleitner, 1992). When Jakob Honegger, a former assistant of Jung's, with whom Jung had made some sort of mutual analysis, committed suicide, Freud dryly remarked: "Do you know, I think we wear out quite a few men" (F/Jun, p. 413). In addition, a good deal of them had drug or alcohol problems (Ruth Mack Brunswick, Otto Gross, Walter Schmideberg …).

Training through love?

We have evidence of many *training* analyses that were or became also erotic relationships (red arrows on the fold-out Chart),[18] and I am

---

[17] Because the dangers inherent in the "constant preoccupation with all the repressed material" stir up "in the analyst as well all the instinctual demands which he is otherwise able to keep under suppression" (ibid.). [Addition] To Abraham Brill, Freud wrote in 1934 that "analysis is a dangerous profession, as deleterious as the handling of X-rays, and I was moved to make the claim, which can't be possibly met in reality, however, that an honest analyst should re-enter analysis every five years or so. It probably does no one good to act the infallible God for six to eight hours a day" (LC).

[18] Or erotic relationships that turned into analyses—it is often difficult to decide.

convinced that what we know is only the tip of the iceberg. Let me name just a few examples: Georg Groddeck and (his later wife) Emmy von Voigt (Will, 1984); Michael Balint and (his later, second wife) Edna Oakeshott (Balint Archives, Geneva); Otto Rank and his wife Beata (Lieberman, 1985); August Aichhorn and Margaret Mahler (Stepansky, 1988); Wilhelm Reich and (his later wife) Annie Pink (Reich, 1988); Rudolph Löwenstein and Marie Bonaparte (Bertin, 1982); René Allendy *and* Otto Rank with Anaïs Nin (Cremerius, 1987; Krutzenbichler & Essers, 1991); Carl Gustav Jung and Sabina Spielrein (Carotenuto, 1980; Kerr, 1993),[19] *and* Toni Wolff (e.g., Donn, 1988), *and* Maria Moltzer[20] (and almost certainly others, too)—Jung also analysed his wife Emma because she "staged a number of jealous scenes, groundlessly" (F/Jun, p. 289); Victor Tausk and Lou Andreas-Salomé (*and* his patient Hilde Loewi) (Krutzenbichler & Essers, 1991); Erzsébet Révész-Radó and Sándor Radó, as well as Sándor Radó and his second wife Emmy (F/Fer II, pp. 357, 362; Krutzenbichler & Essers, 1991; Reich, 1952), and so on.

The interference of affects, in particular sexual ones, with the alleg-edly abstinent atmosphere of an analysis *lege artis* preoccupied the early analysts from the beginning. At a meeting of the Viennese Psychoana-lytic Society in 1909, Hitschmann stated that "the examination of the patient's sex organs by the attending analyst … [was] absolutely nec-essary and it is a sign of prejudice [*Befangenheit*] if Sadger failed to do this" (*Minutes II*, p. 299). Wilhelm Reich even claimed that "there were cases when the psychoanalysts, pretending to examine the genitals, a medical examination, introduced their fingers into the vaginae of their patients. *This happened quite often. I knew that.* … Some psychoanalysts were not honest. … They pretended that nothing specific happened, and then they masturbated the patient during sessions" (Reich, 1952, p. 96; my ital. and trans.). Freud himself advocated a more cautious pro-cedure, well aware of the dangers: "Physical examination is certainly most desirable but unfeasible in analysis; it must be done by another physician" (*Minutes II*, p. 301). It is indeed understandable that Freud

---

[19] [Addition] Their relationship was undoubtedly highly erotically charged. It is irrelevant in this context whether what they called their "poetry" was consummated or not.

[20] Jolande Jacobi stated: "Then I heard from others, about the time before he met Toni Wolff, that he had had a love affair there in the Burghölzli with a girl—what was her name? Moltzer" (in Shamdasani, 1990, p. 54; cf. F/Fer I, p. 446).

found a text on countertransference sorely needed, but at the same time he stated that it had to be *secretly* circulated among analysts only (F/Jun, p. 476) …

The fact that sexual relationships during analyses have been and still are notorious, has gained legitimate attention in the past years (cf. Anonyma, 1988; Fischer, 1977; Krutzenbichler & Essers, 1991). What has been less acknowledged is that sexual relationships have in fact been running as a red thread also through the analytic *training* network from its beginning. I am sure that every analyst could add examples from their own local society, which are usually treated with silence, and only rarely are made semi-public, as in the cases of Masud Khan or Karen Horney. It might prove worth the effort to find out which percentage of analysts married training analysands. But erotic relationships are not the only deviation from "classical" technique, as Ferenczi called it,[21] that we come across.

Familienbande?

Karl Kraus once stated sarcastically that *Familienbande* (family bonds) is one of the deepest words in the German language. Usually used to describe the ties and bonds between family members, it can also be read under the aspect of the second meaning of the word *Bande* in German, namely a gang, a band of gangsters. Kraus's pun could well be used in the context of psychoanalysis, too, because the mingling of analysis with kinship is only too clear (marked in yellow on the fold-out Chart). Not only did husbands or lovers analyse each other, or were analysed by the same analyst, not only did parents have their children analysed by their own analysts or even analysands, but it was common practice that parents analysed their own children, aunts their nephews, men the children of their lovers. In 1925, Lou Andreas-Salomé even remarked to Alix Strachey "that the parents were the only proper people to analyze the child". When Alix reported this to her husband James, she added: "a shudder ran down my spine" (Meisel & Kendrick, 1985, p. 200).

---

[21] [Addition] It was Freud who attributed the expression "classical technique" to Ferenczi in 1924 (*Minutes IV*, p. 170). However, Freud himself had used this expression as early as 1907, when criticising Stekel's technique as "by no means classical" (*Minutes I*, p. 250).

The most famous example is surely Anna Freud's analysis with her father (October 1918 to spring 1922, May 1924 to summer 1925), a fact first put in print by Paul Roazen (1969). In addition to Young-Bruehl's biography (1988), the unpublished parts of the Freud/Lou Andreas-Salomé correspondence and of his letters to Anna herself (both LC)[22] throw light upon this unprecedented procedure. Very early, she started sending dreams to her father ("I have even dreamed of you tonight, but it was not nice at all"; F/AF, p. 82). Of the eighteen such instances between 1911 and 1930, some are very touching, for example, "I dreamed that I had to defend a farm belonging to us against enemies. But the sabre was broken and I was ashamed before the enemies when I pulled it" (p. 154). "Recently I dreamed that you are a king and I am a princess, and that one wanted to bring us apart by intrigues. It wasn't nice and very exciting" (p. 167). "I had a terrible dream. I dreamed that the bride of Dr. Tausk had rented the apartment in Berggasse 20 opposite us in order to shoot you, and each time you wanted to go near the window, she appeared there with a pistol. I was terribly frightened" (p. 221). Freud only rarely responded with short interpretations ("You have to add jealousy to your dream interpretation"; p. 232), he rather did not mention the dreams at all or gave a humorous reply—to her complaints that she suffered from repeated examination dreams, he simply answered: "Very agreeable that your repeated exams are 'tax-free'"[23] (p. 142).

In his letters to Lou Andreas-Salomé (F/AS) Freud frequently wrote about Anna, and also about her analysis with him: "Being inhibited towards the male side because of me, she has had much misfortune in her friendships with women. She has developed slowly, is not only in her looks younger than her age. Sometimes I urgently wish her a good man, sometimes I frighten away from the loss" (3 July 1922). And, on 13 May 1924: "I have accepted a seventh analysis with special feelings: my Anna, who is so unreasonable to cling to an old father. The child causes me much sorrow; how she will bear the lonely life, and whether I will be able to get her libido out of the hiding-place, into which it has crept." A year later, on 10 May 1925: "Anna's analysis will be continued. She

---

[22] [Addition] The Freud/Anna Freud correspondence was published in 2006 (F/AF), so far only in German. Here, the page references now refer to that edition, in my own translation.

[23] Students had to pay a fee—the so-called *Taxe*—for each examination.

is not easy and has difficulties in finding the way to apply upon herself what she sees so clearly now in others. … But, frankly speaking, the whole direction does not 'suit' me. I fear that the suppressed genitality will play her a nasty trick some time. I cannot get her away from me, but then nobody helps me with it."

But Freud was not the only one to analyse a child of his. There were also the analyses of Karl Abraham with his daughter Hilda (Abraham, 1976[1913]), of Carl Gustav Jung with his daughter Agathli (Jung, 1910a), of Ernst Kris with his two children Anna and Tony (Heller, 1992b, pp. 67–68), of Hermine Hug-Hellmuth with her nephew (who later killed her) (MacLean & Rappen, 1991); Melanie Klein analysed all her children and had her grandson analysed by her trainee Marion Milner (Grosskurth, 1986). We know about the inextricable networks of Freud and the Brunswicks (cf. Roazen, 1992). Anna Freud's first patients were two of her nephews, "Heinerle" Halberstadt and Ernst Halberstadt (e.g., Gay, 1987, p. 436) (who was also analysed by her friend Willi Hoffer). Franz Alexander, who had perhaps had some form of training with Freud himself (Rattner, 1990, p. 513), analysed Freud's son Oliver (F/AF, p. 377).[24]

There has been much discussion about whether Freud had had a *liaison* with Minna Bernays, but what I find even more startling is the idea, brought forward by Appignanesi and Forrester (1992, p. 144), that he might have analysed her. Sigmund Freud did not only analyse Marie Bonaparte and her lovers Heinz Hartmann and Rudolph Loewenstein (who himself analysed Bonaparte), but also her daughter Eugénie; her son Pierre was analysed by Heinz Hartmann (Bertin, 1982). Erich Fromm analysed Karen Horney's daughter Marianne, while having a relationship with Horney. As a child, Marianne—as well as her sister Renate—had already been analysed by Melanie Klein; Brigitte, the third daughter (who was to become a known actress), should also have been treated by Klein but, being fourteen years old and strong-willed, she refused to go for analysis at all (see Grosskurth, 1986; Quinn, 1987).

Peter Heller (see Figure 9) was analysed as a child by Anna Freud between 1929 and 1932; his father, Hans Heller, by Ludwig Jekels; his mother, Gretl Heller, by Hanns Sachs. Later, Peter Heller,

[24] Paul Harmat (1986, p. 244) assumes that Alexander analysed Freud's son Ernst, but this is obviously a mistake for Oliver.

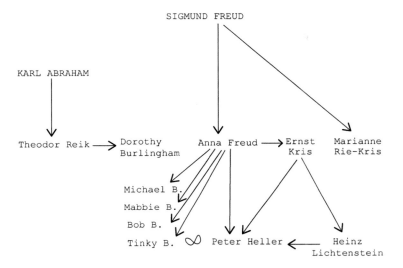

Figure 9.

besides consulting his father's analyst Jekels, was analysed by Heinz Lichtenstein, and by Lichtenstein's own analyst, Ernst Kris, who himself had been analysed by Anna Freud, Heller's first analyst— a fine analytical merry-go-round. When the former patient later discovered that his analysis with Kris did, "however indirectly, … come under her [Anna Freud's] supervision and—still more indirectly— under the purview even of her companion, my mother-in-law [Dorothy Burlingham], who financed the long-drawn-out treatment" (Heller, 1992b, p. 69), when he found out that these people had written about his analysis with the utmost indiscretion in their correspondence, and that these letters were accessible to the public, he partly published them in adding some commentaries (ibid.).[25]

---

[25] [Addition] I had the good fortune of developing a close relationship with Peter, and we had long and animated talks on this and other topics. It was by no means easy for him to go public with all this, and I vividly remember his anxiety before a talk on this topic in Salzburg, when he threatened to cancel it literally in the last minute. We should be all the more grateful to him for surmounting his fears and misgivings. I am also in possession of a tape and a transcript of a talk between him and his friend and schoolmate Ernst Halberstadt Freud, at which I also participated, and in which the topic of the interference of analysis with education in both their lives plays a great role. He also drafted a book

Through Peter Heller's first wife, Katrina "Tinky" Burlingham, this network is tied to another one, the fascinating Burlingham/Freud network (Burlingham, 1989; Young-Bruehl, 1988). All the children of Dorothy Burlingham, the lifelong friend of Anna Freud, were analysed by the latter—at least twice. Of these children, Katrina, in addition, was also analysed by Berta Bornstein, Robert (Bob) by Kurt Eissler, Bob's wife, called Mossik, by Edward Kronold (Kronengold) and by Marianne Kris (daughter of Freud's friend Oscar Rie, analysand of Freud and Franz Alexander), who also analysed Mabbie Burlingham. Michael, the forth child, seems to have been content with his analyses with Anna Freud. Dorothy Burlingham herself was analysed at first by Theodor Reik, and then, this analysis having run into difficulties, by Sigmund Freud himself. This analysis lasted, by the way, from 1927 until shortly before Freud's death in 1939, that is, for thirteen years—during most of which time Dorothy Burlingham lived in the same house as the Freuds. Dorothy's husband Robert, from whom she had separated, was treated by the American analyst Amsden in Budapest, and, possibly, also by Ferenczi in New York (F/Fer III, pp. 285, 288, 342).

Conclusion

In sum, what we find in the factual history of psychoanalysis are repeated patterns of series of affect-laden relationships, be they incestuous, hostile, erotic, or power relations, mixed with varying doses of analysis, leading to much confusion and suffering among those involved. I have not treated hostile relations, which indeed are a chapter *per se*. As for the question of power and its use and misuse in analysis, this is perhaps the most unsettling topic of them all, but it is also the one least studied and the most difficult to grasp, because in most cases it is not as evident as in the case of Gregory Zilboorg and one of his patients, a successful public relations executive (Quinn, 1987, pp. 342–343):

> First there was the watch the patient was wearing (but with a
> different band, at Zilboorg's request), then there were tickets to

---

on the experimental school in Hietzing, Vienna, financed by Dorothy Burlingham, run by Eva Rosenfeld, Joan and Erik Erikson, Willi Hoffer, and others, but he died before he could publish it.

the Joe Louis fight (first or second row, at Zilboorg's request), then a radio. Finally Zilboorg, who needed cash to pay taxes, offered to supplement his analysis of the patient with advice on business undertakings, since the patient—because of his drinking—needed all the help he could get. Zilboorg proposed that the patient pay him a fee of five thousand dollars, in advance and in cash, for his dual role as analyst and business consultant. At this point the patient, even in his dependent state, began to feel used. He paid Zilboorg the first thousand dollars in hundred-dollar bills but then left treatment.

In any case, for the period I primarily studied (until about the Second World War), I have to state that I seldom came across a training analysis *lege artis*, as it was introduced by the Berlin group in 1920 at their institute, and agreed upon internationally in 1925 at the Ninth International Psychoanalytic Congress in Bad Homburg. When theory and practice do not correspond, in fact contradict each other, theory does not *reflect* reality, but stands for ideals not realised in reality, or can even be used to ward reality off and mystify it. According to my material, (1) self-analysis was either not practised after analysis at all, or it did not help much; (2) the dissolution of the so-called transference neurosis hardly ever took place after analysis; (3) hardly ever can one discern something like "abstinence"; (4) the blurring of the borders of professional and intimate relationships was the rule, and not the exception; and (5) even allegedly 'normal', 'unneurotic' people, famous analysts, needed two, three, four, or more long-term analyses—without overcoming certain problems that would almost certainly, were they known, exclude them from analytic training today,[26] and each new biography of a leading pioneer analyst shows with uncanny predictability the dark continent behind the official glamour.

---

[26] "I always play the game (and that's my favourite game) to [say] any time that a training committee [meets]—all the committees make very foolish decisions at times, must, because in borderline cases you can't advise. Impossible. Would say 'Don't be so high up, impressed by your own importance. Let's suppose that the following people would put in an application, and you know everything that you know of them, everything. If it happened today, let's say: Jung, Adler, Stekel, Anna Freud, Melanie Klein, Otto Rank, Ferenczi, Karen Horney. Which of them would you accept? Which of them would you reject?'" (Balint, 1965, p. 47).

Like any other powerful method, psychoanalysis has its in-built dangers. Freud had already drawn the analogy between psychoanalysis and "the effect of X-rays on people who handle them without taking special precautions" (1937c, p. 249). Incidentally, X-rays were discovered by Wilhelm Conrad Röntgen in 1895, the year in which Breuer and Freud's *Studies on Hysteria* were published. And like the early radiologists, the pioneer psychoanalysts—and their patients—suffered the side-effects of the newly discovered method. The more we know about its possible deleterious consequences, the better are we able to take the special precautions required. To do so, however, we have to study the *failed* cases, to learn still more about the dark side of the history of psychoanalysis, without succumbing to the temptation to idealise, to condemn, or to deny our heritage. In this sense, it is my hope that a rewriting of the factual history of psychoanalysis will help us to better understand contemporary problems and to deal with them more efficiently.

Perhaps the time has come to investigate, *sine ira et studio*, the connection between the 'private' lives and experiences of the pioneers and the theories springing from them, to investigate the connection between their experiences (*Erlebnisse*) and insights (*Einsichten*). To do so, the historian must necessarily be indiscreet: like in analysis itself, it is the secret, the repressed, the warded-off, and perhaps precisely the shameful detail that has the greatest explanatory power.

After all, is it not in the best psychoanalytic tradition to let the repressed or disgraceful knowledge "gain a hearing" (Freud, 1927c, p. 53)? And hasn't radical honesty been the trade-mark of psychoanalysis from its inception? "[A]nalysis ... is in the first place an honest establishment of the facts" (Freud & Pfister, 1963, p. 87), and "becoming deceitful and [to] hide the essentials ... is in direct conflict with the spirit of ΨA" (F/Jon, p. 32). And let me conclude with another statement of Freud's saying that

> these psycho-analytical matters are intelligible only if presented in pretty full and complete detail, just as an analysis really gets going only when the patient descends to minute details from the abstractions which are their surrogate. Thus discretion is incompatible with a satisfactory description of an analysis; to provide the latter one would have to be unscrupulous, give away, betray, behave like an artist who buys paints with his wife's house-keeping money or

uses the furniture as firewood to warm the studio for his model. Without a trace of that kind of unscrupulousness the job cannot be done. (Freud & Pfister, 1963, p. 38)

Psychoanalysts and historians might be well advised to take Freud seriously, even when studying him and the one hundred years of the movement he started.

Postscript

Attempting to draw a family tree of psychoanalysis entails at least two major problems: (1) This is not an ordinary family tree. There are not only 'illegitimate children', not only analyses with different 'parents' or repeated analyses with the same 'mother' or 'father', not only reversals in the sense that analysands analysed their former analysts, there are not only mutual analyses, but there is even the case of a son trying to analyse his own physical mother—Jean Piaget (Schepeler, 1993)! (2) Such a map cannot show *which sort of influence* was exerted in these analyses, how this was *experienced* by the analysands, and how they *reacted* upon it. And more:

> Such uncovered filiations will make it that much more complicated to trace the development of … analysts: for not only may the effect of their initiation process be postponed when they are in analysis with someone else; they may be also countertransferentially influenced by the analysts of their spouses and children, or by their patients concurrently or in a delayed manner, or by workshops, ongoing seminars, and so on. (Mahony, 1993)

In sum: the more we know about the past, the more we begin to realise that "it is impossible to write a totally sufficient history of analysis" (ibid.). Not only psychoanalysis itself, but also its historiography might be an impossible profession …

CHAPTER FOUR

Family tree matters*

Through the training analysis, each psychoanalyst becomes part of a genealogy that ultimately goes back to Sigmund Freud and a handful of early pioneers. Evidently, each training and supervising analyst has her or his own theoretical and practical preferences, with which the analysands are confronted and by which they are deeply influenced.[1] Whatever the advantages or shortcomings of this method may be, the point is that a history of ideas in psychoanalysis must take account of the path these ideas have taken. Exploring that path of transmission of theoretical and technical concepts thus becomes a *via regia* for the historical investigator.

---

*[Addition] I have shortened and reworked the original opening paragraphs of this article to avoid repetition.

[1]In addition, there are the influences of the 'sibling' peer group of fellow candidates, etc. All this makes one rather think of schools in the arts or in literature, or even in religion, than of the training in the sciences—although there, too, the borders between theory, practice, and methods on the one hand, and the personal relationship between the trainer and the trainee on the other, are much less distinct than is often believed (cf. Knorr-Cetina, 1981).

Jacob Arlow mentioned that analysts have the habit of tracing their descent from their training analyst (1972, p. 561). Ernest Gellner noted that "the real central emotional bond holding the [psychoanalytic] system together is a striking network of intense binary relations of analysand to analyst" and that it were "both sad and astonishing that little research has yet gone into establishing a full map of these networks" (1985, p. 55). Paul Roazen wrote me that "in the 1960s Geoffrey Gorer tried to get me to construct just such a family tree, but I wilted at the project".[2] Elisabeth Roudinesco has pointed out the filiational networks in her history of psychoanalysis in France (1982, 1986). Recently, Bateman and Holmes have published a small genealogy of British psychoanalysis (1995). Aldo Calanca (Lausanne) has drawn up a family tree for French Switzerland for private use (personal communication), and Victoria Hamilton (Los Angeles) has emphasised this aspect in her teaching (personal communication). In her most recent work, Hamilton has carried out a cluster analysis of responses to a questionnaire, regarding influences of different theories on analytic technique, and has found "a subset of analysts within one orientation, all of whom had been either analyzed or supervised by the same analysts" (1996, p. 9).

In the previous chapter, I presented a provisional draft of psychoanalytic genealogy until about the Second World War, comprising about 500 names, and drew some preliminary conclusions as to the form, structure, and implications of the kind of family tree that emerges.[3] Such a family tree of psychoanalysis is a way to make literally visible, for the first time, the underlying structure of analytic training, as well as the correlational potential and the hidden implications of these data—showing, for instance, the most important training analysts (who were not necessarily the most important theoreticians), by whom today's leading psychoanalysts were analysed, how many analyses were conducted with family members or lovers, which and how many analysts had multiple 'postgraduate' analyses after their initial training, differences between various countries or cities, in which aspects the psychoanalytic training changed over time, and so on.

---

[2] Letter to the author, 7 September 1994.

[3] Let me only add here that a host of clinical papers written at that time are *disguised* accounts of the author's own analysis, of the analysis of a son or daughter, or of a lover, or, perhaps most frequently, of an autoanalysis.

Here, however, I would like to focus on two particular analysts and on their analysands, having a closer look at the impact they have had on contemporary psychoanalysis.

A repressed heritage and the return of the repressed

During the past decades, there has been a debate over core concepts in psychoanalysis, which can be characterised by the following catch-words: drive model versus object relations model, reconstruction of the past versus importance of the present, recovering memories versus creating a narrative, theoretical insight versus emotional experience, inner phantasies versus outer reality, intrapsychical conflict versus environmental deficit, role of the father versus role of the mother, Oedipus complex versus preverbal development, transference versus counter-transference, etc. In this debate, the interpersonal or object relations approach, as opposed to the intrapsychical drive and conflict model, has occupied centre stage.

Could it be that, with some exceptions, there might be one direct line in the psychoanalytic family tree for the interpersonally oriented analysts, and another one for the proponents of drive psychology? In fact, many of the latter, representing the mainstream up to the 1960s or 1970s, can be traced, in their filiation, to Freud himself,[4] and to Freud's daughter *and* analysand, Anna. Those analysts usually acknowledged their debt to and 'descent' from Sigmund and Anna Freud, and considered themselves, and were perceived by many as, representatives of pure or core psychoanalysis. Indeed, what has been called the "Freud factor" has been an important, if unofficial legitimation (see the case of Jean Piaget, who wrongly claimed that his own analyst, Sabina Spielrein, had herself been analysed by Freud, to ennoble his analytic family romance; Schepeler, 1993, p. 261).

On the other side, recent research (e.g., Haynal & Falzeder, 1993; Leitner, 1998; Lieberman, 1985; Rudnytsky, 1991) has shown that influential contemporary, interpersonally oriented concepts in post-Freudian

---

[4]E.g., Marie Bonaparte, Abraham A. Brill, Ruth Mack Brunswick, Dorothy Burlingham, Helene Deutsch, Max Eitingon, Heinz Hartmann, Eduard Hitschmann, Jeanne Lampl-de Groot, Margarete Rie Nunberg, Marianne Rie-Kris, Alix and James Strachey, and many analysands of all these.

psychoanalytic theory and practice go back, to a surprisingly large extent indeed, to two of Freud's first and most intimate colleagues: the Hungarian Sándor Ferenczi and the Viennese Otto Rosenfeld, who called himself Otto Rank—both of whom later became more or less alienated from Freud, and whose work has fallen into oblivion for a long time. Be it the importance of the early caretaker/child relationship, of the preverbal development, be it the splitting into a "good" and a "bad" mother, be it the theory and treatment of sexual child abuse, be it the use of regressive states, and of the repetition of trauma in the analytic interaction, be it the central role ascribed to countertransference and to the use of the analyst's feeling as a tool, be it the interest in nonverbal interactions, the stress on the here and now in the analytic situation, be it the relationship model of therapy as opposed to the interpretation model, be it the concepts of splitting, of double-bind, or, perhaps, most important, the notion about a *non-conflictual core* of early disorders, of a mismatch between the infant's fundamental needs and the environment—all these, and more, can already be found in Ferenczi's and Rank's works.

The idea of a basic, non-instinctual aetiological factor is perhaps best developed in Ferenczi's paper on the "Confusion of tongues" (1933[294]). Ferenczi also drew conclusions as to the changes in therapeutic technique this view entails, stressing what would now be termed the holding and container function, and the therapeutic use of self by the analyst. Such an approach is now usually ascribed to theoreticians, including Michael Balint, Ronald Fairbairn, Erich Fromm, Karen Horney, Heinz Kohut, Harold Searles, Harry Stack Sullivan, William A. White, or Donald W. Winnicott, and, to some extent, Melanie Klein. Their concepts of the "basic fault", "basic trust/mistrust", "existential loneliness", "failing empathy", etc., as well as the following modifications of therapeutic technique, have their historical roots in Ferenczi's and Rank's efforts to counterbalance Freud's stress on the drive paradigm with that on interaction and intersubjectivity.

While some of these views were regarded as dissident when they were propounded in the 1920s and 1930s, they have obviously infiltrated and shaped present theory and practice. With few exceptions, however, the intellectual debts to Ferenczi and Rank have not been acknowledged in the literature—neither by the theoreticians themselves, nor in textbooks and overviews (e.g., Eagle, 1984; Greenberg &

Mitchell, 1983; Mertens, 1981, 1990a, 1990b, 1991). Could it be that it has been inopportune to be associated with those 'heretics'? It makes one wonder that for decades not only the theories of Ferenczi and Rank, but even the subjects they dealt with (e.g., countertransference, object relations, therapeutic relationship), were taboo.

A historical turning point seems to have been the serious personal and scientific conflict within the Secret Committee around Freud in the mid 1920s, which threatened not only to destroy the existence of this 'Old Guard', but even of the psychoanalytic movement itself and of its journals (cf. Grosskurth, 1991; Leitner, 1998; Lieberman, 1985; Wittenberger, 1995). In this conflict, the group represented by Abraham, Eitingon, Jones, and Sachs prevailed over Ferenczi and Rank, with Ferenczi thereafter remaining marginalised in the psychoanalytic movement, and Rank leaving it altogether. The scale was eventually tipped by Freud. Interestingly, some of the new ideas came close to the ones formulated by the young Freud himself. When some of his closest collaborators brought them forward, Freud at first greeted them nearly enthusiastically, then made some ever more cautious reservations, eventually took his distance, and finally espoused the opinion of Abraham and Jones that those concepts were dissident, even heretic and dangerous.

These controversies and the way in which they were treated, acted, as Michael Balint reminded us, as a trauma for the analytic community. A decisive blow on Ferenczi and Rank fell in the 1950s by the hand of Ernest Jones, then the only survivor of this group. Jones labeled both psychotic, and their dissident theories as the outcome of psychotic thinking (Jones III). To quote again Balint: "the aftermath of Jones' biography was a spate of acrimonious publications" (in *Diary*, p. 220).

There were only few to publicly stand up against these allegations. Erich Fromm (cf. 1959) in particular objected to what he called Jones's

> typically Stalinist type of re-writing history, whereby Stalinists assassinate the character of opponents by calling them spies and traitors. The Freudians do it by calling them 'insane'. ... [I]ncidentally, Jones does not seem to be aware of the disservice he does to psychoanalysis. The picture he gives of the central committee is, then, that two members, and the most trusted ones, became insane. Of one, Dr. Sachs, he says that Freud said he should not

have belonged in the first place. Of Eitingon he says that he was not too bright. There remain Abraham and Jones, who were, according to Jones' own testimony, constantly engaged in the pettiest quarrels with all the other members. A beautiful picture of the group of those who claim to represent the sanity which follows from psychoanalysis! (Letter to Izette de Forest, 31 October 1957; Erich Fromm Archives)

This criticism might sound too harsh or exaggerated, but is rather confirmed by an astonishing blackmail letter Jones wrote to one of his critics:

I think it is sheer nonsence [sic] to talk of my having made an attack on Ferenczi simply because there are people who cannot bear the truth. The same of course applies to Freud, Rank, etc. I have all the letters Ferenczi wrote to Freud from 1907 till the end. They make most painful reading as displaying a thoroughly unstable and suffering personality whom I personally had always loved. But the evidence of the increasing deterioration is only too plain. Up to the end Freud wanted him to be President of the International Association, though he advised him to keep back the paper he had written for the last Congress since it would harm his reputation. The President of the Congress refused to admit such an obviously psychopathic paper, and it was only at my intervention that it was allowed. Naturally if anyone attacks me in public I shall have to produce some of the evidence I have taken care to suppress in Ferenczi's own interest. (Letter to Dr. Magoun, 31 October 1957; Erich Fromm Archives)[5]

It is true that the situation has changed: during the past years works on these topics have virtually exploded, while simultaneously interest in Ferenczi, and to a lesser extent, in Rank, has significantly grown. During

---

[5]Izette de Forest astutely commented: "one wonders why Freud, trying to prevent Ferenczi from giving the last paper at Wiesbaden, still constantly tried to get F. accept the Presidency of the Intern[ational Psychoanalytic Association]. Why would Freud want a man suffering from 'mental deterioration' to be Pres.? And why did Jones work to get the last paper published, if it was 'psychopathic' and bad for Ferenczi's reputation and if he loved him so much?" (Letter to Erich Fromm, 3 December 1957; Erich Fromm Archives).

the past ten years or so there has been a veritable Ferenczi renaissance, and there are signs that a similar renaissance is imminent for Rank.[6]

Rank …

During the past years, there has been a growing interest in the work of Otto Rank, who for some is "the most extraordinary catalytic agent that ever hit the psychoanalytic movement" (Kardiner, in Lieberman, 1985, p. 235), or even "the best mind that psychoanalysis contributed to intellectual history" (J. Jones, 1960, p. 219). Recently, Marina Leitner (1998) has shown that the conflict between Freud and Rank was a key conflict in the history of psychotherapy of the twentieth century, and that many ideas usually attributed to Erich Fromm, Karen Horney, Melanie Klein, Margaret Mahler, Donald W. Winnicott, etc., originate in Rank. Esther Menaker (1982, p. ix) sees in Rank's work the "missing link in the historical chain of the development of theory and practice within the psychoanalytic movement". Peter Rudnytsky has pointed out the similarities in Rank's and Winnicott's thinking, and maintains that Rank is "the unacknowledged precursor of contemporary object relations theory" (1991, p. 48). Some philosophers and humanistic and existential psychologists, above all Ernest Becker, but also Paul Goodman or Rollo May,[7] have credited Rank as the source and inspiration of many of their ideas, and his influence on social work is uncontested.

---

[6]Cf. the work on Ferenczi by, for example, André Haynal in Switzerland; Ilse Barande, Thierry Bokanowski, Eva Brabant, Judith Dupont, Wladimir Granoff, Béla Grunberger, Claude Lorin, and Pierre Sabourin in France; Carlo Bonomi and Marco Conci in Italy; Martin Luis Cabré in Spain; Martin Stanton in England; Christopher Fortune in Canada; Lewis Aron, John Gedo, Adrienne Harris, Axel Hoffer, Peter Hoffer, William Boyce Lum, Jeffrey Masson, Arnold Rachman, Ann-Louise Silver, Judith Vida, and Benjamin Wolstein in the US; Michael Ermann, Patrizia Giampieri-Deutsch, Paul Harmat, Rudolf Pfitzner, Michael Schröter, and myself in Germany and Austria. The increasing interest in Ferenczi is also reflected by the publication of the Freud/Ferenczi and the Ferenczi/Groddeck correspondence, of Ferenczi's *Clinical Diary*, by the foundation of the S. Ferenczi Society (NYC), and by the panel on Ferenczi at the IPA Congress 1996 in San Francisco. As to Rank, I would like to mention the work of André Haynal, Ludwig Janus, Robert Kramer, Marina Leitner, James Lieberman, Esther Menaker, Peter Rudnytsky, Jessie Taft, Anton Zottl, and my own. Phyllis Grosskurth and Paul Roazen, although not devoting particular works on Ferenczi or Rank, certainly fostered interest in them. [Addition] The trend has indeed continued, and many works and authors' names would have to be added to this list today.

[7]"I have long considered Rank to be *the* great unacknowledged genius in Freud's circle", Rollo May wrote shortly before his death to Robert Kramer (in Kramer, 1995, pp. 56–57).

Still, most psychoanalysts have, it seems, been loath to acknowledge Rank's pivotal role. His importance for theory and technique, but also for the politics of psychoanalysis up to the mid 1920s, is nearly forgotten today. Besides his scientific contributions, Rank held all strings of psychoanalytic publishing in his hands: he was the editor of the *Internationale Zeitschrift für Psychoanalyse* and of *Imago*, the head of the *Internationaler Psychoanalytischer Verlag*, and co-editor of Freud's *Gesammelte Schriften*. For more than ten years, Rank's name appeared on the cover of Freud's *opus magnum, The Interpretation of Dreams* (1900a). Without doubt, he and Ferenczi were by far closest to Freud, who still in 1924 was "firmly resolved to hand over ... the presidency" of the Vienna Psychoanalytic Society to Rank (F/Ran, p. 196), and, as late as 1927, would have liked to make Ferenczi president of the IPA: "[W]ith you as president, our intentions will be realized. Only in case of strong opposition against you would I like you to support the election of Eitingon, in order to exclude that of Jones" (F/Fer III, p. 324).

Rank started his clinical practice relatively late, in 1920 (ibid., p. 130), but soon rose to be one of the leading analysts. In 1924, he published two important books, *The Trauma of Birth* and, together with Ferenczi, *The Development of Psychoanalysis*. Both works brought forward new, important, and disturbing views, and were at the centre of the scientific and personal conflict within the Secret Committee. When Rank went to the States shortly afterwards (still in 1924), the leading analysts and psychiatrists of New York flocked to him, and he reanalysed "nearly all" (F/Ran, p. 202) of Freud's American analysands along his new theoretical and technical lines. Freud found it "nice" to learn that Rank had taken over his analysands, and added that he recalled their analyses "with no satisfaction at all. It often seemed to me that analysis suits Americans like a white shirt suits a raven" (ibid.).[8]

Rank, however, was spectacularly successful with those ravens, pointing out to Freud (F/Ran, p. 209):

---

[8] Interestingly, in other contexts Freud twice compared psychoanalysis with "whitewashing negroes" (Breuer & Freud, 1895, German edition, p. 262—the expression was omitted in the *Standard Edition*; and in Freud & Abraham, 1965 (p. 40), where it was euphemistically translated as "cleaning up neurotics"). [Addition] This was corrected to "whitewashing" in the 2002 translation by Caroline Schwarzacher (F/Abr, p. 45). On the simile of the raven with the white shirt, also used by Freud elsewhere, see F/Kinder, p. 388 and note 5.

If you interpret the phenomenon of transference starting with the father, then you get homosexual fixation in a man and heterosexual fixation in a woman as the result of analysis—which actually holds for all the cases that come to me from other analysts. The analysts among these patients have felt this both subjectively and objectively: subjectively, since they have lost nothing of their neurosis, and objectively, since they were unable to cure their own patients with this technique. This is attributable not to the people here, who are no better or worse than those in Europe, but to the shortcomings of method and technique. When people saw that their work gets easier and they achieve better results[9] with the modifications I introduced, they praised me as a savior.

Towards his friend Ferenczi, Rank was more outspoken, writing that he had "saved psychoanalysis here, perhaps the life of the whole international movement. The analysts here were for the most part uncured and dissatisfied with Professor's analysis; as they themselves and the whole world said, they came back even worse" (in Lieberman, 1985, p. 245). This attack on her father's technique was not lost on Anna Freud who commented to Eitingon: Rank "is still full of hidden, cheap malice—this becomes clear if you know that the psychoanalyzed patients [sic] he speaks of are all former patients of Papa's" (in Young-Bruehl, 1988, p. 149).

Among Rank's American analysands we find, among others, Thaddeus Ames, Lionel Blitzsten, Harry Bone, Dorothy Hankins, Abram Kardiner, Marion Kenworthy[10] (Lieberman, 1985, p. 268), Anaïs Nin, Martin Peck (ibid., p. 269), John Rosen, Jessie Taft, John Taylor (ibid., p. 287), George Wilbur (ibid., p. 269), and Frankwood Williams,[11] but above all two crucial personalities: Smith Ely Jelliffe (1866–1945; cf. Burnham, 1983) and William Alanson White (1870–1937). (In his

---

[9][Addition] Missing in F/Ran: "both in their own analyses and with their patients".

[10]Who pioneered in the introduction of psychiatry in social work and education.

[11]Frankwood Earl Williams (1883–1936) from New York was an important spokesperson and catalyst, jumping "on three different bandwagons: mental hygiene, Rankian psychoanalysis, and socialism … [His] main motive to undergo psychoanalysis [with Rank] was the positive reaction of his close friend Marion Kenworthy to her own previous analysis in the hands of Rank … [His] apartment in Greenwich Village became a center for Rankian analysis in the United States. … When Rank was in town, he would chair these meetings" (Pols, 1995, pp. 1, 15, 16).

letters to Freud, Rank does not mention his analysands' names, so it is not clear in all cases, which of them had previously been analysed by Freud; Jelliffe and White certainly were not.)

Apart from their important scientific contributions, Jelliffe and White were key figures in psychoanalytic publishing, editing the *Journal of Nervous and Mental Disease*, the *Medical News*, the *New York Medical Journal*, the *Nervous and Mental Disease Monograph Series*, and the *Psychoanalytic Review* (Burnham, 1983). White was for over thirty years the head of St. Elizabeth Hospital in Washington, DC, the main US governmental hospital, and "was of great importance in shaping the entire psychiatric enterprise in the United States and elsewhere" (ibid., p. xiv) and in spreading psychoanalysis. He did keep some distance from Freud,[12] stating for instance that "[t]he time has come to free American psychiatry from the domination of the Pope at Vienna" (in Lieberman, 1985, pp. 174–175), but this very attitude could have contributed to his being receptive to Rank's ideas. White and his wife were analysed by Rank in the States, "and White had promptly published the 'Birth Trauma' lecture in the *Psychoanalytic Review*. ... White wanted to bring out in English the Ferenczi-Rank monograph on technique; Caroline Newton, who was analyzed by Rank in Vienna, had done the translation, which was published before long as *The Development of Psychoanalysis*" (ibid., p. 254).

Another link exists between Otto Rank and Carl Rogers, who is even viewed by some as "the most influential psychologist in American history" (Kirschenbaum & Henderson, 1989, p. xi). Robert Kramer (1995, p. 54) has shown in detail that Rank can be considered the precursor of client-centered therapy, and that it was "a personal encounter with Otto Rank in 1936 [which] revolutionized the way [Rogers] thought about psychotherapy. 'I became infected with Rankian ideas', he told his biographer". When asked "about who had been his teachers, Rogers answered: 'Otto Rank and my clients'" (ibid., p. 78).

... and Ferenczi

When we have a look at Ferenczi's analysands, we find among them, among others, George S. Amsden, Joseph J. Asch,[13] Michael Balint,

---

[12] As did another very important figure, Swiss-American Adolf Meyer.

[13] Joseph J. Asch (1880–1935), Chief of Clinic at the Lenox Hill Hospital, co-founder of the New York Psychoanalytic Society; a previous analysand of Freud's (1922; F/Jon, p. 446).

Therese Benedek, Claude D. Daly, Marga Dubowitz, David Eder, Izette de Forest, Marjorie Franklin, Frieda Fromm-Reichmann, Georg Groddeck (who also analysed Ferenczi in turn), Lewis Hill, Ernest Hoffman, István Hollós, William Inman, Ernest Jones, Edward Kempf,[14] Melanie Klein, Sándor Kovács, Barbara Lantos, Kata Lévy, Lajos Lévy, Sándor Lorand, Erzsébet Révész-Radó, John Rickman, Géza Róheim, Ada Schott, Elizabeth Severn, Eugénie Sokolnicka, Clara Thompson, Rudolf von Urbantschitsch, and Frankwood Williams. Perhaps most crucial in retaining Ferenczi's views within the psychoanalytic community were two of them, Michael Balint and Clara Thompson.

"Ferenczi writes in an unpublished note of 26th of September 1932 ..., when he knew already how ill he was: 'Balint takes up things there where I got stuck'" (Dupont, 1993, p. 212). Balint succeeded Ferenczi as the head of the Budapest psychoanalytic outpatient clinic, he became his literary executor (including the Freud/Ferenczi correspondence and Ferenczi's *Clinical Diary*), and after Ferenczi's death took over his patients. It is interesting, though, that while Balint did credit Ferenczi for some ideas (e.g., the notion of primary object love, or the dismissal of the theory of primary narcissism), he did perhaps not make it sufficiently clear that also his most central contributions are an elaboration of Ferenczi's ideas. For instance, I have tried to show that Balint's concept of the basic fault (Balint, 1968) can be traced to Ferenczi's view of two irreconcilable worlds (that of the infant and that of the adults, that of tenderness and that of passion, that of pre-guilt and that of guilt) (Falzeder, 1986), and that his view of the three phases of trauma (Balint, 1969) is little more than a paraphrase of Ferenczi's ideas as developed in that "obviously psychopathic paper", "The confusion of tongues" (1933[294]). Similarly, Balint's therapeutic technique owes much to Ferenczi: the rejection of the "mirror/abstinence/anonymity illusion" (Cremerius, 1983), the stress on the therapeutical relationship, the

---

Freud did not hold him in high esteem: "[H]e is a pathological fool. His analysis with me was the most miserable you can imagine, without any trace of understanding, either analytic or simple (common sense)" (F/Abr, pp. 501–502).

[14]Edward J. Kempf (1885–1971) worked at St. Elizabeth's Hospital until 1920, and then in private practice in New York City. He developed a form of active psychotherapy for schizophrenia. "When I was analyzed by Ferenczi in 1926 I found that my views were consistent with those of Ferenczi and Freud but I had a far deeper physiological and evolutionary biological orientation than they had" (Kempf, 1974, pp. 8–9; cf. Kempf, 1949). Recommended by G. Stanley Hall, Kempf had visited Freud in August 1923.

importance of the general atmosphere in treatment, the recognition of countertransference as a tool, and the work with regressive states and nonverbal communication. Balint's concept of the "new beginning" also goes directly back to Ferenczi (Ferenczi, 1939[308], p. 271).

Even Balint's interest in medicine and his collaboration with general practitioners in so-called Balint groups is a continuation of Ferenczi's ideas, who, as early as in 1923, had published a paper on "Psychoanalysis in the service of the general practitioner" (Ferenczi, 1923[259]), and in 1926 had written what sounds like a manifesto for Balint groups (*Rundbriefe IV*, p. 309):

> It becomes always clearer that in one way or another one has to take care of the practical training of [medical] colleagues, who are not specialized analysts. Their practice gradually *forces* all doctors to view their cases also from our point of view, and it would be unfair to make them turn to a psychoanalyst for every more or less psychically complicated case. A couple of things could be done by the analytically orientated family doctor himself.

Balint brought these ideas to Great Britain, where they fell on fertile ground in the British "Middle Group" and since have influenced present psychoanalytic thinking, particularly in Europe. Interestingly, Balint also had a considerable impact on post-war psychoanalysis in Germany, analysing or supervising key figures such as Wolfgang Loch, Edeltrud Meistermann-Seeger, Alexander Mitscherlich, and Margarete Mitscherlich-Nielsen. There is even a connection with my home country, Austria, in the person of Balint's analysand Erich Pakesch, founder of the psychoanalytic society in Austria's second biggest city, Graz (and himself analyst of some of Austria's leading analysts: Rainer Danzinger, Angela Kozlik, Gert Lyon, August Ruhs).[15]

Regarding Ferenczi's impact on psychoanalysis in the United States, his stay there in 1926/27 played a pivotal role.[16] For most of the time, he

---

[15]Letter from Gert Lyon to the author, 6 May 1997.—Pakesch had a second analysis (as well as supervision) with Igor A. Caruso, the founder of the *Austrian Study Groups for Depth Psychology*, and co-founder, with Erich Fromm, Gerard Chrzanowski, and others, of the *International Federation of Psychoanalytic Societies* (Caruso, 1982, p. 13). Caruso, a charismatic, but also controversial figure, was my own teacher at the University of Salzburg.

[16][Addition] I might add that all the following information from the Freud/Ferenczi letters and the *Rundbriefe*, both now available in print, was published for the first time in this article, so I went into some detail.

stayed in New York City, where he regularly lectured at the New School for Social Research (*Rundbriefe IV*, p. 320). He also gave talks, among others, at the New York Psychiatric Society (F/Fer III, p. 288), before the National Research Council, the Child Study Association of America,[17] the New York Society for Clinical Psychiatry (*Rundbriefe IV*, p. 332; F/Fer III, p. 291), the Greenwich Psychiatric Round Table Society (a group of psychiatric social workers), at Columbia University, and last but not least at the Hungarian Medical Society in New York (*Rundbriefe IV*, pp. 355–356). In short, he "had the opportunity to meet all leading psychiatrists of New York and Albany, privately and officially" (ibid., p. 331).

This is no exaggeration. From the Freud/Ferenczi correspondence and the *Rundbriefe* we learn that Ferenczi was received very well indeed not only by the psychiatric and academic establishment, but also by influential circles in New York City in general. Not surprisingly, he was on excellent terms with Alvin Johnson,[18] Bernard Glueck,[19] and Frankwood Williams; likewise with William A. White and Smith E. Jelliffe. But he also got to know a host of other persons whose names read, quite literally, like an extract of *Who's Who in America*: Herman Morris Adler (1876-ca.1935), professor at the Universities of Illinois and California; Sanger Monroe Brown (1852–1928), professor at Medical School, Chicago; Sam Adolph Lewisohn (1884–1951), banker and vice-president of the Museum of Modern Art; Adolf Meyer (1866–1950), perhaps the most influential psychiatrist in the United States in the first half of the twentieth century;[20] Edwin Robert Anderson Seligman (1861–1939), professor at Columbia; Thomas William Salmon (1876–1927), also professor at Columbia; Henry Ayres Uterhart (1875–1946), prominent lawyer in New York; and so on.

---

[17]On the relationship between pedagogics and psychoanalysis, at the Waldorf Astoria Hotel.

[18]Alvin Saunders Johnson (1874–1971), famous economist and political scientist, professor at various universities, including Columbia, Cornell, and Stanford; editor of *The New Republic*. Since 1923 director of the *New School of Social Research*, which had invited Ferenczi in the first place.

[19]Bernard Glueck (1884–1972), of Polish extraction, director of the psychiatric clinic of Sing Sing (1915–18), director of the department for mental hygiene at the New School. Known for his works on forensic psychiatry.

[20]Meyer was born in Switzerland. After his emigration in 1892, he had influential posts in Worcester, Ward's Island, and at Cornell University Medical College. 1910–1941 he was a professor at Johns Hopkins University, and Director of its Henry Phipps Psychiatric Clinic (1914).

John Watson (1878–1958), the famous psychologist and founder of behaviourism, found Ferenczi important enough, the latter writes (F/Fer III, p. 294),

> to challenge me to a duel … He gave a lecture in an elegant ladies' club ("Cosmopolitan Club"), had me invited to dinner by the president, and personally apostrophized me in his lecture. … Although unprepared, I had to counter him. It was not difficult to show him the nonsensicalness of his denial of psychic reality (although I doubt whether that would have done him any good). … I would—I said—perhaps send white rats and rabbits, but not people, to Watson for treatment.—The audience seemed as though they were redeemed, and they were happy about the fact that one perhaps doesn't have to give up one's soul after all.

At a dinner in Ferenczi's honour in the Hotel Pennsylvania, "Dr. James Harvey Robinson, Dr. Frankwood Williams, and Dr. Johnson functioned as principal speakers" (ibid., pp. 298–299). Robinson (1863–1936), the famous American historian, was a co-founder of the New School, and professor for history at Columbia. As Ferenczi put it, he was, "next to John Dewey the best-known and most recognized intellectual authority in this country" (ibid.). Robinson gave a talk on the historical significance of psychoanalysis. Unabashed, Ferenczi immediately responded by setting "some of his statements straight. … The evening was actually a celebration in honor of psychoanalysis" (ibid.).

Right before he left, Ferenczi came closest to what he called *Dollarglück*, or "dollar fortune" (F/Fer III, p. 306):

> The dollar millionaire McCormick family … has a member (a man), who … is being treated on an estate in Santa Barbara (Calif.), similar to the way Ludwig II of Bavaria was back then (twice daily music bands, daily cinema performances ad personam, etc.). This [has been going on] for twenty years. They seem to have gotten tired of the thing and are consulting all psychiatrists in order. … [T]he question was also put to me whether I want to make the $\psi\alpha$ attempt … I declined … In my zeal to be conscientious, I also replied hesitatingly to the question of whether I have to visit the patient in order to make a diagnosis, and in so doing misplayed the pleasure trip to California. Dr. Glück—who, strangely, already knew of my

impending mission—asked me to recommend him "in the interest
of the cause of psychoanalysis".

Ferenczi also went to Philadelphia, to talk before the "very conservative" Medical Society there—with great success (*Rundbriefe IV*, p. 356).
And finally, he came to Washington, DC. "I was in Washington for three
days, gave a lecture on sexual and genital theories in the United Ps.An.
and Ps.Pathol. Association. Then *four* long papers for active psychoanalysts on technical questions. Dr. W. A. White was very forthcoming; he
is a reliable friend of psychoanalysis and is influencing his staff of physicians along these lines" (F/Fer III, p. 309).

In addition, he led a busy practice, analysing for eight hours a day
(although only for five on Saturdays …) (ibid., p. 283), like Rank rean-
alysing a couple of analysts who had already previously been with
Freud (e.g., Joseph Asch). And also like Rank, Ferenczi implicitly
criticised Freud—and Freud's 'representative' in this country, A. A.
Brill—when he wrote to him that "[m]any physicians in positions of
leadership told me it is regrettable that I didn't come ten years earlier;
the way in which Ψα was presented to them has scared them away"
(ibid., p. 306).

Ferenczi was also heavily criticised, however, because he made (what
he called) *training* analyses with non-medical persons, with whom he
also met for weekly seminars (*Rundbriefe IV*, p. 334), and whom he
encouraged to organise themselves (F/Fer III, p. 284)—contrary to
the position against so-called lay analysis, taken by the American
Psychoanalytic Association. This led to tensions with the official representatives of psychoanalysis: "The bigwigs: Brill, Oberndorf, Stern,
Kardiner, Monroe Meyer, consistently kept their distance from me"
(ibid., p. 311).

In the wake of his stay in America, some Americans followed Ferenczi
to Europe for analysis, for example, Amsden (ibid., pp. 314, 321), but
above all Clara Thompson. Her role in bringing Ferenczi's ideas to the
United States is comparable to the one played by Balint in England.
She can perhaps be considered Ferenczi's main direct successor on the
North American continent, through her general orientation and more
specifically through her work on countertransference and the role of the
analyst's personality (cf. Thompson, 1956). ("Jones … already has me
labelled as deluded", she wrote to Erich Fromm on 5 November 1957
(Erich Fromm Archives).)

> Thompson had personal analysis with Ferenczi in Budapest
> during the summers of 1928 and 1929, and for two years contin-
> uously from 1931 until Ferenzi's death in 1933. ... Thompson ...
> attributed to Sullivan her decision to seek analysis from Ferenczi.
> "... I would not have gone to Ferenczi, because who would have
> the nerve to go to Budapest all alone, if Sullivan hadn't insisted that
> this was the only analyst in Europe he had any confidence in, and
> therefore, if I was going to Europe and get analyzed I had just better
> go there. So, I went." (Noble & Burnham, 1969, p. 30)

As to Harry Stack Sullivan, it is true that the validity of his theories is
disputed up to the present day, culminating in Steven Marcus's verdict
that "what he had were *terms* that masqueraded as ideas", and that his
views were a "goulash of doubletalk, spiced with drivel and served up
as the blue-plate special of psychobabble", an "incomprehensible nonsense [that] would be no more than good for some laughs today had
Sullivan not been taken seriously by considerable numbers of highly
intelligent people" (1984, pp. 237, 242). Marcus's statement might be as
exaggerated as Chrzanowski's "that history will give Sullivan ... a place
only surpassed by that of Freud" (1977, p. 377), but there is no doubt
that his influence on American psychoanalysis and psychiatry has been
enormous. According to Greenberg and Mitchell, Sullivan is "one of the
most influential, most ambitiously radical, and most frequently mis-
read figures in the history of psychoanalytic ideas" (1983, p. 80).[21]
    The Ferenczian heritage in Sullivan's case is not as explicit as in
Thompson's, but nonetheless discernible and important. He "had been
much impressed by Ferenczi's address on 'Present-Day Problems in
Psychoanalysis' before the American Psychoanalytic Association at its
Christmas meeting in 1926" (ibid.), and it seems that his influencing
Thompson to have analysis with Ferenczi was also motivated by his
idea to have a second-hand Ferenczian analysis in turn. Many of his
core ideas and concepts bear a close resemblance to those of Ferenczi,
while being couched in a different terminology. When Thompson
denies that there was any influence of Ferenczi on Sullivan (1944,
p. 105), she obviously disregards her own close personal and analytical

---

[21] [Addition] Meanwhile, the first intellectual biography of Sullivan has been published
(Conci, 2000).

relationship with both. Sullivan himself "at no time discussed, and only rarely alluded to, anyone who had contributed to his thinking" (Silver, 1993, p. 647).

There is another, perhaps less well known example, where analytical links are mixed with personal ones: When Ferenczi lectured before the Washington Psychopathological Society, he also "gave a series of seminars at the home of Philip Graven" (Noble & Burnham, 1969, p. 15). Graven became the analyst of Ernest Hadley (ibid.), who in turn not only analysed the owner and medical director of the Chestnut Lodge Sanitarium in Rockville, MD (Silver, 1995), Dexter Bullard, Sr., but also Harold Searles (Ann Silver, personal communication). Silver showed (1993, p. 651) how close the concepts of Searles come to those of Ferenczi, while Aron commented, "I believe that Searles may be the contemporary American answer to Ferenczi" (1992, p. 183).

Speaking of Chestnut Lodge, whose pioneering role in the theory and treatment of psychoses is uncontested, would it not be interesting to have a look at the analytic 'family tree' of Searles's predecessor, Frieda Fromm-Reichmann? Her views, too, bear a close resemblance to those of Ferenczi. In an autobiographic taped interview (brought to my attention by Ann Silver), she mentions her first two analysts, Wilhelm Wittenberg from Munich (who later also analysed Erich Fromm), and Hanns Sachs (Erich was analysed by him as well).

In addition, she and her one-time husband (and analysand!) Erich Fromm were deeply influenced by another repressed figure in psychoanalytic history: Georg Groddeck. Frieda worked closely together with Groddeck in the latter's sanitarium in Baden-Baden, serving as hostess at Groddeck's scientific meetings. Erich later stated, if only in a private letter, that

> of all the analysts in Germany I knew, he was … the only one with truth, originality, courage and extraordinary kindness. … I always felt a deep gratitude to him and, if you please, to life, to have had the privilege of having known him, and I am sure that even if I was never his student in any technical sense, his teaching influenced me more than that of other teachers I had. (Letter to Sylvia Grossmann, 12 November 1957; Erich Fromm Archives)

As it happens, Groddeck had been a very close friend of Ferenczi's (cf. Ferenczi & Groddeck, 1982/2006), and the two of them had even occasionally analysed each other. As Ann Silver reminds us (1993, pp. 647–649),

> Ferenczi's major impact on the Washington area occurred with the arrival of Fromm-Reichmann at Chestnut Lodge in 1935 ... [in bringing] the spirit of Groddeck's and Ferenczi's and certainly her own work to the United States through her work at Chestnut Lodge; however she, like Sullivan, did not reminisce about the specific contributions of colleagues who had shaped her views. During those years, Ferenczi's and Groddeck's names had become anathemas; the psychoanalytic applications to treating severely ill patients were often heavily attacked.

In this context, I was excited to find out, in the (then) still unpublished part of the Freud/Ferenczi correspondence, that Fromm-Reichmann did have a *tranche* of analysis with Ferenczi. When Ferenczi stayed with the Groddecks in Baden-Baden after his American trip, she was "coming over to me once a week from Heidelberg. She is an astute, analytically extremely talented person" (F/Fer III, p. 323).

Ferenczi's and Rank's impact

American psychoanalysis in the 1920s and early 1930s was dominated to a great extent by Rank, Ferenczi, and their analysands.[22] How precarious the situation had become for the *echt* Freudians, as they have been called, can be guessed from their cutting Ferenczi, and from their polemical, ad hominem attacks on Rank (for instance by Mary Chadwick and Abraham Brill), publicly calling him "maladjusted", "confused", or even an "idiot" (Lieberman, 1985, pp. 291–292).

Although from a contemporary point of view, Ferenczi and Rank brought similar ideas to the States, they had already broken with each other when Ferenczi came to New York two years after Rank. When they met by chance in Penn Station, Ferenczi cut Rank. "He was my best friend", complained Rank bitterly afterwards, "and he refused to speak to me" (Taft, 1958, p. xvi).

---

[22]Particularly in Boston, Philadelphia, Washington, and Baltimore. There was hardly yet any psychoanalytic movement to speak of on the West Coast.

In 1930, Ferenczi's and Rank's analysands White and Thompson were president and vice-president of the Washington Psychoanalytic respectively, while Sullivan was still vice-president of the American. James Strachey wrote to his wife Alix on 5 October 1924 that "Brill ... gives gruesome accounts of Rank's activities in the States. Only 3 Americans stand out against him: Brill, Frink, and Oberndorf! The others say that one must have one's Father Complex analyzed by Freud & one's Mother Complex by Rank" (Meisel & Kendrick, 1985, p. 80). The New School for Social Research, receptive to Ferenczi's and Rank's ideas, gained increasing importance. The Washington/Baltimore area had, under the influence of Sullivan and White, always steered a more or less independent course. In Boston, in

> 1928–29 the Rankians dominated: Peck, Wilbur, and John Taylor had been Rank's patients and students; Leolia Dalrymple was analyzed by Peck that year. Those psychiatrists attended the Rankian seminars in New York. Forty-five years later Dalrymple recalled the lively sessions in Frankwood Wiliams's large living room in lower Manhattan. The fifteen to twenty participants came from hospitals and universities, from Philadelphia and Boston as well as New York. (Lieberman, 1985, p. 287)

Harvard psychologist Henry Murray, who for some time was involved in the Boston Psychoanalytic Society, was much interested in Rank's work (ibid., p. 345), and in 1935 invited him to speak at Harvard. In Philadelphia, "'*relationship therapy*'—not 'interpretive therapy'—was the emphasis of the Philadelphia School" (Kramer, 1995, p. 59). "[C]hild psychiatrist Frederick Allen [was] an enthusiastic admirer" (Lieberman, 1985, p. 345). Allen (probably an analysand of Rank's) was the director of the Philadelphia Child Guidance Clinic; an important collaborator of his was Rank's analysand Dorothy Hankins, who worked there for over thirty years (Leitner, 1998, p. 225).

In 1929, Brill succeeded White as President of the American Psychoanalytic Association. In 1930, the Boston Society reorganised: "The Freudians took control; the Rankians had to convert or leave" (Lieberman, 1985, pp. 287–288). Finally, with the arrival of the immigrants, the counter-movement fully set in. The European immigrants tended sometimes to adhere to a strict and somewhat limited interpretation of psychoanalysis, wanting to rescue its 'core' from what they viewed as its being watered down, and striving to establish psychoanalysis as a natural science. Having lost their home and home country (many of them for the second or third time), their language, and often their family, psychoanalysis became all the more important to them as a constituent of their identity, which had to be preserved in a 'pure' form. The views of Erich Fromm, Karen Horney, Smith Ely Jelliffe, Harry Stack Sullivan, Clara Thompson, or William Alanson White, were gradually replaced by those of Heinz Hartmann, Ernst Kris, or Rudolph Loewenstein. Fromm, Horney, and Thompson formed their own society (not without splitting themselves later on). Otto Rank was expelled from the American Psychoanalytic Association, of which he had been an honorary member (Lieberman, 1985, p. 263). Persons who had had their training with him or Ferenczi were required to have a re-analysis with an officially approved, medical training analyst in order to qualify.

Paradoxical interventions

So far, I have tried to show that a direct, although forgotten, genea-logical line links theoreticians, who stand for leading paradigms of contemporary psychoanalysis, with two early pioneers. But instead of expanding this further, and to quote more examples, I would like to investigate some cases where this is *not* so. Evidently, not *all* of the object relations theorists can trace their genealogy back to Ferenczi or Rank, and not all of the drive psychologists can trace theirs to Sigmund and Anna Freud.

To start with, it has to be borne in mind that a family tree of psycho-analysis gives a bird's eye view of the channels through which a trans-mission of ideas took place; what it does *not* show is a close-up view, is the *contents* of the transmission, *which sort of influence* was exerted in those analyses, how this was *experienced* by the analysands, and how they *reacted* upon it. Let us have a closer look at some cases of impor-tant psychoanalysts who did *not* take over their analysts' views, and at the interrelationship between how they experienced their training and supervisory analyses, and the kind of theoretical and clinical views they developed.

Perhaps the best example is Ferenczi himself. He started out with the hope of having in psychoanalysis an objective method to clarify human relationships. But this hope was bound to be thoroughly disappointed in the cases of the analyses of his mistress's daughter Elma Pálos with himself and Freud, and in his own analysis with Freud.[23] Instead of solving the problems, the interference with psychoanalysis made those relationships more difficult.

I have tried to show (see Chapter Eleven) that Ferenczi had developed a full-blown transference neurosis towards Freud already before his analysis with the latter, and that, moreover, this transference neurosis was only inadequately dealt with in the analysis itself and therefore could not be dissolved. In these episodes, Ferenczi had to realise painfully that psychoanalysis is not an instrument that can function independently of the person using it. Very probably this played a major role in making him recognise the analyst's attitude as a variable in the therapeutic equation, and therefore placing this very attitude (or, if you prefer, countertransference) at the centre of his interest.

In his relationship towards Freud, Ferenczi clearly identified with the role of the analysand/child, with the person who is not supposed to know what the analyst does know. When he was not helped by the analysis, indeed suffered from it, he reacted like the child suffering from unpredictable or mad parents, turning into their "psychiatrist" (Ferenczi, 1933[294], p. 165).[24] I would like to venture the idea that, also in other cases, those who suffer from their analysts' behaviour are propelled to find an explanation for this very behaviour, tend to focus their interest on the *therapist's* contribution to the analytical relationship, and the therapeutic use of the analyst's self, and will therefore develop a theory of countertransference. Those, however, who take a more parental or narcissistic stance—like Freud—will be more prone to explain why their patients/children make *them* suffer, and will rather develop a theory of transference, that is, a theory that treats the therapist's contribution as a constant factor and thus shifts it out of focus.

Is there further evidence to substantiate this hypothesis? It seems that the first paper ever written specifically on countertransference

---

[23]Ferenczi had at least four 'analyses': with Jung and Freud, and mutual analyses with his colleague Groddeck and his patient Elizabeth Severn (Fortune, 1994).

[24]So far, I agree with Béla Grunberger's (1974) point of view that Ferenczi's theory and technique were a consequence of his failed analysis with Freud, a kind of 'acting out' or an outcome of his 'transference neurosis'. I disagree, however, with Grunberger's conclusion that Ferenczi was therefore *wrong* in his ideas and methods.

appeared as late as 1939,[25] and it was written by Alice and Michael Balint. They cautiously dicuss "personal factors" in the analyst, maintaining that these play a role in shaping the analysand's transference. "The analytical situation is the result of an interplay of the patient's transference and the analyst's countertransference", with the consequence "that something like an 'uncontaminated' [*keimfreie*] analytic method does not exist at all" (ibid., p. 219). After Alice Balint's early death, Michael Balint further pursued this line of thinking, particularly in his book on the basic fault (1968).

I have alread pointed out to what a great extent Balint's technique and theory are a continuation of his analyst's, Ferenczi. Before going to Ferenczi, however, Michael as well as Alice had been in analysis (for two years) with Hanns Sachs in Berlin. Sachs had the reputation of being a very 'strict' analyst, pushing the analyst's abstinence to an extreme. For instance, he is reported to have said not more than a couple of words in weeks of analysis. Michael Balint later told Bluma Swerdloff in an interview (1965) that he was "very dissatisfied" with that analysis, that in fact "it wasn't analysis": "It was rather theoretical. Rather theoretical. One discussed one's dreams. It was very interesting and very illuminating". According to Balint, Sachs "had an excellent taste, really first rate taste— not only in literature but in women and in wine and cigars and what you want. But he was a very neurotic man." Balint decided to go back to Budapest, and continue his analysis there, and he had two more years with Ferenczi. This second analysis "was quite different. [Question:] Did you feel changed? [Balint:] Oh, yes, that's why I became an analyst."

Donald W. Winnicott is usually credited, together with Margaret Little and Paula Heimann, to have (re)introduced the concept of countertransference as a therapeutic tool, in his seminal paper on "Hate in the countertransference", delivered to the British Society on 5 February 1947 (Winnicott, 1949). Winnicott's filiational heritage is thoroughly mixed: he was analysed by Freudian James Strachey, (then) Kleinian Joan Riviere (late 1930s), and supervised by (his wife's analyst) Melanie Klein herself (1935–1940), by her estranged daughter, Melitta Schmideberg,

---

[25]In 1926, Helene Deutsch had published a paper on "Occult processes occurring during psychoanalysis", which also treated countertransference. Deutsch introduced an important distinction which subsequently fell into oblivion, but was later successfully reintroduced by her pupil Racker, to whom it is now ascribed: the concept of "concordant" and "complementary" countertransference.

and by Nina Searl (cf. Grosskurth, 1986; Kahr, 1996; King & Steiner, 1991; Meisel & Kendrick, 1985; Phillips, 1988). Winnicott's ten year-analysis with Strachey was conducted, "[i]n all probability, … on six days of the week" (Kahr, 1996, p. 50). Winnicott wrote to Ernest Jones in 1952 that "Strachey made practically no mistakes and he adhered to a classical technique in a cold-blooded way for which I have always been grateful", even calling him, in his obituary, "my favourite example of a psycho-analyst" (in ibid., p. 55).[26] James W. Anderson, however, "has characterized Winnicott's encounter with Strachey as highly ambivalent. After all, Strachey underlined the vital importance of interpretation as a clinical tool, whereas Winnicott … would eventually become very suspicious of colleagues who interpreted too much" (ibid., p. 54). Kahr mentions Strachey's homosexuality and conjectures:

> In view of Winnicott's sustained childlessness, his lack of professional interest in adult genital sexuality, and his preoccupation with impotence, I suspect that Strachey did Winnicott a great disservice by not analysing fully, if at all, these aspects of his character structure,

and Kahr regards this "neglect" even "as a woeful instance of *malignant countertransference*" (ibid., pp. 51–52; my ital.). One might also speculate that Winnicott's multiple allegiances may have contributed to his thinking about transitional space, transitional phenomena, impingement, etc., and to his central role in the British 'Middle School'.

In "Countertransference and the patient's response to it" (1951), Margaret Little described how she was led to reflect upon countertransference after an interpretation of hers was felt to be off the mark and unempathic by her analysand. In an autobiographic report of her own three analyses (Little, 1990, p. 36) she revealed, however, that this was a disguised account of her *own* analysis with Ella Freeman Sharpe, an interpretation of whom Little had felt "as a massive interference" (ibid.). "I knew that my real troubles had never been touched; instead of empathy there had been 'confusion of tongues' (Ferenczi)" (ibid., p. 37).

Paula Heimann's article on countertransference (Heimann, 1950) appeared at a critical period in Heimann's relationship—both personal

---

[26] [Addition] Note the careful wording: he called him his favourite *example* of a psychoanalyst, not his *favourite* analyst.

and analytical—with Melanie Klein. "Heimann's paper has been accepted as an essential part of the Kleinian corpus [Footnote: Curiously, it was never delivered to the British Society. The paper does not contain a single reference to Klein.]; but few analysts seem to know that Klein and Heimann had a serious disagreement over it, Klein insisting that countertransference is something that interferes with analysis." Heimann claimed, however, that the analyst "must use his emotional response as a key to the patient's unconscious" (Grosskurth, 1986, p. 378). She later told William Gillespie that Klein "had 'seduced' her into analysis" (ibid., p. 381), while simultaneously warning her "against telling anyone that she was in analysis with her" (ibid., p. 383). Regarding Heimann's paper, Grosskurth asks: "Was Heimann in some way telling Klein something about the unsatisfactory nature of her own analysis?" (ibid., p. 379).

Melanie Klein herself is certainly another story, and a very interesting one at that, as she was analysed by two of the most prominent of, but differently orientated among, Freud's disciples at the time, Sándor Ferenczi and Karl Abraham.[27] Her work could be viewed as a unique synthesis of both her analysts' orientations, as on the one hand it is practically about nothing but early object relations, but on the other from the vantage point of drive or one-person psychology.[28]

Conclusion

Unofficially, the importance of psychoanalytic filiations has always been known and acknowledged. This can also be seen from the fact that "[a]s to the matter of appointing certain members of the institute faculty 'training analysts', it is widely known that this issue is the most frequent source of discord within institutes" (Gedo, 1984, p. 176). A well documented example are the so-called Freud/Klein controversies within the British Society (King & Steiner, 1991), which were particularly fought about the question who would be able to exert control over the training

---

[27]The analysis with Ferenczi (appr. 1919; Balint, 1965) took place before Rank had started his analytical practice; the one with Abraham (1924/25) was the obvious choice during her stay in Berlin. Later she had analysis with Sylvia Payne (1933?/34; Grosskurth, 1986), and possibly also with her former analysand Paula Heimann (ibid., p. 242).

[28]As to Rank's case, see the previous chapter, where the dispute about the implications of Rank's not having been analysed is discussed.

of the candidates. As we have seen, such an influence may indeed lead to the desired outcome, and result in the building of a school or of a local orthodoxy, but it may also backfire in that candidates develop contrary or opposed views.

Recently, the president of the IPA, Otto F. Kernberg, has listed "Thirty methods to destroy the creativity of psychoanalytic candidates" (1996), for example, to slow down the processing of applications and the provision of information, no early participation at scientific meetings, a strict separation between undergraduate and postgraduate seminars, a strengthening of graduation rituals, that candidates are never to attend seminars by their training analysts, the reading of Freud and of papers by the leading local members only, the avoidance of exposure to alternative schools, no up-to-date courses on psychoanalytic technique, silent and critical supervisors, fostering paranoid fears, referring all problems "back to the couch", maintaining discretion, secrecy, and uncertainty about how to become a training analyst, etc.

Surprisingly, perhaps the best historical example for an institute that *avoided* much of this is the one in Berlin in the 1920s. The stature and the extremely broad scope of theoretical views held by Abraham's and Sachs's analysands is astonishing indeed. Abraham analysed, among others, Felix Böhm, Helene Deutsch, Robert Fliess, Ella Freeman Sharpe, Edward Glover, James Glover, Karen Horney, Melanie Klein, Hans Liebermann, Josine Müller-Ebsen, Carl Müller-Braunschweig, Sándor Rado, Theodor Reik, Ernst Simmel, and Alix Strachey; with Sachs were Franz Alexander, Alice Balint, Michael Balint, Suzanne Bernfeld-Cassirer, Siegfried Bernfeld, Ella Freeman Sharpe, Erich Fromm, Karen Horney, Hans Lampl, Rudolph Loewenstein, Barbara Low, Heinrich Meng, Josine Müller-Ebsen, Sacha Nacht, and Sylvia Payne. Practically all of these were to become important clinicians and theoreticians in their own right.

A couple of factors seem to have been important: (1) The Berlin institute was the first and only one which offered a more or less standardised training at the time. Consequently, candidates from the most different backgrounds and from all over Europe, from Germany, Austria, Hungary, England, etc., came there. (2) Notwithstanding their theoretical orientation regarding abstinence or their behaviour during sessions, the leading analysts such as Abraham, Eitingon, Sachs, or Simmel, met with their analysands at the institute, at seminars, or socially, even invited them into their houses or paid them visits at theirs. This reminds one rather of the role of the traditional family doctor, and counterbalanced the development and introjection of an idealised transferential image. (3) Training analyses were much shorter than today. (4) The dominating and perhaps intimidating figure of Freud was in Vienna, not in Berlin. (5) There was a vivid communication and interaction within the peer group of candidates. (6) "Abraham was—really I must say that—the very best president I ever met in my life. He was simply magnificent, what he could do. ... Fair, and absolutely firm. No nonsense. And kept the thing very well in hand. ... he was an absolutely reliable, firm, fair man" (Balint, 1965; in Falzeder, 1987). (7) Abraham built no school of his own. He was certainly true to Freud, but although he has been regarded as *the* pillar of orthodoxy, he also succeeded in bringing forward views that differed significantly from Freud's. "Although Abraham was ... among the staunchest of [Freud's] supporters, he was not an idolater" (Good, 1995, p. 1146). Michael Good goes so far as to call "Abraham ... the first psychoanalytic 'rebel', albeit an ambivalent and tentative one" (ibid., p. 1159; for a further elaboration, see Chapters Thirteen and Fourteen).

The golden age of psychoanalysis in the United States, when it was a highly respected branch of science, with its representatives dominating academia and psychiatry, is over. Whether or not one agrees with Alan Stone's diagnosis that its "scientific center crumbles" (Stone, 1997, p. 35), this has become the prevailing opinion, even among some leading psychoanalysts. According to Julia Kristeva (1994, p. 16), two great confrontations endanger the very existence of psychoanalysis as we knew it:

> The first is its competition with the neurosciences: "The cocktail or the word!", which is now the question of to be or not to be. The second is the test to which psychoanalysis is subjected by the desire *not to know*, which converges with the apparent ease offered by pharmacology, and which characterizes the negative narcissism (as André Green said) of modern man.

In my view, it is vital for psychoanalysis, in its present struggle to find its place, to further investigate conditions under which trainees are able to develop along their own creative lines, and to remain open towards new developments in its own field and in neighboring sciences (cf. Haynal, 1991). It is my hope that a rewriting of psychoanalytic history will help to avoid mistakes made in the past and still made today, and that the word and the desire to know will survive.

CHAPTER FIVE

Profession—psychoanalyst: an historical view*

Introduction

The coming into being of psychoanalysis as a psychotherapeutic method and as a profession was perhaps as influential as the impact of Freud's ideas in general. Without doubt, various forms of 'psychotherapy' existed before Freud, for instance, methods using magnetism, hypnosis, somnambulism, automatic writing, occult and spiritualistic phenomena, not to mention religious forms of the talking cure, shamanism, confession, etc. In many respects, Freud's method (and theory) owe much more to these than has usually been acknowledged. Freud succeeded, however, in creating a unique and particularly appealing synthesis, along with an organisational structure by which theoretical and practical notions could be handed down to others. This simultaneously created strong emotional ties between the persons involved, and thereby laid the foundation for a genealogical network still expanding today.

---

*Special thanks to Frances and Bob who put me up in their home in Brookline, Mass., during the time this article was written.

Freud founded, in other words, a *secular profession and organisation* of psychotherapy that soon occupied centre stage and overshadowed any competing movements (such as the Emmanuel Movement in the United States, to name but one example; cf. Gifford, 1997). Psychoanalysis became a professional identity of its own, along with medicine, psychology, neurology, etc., and a considerable number of people eventually devoted their professional lives to it and earned their living from it. Many contemporary forms of psychotherapy have been influenced by psychoanalytic theory and technique (having developed as a direct offspring, or as a sideline, or in opposition to it). Moreover, they have also taken over its unique form of training: the future psychotherapist's personal experience of the method they will then use on others, and the supervision of the therapist's first cases.

The present form of psychoanalytic training goes back to the 'tripartite model' developed in Berlin in 1920 (personal analysis, theoretical courses, and supervision of clinical work). This model was taken over by the International Psycho-Analytical Association in 1925. This means, for instance, that "American societies admitted unanalyzed persons to membership as late as 1925" (Lewin & Ross, 1960, p. 28). Even afterwards, at least as long Freud lived, there were many exceptions. But how did one become a psychoanalyst in the thirty years before that?

The first psychoanalyst ever became one (or claimed to have become one) through self-analysis. But what about his first colleagues? Did they follow Freud's model, or did they already have something like today's training analysis? And if not, where does training analysis come into the picture? What was the very first training analysis?

Two early pupils

Perhaps Freud's very first 'Freudian' pupil was Felix Gattel (1870–1904; cf. F/Fli; Scharnberg, 1993; Schröter & Hermanns, 1992a, 1992b; Sulloway, 1979, pp. 513–515). For some time, Freud was "greatly please[d] … by his intelligence" (18 June 1897; F/Fli, p. 253), and spent much time, even his holidays, with him. But their collaboration ended on a sour note. On Freud's instigation, Gattel collected material on the sexual causes of neurasthenia and anxiety neurosis at the psychiatric ward of the *Allgemeine Krankenhaus* in Vienna. When he planned to include, in his forthcoming publication, "a large treatise in which he deals with the theory of hysteria, with the sexual substance and the like" (ibid., p. 297), Freud felt plagiarised: "[E]ven if he has pursued these matters further, he cannot possibly publish them as his own work" (ibid.). "The 'large treatise' ... never found its way into Gattel's monograph" (Schröter & Hermanns, 1992a, p. 98). Gattel's conclusions were obviously largely based on short anamnestic interviews, but he also reports the "analysis" (Gattel, 1898, p. 57) of one case, Fräulein Ella E., in nine sessions (of which she cancelled one; English translation in Scharnberg, 1993, pp. 44–47). According to Jones (I, p. 334), Gattel also became Freud's patient. I was not able to verify this; it is conceivable that Jones inferred this from Freud's statement towards Fließ that "[p]upils à la Gattel are easy to come by; in the end they regularly ask to be treated themselves" (F/Fli, p. 347).[1]

An interesting example of the opposite case, that is, of a patient turning into a pupil, is that of the person who was probably Freud's first trainee (as opposed to pupil). She was the fourth of nine children of a wealthy family of Jewish paper manufacturers. The family "combined the best traditions of liberal thinking with a warm-hearted social consciousness. Sigmund Freud and Victor Adler were among the friends of the family" (Glaser, 1981, p. 56). She was active in the women's movement, and two of its prominent proponents, Rosa Mayreder (1858–1938) and Marie Lang (1858–1934), were among her friends. Her name can also be found on the list of the founding committee for the "*I. Wiener Frauenklub*" (The First Viennese Women's Club) (Huber, 1986a, pp. 68–69). She remained unmarried and was, according to her nephew, "very beautiful," possessing "unusual qualities" (Hirst interview; LC).[2] (This nephew, by the way, would also become an analysand of Freud's as an adolescent a couple of years later.)

---

[1] At around the same time, "in 1898 or 1899", Ludwig Jekels met Freud for the first time. He was in Vienna, calling on a number of well known physicians to get recommendations of patients for his sanitarium. Jekels included Freud simply because his name was listed among the *Dozenten* of the University. "I arrived in the early afternoon hours—the busiest time of the day for a renowned physician ... [T]he waiting room was completely empty. ... I explained the object of my visit. Freud was not impolite, but ... he made it clear that in matters of current therapy of nervous patients he 'thought completely different'. My visit was evidently without any success. And a few moments later, I took my leave greatly relieved despite my failure" (Memoirs; LC). Jekels met Freud again around 1905, when he moved to Vienna and attended Freud's lectures at the University. He, too, became an analysand of Freud's.

[2] Partly published by Masson (1984).

Her name was Emma Eckstein, and Freud treated her in the mid 1890s resulting in, again according to the nephew, "Freud's first spectacular success" (ibid.). She did, however, suffer a relapse, reproached Freud for having ended her treatment, wanted to continue it, and demanded that he treat her gratis. Freud at first declined to take her on—on grounds that he had too much to do at that time—and wrote that her request to treat her "without expecting money from you is something which seems to be so foreign to you that I am convinced this is the first thing you will take back" (20 November 1905; LC).[3] Later, however, "Freud would come to her and try to continue the analysis" (Hirst interview), with Freud insisting that her troubles were of psychic origin, while she was convinced that they were of organic nature; the nephew also claims that he treated her, "I am sure, without pay ... Also, and that was most unusual for him, he treated her at her home, not at his office" (ibid.). On 4 August 1906, Freud wrote her: "I am not satisfied with you, and I would like to be" (LC). He wrote this during his holidays in the South Tyrol, and confessed that the reason for his writing to her was "a dream the night before" (ibid.)—a countertransference dream. Already once, this patient had triggered a countertransference dream in Freud that was to become of paramount importance to him ...

Freud's treatment ended, according to the nephew's memoirs, when a woman physician, befriended with Eckstein, "pretended to operate" (Hirst interview) on an alleged ulcer or abscess, or "drained it" (Hirst autobiography; in Masson, 1984, p. 257). The symptoms were suddenly gone. Freud was furious about the interference, stopped the analysis, and predicted that the patient would remain neurotic and bedridden for the rest of her life. This prediction proved to be true—with the interesting exception that for a short period of time she did lose her symptoms and cared for her relatives, who themselves were bedridden during a flu epidemic. "There was a complete break between Freud and her" (Hirst interview) although, interestingly, she preserved his letters, and even made special provisions in a suicide note that they were to be given to her nephew.

Although Emma Eckstein (1865–1924; cf. Huber, 1986a; Masson, 1984, esp. pp. 241–258) achieved fame mainly for her role in the Freud/Fließ relationship, for nearly dying after Fließ had forgotten a piece of

---

[3] Extracts of this correspondence were also published by Masson (1984).

gauze in the operation wound, and for her alleged importance with regard to the dream of "Irma's injection" (Freud, 1900a, pp. 106–121),[4] it is worth remembering that she became also a therapist in her own right. We know from the Fließ letters (F/Fli, p. 286) that she treated a young woman or girl along Freudian lines, but only further investigation might show for how long and how seriously she worked as a therapist. Perhaps this was only a brief interlude. It should, however, be pointed out that her treatment with Freud was her only form of training. In addition, she published a couple of papers, notably an early review of Freud's *Interpretation of Dreams* (cf. Huber, 1986b), and a psychoanalytically inspired monograph on *The Sexual Question in the Education of Children* (Eckstein, 1904). Freud closely supervised the writing of the latter, made his library available to Eckstein, and planned to write a review for the *Neue Freie Presse*.

Freud as the "other"

After Freud had developed his dream theory, he thought that other people could simply follow his own example—to undertake a self-analysis by analysing their dreams. At the same time, Freud seemed confident about being able to intellectually convince other people of his views without meeting strong resistance. Only gradually did he conclude that reading his works and self-analysis were not enough, or did not really work, and would have to be complemented or even be replaced by psychoanalysis itself.

There are conflicting statements of his on this issue, showing his ambivalence and uneasiness, but also his awareness of the problematic consequences this entailed. In 1910, for instance, Freud held that "[a]nyone who fails to produce results in a self-analysis … may at once give up any idea of being able to treat patients by analysis" (1910d, p. 145). Two years later he acknowledged the need for a training analysis (see below), but then in 1914 claimed that a self-analysis with the help of dreams would be possible and would "suffice for anyone who

---

[4] "[T]he first dream which [Freud] submitted to a detailed interpretation" (1900a, p. 106) on 24 July 1895 (ibid., p. 121). Only a few weeks earlier, Freud had written a note to Eckstein, his "very dear and good Fräulein" (12 June 1895; LC), that he had to cancel an appointment because he had to meet guests at Bellevue.

is a good dreamer and not too abnormal" (1914d, p. 20). It should be noted that Freud never advocated that a training analysis should be as long and deep-probing as a patient analysis, or even more so (as Ferenczi later thought). As late as 1937, Freud felt that a training analysis "can only be short and incomplete" (1937c, p. 248), and that it would fulfill its purpose if it convinced the candidate of the existence of the unconscious, and showed him how the technique worked (ibid.).

Freud's book on dreams, which held out the promise of describing a replicable method of dream analysis, contained not one single full analysis of a dream. In fact, it did not even convincingly demonstrate its main thesis that the dream is the fulfillment of an unconscious (probably infantile) wish, because Freud did not disclose that wish, let alone the "navel" (1900a, pp. 111, 525), for any of his dreams. Even the interpretation of the "specimen" dream of Irma's injection (ibid., pp. 106–121) is thoroughly wanting in this respect. When Abraham asked "whether the interpretation ... is incomplete on purpose" and ventured some speculations of his own: "the dirty syringe (!!)" (F/Abr, p. 19), Freud gave a few more clues, but then declared the discussion closed: "All sorts of intimate things, naturally" (ibid., p. 21).

Thus, if one wanted to get a firsthand knowledge of Freud's method, and the conviction he claimed would go along with it, the best way seemed to have the method tried out on oneself with the help of another person, and the only one to approach for such an endeavour was Freud himself. Inevitably, a therapeutic or quasi-therapeutic relationship ensued.

Freud, for his part, was ready to offer such assistance, as in the case of Heinrich Gomperz (1873–1943), son of Freud's ex-patient Elise and of philologist Theodor Gomperz, who had mediated Freud's translation of John Stuart Mill. Obviously, Freud hoped to be able "to turn [Heinrich Gomperz] into a student" (editorial note in F/Fli, p. 388), when he suggested to his fellow academic to make him an analysand (1960a, pp. 239–240):

> Dear Doctor, ... If you can disregard this obstacle [that an analysis might disturb or interrupt your work] and forgive me for the indiscretion with which I should have to explore you and for the unpleasant effects I shall probably have to arouse in you—in short, if you are willing to apply the philosopher's unrelenting love of truth also to your inner life, then I would be very pleased to play the role of the "other" in this venture. ... The prospect of convincing

you to any extent of the correctness of my findings is very tempting to me, and your hint you may perhaps approach the suject scientifically sounds to me almost like a wish fulfillment for me. ... I consider you a person subject to hysteria—which of course does not prevent you from being healthy and resilient as well. No doubt we shall run into difficulties—I don't know of what nature, for someone of you intellectual constitution has so far never put himself at my disposal.

Unfortunately, the experiment failed and Freud "did not ... succeed in convincing [his] philosopher" (F/Fli, p. 391). Gomperz later claimed that Freud told him he was one of the two persons whose dreams he could not analyse (in ibid., p. 388).

Freud's analysis of another colleague, psychologist Hermann Swoboda (1873–1963), was not entirely successful either. Today Swoboda is chiefly remembered in psychoanalytic circles for his role in the conflict over plagiarism between Freud, Fließ, and the late Otto Weininger, but it is worth remembering that he was also one of Freud's fellow academics whom Freud treated as a patient, while failing to convince him of his ideas. In 1906, at the height of the priority conflict, Freud put much of the blame on his ex-patient. Swoboda was upset by the publication of extracts of Freud's letters to Fließ,[5] which contained Freud's unflattering remarks about Swoboda (cf. F/Fli, p. 464). Freud defended these remarks as entirely justified, and chided Swoboda again for his "neurotic gratitude" (19 July 1906; LC), for his "rude manners", and for being a "racial anti-Semite". He felt "deceived and hurt" by Swoboda's behaviour and signed: "Dr. Freud" (6 August 1906; LC).

In 1903, the German psychologist and psychiatrist Willy Hellpach (1877–1955) had published a critique of Freud's dream theory in the newspaper *Der Tag*. Freud sent him a rejoinder (9 October 1903; LC), attributing the criticism largely to misunderstandings ("If someone wanted to formulate the contents of my dream theory as follows: The dream is the fulfillment of a wish or of its opposite—anxiety, fear [*Befürchtung*]—I would have no objections [sic!]"; ibid.). A correspondence ensued. Freud was eager to persuade Hellpach, interpreted one of his dreams by mail (10 June 1904; LC), and hoped that he would eventually take over Freud's theory of hysteria, if only he were willing

---

[5] By Fließ himself (1906, pp. 18–23), and by Pfennig (1906).

"to let own experience and later following communications have an influence on the change of [his] views" (ibid.). On 30 November 1904, Freud again pleaded with Hellpach, in the hope that the latter would "be as surprised by the role sexuality plays in the neuroses as I was who, as a pupil of Charcot's, was certainly not prepared for it. I have the trust in you—and much is said with this—that you will then not hesitate to admit it" (LC). Even after reading Hellpach's *Grundlinien einer Psychologie der Hysterie* (1904), which criticised the sexual theory and Freud's concept of the unconscious, Freud sent him a very friendly letter and wished the book "great success" (5 February 1905; LC).

By 1910, however, Hellpach had become an opponent, "lurking in wait" (F/Jun, p. 367) for signs of "the inevitable collapse of the Freudian movement" (Hellpach, in ibid.). Freud was annoyed by his "prattle" (F/Abr, p. 114), and Jung was "staggered by the incredible megalomania of this miserable pen-pusher" (F/Jun, p. 385).

As late as 1907, Freud analysed the character of psychologist Wilhelm Betz (cf. Betz, 1918, 1927) on the basis of a book manuscript and their correspondence (4 November 1907; LC), while adding: "I hope to learn more from your dreams and I am willing to let drop this first diagnosis altogether when I will have better information" (ibid.). On 24 November 1907, Freud did in fact send Betz a short analysis of the latter's dreams (LC)—another analysis by correspondence.

In those early days, one cannot yet speak of 'psychoanalysts'. Freud tried to convince other colleagues—doctors, psychologists, psychiatrists, philosophers—of his theory that, he was certain, "one day must bring about a reversal of psychology" (to Hellpach, 9 October 1903; LC), and that "one day will surely become common knowledge" (to Sadger, 20 March 1902; LC). Then, as indeed until the end of his life, he was much more concerned with founding a new science of man than merely a branch of psychiatry. And he tried to convince others by demonstrating his method *in vivo*.

In sum, if one wanted to learn psychoanalysis or even use it in practice, one could either start out as an intellectually interested colleague or disciple, and probably end up as a patient, or as a patient, with the option of turning into a psychotherapist afterwards.[6] In fact, treatment

---

[6] This of course is not very different from today, with the important exception that the procedure of making trainees into patients has been institutionalised, while the path of

and teaching (or training, if training it can be called) were virtually indistinguishable.

Freud himself was ambiguous about this mixture. On the one hand, he unreservedly made himself available to certain colleagues,[7] on the other his craving for recognition was counterweighed by a "horror of the uncritical adulation of the very young" (F/Fli, p. 347), which gave him a "feeling of disgust" (Freud, 1900a, p. 470), and the blurred borders between instruction and therapy made him uneasy. In any case, he neither attracted a noteworthy number of followers, nor did hardly any of those very early patients/pupils stay with him or within the psychoanalytic fold. Obviously, Freud's experimental and somewhat contradictory way of trying to convince others of his ideas by a mixture of writing, teaching, and treatment was not very successful.

The group

After the publication of *The Interpretation of Dreams* (1900a) and the cooling off and eventual break of his relationship with Fließ, Freud was at a cross roads. He was nearing his fiftieth year, and looked back at a series of dead-end streets and failures. Practically all his relationships with potential supporters or followers (e.g., Josef Breuer, Emma Eckstein, Wilhelm Fließ, Felix Gattel, Heinrich Gomperz, Hermann Swoboda) had ended, or were about to end in separation. The personal friends who remained (Emanuel Löwy or Oscar Rie, for example) had nothing to do with psychoanalysis. His academic career, too, had come to a stalemate. This was partly due to a hostile or at least not welcoming attitude of the powers that be, but it is equally clear that Freud had not pursued a straightforward career. He had speculated about, or tried and given up, careers as a philosopher, as a zoologist, as a politician, as a paediatrician, as a psychopharmacologist, and as a neurologist. Although he had twice come very close to fame, in one instance he had missed the chance to make an important discovery, and in the second

---

making patients to trainees is regarded to be the less desirable one, although it happens often enough.

[7] He refused to take on others, however, for instance his student Robert Bárány, the later Nobel Prize winner, whom Freud "rejected as a pupil because he seemed to [him] to be too abnormal and disagreeable" (F/Fer II, p. 86).

instance had wrongly claimed he had in fact made such a discovery. It was not Freud, but his friend Carl Koller who discovered the medical use of cocaine, while Freud remained mainly known as the one who had imprudently and indiscriminately recommended the use of this drug, for instance, for curing morphinism, with disastrous results. And shortly after declaring his so-called seduction theory the discovery of the "*caput Nili*" (Freud, 1896c, p. 203; F/Fli, p. 184), he had to retract it, if only privately.

There remained psychoanalysis. Without a following, being disappointed by the failing support of his colleagues of about his age or what could have been his scientific 'fathers', Freud for a while turned to the B'nai B'rith 'brotherhood'. The B'nai B'rith was a very respectable society, to which practically all the prominent members of the Viennese Jewish community belonged (Klemperer interview; LC). For some time, this was Freud's chief audience. Thus, he there spoke on "Interpretation of dreams" (7 and 14 December 1897; cf. Klein, 1981, pp. 155–157) before having published on the subject. He always remained grateful for the support and for the feeling of belonging this lodge gave him, but this was not the circle from which to recruit pupils or followers.

If Freud's "splendid isolation" (Freud, 1914d, p. 22) was probably not as complete as he later implied, it was not as splendid, either. He evidently went through a serious crisis: this was the only prolonged time in his adult life when he did not publish.[8] Except for a couple of book reviews and a few lines, he published nothing at all in the years from 1902 to 1904. Freud himself claimed that it was the "manifestations of malicious superior air, which were the only reaction [he] could wrest from his Viennese colleagues", that had "kept him from further publications" (to Hellpach, 30 November 1904; LC), but there is no evidence that he held back any notable works except the "Dora" case history (Freud, 1905e). It seems, in fact, that for some time he did not write.

As a *Privatdocent* (since 1895), Freud had already lectured for many years at the Vienna University. Without going into detail (cf. Eissler, 1966; Gicklhorn & Gicklhorn, 1960; Klemperer memoirs, LC; Sachs, 1944), it is of interest that his audience was usually very small (so that he sometimes had trouble in having the three students required for a

---

[8] Not counting the pauses due to illness and fatigue in his last years.

course to take place—'*tres faciunt collegium*'), and that it included many non-medical students. Moreover, only very few of these early students stayed on in the psychoanalytic movement.[9]

A turn of events came in November 1902. Freud invited a handful of colleagues—no longer students, but younger than he—to discuss "the topics of psychology and neuropathology that interest us" (to Adler, 2 November 1902; LC):[10] Alfred Adler (1870–1937), Max Kahane (1866–1923), Rudolf Reitler (1865–1917), and Wilhelm Stekel (1868–1940).

The priority of having been the first MD to undergo a short-term analysis with Freud probably goes either to Felix Gattel or to Wilhelm Stekel. The latter had eight sessions with Freud because of impotence (cf. Stekel, 1950, pp. 107–108, 115), after which it was he who proposed a discussion group. (Stekel's account is not always trustworthy, but that it was indeed his initiative is evidenced by Freud's letter to him of 4 February 1904 [LC], in which Freud speaks of "the psychological society founded by you".) Stekel did become one of the very first practising analysts and, for some years, one of Freud's most important followers.[11]

These men met privately in Freud's apartment and formed the nucleus of what became known as the Wednesday Society. All of these founding members were medical doctors with a special interest in neuroses, but they were not psychiatrists. With the exception of Stekel, there is no indication that any of them had had a personal analytic experience. Adler and Stekel are well known today, but Rudolf Reitler and Max Kahane are practically forgotten. Both had visited Freud's early lectures at the university, and both were physical therapists: "It had not been

---

[9] In 1902, Freud was appointed *Professor extraordinarius*. This was a merely nominal title, and there were no prospects of tenure, but it did give prestige, and was bound to attract more patients.

[10] [Addition] In 1992, I published an article together with Bernhard Handlbauer that was the first to draw on Freud's letters to Adler, which had become accessible in the LC shortly before, and to reprint practically all the relevant passages. It came out in French, because the leading German psychoanalytic journal, *Psyche*, rejected it at the time as "not interesting enough". In 2011, there appeared the first complete edition of this convolute in an Adlerian journal (in German; F/Adl).

[11] [Addition] In his recent book, Clark-Lowes even maintains that "he arguably played the most prominent part of any member [of the Vienna Society] up until the time of his resignation in November 1912" (2010, p. 11). See also Bos & Groenendijk (2007).

long since neurotics were treated only with electricity and hydrotherapy; therefore physical therapists like Reitler and Kahane were among Freud's earliest followers" (Hitschmann, autobiographical note; LC). Reitler was head of a sanitarium in Vienna; according to Jones, he "became the first person to practice psychoanalysis after Freud" (II, p. 7).

"Kahane had been an intimate of Freud's early days" (Wittels, 1924, p. 132). It is likely that they worked together in the Children's Clinic of Kassowitz (Hochsinger, 1938, pp. 13, 46).[12] Interestingly, Kahane was the translator of the second part of Charcot's lectures into German, the first part of which had been translated by Freud (Charcot, 1892, 1895). He worked at the *Allgemeine Krankenhaus* in Vienna, and founded and headed an "Institute for physical treatment methods". Kahane was an extremely prolific author (cf. Kahane, 1892, 1901a, 1901b, 1902, 1904, 1905, 1906, 1908, 1910, 1922; Kahane & Pietschmann, 1907), mostly of medical textbooks for practitioners and students. He did not publish any psychoanalytic works, left the group in 1907, and fell out with Freud not long afterwards. (Wittels gives two different dates for Kahane's breach with Freud: "[a]bout fifteen years before his death"—which would be around 1908—or "towards 1912"; 1924, pp. 132, 216.) In his book on *Therapie der Nervenkrankheiten* (*On the Therapy of Nervous Diseases*) (1912), Kahane listed pharmacological, hygienic, dietary, climatological, electrotherapeutical, thermal, hydrological, mechanical, and surgical methods, but not psychotherapy, let alone psychoanalysis. He even raved against

> laying all too much stress on *sexuality*, [which would be,] even in the *guise of a scientific presentation*, a factor significantly *harmful to culture*, because only *work, temperance* and *righteousness* represent the basis of a salutary material, intellectual and ethical development, whereas a *preponderance of sexuality*, a fight against *marriage* and *procreation*, and a rampant growth of the *sexual* element in literature and art are absolutely to be seen as *symptoms of decline*. (Ibid., p. 81; my ital.)

From this early circle only Rudolf Reitler stayed an adherent of Freud's.[13] Without doubt, this forum was very important to Freud, but it was

---

[12] I am indebted to Carlo Bonomi for drawing my attention to this.

[13] On these four pioneers, as well as on the other members of the Vienna Psychoanalytic Society, see Mühlleitner, 1992.

without much impact on larger circles. Such were the inconspicuous beginnings of a movement which, some thirty years later, listed 374 active full members[14] in fifteen countries all over the globe (USA, Germany, India, Israel, Hungary, Netherlands, Norway, Denmark, Sweden, Finland, France, Russia, Switzerland, Japan, Austria),[15] nearly all of them practising psychoanalysis as a profession, and today counts some 10,000 analysts in the United States alone, about a third of which are members of the International Psychoanalytic Association founded by Ferenczi and Freud in 1910. But let us return to the beginnings.

The Swiss connection

While Freud and his early followers met on Wednesdays, discussing a wide range of topics, from smoking to friendship, from female sexuality to autobiographical confessions about the years before marriage, a major shift occurred, moving the centre of psychoanalysis away from Freud and Vienna.

There is no doubt that a very important new hope appeared on Freud's horizon when two young Swiss, Carl Gustav Jung (1875–1961) and his student Ludwig Binswanger (1881–1966), visited him in March 1907 as emissaries of the Burghölzli, the psychiatric university clinic in Zurich/Switzerland, headed by Eugen Bleuler. This opened up the prospect that the doors of psychiatry and academia could be opened via Bleuler, professor at the Zurich University, and also through Binswanger's uncle, Otto Binswanger, professor and director of the psychiatric clinic at the University of Iena/Germany.

It was Bleuler, not Jung, who had introduced psychoanalysis at his clinic, and who had recruited a staff open to dynamic psychiatry in general and to this new discipline in particular, among them Carl Gustav Jung. And it was Jung, not Freud, who first recommended, as a general requisite, the analysis of the analyst, as Freud himself acknowledged (1912e, p. 116).

We have a well documented case of what would eventually be a 'training' analysis at the Burghölzli that contained some unusual

---

[14] The actual number is slightly lower, because of a few cases of double membership (IPA, List of Members 1935; LC).

[15] The biggest component society by far was, by the way, still the one in Vienna (fifty-three full members).

features. It was the analyst's first psychoanalytic clinical case, begun in 1904 (F/Abr, p. 216); and it turned out that the person who had begun as a patient with severe, near-psychotic symptoms became a well known and respected analyst. I am, of course, speaking of Sabina Spielrein's analysis—and more—with Carl Gustav Jung (cf. Carotenuto, 1980).[16]

As for other colleagues, Jung 'analysed' a couple of them, for instance Seif of Munich ("for 3 days"!; F/Jun, p. 280), or Sándor Ferenczi (see p. 54). A kind of therapeutic marathon, for hours on end, sometimes turning into a mutual analysis, took place between Jung and Otto Gross,[17] ending eventually in Gross's escape over the walls of the Burghölzli. Another 'mutual analysis' occurred between Jung and his collaborator Jakob Honegger.[18]

The first generation of physicians who practiced psychoanalysis as a profession came to Freud almost exclusively via Jung and Bleuler. Freud himself stated in 1914 that "[m]ost of my followers and co-workers at the present time came to me by way of Zurich" (1914d, p. 27). The Burghölzli was *the* place in the world to go for any young, ambitious, open-minded psychiatrist. Take, for instance, the case of Karl Abraham from Germany: "In Zurich I could breathe freely again. No clinic in Germany could have offered me even a fraction of what I have found here" (F/Abr, p. 10); or that of Ernest Jones from Great Britain; or of Smith Ely Jelliffe, Trigant Burrow, and Abraham A. Brill from the United States. The Burghölzli went truly international, with staff members from, for example, Germany, Great Britain, Greece, Italy, Holland, Hungary, Luxembourg, Poland, Russia, Scandinavia, and the United States; and, of course, its distinguished Swiss collaborators such as Ludwig Binswanger, Jakob Honegger, Carl Gustav Jung, Alfons Maeder, Emil Oberholzer, or Franz Riklin.[19] The only clinic and name rivaling Bleuler, Jung, and

---

[16] [Addition] This was written before the publication of Kerr's book (1993) (and the Hollywood film based on it) and the fine biography by Richebächer (2005).

[17] "Whenever I got stuck, he analyzed me. In this way my own psychic health has benefited" (25 May 1908; F/Jun, p. 153).

[18] "He has also done a lot for me personally: I have had to hand over some of my dreams to him" (30 January 1910; F/Jun, p. 289). Brill dated the inception of training analysis to the mutual dream analyses at the Burghölzli (Brill, 1944, p. 42).

[19] See *Verzeichnis der seit 1. Juli 1870 im Burghölzli tätig gewesenen Direktoren, Sekundar-, Assistenz- und Volontärärzte* (with thanks to Sonu Shamdasani). [Addition] In the

the Burghölzli was that of Kraepelin in Munich—but Kraepelin's classifying approach to psychiatry was clearly losing among the younger generation to the dynamic views endorsed by the Burghölzli people.

The first international meeting of analysts, 1908 in Salzburg/ Austria, strengthened the bond with Zurich. "Bleuler was very, very celebrated. ... I remember the pleasure of Freud that Bleuler came. Everybody was introduced to Bleuler, and Bleuler was the center of the Congress" (Klemperer interview; LC). Bleuler also became co-editor, with Freud, of the first psychoanalytic periodical, the *Jahrbuch für psychoanalytische und psychopathologische Forschungen* (*Yearbook for Psychoanalytical and Psychopathological Research*). Its first half-volume (March 1909) contained, besides Freud's case history of Little Hans, only works by authors linked with the Burghölzli: Abraham, Maeder, Jung, and Binswanger. Freud was pleased about this "preponderance of the Zurich school" (F/Abr, p. 89). Although Bleuler already expressed certain reservations against the nascent psychoanalytic "movement", for some time the contacts between Zurich and Vienna became even stronger. After visits of members of his staff (Eitingon, Jung, Abraham, Binswanger), Bleuler himself paid a visit to Freud in October 1908, accompanied by his wife.

One major factor for Bleuler's eventual decision not to fully endorse psychoanalytic theory and to leave the psychoanalytic movement, was that he had asked Freud to analyse his dreams, and that this *experimentum crucis* failed. As in the above quoted cases, an *analytic* relationship, in addition to a teacher/pupil relationship, runs as a red thread through the diffusion of (or break with) psychoanalysis.

One can hardly overestimate the importance of Bleuler's dissension. I would even go so far as saying that the break with Bleuler was more important for the course and shape the psychoanalytic movement has since taken than that with Jung or Adler. Freud was well aware of Bleuler's importance; in fact, Bleuler was the only person whom Freud ever repeatedly tried to *persuade* to stay within the movement, meeting with him, and writing many long letters to that effect. When he

---

meantime, Annatina Wieser's authoritative dissertation (2001) on the beginnings of psychoanalysis in Switzerland, drawing extensively on the Burghölzli's archives, has been published online (link on the homepage of the journal *Luzifer-Amor*).

did not succeed, it meant that psychoanalysis would develop *outside* of universities and academia, and outside of psychiatry, psychiatric hospitals, and university clinics—at least in Europe.

This also had considerable consequences for the training and accreditation system. In the case of a link between psychoanalysis and academia and medicine, it is likely that the formation of psychoanalysts would have included some features of professional academic and medical training. This was, in fact, the case at the Burghölzli. Apart from short-term 'analyses', there were courses at the university. There was research: Jung was deep in his research on the association experiment, which made for a large part of his 'psychanalyses' (Jung's preferred term). Nearly all of the collaborators, colleagues, and visitors participated in this research, serving for example as test persons. (Still in 1913, for instance, David Forsyth's description of "Psychoanalysis" in the *British Medical Journal* was essentially a description of the association experiment.) There was the community of senior and younger doctors, and of nurses, and there was the hospital itself, with all the opportunities it offered to learn diagnostics, various forms of treatment, and bedside manners.

In contrast to the development in Europe, strong ties developed between psychoanalysis and medicine, psychiatry, and academia in the United States. For instance, "[b]y 1962, over half of the chairmen of departments of psychiatry in medical schools were psychoanalysts" (Bettinger, 1986, p. 1). And here, too, an analytic relationship was at the beginning of such development: Freud's demonstration of his method—this time successful—on James Jackson Putnam, the eminent Harvard neurologist (1846–1918; cf. Bettinger, 1986; Dolin, 1963; Hale, 1971a, 1971b, 1978; Jones, 1920; Lucado, 1994; Oberndorf, 1953; Quen & Carlson, 1978; Vasile, 1977).

Putnam "spent six hours in analysis with Freud in Zurich" (Hale, 1971b, p. 39), where they met in 1911 before travelling to the Third International Psychoanalytic Congress in Weimar, September 21–22. Putnam later referred to these "few conferences at Zurich" in a letter to his cousin Fanny Bowditch, recalling how "in the very first" of these sessions Freud had pointed out to him that he "was a murderer!" (ibid., p. 40). "Putnam returned home with a keen sense of the importance of the analysis of the analyst" (ibid., p. 39), calling it "very important, indeed almost essential" (Putnam, 1914, p. 201). He also "began to pursue self-analysis assiduously" (Hale, 1971b, p. 39).

Fortunately, we are able to trace some more elements of Putnam's analysis in his disguised account of it: "Remarks on a case with Griselda phantasies" (Putnam, 1913). It deals with a patient's depression and his "strong love-hate complex" (pp. 176, 186) in respect to his daughter, linking them to infantile sadomasochistic tendencies as revealed in day-dreams, dreams, masturbation and coitus phantasies. That this paper is indeed autobiographical is evidenced by two remarks of Freud: one to Ferenczi that Putnam's "17-year-old daughter (not Griselda)" had died (F/Fer I, p. 532), and the other, even more convincing, to Jones: "Putnam ... is a man of doubt, we know by his self-analysis (you remember the Griselda paper)" (F/Jon, p. 252). Given that Putnam did have analytical talks with Freud, it is very likely that this was not a pure self-analysis. Freud may also have been reluctant to disclose that fact, particularly towards Ernest Jones. In any case, Putnam acknowledged that "the psycho-analytic investigation ... was extremely helpful to him, in respect both to his feelings regarding his daughter and his tendency to depression, not to mention his general attitude towards life" (Putnam, 1913, p. 185).

There is general agreement that Putnam's "conversion" (Hale, 1971a, p. 203) was instrumental in preparing the ground for the spread of psychoanalysis in America, particularly among the medical profession. "[H]e secured a hearing for Freud's views among the nation's neurologists" (Hale, 1971b, p. 1). He was the "catalyst of the American psychoanalytic movement", and "smoothed the path for Freud's medical reception in the United States" (Hale, 1978, p. 162). Being "a landmark of credibility for the psychoanalysts", he "enabled psychoanalysis to come crashing down with such force upon America's shores" (Lucado, 1994, p. 67). He was "the chief promulgator of psychoanalysis and the leading proselytizer (along with A. A. Brill) for its movement in the United States" (Dolin, 1963, p. 23). Freud referred to him as the "chief pillar of the psycho-analytic movement in his native land" (Freud, 1914d, p. 32).

None of the 'analyses' mentioned so far, however, be it that of Eckstein or Spielrein, of Ferenczi, Gross, Stekel, or Seif, of Bleuler or Putnam, could in any way qualify as a training analysis in contemporary standards. So what was the first analysis of a colleague with the explicit aim of more or less duplicating a patient's analysis in length and depth?

Nothing to be ashamed of

Ernest Jones claimed that he was "the first analyst to undergo a training analysis" (II, p. 127), slightly exaggerating its duration ("summer and autumn") and its originality ("it was a revolutionary idea") (Jones, 1959, p. 199). Jones's analysis with Ferenczi in Budapest took place for two months in the summer of 1913, for two hours a day (cf. F/Fer I; F/Jon).

Jones is not only mistaken about the duration of his own analysis, but also about his priority. Let me give a few details about two other analyses of colleagues, conducted by Freud before the one Jones had had with Ferenczi. (At around the same time, in 1913/14, Clarence Oberndorf was analysed by Paul Federn, who was then in the United States; Lewin & Ross, 1960, p. 13).[20]

On 11 August 1911, Freud wrote to Ferenczi from his vacation in Klobenstein in the South Tyrol (in response to a missing communication of Ferenczi's) that "[i]f Dr. Spitz is to be taken seriously, I am ready. But that is a condition for treating him; otherwise it would be too unpleasant to take on a physician as a patient. Since you recommend him warmly, it certainly seems to be in order" (F/Fer I, p. 300). This refers to the later famous psychoanalyst and developmental psychologist, René A. Spitz (1887–1974), who started analysis with Freud in October 1911. Freud kept Ferenczi informed: "Dr. Spitz is very interesting; the window-dressing is over, and he is behaving quite properly neurotic, with strong resistances" (ibid., p. 309). "Dr. Spitz made a bit of a play of grandiosity and was penalized for it by being deprived of three hours, and since then he seems to want to take it more seriously. The mainsprings have been weakened considerably, since he wants to give in to his father and doesn't want to remain a physician. Still, he is quite nice" (ibid., p. 317).

About three months later, the young Swiss doctor Emil Oberholzer (1883–1958) wrote to Freud. I was not able to find his letter, but his request can be deduced from Freud's reply of 1 March 1912: "I certainly approve of your plan, and will myself, in a publication, endorse that each analyst should have undergone an analysis himself. So if you think that you are in need of my help, I will be only too happy to give it to you" (LC). Freud even proposed to interrupt the treatment of one of

---

[20] Hans Zulliger writes that he went through an analysis in 1912 (Zulliger, 1966, p. 171).

his patients to make a place free for his colleague, but was not willing
to suffer a substantial loss in income: "Unfortunately, I am ... in the
embarrassing situation that I have to ask for a fee also from colleagues,
whom I would prefer to give my full interest without being paid for"
(ibid.). In addition, there was the question of discretion, and of whether
this analysis should or could be kept secret: "Dr. Jung will not be
informed of your suggestion, nor will anybody else, although I think
that your presence in Vienna can hardly be kept secret. But then, an
analysis is nothing to be ashamed of among ourselves" (ibid.).

Again three months later, Oberholzer started his analysis and, to
be sure, Freud did not only hasten to inform Jung (F/Jun, p. 511), but
also immediately reported to Oberholzer's wife Mira, née Gincburg
(1887–1949), herself one of the first woman analysts in her own right,
who had sent Freud some further information about her husband.
Freud had deliberately not read these notes, he told her, because he had
decided "to treat him as correctly, that is, as severely as possible, and
for such an undertaking any information which does not come from
the patient [sic] himself is interfering" (6 June 1912; LC). He further
offered his opinion (ibid.), which can have hardly been reassuring to
Mrs. Oberholzer, that her husband would suffer from

> very serious disturbances. Unfortunately, 5 weeks are not sufficient
> a time to bring about a change. What I can do is to stir him up as
> profoundly as possible. In the first session he has shown himself as
> very nasty, and thus has shown me many hidden things. But then
> in the second hour he was nice, which makes me fear that he will
> now hide his resistances from being discovered. But I promise to
> have a keen eye on him.

Seven years later, this former 'patient' was about to become president
of the Swiss Society. Freud was not in favour, and voiced his strong disapproval toward Ferenczi: Oberholzer, "as a *severe* neurotic, is ... very
questionable to me. In Switzerland they certainly have a very special
pure strain of fools" (F/Fer II, p. 329; my ital.).

Nevertheless, Oberholzer did become co-founder, in 1919, of the
"Swiss Society for Psychoanalysis" (which is still in existence today),[21]

---

[21] On February 10, in a circular letter, Pfister and Mira and Emil Oberholzer proposed the
founding of a Swiss Society for Psychoanalysis. The organisational meeting subsequently

and he did become its first president, remaining in this office until 1927, when he and nine others split from it, founding their own purely medical psychoanalytic group. On that occasion, Max Eitingon repeated that it would have been "quite clear to all of us" that Oberholzer was "a completely untreatable neurotic" (circular letter of 16 February 1928; Archives of the British Psycho-Analytical Society). Oberholzer's group eventually dissolved after his emigration in 1938. He and his wife went to New York City and joined the Society there.

Spitz and Oberholzer were among the first to actively seek the experience of a proper 'training' analysis (Jones having been more or less ordered by Freud to do so), and soon a couple of others followed. This was still a rare exception, however, certainly not considered as a mandatory prerequisite for practising psychoanalysis, and was practically confined to members of the 'second generation'. Of the prominent members among the first generation, Jones and later Ferenczi—whose three short *tranches* of analysis with Freud during the First World War are by now well known (cf. Dupont, 1993; Hoffer, 1996; and Chapter Eleven)—came nearest to having an analysis *sensu stricto*. In late 1909, Eitingon was in Vienna and let Freud "analyze him in the course of evening walks" (F/Jun, p. 255).[22] Freud analysed van Emden during afternoon walks when they vacationed together in Karlsbad (F/Fer I, p. 294). Also Abraham A. Brill "and Freud would take long walks, discussing psychoanalysis, relating their dreams to each other, and analyzing them" (Romm, 1966, pp. 212–213). Freud, Ferenczi, and Jung analysed each other's dreams on board the ship that brought them to America in 1909. Rank, feeling depressed, had planned to go to Jones in England for analysis in 1914, but this plan came to naught because of the outbreak of the First World War. C. G. Jung maintained, in his letter to Freud of 18 December 1912, that he had "submitted *lege artis et tout humblement* to analysis" (F/Jun, p. 535), but it seems highly unlikely that

---

took place on March 21; the first meeting, with guest lectures by Jones, Rank, and Sachs on "Psychoanalysis as an intellectual movement", took place on March 24; affiliation with the IPA was also decided upon there. The first chair was Emil Oberholzer, second chair, Hermann Rorschach; other members of the board were Binswanger, Morel, and Pfister (cf. Haynal & Falzeder, 2011).

[22] In February 1910, Eitingon gave Freud Dostoevski's Collected Works as a kind of honorarium, which reminded Freud of those "interesting walks which actually served my health" (F/Eit, p. 59).

this was a prolonged, in-depth analysis (probably with Maria Moltzer, later a prominent Jungian analyst). Karl Abraham, Alfred Adler, and Hanns Sachs were not analysed at all.

In their clinical practice, practically all of these pioneers experimented and often ran into difficulties with their patients, although this was not written about in the literature. Again, many of them came to Freud for advice. If early analysis was carried out, to a considerable extent, by exchange of letters, so were the beginnings of *supervision*: Freud's professional correspondence of that period is largely supervision by mail.[23]

The Freud/Edoardo Weiss letters are aptly called *Freud As a Consultant* (F/Wei). The Freud/Pfister correspondence (Freud & Pfister, 1963; F/Pfi) revolves around two crucial cases (that have been censored in the published version). Immediately after his first visit to Freud, Ferenczi asked Freud about his opinion about the treatment of a paranoid woman, and if institutionalisation could be dispensed with (F/Fer I, p. 3). The Freud/Jung correspondence starts on the somber tone of Jung's veiled account of a difficult analysis with a Russian student—Sabina Spielrein. A crucial topic in their exchange was also the case of Frau Hirschfeld, both Freud's and Jung's patient (see Chapter Two). Abraham wrote to Freud on 8 January 1908 that he had taken into analysis a case of obsessional neurosis, had succeeded in uncovering a couple of memories, but had now reached an impasse. "This is as far as I got in two sessions without resistances that were too great. But now I am stuck. ... I am certain that I have uncovered only a part of the repressed material, but up to now I have found no way of access. Perhaps you know from similar cases how to find a way to these deeper layers" (F/Abr, pp. 17–18). Freud answered by return of the post (pp. 20–21):

> I write to you hurriedly, formlessly, impersonally, to enable you to make use of my technical information as soon as possible. Sorry you are afraid of getting stuck. Doesn't happen to me all year round. I must get those technical rules of mine out soon. ... The chief rules are: [(1.)] Take your time ... Dissatisfied after only two sessions.

---

[23] "The history of supervised practical work began with the numerous letters written by Freud in answer to colleagues asking his opinion on psychoanalytic cases" (Pomer, 1966, p. 55).

At not knowing everything! (2.) A problem like: How do I go on? must not exist. The patient shows the way, in that by strictly following the basic rule (saying everything that comes into his mind) he displays his prevailing ψ surface.

Witnessing the problems of his followers, Freud started in 1908 to write the text alluded to in his letter to Abraham, a comprehensive "General Methodology of Psychoanalysis" (F/Fer I, pp. 29–30). He then abandoned this project, however, and instead wrote a series of six short, unsystematic papers on technical "recommendations" between 1911 and 1914. He later qualified these recommendations as meant for "beginners" (Blanton, 1971, p. 48) and "essentially negative" (F/Fer III, p. 332). And that was it, as James Strachey noted: "in the twenty years that followed their publication he made no more than a couple more explicit contributions to the subject" (in S.E. 13, p. 86)—with one exception, to which we will come in a moment.

The Institute

The First World War put a temporary end to the spread of psychoanalysis. The journals were stopped or reduced in frequency and length. Publishing was nearly impossible because of lack of paper. Most of Freud's patients, colleagues, and pupils were called to arms. At the same time, however, the war furthered psychoanalysis, much as the Second World War would do later.[24]

The Fifth International Psychoanalytic Congress in Budapest, in September 1918, was a highlight for the psychoanalytic movement. It was closely connected with the war; its subject: the so-called war neuroses. High-ranking military officials and the mayor of Budapest were among the participants, nearly all of the analysts (with the exception of Freud) were in uniform.

Official reception by the burgomaster, first class banquet, with the head of the public health department of Budapest, an Austrian general and two official representatives of the German War Ministry

---

[24] "World War II stands as the single most important factor in the meteoric rise of psychoanalysis" in the United States (Bettinger, 1986, p. 4).

in attendance, the loan of the conference hall of the Academy of Science. … They now believe that they can use us for practical purposes, but they seem to have no understanding of the value of a scientific study of the war neuroses. (F/AS, pp. 83–84)

Freud gave a talk on "Lines of advance in psycho-analytic therapy" (1919a) that can be considered his swan song on the topic. In this paper, Freud stated that a "new technique … is still in the course of being evolved", and that this new development in therapy would proceed, "first and foremost, along the [line] which Ferenczi … has … termed 'activity' on the part of the analyst" (pp. 161–162).[25] Freud himself did not further venture into explorations of technical innovation. With a few exceptions, he also gave up therapeutic analyses and confined himself to didactic ones.

Ferenczi was elected president, and von Freund secretary of the International Psychoanalytic Association. Anton von Freund (Antal Freund von Tószeghi) (1880–1920), PhD, was the wealthy director of a beer brewery in Budapest. He had been in analysis with Freud intermittently from 1915 onward (von Freund to Freud, 4 January 1916; FML). On 7 April 1918, Freud wrote to Ferenczi that "Dr. Freund is now sorting out a piece of his old neurosis here. He is free of delusion, but still in an uneven mood. His desire to help is now coming to the fore; he also wants to help me, and in the process he has expressed an intention about which I would even have very much liked to hear your view. His overpayment is also worthy of note" (F/Fer II, p. 275). Shortly afterwards, von Freund indeed donated a sum of almost two million crowns for the advancement of psychoanalysis.

The Budapest Congress nourished the illusion that psychoanalysis would gain public recognition and support, that polyclinics could be founded, and that the psychoanalytic movement could maintain its independence with the help of von Freund's money. Freud even "expected that Budapest will now become the headquarters of our movement" (F/Abr, p. 382). The talks at the congress were published as the first book of the *Internationaler Psychoanalytischer Verlag* which had been founded with von Freund's fund. Ferenczi was soon to be

---

[25] [Addition] On the development of psychoanalytic technique see the authoritative study of Leitner, 2001.

appointed the world's first university professor for psychoanalysis, and to head a psychoanalytic clinic.

It was at this same Budapest Congress in 1918 that Nunberg first publicly stated "that no one could any longer learn psychoanalysis who had not been through an analysis himself" (Eitingon, 1937, p. 197). As Eitingon later put it: "As these words left his lips, we realised that something extraordinarily important had been said, which should at once become a general goal and very soon also reality" (ibid.).[26]

It was Eitingon himself who put this into action. With the end of the war, political upheaval, the fall of the Council Republic in Hungary, and the ensuing White Terror, the plans in Budapest came to naught. The clinic was closed, Ferenczi lost his professorship, he was excluded from the Hungarian Society of Physicians, and for weeks could not even show himself in public. Anton von Freund died of cancer, most of his foundation was frozen by the government, and devalued by inflation to boot. In this situation, Eitingon, a rich man, founded the Berlin clinic and institute with his own funds on 14 February 1920. Instead of Anton von Freund it was Eitingon who received the ring from Freud, the sign that he had now been admitted to the inner circle, the Secret Committee.

For the first time, there was a standardised training curriculum for psychoanalysts. Freud was not entirely happy with this somewhat 'Prussian' institutionalisation of analytic training, but eventually endorsed it. It was the Berlin of Abraham, Sachs, Simmel, and Eitingon, not Ferenczi's Budapest or Freud's and Rank's Vienna, that became the new centre of psychoanalysis; it was the Berlin institute after which practically all following ones were modeled. Sándor Radó, for example, was invited to come to New York to create an institute along the Berlin lines.[27] For years, Eitingon and Sachs ran the training in Berlin.

It is worth noting that these two men, who developed and oversaw what has become the model for psychoanalytic training all over the world, as well as Karl Abraham, under whose presidency this

---

[26] Sonu Shamdasani (private communication) points out that both Nunberg and Eitingon had worked at the Burghölzli, and that Nunberg's proposal met with strong resistance on the part of Victor Tausk and Otto Rank.

[27] André Haynal (private communication) notes the interesting fact that although the psychoanalytic movement had left the academic world, the Berlin Institute, and later ones modeled after it, imitated an academic setting and curriculum.

took place, had never been analysed themselves.[28] I would suggest viewing their training model as a reaction rather than a positive evaluation of what should be included in such training; a reaction, that is, to the countless transgressions and violations of boundaries that pervaded the early history of psychoanalytic training (see Chapter Three; cf. Gabbard, 1995; Gabbard & Lester, 1995). Training was institutionalised following certain rules meant to tame, through that process, those repeated patterns of highly charged analytic relationships.

This was only partly successful, and brought other dangers with it. With the Berlin Institute, however, the prehistory of psychoanalytic training ends. Whether or not the further development to a highly institutionalised and controlled training system has been able to circumvent the pitfalls of the pioneering epoch, is another question.

---

[28] If we do not count Eitingon's 'analytic walks' with Freud.

PART III

IS THERE STILL AN UNKNOWN FREUD?

CHAPTER SIX

Whose Freud is it? Some reflections on editing Freud's correspondence

It seems to me that the world has no claim on my person and that it will learn nothing from me so long as my case (for manifold reasons) cannot be made fully transparent.

—Freud to Fritz Wittels, 18 December 1923; Freud, 1960a, p. 346

What she [Simone Weil] gives us to think about, we *should* think about. We can safely disregard her personality, we do not miss anything that would be important or revealing.

—Anna Freud, in Coles, 1992, p. 21

In 1965, a selection of the letters of Sigmund Freud and Karl Abraham appeared with The Hogarth Press and The Institute of Psycho-Analysis, under the title *A Psycho-Analytic Dialogue*, edited by Abraham's daughter Hilda and Freud's son Ernst, translated by

132   PSYCHOANALYTIC FILIATIONS

Bernard Marsh and Hilda Abraham.[1] After the letters to Wilhelm Fliess (Freud, 1950a), the correspondence with Oskar Pfister (Freud & Pfister, 1963), and a selection of Freud letters to various correspondents (Freud, 1960a), it was the fourth volume of Freud letters to be published. There followed the exchanges with Lou Andreas-Salomé (Freud & Andreas-Salomé, 1966), with Arnold Zweig (F/AZ), with Georg Groddeck (Freud & Groddeck, 1970), and with Edoardo Weiss (F/Wei).

None of these, however, was a complete, unabridged edition; whole letters were left out, and passages were cut that were considered unimportant, repetitive, indiscreet, offensive, or not worth printing for whatever other reason. Sometimes the places where something was omitted were marked, sometimes not; in no case was it indicated how many words, phrases, or paragraphs were omitted. In some places even the original wording was changed in order to cover up the omissions. Patients' names, but in some instances even names of analysts and colleagues, were anonymised, either by their last initial, or by arbitrary letters or combinations of letters; in addition, it is important to note that the various editors did not use the same pseudonyms for the same patients or analysts. The transcriptions of the originals, on which these publications were based, contained numerous errors— errors that sometimes even altered the meaning or turned it upside down. The editorial notes, if there were any, were sparse, often misleading or outright wrong. The English translations, as a rule, added a further distortion. They either suffered from a poor command of German (in particular of Freud's Jewish-Viennese variety of it), of English, of the theory and history of psychoanalysis, psychiatry, neurology, arts, and literature—or of a combination of these. In addition, there was a tendency to downplay or water down—or to launder— Freud's emphatic, often indiscreet, offensive, or pejorative remarks about third persons. As a result, what the reader, and the English-speaking reader in particular, took for Freud's letters until the mid

----

[1][Addition] This article was written at a time when I was working on the edition of the complete Freud/Abraham correspondence. In the rest of the book, I have changed the pertaining references to this completed edition (F/Abr), but here I will have occasion to repeatedly refer to the older, censored one (Freud & Abraham, 1965, cited hereafter as *Dialogue*), as well as to other abridged editions of Freud's letters, which will be referenced in the usual, not abbreviated, style.—Bernard Marsh is a pseudonym for Eric Mosbacher (Roazen, 1971, p. 552).

1970s, was not Freud, but a censored and distorted version of what he had actually written.

In the introduction of the 1965 edition of the Freud/Abraham letters, for instance, the editors (Hilda Abraham and Ernst Freud) state (p. vii):

> Omissions and cuts have been made for reasons of discretion where names and facts might lead to recognition of patients or their families, or where the people discussed would not be of any interest nowadays; furthermore to avoid repetition or details about the various psycho-analytical organisations which were of purely local interest and, finally, to avoid unimportant personal details about the writers and their families, which do not contribute to the knowledge and understanding of their personalities and of their scientific work.

They also thank "Miss Anna Freud, Ll.D., for advising us on the selection of material" (p. viii).

We should bear in mind, however, that when these abridged editions appeared, many of the persons involved were still living, and that the editors—relatives, friends, or disciples of the correspondents—had a quite understandable interest to preserve what they considered a modicum of privacy and discretion. Moreover, they were not professional editors and could devote only a fraction of their time to edit and annotate those letters. In general, these editions were, despite their shortcomings, a valuable addition to the literature, and served a purpose. Let us only remind ourselves, for example, of the first edition of the Fliess letters, which were saved by Marie Bonaparte from Freud's intention to destroy them, and which instigated a large number of investigations on the origins of psychoanalysis.

On the one hand, it is understandable and perhaps inevitable that those early editors tried to control the publications, and judged what merited publication and what not in their opinion. On the other hand, it is equally clear that to the extent a person such as Freud gradually becomes the 'property' of the general public, he is subject to ever closer scrutiny, and step by step loses the protective cloak of privacy. Before the background of these two conflicting tendencies emerges the picture we gain of Freud, a picture which is often one-sided. Are there two Freuds, one the private person, to be treated with discretion, and the other the writer and scientist? Is he the hero of a legend, the villain of the piece, or is he, after all, returned to his own history? Whose Freud is it?

Unfortunately, the early editorial policy, as well as attempts to lock away archival material for decades to come, have contributed to what could be called, with only slight exaggeration, a war between Freud historians. Sadly, yet also interestingly enough, these fights are at least as bloody as the conflicts in the history of psychoanalysis about which they are fought. The one great Freud biography, whose author had been given unrestricted access to unpublished material (Jones I–III), did not calm the waters, but rather fueled an interest in alleged bodies in the closet in other scholars who had been denied that privilege.

Easy as it is to understand, and to sympathise with, the wish to protect the privacy of the protagonists, their families and their patients, it is but one small step from this to censorship and the cultivation of certain myths. And as justifiable as an attempt to fight censorship and to divest the history of psychoanalysis of its treasured myths is, one has to be careful not to cast away the good with the bad, and construct an equally biased account. Historiography is not a football match, and there are no winners who could lay claim to possessing The Historical Truth.

In 1974, the nearly unabridged Freud/Jung letters appeared, meticulously edited by William McGuire (F/Jun). For the first time, there was a reliable and almost complete text[2] of a correspondence of Freud's, substantially enriched by generous and accurate notes. Indeed, the editorial apparatus of McGuire was for years to come one of the most important references for the background of psychoanalytic history. There followed the complete letters to Fliess (F/Fli) and Silberstein (F/Sil), and, recently, the exchange with Binswanger (F/Bin), the first two of three volumes of the Freud/Ferenczi correspondence (F/Fer I, II), and the letters with Ernest Jones (F/Jon), all of them as complete as possible. After the Fliess letters, the Freud/Abraham correspondence will now be the second one to appear at first abridged, then complete.

---

[2]Some rude remarks about Eugen Bleuler in Jung's letters were omitted on request of the Jung family, out of consideration for Bleuler's son Manfred, then still living. In accordance with the heirs, patients' names were anonymised (A, B, C, etc.). There are plans for a new edition, filling in the few suppressed passages, and giving the full names of the analysands (letter of William McGuire to the author, 4 March 1996). [Addition] This plan has so far not been realised.

As to the Fliess letters, I cannot go into detail here. As far as I know, no systematic study and comparative analysis of the two editions has been made so far. It could be helped by taking into account the correspondence between Anna Freud and Ernst Kris, the editor of the first edition, recently made available in the Library of Congress. These letters bear witness of Anna Freud's far-reaching influence on this publication, and contain numerous examples of what she suggested to, indeed ordered, her analysand Ernst Kris to exclude from the book.

Apart from being an important step towards making available to the public the whole story, and not only a version *in usum delphini*, the unabridged editions allow the reader to *compare* them with the previous ones. Both of them are not only highly important source material for the history of psychoanalysis, but are, at the same time, a reflection of changing attitudes towards how this material should be presented—so that those editions represent themselves a part of the making and construction of the history of psychoanalysis.

It will become clear that the omissions, alterings, and misunderstandings in the cut versions sometimes affect major issues, sometimes minor ones. But even these seemingly minor points have significance, and may give us a surprising insight which the major ones do not. They are more than *lacunae* and unimportant trifles. Moreover:

> In its implications the distortion of a text resembles a murder: the difficulty is not in perpetrating the deed, but in getting rid of its traces. We might well lend the word *"Entstellung* [distortion]" the double meaning to which it has a claim but of which to-day it makes no use. It should mean not only "to change the appearance of something" but also "to put something in another place, to displace". (Freud, 1939a, p. 43)

But such a distortion—like repression—not only changes the appearance of the text and puts the suppressed in a hidden place, but simultaneously *preserves* the concealed. Secrets do not evaporate in their well-guarded hiding places, and the traces leading to them stand out as fresh as when they were made.

As a first example, let us have a look at the Freud/Pfister correspondence, published in 1963. Its co-editor Ernst Freud states in his preface (Freud & Pfister, 1963, p. 7):

> We had hoped to publish [Freud's] correspondence with Pfister in its entirety but, though Freud's original letters have survived,

> Pfister's have not. … However, surviving shorthand notes of
> Pfister's have made it possible to reconstruct his letters and hence
> fill in a number of important gaps.

This is an at least misleading statement, as it suggests that what had survived had in essence also been published. But there is a list in Anna Freud's handwriting (SFC), running over six pages, and listing seventy-eight letters of Pfister's to Freud from 22 February 1918 onward. After the respective date of the letter, Anna Freud made short comments (mostly a simple "no", or "uninteresting", "good passage about Groddeck", "too positive", "this is all too unimportant", "interesting about the patient, but no good for publication", "the theoretical aspects good, the personal ones no"). A comparison with the publication shows that these remarks were indeed decisive for the choice finally made, a choice that suppressed nearly all of Pfister's letters. The extant material, however, would have permitted to print a factual *exchange* of letters, all the more so, in that Pfister's own stipulation when handing over Freud's letters to Anna Freud was just "that nothing should be published that might give offence to any living person" (Freud & Pfister, 1963, p. 11).

As to Freud's side of this correspondence, Ernst Freud initially opted for a quite liberal editorial policy:

> In my view, the Freud letters must be seen as documents, in which
> omissions and alterations are permissible only for very good rea-
> sons. Such reasons could be possible law suits, the hurting of per-
> sons still living or of their descendants (Oberholzer), indiscretions,
> etc. I would rather like to include allusions to and remarks about
> both the patients Hirschfeld and Lieberman—under pseudonyms,
> of course—, as well as all the remarks about the Jung conflict. I see
> no reason why the fact that psychoanalysts' opinions about cer-
> tain points have changed or undergone a development should be
> a motive to suppress Freud's original remarks about them. Simi-
> larly, the discussion about religious resp. irreligious attitudes must
> remain as is. (Letter to Heinrich Meng, 23 January 1961; SFC)

Shortly afterwards, however, he concedes to Meng: "After careful consideration, I finally agree with you that the whole Hirschfeld affair has to be omitted after all" (20 April 1961; ibid.), while maintaining that

WHOSE FREUD IS IT?

"the case of Lieberman should remain fully standing, if at all possible" (no date, possibly 28 July 1961; ibid.).

A comparison of the published book and the originals,[3] however, shows that there is much more that was censored. Why, for instance, was Freud's letter of 9 June 1910, which discusses nothing but a painting of Leonardo da Vinci's, omitted? Why the following paragraph in the letter of 3 March 1913: "Should you have to deal with America after all, you will surely be taken in. In business matters, they are head and shoulders above us!"? Why the letter of 4 March 1923, in which he advises Pfister against publishing a certain essay? Why the letter of 8 February 1927, in which Freud praises Wilhelm Reich and asks Pfister to refer patients to him? Why the one of 27 February 1934, in which Freud criticises Reich's new ideas, in adding: "One can spare oneself the refutation with the help of arguments in the case of a large number of authors, if one knows how abnormal they are themselves"? And why the letter of 15 May 1932, in which Freud thanks Pfister for his aid to the *Internationaler Psychoanalytischer Verlag* and, referring to favourable news about Pfister's marital life, adds some remarks about "the dragon of folly", which he, Freud, had not been able to kill at the age of seventy-six, and which would surely also survive in further battles—"It is tougher than we are"? Why were eventually almost all references to three psychoanalytic cases omitted, which are pivotal for understanding the relationship between Freud and Pfister, for Pfister's attitude towards psychoanalysis, and which are of paramount importance for the history of the evolving theory and technique of psychoanalysis? In fact, the passages pertaining to these three cases constitute the bulk of the omissions.

My second and main example will be the 1965 edition of the Freud/ Abraham correspondence. I have chosen to look in greater detail at the first fifty letters, as well as at those of the decisive years 1924 and 1925. I have at my disposal a microfilm of the originals (LC), and a copy of the typescript of the correspondence, on which the editors of 1965 obviously based their publication. In the typescript, the passages that eventually were not printed are struck out by hand, and it already contains handwritten footnotes which were more or less taken over into

---

[3] Of Freud's letters to Pfister (LC). So far, I could not find out about the whereabouts of Pfister's side.

the publication. Apart from being able to actually *see* the well-preserved traces of distortion—the lines that decided the fate of passages to be or not to be published—and to check the transcript for misreadings, I could also find out which of the omissions in the book were due to deliberate decisions, and which to errors in the transcription. These errors are partly due to oversight—so that every now and then a word, half a sentence or more are missing—, partly to misreadings.

Let me give one example for each. In Freud's letter of 21 October 1907, the words *der das Wesentliche ist* (which is the essential characteristic of it) are missing after *den Mechanismus, der ihn dement macht* (the mechanism that makes the dream demented). This is not only the essential characteristic of the dream mechanism, but also the essential statement in this sentence! A seemingly minor misreading occurred in an often quoted line in Freud's letter of 23 July 1908, which reads in *Dialogue*: "May I say that it is consanguineous, Jewish traits that attract me to you [*in Ihnen*]?" (p. 46). In this form, the reader cannot appreciate that Freud is subtly referring to something which Abraham had written to him on 11 May 1908 (p. 36):

> I freely admit that I find it easier than Jung to go along with you.[4] I, too, have always felt this intellectual kinship. After all, the Talmudic way of thinking cannot disappear in us just like that. Some days ago a small paragraph in *Jokes* strangely attracted me. When I looked at it more closely, I found that, in the technique of apposition and in its whole structure, it was completely Talmudic.

A couple of weeks later, Freud actually wrote (now in F/Abr, p. 53):

> I value so highly the resolute tone and clarity of your writings that I must ask you not to think that I overlook their beauty. May I say that it is consanguineous Jewish traits that attract me to *them* [*in ihnen*]? We understand each other, don't we?

Thus, he does not refer to an unspecific 'Jewishness', which would attract him to Abraham, but to a particular point raised by the latter,

---

[4] Wrongly translated in *Dialogue* as: "I find it easier to go along with you rather than with Jung."

implicitly acknowledging Abraham's view of Freud's "Talmudic" way of writing, and returning the compliment. A difference that looked negligible at first sight, suddenly opens up new perspectives.

Now to the deliberate omissions. The first sixteen letters—which are about theoretical and therapeutical questions—are reprinted complete. Then, in Abraham's letter of 15 January 1908, a postscript is left out,[5] referring to two dreams of Abraham's wife, mentioned above in the letter: in case of publication, Abraham wrote, he would like "to disguise a few points, without harming the value of the dreams. I wanted to tell *you personally* about the dreams and their interpretation without changing them in any way." Similarly, Freud's response was omitted: he would rather not publish those dreams at all, he wrote, because "I have no lack of material, and should like to avoid distortion as far as possible." Thus, the first passages that were cut are about the question of discretion, what Abraham wanted to tell Freud *personally*, and about what Abraham called disguise and Freud distortion!

In the following letters, we find a wide variety of what the editors found not worth printing: personal details and family news, business questions about the goings-on in psychoanalytic politics and about the *Jahrbuch*, also quite a few scientific points, particularly concerning Abraham's monograph on *Dreams and Myths* (1909[14]) and Freud's suggestions for alterations and changes in it, remarks about third persons such as sexologists Magnus Hirschfeld (positive)[6] and Albert Moll (negative),[7] psychiatrists Eugen Bleuler and Hermann Oppenheim, or the Viennese writer Alfred Polgar.

As a second sample from the Freud/Abraham correspondence I have taken the letters of the years 1924 and 1925. These years mark the climax of a serious conflict within the Secret Committee, with, in various degrees of involvement, Rank and Ferenczi on the one side, and the Berliners (Abraham, Eitingon, Sachs) and Jones on the other. This conflict threatened not only to destroy the existence of this "Old Guard" but also of the psychoanalytic movement itself. At the same time a heated theoretical discussion was led, the outcome of which would

---

[5] Apart from a passage informing Freud and his wife about hotel prices in Berlin.

[6] "I hope you will not be influenced by the opinion of the official mob in Berlin about him."

[7] Alluding to the Latin *cave canem* (beware of the dog): "*Caveas!* M. bites too."

influence the history of ideas for decades to come. It is to the credit of the editors that they published much of this material, and even included two *Rundbriefe* (circular letters) of Freud's. Nevertheless, there is also much that was left out in the letters of 1924—remarks about the meeting of the Committee on the occasion of the 1924 congress in Salzburg, a very detailed account of this congress (the first Freud did not attend) by Abraham, various remarks about Rank and Ferenczi, about plans to re-establish the Committee and the *Rundbriefe* without Rank, etc. In addition, most about the preparation of a meeting and the meeting itself of German analysts in Würzburg was omitted; as was Freud's warning Abraham not to go to America on the invitation of an American analyst, Asch, "a pathological fool"; details about Abraham's and Freud's interest in the symbolical meaning of the number seven; a passage in which Abraham half defended Dr. Felix Deutsch for not having disclosed to Freud the truth about his cancer; some commentaries on Alix Strachey's analysis with Abraham[8]; remarks about Urbantschitsch, Federn, Helene Deutsch, Hitschmann, and others; and, again, family news, holiday plans, etc.

Most of Freud's and Abraham's emphases, such as exclamation marks and underlinings, though being in the transcript, were not printed. In his letters of 1924 and 1925, Abraham refers to the other members of the Committee by their *first* names. In the publication, the *family* names were printed instead, and so the reader cannot appreciate the subtle change in Abraham's attitude who, in his letter of 12 November 1924, reverts to the family name when speaking of the "divorce from Rank".

As to the letters of 1925, the most interesting among the ones that were left out deal with, again, Rank and Ferenczi, but above all with the "film affair" (cf. Ries, 1995). The correspondence ends on a bitter note. In his very last letter of 27 October 1925, the terminally ill Abraham stands up for his opinions and decisions against Freud, in a way he had

---

[8]For instance: "Perhaps, dear Professor, you may be interested in hearing something about the psychoanalysis of Mrs. Str. from London. It struck me from the very beginning that the long years of work with you are like extinguished. We have to discover everything afresh, as all the facts elicited by the first analysis have disappeared, while the general knowledge of psychoanalysis is intact. You will remember that the patient lost her father in the first weeks of her life, and has no memories of her own of him. Besides other reasons for the amnesia there is a complete identification of your person with her father—she does not remember either of you. On the other hand she has directed to you the same rescue phantasies as to her father."

hardly ever done before. In a cut passage that runs over several pages, he reaffirmed that nothing he (and Sachs) had done would justify Freud's "unpleasant aftertaste" (Freud to Abraham, 11 September 1925), that he had informed Freud "even though I was already ill in bed", that "Sachs and I have not done the slightest thing that would have been open to ethical objections", that he had a completely different (negative) opinion of Bernfeld and Storfer than Freud, that he rejected Freud's accusing him of "harshness", while concluding with: "This whole affair is to me a bagatelle which I should have liked to pass to the order long ago." Freud, in his rejoinder of 5 November 1925, maintained his position, and directly accused Abraham of not saying the truth: "Because of your complaint that St.[orfer] did not comply after Eitingon had reached his decision, I turned directly to Eitingon for information and from him I learned the contrary."[9] The correspondence ends with a (printed) sentence of Freud's, allegedly alluding to Abraham's health: "in any case let the outcome be that you cause us no more worry" (*Dialogue*, p. 399). In the light of their serious controversy, however, which could no longer be settled, these words have an uncanny ring …

* * *

For practical reasons, one can divide the omissions as falling into three categories: (1) unimportant details; (2) references to third persons, to psychoanalytic politics, and to inner conflicts; and (3) intimate data about the letter writers, their family members, colleagues, and patients.

Many of the omissions seem indeed to be trifles at first sight. It could be argued that, on the whole, the reader of the abridged editions does not miss a great deal. Why should the editors not leave out references to "people of no interest nowadays", "repetitions", "details of purely local interest", and "unimportant personal details"? But, then, why should they? Unimportant in themselves, some might prove to be key pieces in a bigger puzzle; and which of them it is impossible to say in advance. What makes one wonder, moreover, is that sometimes these details *were* published, and sometimes not. Why were Freud's pejorative remarks

---

[9]On 20 October 1925, Freud had sent Abraham's letter of 27 October to Eitingon with the request "to hear from you, who witnessed everything, if I really do A. an injustice and if I am mislead by sympathy for those who live nearer to me" (SFC). Eitingon's answer of 3 November sharply criticised Abraham, his "harshness", "lack of humour", "love for himself", "intellectual self-righteousness" and "moral contendendness" (ibid.).

on America to Pfister cut, while his terming America "Dollaria" in his letter to Pfister of 20 August 1930, which neatly sums up his opinion in one word, was not? Why is an influenza not mentioned, but Freud's self-diagnosis—in connection with the dream of Irma's injection—of "sexual megalomania" is (*Dialogue*, p. 20)? Why can we read about plans for one scientific project, but not about another? Why should it be important to learn about Freud's general reaction to a work of Abraham's (ibid., pp. 39–40), but unimportant to read a more detailed discussion of it (17 July 1908)?

As far as these 'unimportant' details are concerned, one can hardly make out a guiding principle; we are rather confronted with a mixture of arbitrary decisions and sloppiness. There is one important effect to this, however. Once a decision had been made not to print a question, a statement, an advice, an expression of thanks, etc., its consequences were *not systematically drawn*. Thus, sometimes we find questions, but not the answers, sometimes we read answers to questions we have to reconstruct. While the correspondents themselves did lead a very careful dialogue, meticulously referring and alluding to, expanding on, and answering each other's questions and statements,[10] the overall effect on the reader of *A Psycho-Analytic Dialogue* is rather the opposite of this title: this correspondence, as published, is not a real dialogue, let alone a psychoanalytic one.

More eye-catching are the omissions concerning third persons and conflicts within the psychoanalytic movement. Wilhelm Reich and his status as a psychoanalyst might be sensitive subjects; but instead of letting the reader have examples of Freud's changing attitude towards Reich, references to him are omitted altogether in the edition of the Freud/Pfister letters. This is regrettable, since the *effect* of such a policy (intended or not) has been the *Totschweigen* of key figures in psychoanalytic history. Still in 1987, in Peter Gay's monumental Freud biography, Reich is not even *mentioned*. The cut passage about Reich's being "abnormal" quoted above, is also an example of a not uncommon strategy in the history of psychoanalysis, namely, to "pathologise" opponents (Leitner, 1998, pp. 180–196), and then spare oneself the effort to refute the theory of the "abnormal" colleague "with the help of arguments".

---

[10] As in the above quoted remarks about Jewish traits in both their writings.

In the Freud/Abraham correspondence, many of the cut passages refer to two areas of conflict and controversy—the Rank and the film affairs—which overshadowed the relationship between Freud and Abraham during the last years of the latter. (Freud stood by Rank for a long time, while Abraham vehemently criticised him; Abraham supported a film project about psychoanalysis, loading heavy criticism of Freud's on his head.) Evidently, the editors tried to take the edge off the whole story, in printing conciliatory remarks of Freud and Abraham rather than acerbic ones, in omitting the more hostile remarks against each other and about third persons, and in cutting indiscretions. But theirs was essentially a thankless job, because they did have to print many other references to these topics; had they not, the remaining torso would have made no sense. The effect is that the reader learns that there were serious conflicts, but without being given many of the details, so that she or he cannot really *follow* the events as they developed.

The most delicate issues, however, are without doubt the passages dealing with intimate personal details and with patients. In fact, the reason why Pfister's letters of 1912 did not survive is that they were destroyed by Freud on Pfister's own request. In order to protect Pfister's privacy, the editors tried to omit references to why he wanted to have them destroyed, but the 'secret' leaks through every now and then, and the reader of the 1963 edition need not be a Sherlock Holmes to make a good guess. Counteracting the goal of discretion, the reader is rather invited to speculate, when reading that some letters were not of "impersonal content" and that Pfister had been in danger of committing "stupidities" (Freud & Pfister, 1963, pp. 108-109). Freud's report of 1 June 1927, that he had fulfilled the "hangman's job" of destroying these letters, is duly reprinted, but not a paragraph in the same letter in which Freud assured Pfister (F/Pfi):

> I have accomodated to your wish, although I have the intention to prevent a literary utilisation of my correspondence through a certain expression of my will. I want to bother the folks [*Leutchen*] as little as possible with my person. To tell the very truth: the present generation really sickens me too much, and I have no reason to believe that the future generations will be different.

Thus we are faced with the interesting situation that Freud's heirs made "literary utilisation" of his letters by publishing them, while cutting the paragraph in which Freud said he wanted to prevent precisely this.[11]

As to medical discretion, while we would all agree that medical discretion is a great good, perhaps even the quintessence of discretion, the real problem lies in the particulars. In view of the significance of the matter, some general remarks might be in order. Should one omit *all* references to patients? Or just those to certain patients? Or bring only those details which one considers not to be offensive? Or not abridge comments on cases, but anonymise the patients' names? After which period would it be possible to publish these names?

Obviously, opinions diverge. Some seventy years after the "Rat Man's" death, for example, Patrick Mahony published his name, Dr. Ernst Lanzer, as well as those of his siblings (Mahony, 1986, pp. 2–3). In the following year, 1987, the *Nachtragsband* to the German *Gesammelte Werke* came out, including the original notes on this case (Freud, 1955a) in a new transcription. In this edition, the pseudonyms originally chosen by James Strachey were kept. Curiously enough, this very edition also brings a facsimile of one page of the manuscript, in which a couple of names are clearly legible that are anonymised in the transcribed text on the facing page! Thus, a footnote such as the one on page 540 ("The original name is that of a well-known public figure in Austria"; p. 277 in S.E. 10) is rather pointless, when we already know from the facsimile that the pseudonym Hertz stands for Adler (Dr. Victor Adler in this case).

Archivists are faced with the same question. One way to deal with this is to make accessible only photocopies of the originals, in which the names of patients are blotted. This is the way it is done in the by far biggest collection of Freud letters, the Freud Archives in the Library of Congress. Although this might seem to be a sensible procedure, it entails all sorts of problems. It is a more amusing arabesque that the name of a literary personnage was blotted because it was mistaken for a patient's name, but it leads us to the fact that the person(s) responsible would have to have a complete—thus, impossible—knowledge of psychoanalytic history to fulfil the task efficiently.

---

[11]Cf. Ernst Freud's letter to Heinrich Meng of 26 October 1961: "I would rather not justify the publication [in the preface]. This is a delicate issue, and had we taken into account the wishes of my father, a publication would not have been possible at all" (SFC).

To quote one example from my own experience: in preparing the Freud/Ferenczi letters for publication, I came across the following passage in Ferenczi's letter to Freud of 20 January 1912: "I suspect that he [Jung] has … an unlimited and uncontrolled ambition, which manifests itself in petty hate and envy toward you, who are so superior to him. The case of Hirschfeld is proof of that" (F/Fer I, p. 332). This could well have been an allusion to the Berlin sexologist Magnus Hirschfeld, who had declared his resignation from the Berlin Psychoanalytic Society after a remark by Jung at the Weimar Congress, supposedly an allusion to Hirschfeld's homosexuality (Freud & Abraham, 1965, p. 108; F/Jun, pp. 453–454). Only later I found out that it referred to a patient of both Jung's and Freud's, whose treatment had been at the centre of the personal conflict and eventual break between the two men (see Chapter Two). At the outset, this was not clear at all, and only detailed research led to the discovery of this important case. Such a research would have to be done in every similar instance by the archivist, but such a research would be nearly impossible for any other scholar once the name were blotted.

Another possibility would be to give scholars unrestricted access to the material, but letting them sign a waiver that they would not publish patients' names.[12] Apart from ethical and practical problems (Who is entitled to exercise such a control? Who is a scholar?[13] How could one prevent publication in other countries and languages or in the Internet?),

---

[12]The attempt to exert control over the use of archival material has been pushed to an extreme by the archives of the British Psycho-Analytical Society. Each scholar who wants to do research in those archives has to sign the following waiver: "I understand that material from the Archives will be made available to me on the condition that I observe scrupulously the Regulations of the Archives and the following guidelines. 1) I undertake not to use for publication in any form, abstract, paraphrase or any other means, material obtained from the Archives without the written permission of the Honorary Archivist of the British Psycho-Analytical Society. Such permission can only be granted on receipt of a written application accompanied by the pages of the manuscript containing the citation as well as the two preceding and the two following pages. 2) I undertake to provide a copy of the entire manuscript, or any part therof, if requested to do so by the Honorary Archivist" (Rules and Conditions of the Archives of the British Psycho-Analytical Society).

[13]The Freud Archives have recently somewhat loosened their restrictions, in granting confidential access to patients' names for editors of Freud's correspondence. An author, however, preparing a historical novel about one of Freud's patients, was denied such an access, although she promised to treat the name confidentially.

one question remains: *Who is a patient?* In Freud's correspondence, there are numerous discussions of analyses of colleagues, sometimes of very prominent ones (Anna Freud, Ernest Jones, Anton von Freund, Kata Lévy, René Spitz, Max Eitingon, Ernst Simmel, Karen Horney, etc.). Should one anonymise *their* names? Or give them pseudonyms when they are mentioned as analysands, and give them their proper names when not? To return to Frau Hirschfeld: anonymising her name would also have meant that her status as one of the very few co-authors of a work of Freud's would have been denied to her.

Or should one provide even more information than the correspondents themselves? In the 1986 edition of the letters between James and Alix Strachey from 1924 and 1925, references to analysands were not only not cut, but abbreviations by the letter-writers were completed in brackets. Thus we read, for instance: "It does seem horribly difficult to see what's best to be done. Perhaps fresh data will turn up—Mrs. D[isher] will solve all, or Mr. W[innicott] will die or f-ck his wife all of a sudden, & Mr. H[artsilver] likewise" (Meisel & Kendrick, 1986, p. 166). Does this go too far?

And where is the dividing line between a 'training' analysis and a psychoanalytic 'cure'? Actually, training and treatment were inseparably linked from the beginning (see Chapter Five), and it would be a distortion of history if one treated the two as separate issues in retrospect. There is also at least one instance in Freud's writings that the name of an *analyst* was omitted by the editors. In the posthumously published paper "Psycho-analysis and telepathy" (Freud, 1941d) we read: "The girl ... behaved more and more in a contradictory manner, and it was decided that she should be analysed" (p. 192); the original manuscript adds: " ... by Dr. Deutsch".[14]

In summarising, it can be safely assumed that the editors were guided by the assumption that what should be published were primarily *theoretical* ideas and discussions, and partly also personal affairs and opinions, when they shed a humane or humorous light on the correspondents, but that more intimate details about them and their

---

[14]In the German original the difference is even greater: ... *sie einer Analyse zuzuführen* (p. 43) instead of *sie der Dr. Deutsch zur Analyse anzuvertrauen*. The original manuscript, which I consulted at the Library of Congress, further contains unpublished passages about this and another case.

analysands as well as outright aggressive remarks should be left out. As reasonable as this sounds, there are nevertheless some tricky aspects to it. The most important one, in my opinion, is that in doing so, a distinct, if implicit *dividing line* is drawn between *theory* on the one hand, and *personal experience* on the other. The first is seen as fit for the public, the second as in need of discretion. And more: the son of Sigmund Freud and the daughter of Karl Abraham, herself a fully fledged analyst, even stated that "certain personal details about the writers and their families" had not only to be omitted for reasons of discretion, but "do not contribute to the knowledge and understanding of their personalities and of their scientific work" (*Dialogue*, p. vii). Are there two different kinds of *personalia*, those which contribute to the understanding of a person and his theory (but unfit for print because of discretion), and those which do not (but too unimportant to be printed)? However this may be, the outcome is that in the remaining text we read very little about undiluted love and hate, but much about sublimation. But just as sexuality does not enter "into children at the age of puberty in the way in which, in the Gospel, the devil entered into the swine"[15] (Freud, 1910a, p. 42), psychoanalytic theory does not enter into analysts' heads like a demon from nowhere, but springs precisely from their personal and most intimate experiences. In cutting these, the *missing links* between the theoreticians and their theories can no longer be deciphered.

One concluding reflection might be appropriate. In the first two volumes of the Freud/Ferenczi correspondence, the analysand about whose intimate life and troubles we learn most, sometimes in a very indiscreet way indeed, is Ferenczi himself. This also holds true, to a somewhat lesser extent, for the analyst, Sigmund Freud. The whole correspondence revolves around their quasi-analytical and analytical relationship, and its publication, however abridged, would have been impossible had one preferred to treat that with discretion.[16] Or should one have published it as the "Freud/X. letters" (Shamdasani, 1997, p. 365)? Or even—given the fact that there are numerous details about Freud as a patient (although not an analytic one)—as the "X/Y

---

[15] Cf. Matthew, 8, 28–34; Mark, 5, 11–17; Luke, 8, 32–33.

[16] This is, in fact, one reason for the delay in publication. Although the heirs had agreed upon bringing out a selection of letters already decades ago, nothing came of it because of the impossibility of such a selection.

letters"?!¹⁷ As far as I know, no one has so far objected to the publication of these letters as such—on the contrary, they were greeted enthusiastically by the scientific community and the public—although there were some objections against the publication of patients' names (but not against those of Freud and Ferenczi). This is a double standard; either one decides to publish it as it is, or one should try to prevent its publication altogether.

It is my conviction that the best way to deal with the situation today, a century after the birth of psychoanalysis, is to make accessible and publish primary material. It might turn out that many of the 'big secrets'¹⁸ do not exist at all, or that *parturiunt montes, nascetur ridiculus mus*, while other details, unimportant in themselves, gain unexpected importance in a larger context. Although the situation is still far from being satisfactory, there are undeniable signs that archival restrictions have been loosened. Moreover, important writings and letters are now being prepared for publication, apart from the Freud/Abraham correspondence, for example, Freud's neuroscientific papers, various correspondence with family members, with Max Eitingon, Sándor Ferenczi, and Otto Rank, as well as the circular letters of the Secret Committee. The final goal is naturally a complete, unabridged, and annotated edition of both Freud's writings and letters—although there is still a long way to go, if we consider estimates that Freud wrote more than 20,000 letters during his lifetime.

Perhaps the time has come that the manifold reasons why Freud's case could not be made fully transparent have faded away, and that we may learn from it.

---

¹⁷To the best of my knowledge, no one has protested against publication of intimate details about Freud's medical record (e.g., Jones III; Romm, 1983; Schur, 1972). Schur discusses in length the question of discretion, in concluding that it would not be in Freud's spirit to withhold any details of his suffering and dying (ibid.).

¹⁸One of the finer examples is the world-shaking question how big Freud's penis really was (Berthelsen, 1987, p. 38).

CHAPTER SEVEN

Is there still an unknown Freud?
A note on the publications of Freud's
texts and on unpublished documents*

It is one paradox of historical research that the longer the object of that research dates back to the past, the more we know about it. Today, we know (or *could* know) substantially more about Freud than we did ten years ago, and we will know even more about him in the future. And yet the writing of history may well be another impossible profession: the judgement of contemporary witnesses is biased by their own interest, their involvement, and their lack of distance, and that of later generations by the ever-growing temporal and emotional distance and, in many cases, by interests of their own that often have little to do with a truly historical perspective.[1] Although it may be argued that the resulting view of history is more objective than that of contemporaries, this is counterbalanced by the fact that it becomes evermore difficult to empathise, to 'feel ourselves' into that now distant and alien

---

*[Addition] Obviously, even more materials have been published since this was written. I have left the text standing as a kind of 'stocktaking', so to speak, of the situation at the time, and I think that the conclusions that I drew are still valid.

[1] As in so-called "Whig history", for example, an interpretation of history that looked at much of history, through British Whig eyes, as having been a course of progress away from savagery and ignorance towards peace, prosperity, and science.

past, and to reconstruct it from 'within'. The situation is comparable to that of infant research. The research subjects can no longer, or not yet, speak, and we have to lend them our own voice. Or, differently put, both infants and silent documents do have something important to say, but we have to learn and to respect their own peculiar language to understand them, without forcing our own agendas on them.

The past years have seen a veritable avalanche of publications of and on Freud: hitherto unpublished correspondence, other primary materials, and a mass of secondary and tertiary literature. It is virtually impossible to give a complete survey of all the literature churned out by the "Freud Industry"[2] in many languages. On the occasion of his 150th birthday in 2006, the speed with which these volumes appeared has even been increased, not to mention the hype generated in the mass media, second only to the one about Mozart. As is well known, however, this huge quantity of materials has not led to an agreement between scholars, neither about Freud's personality and trustworthiness, nor about the validity or usefulness of his theory. In this situation, it seems a good idea to turn to the primary sources. After all, it is indisputable that any historiography worth its salt has to be based on those primary sources, of which anything Freud wrote himself is surely to be considered first. Passing judgement on him without an intimate knowledge of his writings would indeed be, as John Stuart Mill wrote in his *System of Logic*, "an abuse of the privilege of writing confidently about authors without reading them" (p. 241, 1843). So here I would like to concentrate on a seemingly simple question: How much do we actually know by now about what Freud wrote and said?

What Freud wrote

Works

First of all, anybody interested in what Freud wrote will have to turn to the works he wrote and published himself. Surprisingly, to this date there is no complete edition of those texts in any language, from his first

---

[2] It is not clear who first used the term "Freud Industry". "The term 'Darwin Industry' was arguably introduced in 1974 by Michael Ruse in 'The Darwin Industry—A Critical Evaluation,' *History of Science*, 12 (1974): 435–458, who … was using the model of the 'Newton Industry' that was already so named" (Burnham, 2006, p. 231).

publication in 1877 (1877a) to his last papers in 1939, not to mention manuscripts not printed during his lifetime. In the original German, there are two editions of collected works. The nineteen volumes of the *Gesammelte Werke*, including an index volume (1968), and an unnumbered *Nachtragsband* (supplement volume; 1987), contain his psychological and psychoanalytic works in chronological order, but are (with the exception of the *Nachtragsband*) not annotated. The second edition is the so-called *Studienausgabe* in eleven volumes (1969–1975), which is partly annotated,[3] but presents only a selection of his psychoanalytic texts.

What is still missing, is a critical and historical edition of his complete works, including his many pre-psychoanalytic writings, although some of them, such as his cocaine papers (Byck, 1974), or the monograph an aphasia (Freud, 1891b), have been reprinted separately.[4] There are, however, some separately published paperback editions in the original German of specific works that meet the standards of a scholarly, historical-critical edition. Such an edition is all the more desirable as the importance of the fact that Freud changed many texts—in the light of his own development and the reactions they received—has been increasingly realised (see Marinelli & Mayer, 2002).

In English, there is the well known *Standard Edition of the Complete Psychological Works of Sigmund Freud* (24 volumes), translated and annotated by James Strachey and his co-workers. This edition became available on CD and on the Web in December 2006 through PEP (Psychoanalytic Electronic Publishing; http://www.p-e-p.org/). At present, new translations of these texts by different translators appear in paperback format with Penguin. A collection of more than 120 pre-psychoanalytic works is being prepared for publication by Mark Solms. In French, the situation had long been unsatisfactory, as editions of Freud's writings were scattered, translated by different translators, and published by different publishers. However, the publication of the *Œuvres Complètes*, in a new translation, is now well under way. In Spanish, the *Obras completas*, the first translation of Freud's Collected

---

[3] Only about one half of the volumes are sufficiently annotated (see the discussion of this question in Richards, 1969, and Grubrich-Simitis, 1993, pp. 75, 88–89).

[4] [Addition] In the meantime, a DVD with Freud's complete writings, including the pre-psychoanalytic ones, has appeared in German (Freud, 2010).

Works into a foreign language, are available both in print and on CD. All editions of his collected works usually also include a few posthumously published works.

Indispensable working tools are the concordances for both the German *Gesammelte Werke* (including the *Nachtragsband*) and the English *Standard Edition*, both compiled by Guttman et al. (1983, 1995). With their help, one is able to find instantly the reference to any quote, of which one remembers just two words; or one can immediately find out if, or how often, Freud used this or that term.[5] As Fichtner and Meyer-Palmedo's authoritative Freud bibliography (1999) also contains a page converter for the two German editions and the *Standard Edition*, one can easily switch between these three.

Letters

A prime source on Freud is his vast correspondence. There are some particular features of Freud scholarship with regard to those letters and their use. First, for a long time only a fraction of them was published, and many of those publications were unreliable, full of errors in transcription, translation, and editorial notes. Second, many letters had long been locked away in archives, many of which have only recently been derestricted. Third, even those that were indeed accessible in archives were not used to the extent it would have been possible and desirable. This is at least partly due to the banal reasons that many Freud scholars have no, or only a very limited, command of German, in which most of the letters are written; that most of them are written in so-called Gothic or Sütterlin script, which fewer and fewer persons are able to read; and that the bulk of them has been transferred to English-speaking countries, particularly to the Library of Congress in Washington, DC. Many

---

[5]One may be chagrined at the thought that the *Konkordanz* renders useless the 1099 pages of the existing Index of the *Gesammelte Werke* by Lilla Veszy-Wagner, fruit of long years of devoted labour in pre-computer times. But this is not so; the Index provides what could be called an 'analog' index, while the *Konkordanz* provides a 'digital' one. For instance, the Index lists several references under *Liegen* (lying)—in analysis, during coitus, when sleeping, etc.—without the word *Liegen* actually occurring in most of the quotes, and thus not to be found among the entries for *Liegen* in the *Konkordanz*. On the other hand, the 175 entries for *Liegen* in the latter surpass by far the eight ones in the Index. Anyone interested in what Freud had to say about a specific *topic* is well advised to consult both Index and *Konkordanz*.

of those who were able to spend some time there were hindered by the above-mentioned personal limitations, while many of those who were not so hindered simply did not have the resources to go there.

The first correspondence of Freud's to appear, selected letters to Wilhelm Fließ, came out eleven years after his death (Freud, 1950a). There followed a selection of letters to various correspondents (Freud, 1960a) (including some letters to his fiancée), the correspondence with Oskar Pfister (Freud & Pfister, 1963), Karl Abraham (Freud & Abraham, 1965), Lou Andreas-Salomé (Freud & Andreas-Salomé, 1966), Arnold Zweig (F/AZ), Georg Groddeck (Freud & Groddeck, 1970), and with Edoardo Weiss (F/Wei). None of these was a complete, unabridged edition; entire letters were left out, and passages that were considered unimportant, repetitive, indiscreet, offensive, or for whatever other reason not fit for print were cut (see the previous chapter).

A landmark change happened in 1974, when the nearly unabridged Freud-Jung letters appeared, meticulously edited by William McGuire (F/Jun) (out of consideration for Bleuler's descendants, a few rude remarks about him were left out). The following editions appeared all unabridged:[6] the (now complete) letters to Fliess (F/Fli), to Eduard Silberstein (F/Sil), the correspondence with Ludwig Binswanger (F/Bin), with Sándor Ferenczi (F/Fer I-III), Ernest Jones (F/Jon), with his nephew Sam and other relatives in Manchester (conducted in English, so far only published in French and Spanish) (Freud, 1996g), the completed correspondence with Abraham (F/Abr), and the so-called circular letters (*Rundbriefe I-IV*) between the members of the "Committee", whose final volume has just appeared. There followed Freud's letters from his various travels to members of his family (Freud, 2002), his correspondence with Max Eitingon (F/Eit), with his sister-in-law Minna Bernays (F/MB), and the exchange with his daughter Anna (F/AF). (One could also add the letters between Lou Andreas-Salomé

---

[6]Although many of them did not publish the names of mentioned patients. While the editors of the Freud/Jones, Freud/Ferenczi, and Freud/Abraham letters, for instance, chose to disclose those names, more recent editions have again reverted to the policy of rendering them anonymous. There is an ongoing discussion of this sensitive issue of medical discretion versus public and historic interest (cf. Eissler, 1995; Fichtner, 1994; Haynal, 1995; May, 2007; Schröter, 1995a; and the previous chapter). Suffice it to say here that there is probably no completely satisfactory solution to this dilemma, but that in my opinion the arguments in favour of full publication, a hundred and more years after the fact, seem to prevail.

and Anna Freud; Andreas-Salomé & A. Freud, 2001.) Soon to appear
are the German editions of the complete Freud/Abraham correspondence (F/Abr), that between Freud and his fiancée Martha (Freud &
M. Freud, in prep.), and the letters to his children besides Anna.[7] Many
of the mentioned editions also came out in other languages: Portuguese,
Norwegian, Danish, Japanese, Hungarian, Romanian, Dutch, Serbian,
Czech, Korean, Chinese …[8]

Added to these are books and articles containing a more or less large
number of Freud letters; to name only a selection, and in chronologi-
cal order of their publication: to Hilda Doolittle (Aldington) ("H.D.")
(Freud, 1956c), Theodor Reik (Reik, 1956), Ernst Simmel (Freud, 1964a),
Emil Fluß (Freud, 1969a), Paul Federn (E. Federn, 1971), James Jackson
Putnam (Hale, 1971a), René Laforgue (Bourguignon, 1977), Sabina
Spielrein (Carotenuto, 1980), Smith Ely Jelliffe (Burnham, 1983), Anna
von Vest (Goldmann, 1985), Stefan Zweig (Zweig, 1987), Alphonse
Maeder (Maeder, 1988), G. Stanley Hall (Rosenzweig, 1992), Joan Riviere
(Hughes, 1992), Alfred Adler (Falzeder & Handlbauer, 1992),[9] Romain
Rolland (Vermorel & Vermorel, 1993), Sándor Radó (Roazen & Swerdloff,
1995), Paul Häberlin (Häberlin & Binswanger, 1997), Hermann Swoboda
(Tögel & Schröter, 2002), his sister Maria ("Mitzi") in Berlin (Tögel &
Schröter, 2004a), and to his niece Lilly Freud-Marlé (Freud-Marlé, 2006).

An invaluable guide to anything published by Freud, including
the letters, is the continuously updated complete bibliography on
him (Fichtner & Meyer-Palmedo, 1999), of which a new edition is in
the making.[10] Earlier discussions of Freud as a letter writer, based on
materials then available, have been undertaken by Martin Grotjahn
(1976), Gerhard Fichtner (1989), and Alain de Mijolla (1989). Recently,

---

[7][Addition] The letters to his children have appeared in the meantime (F/Kinder), as
have two of five volumes of the correspondence with his fiancée (F/Martha I, II).

[8]Email of Ekaterina Chekulaeva of Paterson-Marsh, formerly S. Freud Copyrights, 18
May 2006.

[9]The full text of the letters to Adler should be out shortly, as will be that of the Freud/
Ehrenfels correspondence (courtesy Wilhelm Hemecker). Both correspondences are quite
short, however. [Addition] The letters to Adler appeared in 2011 (F/Adl), the Freud/
Ehrenfels is still not out.

[10][Addition] This plan could not be realised. After Fichtner's death, his successor Albrecht
Hirschmüller kindly made available an updated version (2013) in electronic format to the
scientific community, however.

an excellent overview on Freud's letters has been provided by Michael Schröter (2006).

How many letters[11] did Freud actually write in his lifetime, how many of the written ones have been preserved, how many of the preserved ones have been published, and, finally, how reliable and accessible are those editions? In 1989, Fichtner estimated, on the basis of an intimate knowledge of the material, that Freud wrote about 20,000 letters during his lifetime, of which more than half he believed to be still extant (Fichtner, 1989, p. 810). Naturally, Freud received at least as many letters himself. Fichtner notes that he is still standing by these earlier estimates, although there might be minor shifts in the light of further discoveries. To this date he has counted 14,147 known letters to and from Freud, of which "the by far greater number" was written by Freud.[12] When all these letters will have been published, the quantity of Freud's theoretical works will pale in comparison.[13]

How many letters from Freud's own pen have been published so far? It is again with my thanks to Gerhard Fichtner that I am able to tell you the exact number: as of 21 September 2006, there are 5,666 Freud letters or parts thereof in print. Let us break down this number. Of correspondence published in book form[14]—and thus easily accessible—there are 225 Freud letters to Karl Abraham (of a total of 501

---

[11] Among "letters" I also include telegrams, postcards, picture postcards, and other communications such as referral notes on calling cards, etc.

[12] Emails of 19 and 20 September 2006.

[13] Future historians, who will write the history of our age of the email and the mobile phone, will have to make do without that unique source of information, now rapidly disappearing. Communication by email, texting, or social networks differs substantially from a classical correspondence by letters. It is fascinating to see, for example, how accurately Freud responded to others, and how well he remembered what he himself had written, and this in view of the often considerable time lag between the letters, and the fact that he usually kept no copies of his own. Another source of information that is gradually being lost are handwritten or typed manuscripts, with all their slips of the pen, typos, corrections, insertions, etc.

[14] The following list is not complete, although I have tried to include the most important editions. I have not included, however, secondary literature in which, often many, Freud letters or parts thereof are quoted (e.g., Jones I-III; in the German translation most of those quotes are taken from the originals). The numbers given should also be taken with a grain of salt. Errors in my hand-counting them could have occurred. My aim is to demonstrate the approximate proportions, and what they tell us, not to give exact figures down to the last letter.

for both correspondents); to Lou Andreas-Salomé 97 (226); to Minna Bernays 97 (199);[15] to Ludwig Binswanger 116 (195); to Max Eitingon 365 (821); to Sándor Ferenczi 540 (1247);[16] to Wilhelm Fließ 284 (287); to Anna Freud 157 (298); to his nephew Soloman ("Sam") Freud in Manchester 69 (138); the 248 letters[17] he wrote from his various travels to members of his family; to Georg Groddeck 42 (88); to Paul Häberlin 10; to Smith Ely Jelliffe 20 (42); to Ernest Jones 306 (671); to Carl Gustav Jung 164 (359); to Oskar Pfister 99 (130); to James Jackson Putnam 32 (88); to Theodor Reik 46; to Eduard Silberstein 80; to Sabina Spielrein 20 (31); to Edoardo Weiss 45; to Arnold Zweig 56 (137); and to Stefan Zweig 45 (79).

There are also the editions of letters presently in preparation: some 400 plus letters to his children besides Anna; the correspondence with his fiancée (ca. 770 [1542])[18]; and the exchange with Otto Rank (ca. fifty [250]).[19] Of the ca. 315 letters to various addressees reprinted in the anthology of 1960, most have been published, or will soon be, in the mentioned editions and other publications. A somewhat exceptional position is occupied by the so-called *Rundbriefe* (circular letters) between the members of the Committee, not included in this overview. The letters from Vienna were usually drafted by Otto Rank, and then co-signed by Freud. Only twice Freud wrote letters himself. It was only after the break with Rank and the re-founding of the Committee that Freud dictated the letters to Anna, who then co-signed them.

It can be stated that, of the above-mentioned 5,666 Freud letters, about 3,200 can be found in easily accessible editions, and in the near future this number will be increased to about 4,400. To this must be added a few hundred letters that appeared elsewhere in the most scattered, but still more or less accessible places, such as scientific journals, or that were quoted in the secondary literature. And if we finally also

---

[15] Including some letters addressed to both Minna and her mother or her sister.

[16] In the book, the count is 1246, but one unnumbered letter had also be included.

[17] Of which some had already been published elsewhere.

[18] According to Gerhard Fichtner, co-editor of the upcoming edition, the estimated total, which may still slightly change, is now at 1,542, of which about half are Freud's (email of 20 September 2006). Michael Schröter speaks of "ca. 750" letters on Freud's side (2006, p. 220).

[19] Numbers according to Schröter (2006, p. 221). These letters will first appear in English. [Addition] See F/Kinder; F/Martha I, II; F/Ran.

add the letters reprinted in remote places, such as auction catalogues etc., the total of Freud letters soon in print will exceed 6,900. We have to bear in mind, however, that a great many of them are still reprinted in abridged form or in translation only, that many contain transcription errors, that many are not annotated at all, and that the editorial notes to those that are annotated differ greatly in quality and quantity. Moreover, there are various policies on how to present them: be it in modernised grammar and orthography, or true to the original, be it with or without text-critical notes regarding crossed-out, inserted, or underlined words, margin remarks, etc. It is beyond the scope of this article to enter into a discussion about the accuracy and quality of Freud translations, particularly into English (see, e.g., Bettelheim, 1983; Ornston, 1992) and French. Obviously, this adds another layer of possible distortion.

In any case, about two thirds of his extant letters, including practically all of Freud's 'big' correspondences, are now, or will shortly be, in print. Schröter states that "the large correspondences of Freud with friends and disciples have nearly all been published" (2006, p. 221). There remain only a few important lacunae, for example, the letters to Franz Alexander, Eugen Bleuler,[20] Marie Bonaparte, Abraham A. Brill, Ruth Mack Brunswick, William Bullitt, Jeanne Lampl-de Groot, or Irmarita Putnam. There are, of course, many minor textual residues, individual letters, notes of thanks for birthday greetings or books received, referral notes, etc. Perhaps the greatest desideratum, as far as his letters are concerned, is completed editions of exchanges so far only published in an abridged form, as has already been done with the Freud/Fließ and the Freud/Abraham letters.

Other Freud texts

Other texts from Freud's pen not meant for publication include manuscripts and drafts, entries in diaries and calendars, dedications and margin notes in books, case notes, and appointment calendars.

Some of his manuscripts, such as the talk he gave before the Committee on telepathy in 1921 (Freud, 1941d), were reprinted posthumously (though in an edited and abridged version) in various editions of his Collected Works. Ilse Grubrich-Simitis (1993) has given an excellent

---

[20] Apart from a few extracts of Freud's letters (in Alexander & Selesnick, 1965), only Bleuler's side has so far been accessible. [Addition] In the meantime, the extant letters were published by Michael Schröter (F/Bleu).

overview of the extant Freud manuscripts, and of the way Freud worked.[21] She also published passages that were left out by the editors in the above-mentioned text on telepathy[22] and in other manuscripts, such as a "Postscript to the question of lay analysis", in which Freud polemically discusses the situation regarding this question in the United States (ibid.). Freud's until then missing manuscript of the twelfth metapsychological essay on the transference neuroses was discovered among the Freud-Ferenczi letters, when a committee met in London to discuss their future publication, and was published in English under the title: *A Phylogenetic Phantasy* (Freud, 1985a).[23] Freud's expert opinion "On the electrical treatment of war neurotics" (1955c) appeared first in English translation in the *Standard Edition*, and is now also contained in the German *Nachtragsband*. The Fließ letters contain numerous drafts as well as the so-called *Project for a Scientific Psychology* (Freud, 1950c). Added to these are various notes and observations, such as his "Remarks on faces and men" (*Bemerkungen über Gesichter u Männer*), jotted down in 1908 in the National Portrait Gallery in London (in Freud, 2002, pp. 250–255), or remarks on "The individual characteristics of my dreams" (*Meine individuelle Traumcharakteristik*) (in Grubrich-Simitis, 1993, pp. 144–146). A few of the original manuscripts remain still unpublished, such as those of *Beyond the Pleasure Principle* (Freud, 1920g) and *The Man Moses* (1939a), or Freud's original contributions to the book he co-authored with Bullitt on Thomas Woodrow Wilson (Freud & Bullitt, 1967).[24] It is unlikely, however, that many more such manuscripts will be discovered, since "Freud was definitely not one of those authors who, hoping for posthumous recognition, produced texts to be put in a drawer. He wrote

---

[21] For a discussion of Freud as a writer, see Mahony's classic book (1982). Walter Kaufmann gives the following list of six writers "who wrote the best German prose after Luther ...: Lessing and Goethe, Heine and Nietzsche, Freud and Kafka" (1980, p. 15). I would also add Arthur Schopenhauer.

[22] The publication of Freud's "Postscript" to this text is being prepared by Dr. Maria Pierri (email of 5 October 2006).

[23] [Addition] André Haynal, who was present at the meeting, described how "Mrs. Ilse Grubrich-Simitis laid her hands" (2008, pp. 32–33) on the manuscript and had it published.

[24] The extent of Freud's co-authorship, or even the question whether he contributed anything at all besides the preface, has long been contested. The late Paul Roazen discovered Freud's manuscript among the Bullitt papers, however, which I transcribed and translated for him, and about which he drafted a book. At the moment, it is unclear whether it will still be published after his death.

for straight and immediate publication" (Grubrich-Simitis, 1993, p. 289), and he destroyed many of his manuscripts once they had been printed.

As far as private notes are concerned, Freud's diary of his trip to America in 1909 and his "travel calendar" of his last visit to Rome in 1923, together with his daughter Anna, were reprinted by Christfried Tögel in the volume with his travel letters (Freud, 2002, pp. 283 sqq., 378–381, also in facsimile). Michael Molnar, former archivist and then acting director of the Freud Museum in London, published Freud's diary of his last years (*Kürzeste Chronik*), together with a wealth of additional information and photographs (Freud, 1992i). Comparable "calendar notes", made by Freud during the First World War, are accessible in the Library of Congress.

J. Keith Davies, also of the London Freud Museum, and Gerhard Fichtner recently published a comprehensive catalogue of Freud's library on CD (Davies & Fichtner, 2006), containing images of hundreds of covers and pages of books in his library, with dedications, margin notes, etc. Thus we not only get an excellent overview of *what* Freud read,[25] but also some revealing insights into *his reactions* to his reading. For example, his first biographer Wittels wrote about the Weimar Congress in 1911, in which Adler no longer participated. With reference to the Schreber case, Freud talked about the symbolism of the eagle, and that the eagle would be the only animal that could look straight into the sun. Wittels added that Stekel got a laugh when he pointed out that Freud had left an *Adler* (eagle) at home who had dared look into the sun. To which Freud remarked in the margin: *nicht wahr! Er sprach von Schlange am Busen. Lüge v. St.* (not true! He talked of the snake at the bosom. Lie of St.) Apart from providing such glimpses into his spontaneous reactions, Freud's underlinings and margin notes can also be of great value for a study of his sources and how he made use of them. Frank Sulloway, for instance, said that, for his Freud book (1979), he "based his historical conclusions on a detailed study of the notes Freud made in the books of his library" (Sulloway, 1994, p. 61).[26]

---

[25] See also Peter Brückner's early (1975) and Rohrwasser's recent book (2006) on Freud's private reading.

[26] For the point here made it is irrelevant whether or not one actually agrees with Sulloway's conclusions. The point is that such research no longer requires travels to London, New York, and Vienna, but can be done at one's desk with a few keystrokes.

Books that Freud dedicated to other persons are naturally harder to trace, but we know for instance of his translation of a set of Charcot's lectures (Charcot, 1886), which he dedicated to Josef Breuer with the words: "To his most highly esteemed friend, Dr. Josef Breuer, secret master of hysteria and other complicated problems, in silent dedication, the translator" (in Swales, 1989, p. 292).[27] There has been some discussion about Freud's dedication of his exchange of letters with Einstein, *Why War?* (Freud, 1933b), to Mussolini: "From an old man who greets in the ruler the hero of culture" (F/Wei, p. 20).[28] One alleged inscription has turned out to be a myth, however, namely, that Freud, when he was requested to sign a document that he had been treated correctly by the Gestapo, is said to have added: "I can heartily recommend the Gestapo to anyone" (Jones III, p. 226).[29]

Of case histories, perhaps one of the most interesting and revealing ones seems to be lost. I am referring to that on Frau Elfriede Hirschfeld, Freud's "grand-patient" and "chief tormentor" (see Chapter Two). Freud had written her "secret history for her," an "essay about her illness" (3 July 1911, 9 February 1912; F/Pfi). Of the surviving case notes, arguably the most important ones are the original notes on the Rat Man case (Freud, 1955a), published in both the *Standard Edition* and the *Nachtragsband* of the *Gesammelte Werke*. To give but one example of the synergetic possibilities of the working tools now available: Not only is it possible to compare in general terms how Freud's case notes differ from his printed account, but with the help of the *Freud Concordance* we are for instance able to find out that Freud mentioned

---

[27] *Seinem vor Allen hochgeehrten Freunde/Dr. Josef Breuer/geheimem Meister der Hysterie und anderer complicirter Probleme,/in stiller Widmung/der Übersetzer.* According to Swales (ibid.), writing in 1989, the copy of the book had been offered for sale a few years before by an American bookdealer, probably John Gach.—With thanks to Richard Skues.

[28] *Benito Mussolini mit dem ergebenen Gruß eines alten Mannes, der im Machthaber den Kulturheros erkennt. Wien, 26. April 1933*—Freud (F/Wei, p. 34). Weiss told Jones about this, who mentioned it in his Freud biography (Jones III, p. 180), despite Weiss's request that it should not be published. See the discussion in Roazen (2005, pp. 31–41).

[29] *Ich kann die Gestapo jedermann aufs beste empfehlen.* Jones actually only writes that Freud *asked* if he might add that sentence, without saying whether he really did so, but this has often been treated as a 'fact' ever since. Peter Gay even speculates about Freud's motives in sarcastically challenging the Gestapo, and thus to endanger his life: "Was there something at work in Freud making him want to stay, and die, in Vienna?" (1987, p. 628). Nothing like this was found in the actual document, however (Roazen, 1993, p. 47).

the "mother" sixty-seven times in the notes, but only sixteen times in print! This might also help to explain why Rank, in the first discussion of this case in the Vienna Psychoanalytic Society, could state that "all aspects clearly point to a love of the mother" (*Minutes I*, p. 233)—whose traces had then been nearly obliterated in the published version. From Freud's pre-psychoanalytic time, Albrecht Hirschmüller published forty-five short psychiatric case histories, written when Freud worked at Meynert's clinic in the *Allgemeine Krankenhaus* in Vienna (Hirschmüller, 1991, pp. 233–485; cf. Hirschmüller, 1978). Naturally, there is always the possibility that new documents will turn up. Just recently, for instance, Angela Graf-Nold discovered a long referral letter of Freud's to a colleague of 1893, containing a detailed description of the patient's case history and of the treatments applied.[30]

One of the most interesting recent finds are Freud's lists of analytic treatments of the years 1910 to 1920, which were found in the Freud Museum in London. For the first time, it is now possible to reconstruct exactly, with whom, when, for how long, and with what frequency Freud worked during those years (May, 2006, 2007; Tögel, 2006). Another very recent discovery, made by Franz Maciejewski (2006), is Freud's handwritten entry in the guest book of the hotel in the Engadine, in which he stayed with his sister-in-law Minna Bernays in August 1898: "[double room number] *11/Dr. Sigm Freud u Frau* [and wife]/*Wien*", thus adding fuel to the long-discussed question of whether or not Freud had an affair with Minna (cf. Swales, 1982, 1992, 1993, 1998, 2000).

What Freud said

This is a wide field, ranging from detailed proceedings of scientific meetings to apocryphal and, in all probability, fabricated quotes, such as the infamous "Sometimes a cigar is just a cigar" (cf. Elms, 2001). The most important source in this respect is arguably the four volumes of the *Minutes of the Vienna Psychoanalytic Society* (*Minutes I-IV*; cf. also Fallend, 1991; Lobner, 1992), painstakingly compiled by Otto Rank, a rich source that is, interestingly, rather under-used in Freud studies. In addition, there are many other records of his contributions in various settings. Let me only mention as examples the proceedings of the meeting of the *K. k.*

---

[30] [Addition] See Falzeder & Graf-Nold, 2010.

Gesellschaft der Ärzte in Wien on 15 October 1886, when Freud gave his famous paper on male hysteria (*Wiener Medizinische Presse*, 1886, 27: col. 1407–1409); or Freud's contributions as an expert witness to the hearings in the case of Wagner-Jauregg and the treatment of war neuroses (in Eissler, 1979). We know of sixteen published interviews. To name just three of them: One he gave the *Boston Evening Transcript* on the occasion of his lectures at Clark University in 1909, conducted by Adelbert Albrecht (Freud, 1909f), one was with George Sylvester Viereck (Freud, 1927h), and one with "N. B." (Nicolas Bandy?), published in the *Neue Freie Presse* (Freud, 1932g).[31]

Quite numerous are notes, diaries, and recollections of his analysands, be they patients or (later) analysts.[32] Probably the most detailed account published so far are Ernst Blum's notes of his analysis with Freud, written with Freud's consent after each session, which have recently come out (Pohlen, 2006). We learn, for instance, what Freud said after Blum disclosed his phantasy to marry Anna: "I wouldn't mind if you wished to marry my daughter; you are a young man with good manners, you are an analyst, you are Swiss—which are all qualities that I like"[33] (ibid., p. 247). Of other books let me mention those by the poetess "H.D." (Hilda Doolittle) (1956) (with the well known scene in which Freud complained that he was too old to be loved by her; p. 47); Smiley Blanton (1971) (with many quotes from the analytic hours); Helene Deutsch (1973); Roy Grinker (1975); John M. Dorsey (1976) (with a precious snippet for those who still believe that Freud detested music: "I recall during a session his leaning over the couch to sing [!] one or two strains to me from Mozart's *Don Giovanni*"; p. 51); Abram Kardiner (1977) (the fact that Freud talked with him "all the time" during the analytic hours made John Rickman and James Strachey ask him how he "did" it, because to them "He never sa[id] a word"; pp. 77–78); and Joseph Wortis (1954) (who reports that Freud called *Don Giovanni* "the greatest opera there is"; p. 161). Kata Lévy-Freund wrote about her analysis with Freud in Budapest. One day she happened to fall asleep right in the middle of the analytic session. The Professor was quite indignant, telling her that

---

[31] Cf. also Ackermann, 1989.

[32] A distinction which is often hard, if not impossible, to draw. I will not enter into a discussion of this question, as it is not germane to the topic of this article.

[33] This quote does not appear in the actual notes written down after the sessions, however, but was recalled much later by Blum during talks with the editor of the book.

although this had indeed occurred to himself already, it was unheard of in a patient (Lévy-Freund, 1990, p. 40)! Marie Bonaparte kept (still unpublished) diaries of her long-term analysis with Freud, rushing to her hotel room after each session to write down what she remembered of Freud's words; sometimes she even made notes during the analytic hours themselves (cf. Bertin, 1982). On 8 December 1925, she recorded for instance the dictum that has since become famous: "What does Woman want?" (Elms, 2001, p. 87).

Among his patients, Sergej Pankejeff, known as the "Wolf Man," wrote down his memories of Freud (in Gardiner, 1971), and told the journalist Karin Obholzer about his analysis with him (Obholzer, 1980). Still unpublished are the recollections of the painter and graphic artist Rudolf Kriser (written in exile in Argentina in 1954). Towards the end of the analysis Freud let himself be portrayed by his patient, and treated him gratis for the last ten hours (LC; cf. F/Abr, pp. 378–379). In the 1960s Paul Roazen not only "tried to meet all the living members of the early psychoanalytic movement and some of Freud's immediate family" (Roazen, 1971, p. xxii), but also former analysands, which resulted in his books, *Freud and His Followers* (ibid.), now considered a classic, and, more recently, *How Freud Worked* (1995). Kurt Eissler conducted numerous interviews with former analysands of Freud's and other persons who had known him. Many of these interviews are still restricted.[34] We know, however, of the one he made with the later wife of Richard Tauber, the famous Austrian singer, who had been in analysis with Freud because of impotence. She told Eissler: "Freud said I will give you an advice. Tell him you dont [sic] like intercourse + refuse it. He will stop thinking of himself + will be potent. Mrs. T. carried out the advice + RT was potent. (When I admiringly said Freud achieved it in 2 sessions + the telephone conversation with you, the blonde exclaimed I achieved it)" (LC).

---

[34] Eissler's policy of restricting the transcripts of those interviews for decades to come has led to criticism, as well as to speculations about possible bodies in the closet he might have wanted to hide from the "FBI" (his acronym for "Freud Bashers International"). A librarian at the Library of Congress once told me in an aside that he had looked at a transcript of one of those restricted interviews, and had wondered why it had been classified at all, given its innocuous content. In it, Eissler assured the woman he interviewed that she could feel free to be completely frank, because the interview would be locked away anyway—which made the lady ask: "But why do you interview me at all, Dr. Eissler, if nobody can read it?"

Or Max Graf, the father of "Little Hans", told Eissler that when Hans was cured from his horse phobia, Freud made him a special birthday present: he climbed the four floors to the Grafs' apartment with a rocking horse under his arm (interview of 16 December 1952; Balint Archives, Geneva).[35] David J. Lynn gave an account of "Sigmund Freud's psychoanalysis of Albert Hirst", the nephew of Emma Eckstein, on the basis of Hirst's unpublished autobiography and typescripts of Eissler's interviews (Lynn, 1997). The treatment started in 1903 when Hirst was sixteen years old, and began with "Hirst sitting in a chair: 'He ordered me to assume in that chair the position in which I masturbated.' Hirst had no thought of disputing such an order. Freud reassured him that masturbation was not destructive, and Hirst felt immediate relief" (ibid., p. 74).

Many family members also wrote about their memories of what Sigmund Freud had said. My favourite quote is reported by his niece Lilly Freud-Marlé: "Sometimes he did not want to comment, however, and, when one looked inquiringly at him in expectation of a remark, he pressed his lips together with much charm, then opened them slightly— and surprised one by uttering: 'Woof-woof, woof-woof'" (Freud-Marlé, 2006, p. 195). Martin Freud paid tribute to his father in his book, *Glory Reflected* (M. Freud, 1957), providing charming descriptions, for instance, of the holidays spent together in the Austrian and Bavarian mountains when he and his siblings were children, for example, of the one and only occasion when Sigmund Freud went shopping for groceries: Because of flooding, many villages were cut off, and the supply of food ran out. Freud began a foraging expedition over the mountains to find shops that were still open, and after a long time returned with a full load in his knapsack, including an enormous salami, still remembered by his children in their old age. He must have had a difficult time, however, because "he, usually eager to entertain us", remained taciturn about the details of this adventure (ibid., p. 63).

The memoirs of Freud's sister Anna Freud-Bernays, including her recollections of Sigmund, were edited by Christfried Tögel (Freud-Bernays, 2004). There is her amusing memory of schoolboy

---

[35] In an earlier article, however, Graf ante-dated this episode to Hans's third, not fifth, birthday (Graf, 1942), thus leading to speculations whether Freud had actually triggered the horse phobia himself with his present (e.g., Rosenzweig, 1992, p. 162)! Eissler's interviews of Max Graf and of "Little Hans" Herbert Graf have now been derestricted.

Sigi in his room, humming Viennese folk songs during his studies: "There's one thing, dear Lord, I'm asking for, though, send me a fiver, I'm needing some dough" (ibid., p. 221). His granddaughter Sophie Freud described Freud in the biography of her mother, Esti, wife of Martin (S. Freud, 2006). When Esti paid her first respects to the Freud family, Freud turned to Martin and whispered: "Much too pretty for our family" (ibid., p. 66). Later, however, he called her "not only malignantly *meshugge*, but also insane in the medical sense" (ibid., p. 214).

Additional information can be gleaned from letters of family members to third persons, as in the letters from Anna Freud to Andreas-Salomé (2001), or to her friend Eva Rosenfeld (in Heller, 1992a). The actor and journalist Detlef Berthelsen interviewed the maid and housekeeper of the Freuds of many years, Paula Fichtl (1987), including a discussion of the world-shaking question of how big Freud's penis really was (p. 38). Fichtl also remembers that Freud relied on the judgement of his dog: "The Professor always said: 'There's something wrong with people whom Jofie does not like' … And of course 'Jofie was always right'" (p. 34).

Many of his followers—regardless of whether they later broke with him or not—wrote about Freud and their memories of him, or recounted them in interviews. Regarding the latter, the work on oral history done by Eissler and Roazen must again be mentioned (notwithstanding the fact that they had different, and often antagonistic, aims in mind). Some of Eissler's interviews with those persons did see the light of day, for example the one with Wilhelm Reich (Reich, 1952).[36] In 1973, Hendrik M. Ruitenbeek edited a collection of recollections, memories and impressions of Freud, *Freud As We Knew Him*, selections of pieces that had already appeared elsewhere. Lou Andreas-Salomé published a "Freud Journal" of the year she spent in Vienna (1958). Admiring, or not so admiring disciples, wrote down their memories of Freud, for example, Hanns Sachs (1944), Theodor Reik (1956), Wilhelm Stekel (1950), Ludwig Binswanger (1956), Richard Sterba (1982), or Isidor Sadger, whose memoirs were recently refound and published (2005).

---

[36] It was published without authorisation, against Eissler's intention to restrict it for one hundred years, and against the protestations of the Freud Archives (cf. Schwartz, 1970). It should again be noted that it is beyond the purpose of this article to discuss the question of the conflicting interests between historical research and personal discretion.

Letters between Freud's colleagues naturally also often dealt with him and what he said, for example those between Ferenczi and Groddeck (1982/2006),[37] between Ferenczi and Rank, or Abraham and Jones (both not yet published in their entirety). Much of Ferenczi's *Clinical Diary* is devoted to a discussion of his relationship with Freud, quoting from conversations with him.

In addition, hundreds, if not thousands, of canonised or apocryphal quotes can be found in the literature, which it is impossible to review here. So let me randomly pick only two of those quotes. When Freud was guest of G. Stanley Hall in 1909, Hall asked Freud for his professional opinion on an agoraphobic man of Hall's acquaintance. When Freud judged that one reason for the neurosis was the man's wish to be financially supported by his father, he jokingly told Hall the remedy: "Kill his father" (Jones II, p. 58). In a letter to Hitschmann Freud added: "Hall was flabbergasted, and I had to reassure him that I had not told this to the patient himself" (6 November 1935; LC). When Ernst Simmel gave a paper "whose meager content was disproportionate to its length, Freud noted in the margin of his program: 'That's what is called milking a buck'" (Lévy-Freund, 1990, p. 44). There is also one recording of Freud's voice, which is played in the Freud Museums in London and Vienna.

With regard to other materials, let me just mention that, apart from his books, many of Freud's possessions have survived, such as his collection of antiquities (cf. Gamwell & Wells, 1989) or his furniture, including the famous couch. And of course there are many photographs, and even some films, taken of him (e.g., Engelmann, 1976; E. Freud, L. Freud, & Gubrich-Simitis, 1976; Freud, 1992i; Lehrman Weiner, 2005). In an ongoing series in the journal *Luzifer-Amor*, Michael Molnar presents and comments upon photographs from the holdings of the London Freud Museum (2004a, 2004b, 2005a, 2005b, 2006a, 2006b).

Freud's life

Lives

The first to write about Freud was Freud himself, in a mixture of openness and concealment, as in "Screen memories" (1899a), *The Interpretation*

---

[37] A first edition appeared in French translation (1982; German 1986), followed by a completed and corrected edition in English (2000), and an authoritative edition in German (2006).

of Dreams (1900a), or *The Psychopathology of Everyday Life* (1901b). His autobiographical writings proper were always written with an eye on "the Cause" founded by him, most famously in his *History of the Psychoanalytic Movement* (1914d), which set the tone of much of later psychoanalytic historiography, or in his "Autobiographical Study" (1925d).[38]

The first biography proper to appear was written by his erstwhile follower Fritz Wittels (1924) (who later came back into the fold), an essay that is avowedly "subjective through and through" (p. 260), but which many find still worth reading, not least because of Wittels's first-hand acquaintance with Freud and his sharp pen. Freud himself found it "by no means hostile" and "not unduly indiscreet". Although he criticised "positive distortions", he acknowledged that Wittels "detect[ed] many things which are well known to myself" (in ibid., pp. 11–13). We know about the details to which he objected and, perhaps even more interesting, to which he apparently did not, from a list of corrections he sent to Wittels (LC), and from the notes he made in his own copy (see above). Still during Freud's lifetime there followed appraisals by Edgar Michaelis (1925) (critical and ironical), Charles Maylan (1929) (ad hominem and antisemitic),[39] and Stefan Zweig (1931) (an admiring homage). Freud was pleased by Zweig's statement that his achievements were "less the result of intellect than of character", but objected that "[t]he fellow is actually somewhat more complicated" (Freud, 1960a, p. 402).

After Freud's death, Emil Ludwig published *Doctor Freud, An Analysis and a Warning* (1946), an example of 'history lite'—fact free history—since Ludwig's only sources on Freud's life were the latter's

---

[38] In fact, much of the fodder for many of Freud's harshest critics, who see him as "willful and opportunistic, … lacking in … empirical and ethical scruples", and "stooping to low tricks" (Crews, 1995, pp. 35-36), is coming from the "tantalizing autobiographical clues" (ibid.) he himself provided. Peter Swales's brilliant analyses of "Herr Aliquis" (e.g., 1998)—the conclusion of which has been heavily contested, but never disproven—may serve as an example.

[39] About which Freud wrote in a letter to Walter Kluge (30 April 1929; LC): "Regarding such incorrect applications of analysis one knows, after all, how much the eagerness of causing a sensation and of giving offence play a part in this, and one plays into the hands of its originator if one pays much attention to his achievement." And, to Abraham A. Brill: "I only know he went into analysis at Berlin and was sent away as a queer, abnormal customer unfitted for our work. The book is his personal revenge" (8 October 1929, LC; in English in the original).

own published works, although it contains some interesting snippets, such as his account of his visit to Freud in 1927.[40] Helen Walker Puner's *Freud, His Life and Mind* (1947) solicited very mixed reactions. While Erich Fromm, for instance, was "sure that her biography will help greatly to disseminate a true and inspiring picture of the founder of psychoanalysis" (in ibid., p. xvi), and Paul Roazen even called it "outstanding" (in ibid., p. ix), it was severely criticised by the 'inner circle', and it was one of the reasons that moved Anna Freud to authorise an 'official' biography, Ernest Jones's *opus magnum* (Jones I-III), in which he explicitly took Puner's work to task.[41] Before Jones, analyst Siegfried Bernfeld and his wife Suzanne had already started on a biographical venture, particularly of Freud's early years (1981), but were not able to finish their work. They put their material at Jones's disposal, who did in fact heavily draw on it, although he did not always fully acknowledge this fact.

Jones's biography has long been the object of heated debates. The dominant emerging view seems to be that it is a hagiography of Freud and idealises him, while simultaneously painting a spiteful picture of many of his followers and the movement's dissidents. Practically all the latter are diagnosed as mentally insane.[42] This may be so but, when asked to name the best Freud biography to date, many of Jones's critics still mention his work. The fact remains that it is still a mine of information, the starting point and first source of reference for Freud's life, and it is unusually well written to boot. Literary skill and mastery of an immense amount of material by the ageing and ailing Jones, invaluably supported by his wife, command respect (cf. Maddox, 2006).

There followed literally thousands of books that were either full-scale biographies or dealt with particular periods or aspects of Freud's life. Again, it is simply impossible to list even all of the full-scale biographies, not only for reasons of space, but also because I am sure that some of them must have escaped my notice (if only perhaps

---

[40] Freud wrote to George Sylvester Viereck about that visit: "We really did not get along well. I accused him of taking the easy way out by applying amateurish psychology to his heroes or victims" (7 February 1928; LC).

[41] Still in 1996, Emilio Rodrigué dismissed Puner and her work: "Do not consult her book" (1996, p. 567).

[42] [Addition] See Erich Fromm's assessment of the picture Jones gives of the Committee, quoted on pp. 81–82.

because they appeared in languages I do not read). Let me mention only the books by Erich Fromm (1959), Marthe Robert (1964), Octave Mannoni (1968), Henri Ellenberger (1970), Irving Stone (1971), Max Schur (1972), Ernst Freud, Lucie Freud, and Ilse Gubrich-Simitis (1976), Ronald Clark (1980), Peter Gay (1987), Richard Webster (1995), Emilio Rodrigué (1996), Paul Ferris (1997), or Louis Breger (2000).

One of the first useful overviews of the literature is "Freud as reflected by his biographers" by Martin Grotjahn and Jürgen vom Scheidt (1976). Gay's "Bibliographical Essay" in his Freud biography (1987, pp. 741–779), although rather questionably replacing and in lieu of a standard bibliography, is another helpful overview. Already in 1987, Gay could note that the "secondary literature on Freud is vast, rapidly growing, almost out of control", and readily admitted that he had "not tried for completeness" (ibid., p. 741)—because, I would argue, the situation was indeed already out of control. The essay does list most of the important contributions, although it tells us more about Gay's judgement of them and their authors than about their contents. Elisabeth Young-Bruehl contributed a "History of Freud Biographies" (1994). Elke Mühlleitner has summarised the history of Freud biographies in her entry on "Psychoanalysis, History of" in the *International Encyclopedia of the Social and Behavioral Sciences* (2001). Another attempt was made by Louis Breger in his chapter on "Background and Sources", appended to his Freud biography (2000, pp. 375–386). It is much less inclusive than Gay's, and severely limited by a fact which the author openly confesses: "I do not read German"—and no other language than English, as one is forced to conclude, since no works in any other language are quoted in his book.[43] Christfried Tögel has established a valuable select bibliography on biographical works on Freud (in *Sigmund Freud*, 2001).

Further documentation

In addition, there are literally thousands of articles and brief communications on "Freudiana" that present snippets of primary

---

[43] Breger is by no means an exception. It is a peculiar characteristic of Freud studies that a great number of "Freud scholars" are not able to read his works in the original, let alone his handwritten letters. What would one think about Shakespeare scholars not being able to read English, or about Proust scholars without a perfect command of French?

material. To name but two interesting recent examples: the already mentioned list of analytic treatments of the years 1910 to 1920, and a documentation on the stay of Freud's father and his family in Leipzig (Tögel & Schröter, 2004b). Since 1989, Christfried Tögel has worked on a "Freud diarium" (http://www.freud-biographik.de/frdbio.htm), a documentation that tries to list all datable events in Freud's life. Tögel is also on record for minutely reconstructing Freud's travels, sometimes down to the minute when his boat or train left the harbour or station. A wealth of information on Freud has been amassed by scholars such as Gerhard Fichtner (†), Professor Emeritus at the University of Tübingen, and his collaborators at the Institute for the History of Medicine, notably his successor Albrecht Hirschmüller, and by independent Freud scholars such as Peter J. Swales and Anthony Stadlen. Alas, Fichtner's holdings are not accessible to the public, Swales has published only a fraction of his materials, while many of his writings are privately circulated, and Stadlen has published even less.

During a nine-month-long stay at the Library of Congress in Washington DC, in 1997/98, I myself transcribed into the computer what was then accessible in their Freud Archives, the by far greatest collection of Freud materials in the world. There are now plans to put those archives online, that is, to offer high resolution images as well as a transcription of every page on the Internet. Other archival deposits are at the Freud Museums in London (a list is available on their website at www.freud.org.uk) and Vienna, in the archives of the British Psychoanalytical Society, in various archives of other psychoanalytic societies, or the former holdings of Sigmund Freud Copyrights (now at the University of Essex), to name only the most important ones.

Works on related topics and literature on Freud

Let me mention, just for the sake of completeness, that there are literally thousands of works on "Freud and ..."—Freud and Judaism, Freud and religion, Freud and women, Freud and politics, Freud and *fin-de-siècle* Vienna, Freud and his followers, Freud and writing, Freud and his patients, Freud and his family, Freud and his influence, Freud and his reception in various countries, Freud and various aspects of his theory, Freud and psychology, philosophy, medicine, psychiatry, music, Freud and travelling, Freud and his eating habits ...—the list is endless.

"The number of words devoted to Freud's habit of smoking cigars, for example passes credibility" (Burnham, 2006, p. 216).

Conclusion

First, all the *works* Freud published during his lifetime are accessible one way or another, even if his pre-psychoanalytic writings are not yet presented in one collection. Second, in little more than a decade, many more Freud documents (such as letters) have appeared than in the fifty years before. The most important primary materials are now, or will shortly be, in print. This is also due to the fact that the copyright for Freud expired in 2010, so that there was a financial interest to sell as many rights as possible before that date. Third, a wealth of other documents and eye-witness accounts has been published. Fourth, after decades of attempts to lock up and render inaccessible unpublished archival materials, such as letters or interviews, the restrictions have now been considerably loosened. And finally, there is an incredible quantity of secondary literature.

Already in 1971, Paul Roazen, in quoting Henry Murray, stated that the available documentation on Freud surpassed in specificity and depth of insight the extant material on any other human being in history (Roazen, 1971, p. 10).[44] This is even more to the point today. I think there might be agreement that Freud scholars, at last, would now be in a privileged position indeed to go about their work, as compared with researchers of other historical figures. The topic of Sigmund Freud should by now be any historian's paradise.

In reality, however, much, if not most, of the literature on Freud has been written with an agenda, with the intention either to condemn or to idealise him. In this process, historians have tended to underline, exaggerate, construe, or outright invent facts that suited their view, and conveniently to omit others that might have challenged their position.

Let me give you one example: Before the publication of the Freud/Jung letters, Anna Freud had prepared a list of proposed cuts (cf. Shamdasani, 1997). Many of her propositions referred to the most frequently mentioned patient in that correspondence (Frau Hirschfeld;

---

[44] This may be an exaggeration, however. Let us only think of the thousands of works on figures such as Goethe or Thomas Mann.

see Chapter Two). In particular, Anna Freud was concerned about remarks that might "easily be misunderstood". For instance, Freud wrote to Jung about that patient that he found her "analytically of no use for anybody", but that he would nevertheless continue to have her in analysis because it would be "her duty to sacrifice herself to science" (F/Jun, p. 474). Anna Freud reasoned that this "is, of course, not meant in this way, but will be understood like this" (in Shamdasani, 1997, p. 361). Against her wishes, however, the correspondence was published virtually complete and, sure enough, her prediction came true: Frederick Crews used this very quote to drive home his point that Freud "was indifferent to his patients' suffering" and that he did not "care very much, except from a public relations angle, whether those patients improved as a result of his treatment" (1995, p. 39). What he did not write is what Freud had to say about the same patient on other occasions: that she was a "particularly fine, good and serious woman", that she was "more than sympathetic, rather of high principles and refined", that her case was indeed "more interesting and her person more valuable than others" (all in F/Pfi), and so on.

In the present controversies, each of the parties or camps seems to have construed a 'Freud' of its own. Thus, for some he is the hero of a legend, for others, the villain of the piece. He can be the relentless, heroic searcher for truth, or the inveterate liar and falsifier of case histories. We have heard nearly anything about Freud: that he was the greatest psychologist ever, or the criminal who attempted to murder his best friend; that he was a superhuman being who had achieved what no other living creature before him had achieved—to descend into his own deepest depths, wrestle with the angel of darkness, and thereby heal himself, transforming himself into a different man—or a drug addict whose 'theory' is nothing but wild speculations made 'Under The Influence'. Was he an ascetic bourgeois, or someone obsessed, at one time, with "masturbation" (Crews, 1995, p. 124), at another "with copulation from the rear" (ibid., p. 48), frequenting prostitutes, and sleeping with his sister-in-law? Was he a wise and successful therapist, or did he botch nearly all his cases? Was he a mildly mannered, tolerant, benevolent friend, or a bitter, acerbic person, whose friendships all ended in a break-up? Was he a model husband and father, or a family tyrant? Was he a revolutionary, paving the way for sexual liberation, anti-authoritarianism, pacifism, women's lib, or was he a counter-revolutionary, reactionary, phallocratic, undemocratic, and adamantly opposed to women's emancipation—indeed "the male chauvinist par excellence" (ibid., p. 206)?

Perhaps the most important of these controversies is fought over the question whether Freud was a trustworthy, reliable scientist, or someone who lied, cheated, and falsified or invented his case histories, who changed reality to suit his theory, someone, in short, who sacrificed truth for fame. Even those biographers who openly proclaim how unbiased they are, offer a rather curious middle position: "'Charlatan' is too strong for my taste; 'ruthless' and 'devious' seem acceptable" (Ferris, 1997, p. xi). Writing the history of psychoanalysis has become *instrumentalised*, has been used as a weapon in a very contemporary fight. The field has become a battleground, and we are faced with what has been called the "Freud Wars" (cf. Forrester, 1997). As a matter of fact, empirical and moral judgements have become completely confused.

Freud's critics have an agenda: to relegate psychoanalysis "to history's ashcan" (Crews, 1995, p. 223). As John Forrester observed, the harshest among them have a "heartfelt wish that Freud might never have been born or, failing to achieve that end, that all his works and influence be made as nothing" (1997, p. 1). But "why should a historian care whether or not Freud or C. G. Jung or someone else was 'right' or 'wrong'? ... The combination of overproduction and unseemly controversy in this way tended to trivialize an important subject: the impact of a major historical figure in Western and, to a surprising extent, world thinking" (Burnham, 2006, p. 217).

So, is there still an unknown Freud? Let me close with one of the answers to that question that I got from colleagues. Richard Skues wrote me, wittily (email of 19 September 2006):

> Surely the answer has to be "yes" and the reasoning is as follows. 1. The sum total of our knowledge is contained in all publications on and about Freud. 2. Most of these publications are rubbish. 3. The amount of rubbish is increasing exponentially year by year. 4. Therefore our non-knowledge of Freud is increasing accordingly. Ergo 5. The unknown Freud not only exists but is increasing exponentially. Corollary 6. Eventually we shall end up knowing nothing about Freud.

Let us hope that this judgement is too severe. There are signs that a historiographical shift is about to occur, for which John Burnham (2006) has coined the term "New Freud Studies"—an effort to put Freud much more fully into historical context, and thereby to find larger dimensions and configurations in Western thinking that are fresh and intriguing on many levels.

It is incontestable that Freud has had an enormous influence. Practically no field in Western culture has escaped this influence. In fact, he is still very much present in our everyday lives, whether we like it or not. Is it really important whether Freud was a nice guy or not? What percentage of his theses is still valid? For the intellectual historian this matters no longer. There is no need to either defend or attack Freud (or perhaps only when stupid people accuse him of stupid things, or, conversely, when one feels compelled to counter those who sanctify him). What matters is placing Freud in the historical context, in studying the truly amazing history of the ideas he helped to set in motion, and how this shaped and influenced our culture. I am not interested in participating in the heated controversies he can still provoke, but rather in the question why such a peculiar and untimely phenomenon can still happen. If nothing else, this is a tribute to his ongoing influence.

PART IV

FREUD, BLEULER, JUNG

CHAPTER EIGHT

The story of an ambivalent relationship: Sigmund Freud and Eugen Bleuler

A year or so before the first international meeting of psychoanalysts in 1908 in Salzburg/Austria, at a time when Freud and a handful of his early followers privately met every Wednesday and discussed a wide range of topics, from new books to smoking, from male friendship to female sexuality, when they shared personal confessions about the years before marriage or occasionally tried out psychoanalysis on the Master himself, two strangers appeared on the scene, marking a major shift that was about to move the centre of psychoanalysis for a number of years to come away from Freud and his all-male, all-Jewish, all-Viennese[1] group.

Mutual interest

Two Swiss came to visit Freud in March 1907, Ludwig Binswanger and Carl Gustav Jung. They had been preceded by a first emissary,

---

[1] Only few of these Viennese, however, came from Vienna. Many of them were born in the Eastern provinces of the Habsburg Empire, and were brought to the capital by their parents—like Freud himself. Practically all of those who lived long enough to see their lives threatened emigrated for a second (or third) time, if they were lucky.

a stammering young Russian, Max Eitingon, then also in Switzerland, but Binswanger and Jung were of a different calibre. They were two brilliant young Gentiles with all the right connections. Binswanger was the upstart member of a dynasty of important psychiatrists, professors, and sanitarium owners at Kreuzlingen on Lake Constance; his uncle Otto Binswanger headed the psychiatric clinic at Jena/Germany, and was a professor of psychiatry at the university there. Young Binswanger was at the time Jung's assistant.[2] Jung himself was already a well established figure in international psychiatry and academia— actually more so than Freud, nineteen years his senior. Jung was quite correct in stating that "Freud has only a few adherents in German speaking countries, and a handful in the United States, otherwise he is unknown or heavily attacked" (van Wayenburg, 1908, p. 275). When Jung defended Freud's views at the important Amsterdam Congress later that year (2–7 September 1907), the "duel Jung-Aschaffenburg" was eagerly awaited, because "the former is known as one of the most fiery adherents of Freud's teachings on hysteria, and the latter as their fierce opponent".[3] And it was no coincidence that the young and energetic Jung was considered a worthy opponent of the venerable representative of official German psychiatry. Jung was *Privatdocent* (roughly the equivalent of an associate professor) at Zurich University, and held the second highest position at the Burghölzli, the psychiatric university clinic in Zurich. The Burghölzli had openly, and much to the surprise of many German colleagues, endorsed some of Freud's views. It was headed by Eugen Bleuler, who also held the chair for psychiatry at the University.

Bleuler's support for Freud can hardly be overestimated. He was indeed the very first university professor to support Freud's views. When Jung returned from his visit in Vienna, Bleuler wrote to Freud that "colleague Jung came back full of enthusiasm & I, too, profit by what he has taken with him from you", and, even more gratifying: "the

---

[2] "[My father] made his dissertation on Jung's suggestion about the Galvanometer matrix experiment, so there he was doing his thesis under Jung who was very interested, of course, in having such a dissertation. But I don't know if there was any real contact. There must have been, otherwise, Jung wouldn't have taken his pupil, his young assistant with him to Vienna" (interview Ludwig Binswanger jun., CL).

[3] Congress report in *Monatsschrift für Psychiatrie* etc., p. 565.

symptomatology of this illness [schizophrenia] has become a panegyric for your ideas" (21 March 1907).[4]

What exactly had attracted Bleuler to Freud's thoughts in the first place is not entirely clear. Both were interested in neuropathology, in particular syndromes such as aphasia (Bleuler, 1892; Freud, 1891b), in hypnosis, and, possibly, also in parapsychology (interview Carl A. Meier, CL). Bleuler had authored a positive review of the *Studies on Hysteria* (Breuer & Freud, 1895), declaring the book to be "one of the most important recent publications in the field of normal and pathological psychology" that would offer "a new insight into the psychic mechanism" (Bleuler, 1896, p. 525; also in Kiell, 1988, p. 74). When *The Interpretation of Dreams* (Freud, 1900a) came out, Bleuler was greatly impressed, "realised its correctness after the first reading" (F/Bleu, p. 74), and invited Jung in 1901 to give a talk on Freud's dream theory in the Burghölzli. In 1904, he published another defence of Freud's views: "Freud ... has shown us part of a new world" (p. 718). "[A]n absolutely stunning recognition of my point of view ... by an official psychiatrist, Bleuler, in Zurich", Freud wrote to Fließ. "Just imagine, a full professor of psychiatry and my ††† studies of hysteria and the dream, which so far have been labeled disgusting!" (F/Fli, p. 461). For Freud, it must have been the wish-fulfilment of a dream.

MB: Freud had a great, great (more than nowadays) respect for a university. It meant a great deal to him that a professor of a university was interested in his work.

INT: I see, and your father would have been one of the few professors?

MB: Oh, he was the *only one* for many years.
      (Interview Manfred Bleuler, CL)

Bleuler "discovered ... that this man Sigmund Freud had something to say ... He was the first in Europe to consider Freud. Bleuler opened his clinic to Freud" (interview Ludwig Binswanger jun., CL). On 21 September 1904, their correspondence began.[5]

---

[4] If not mentioned otherwise, these and the following quotes are from letters held at the LC. [Addition] The extant Freud/Bleuler correspondence has been published in the meantime (F/Bleu), the quote on p. 103.

[5] Date given by Alexander & Selesnick (1965, p. 6). The quoted letter to Fliess and other material available to us also suggest a beginning of their correspondence not before 1904, and not in the early 1890s, as Bleuler's son maintained (CL). [Addition] There is one short

It seems safe to say that Bleuler's interest was mainly a scientific and practical one: a wish to understand his psychotic patients better, to find meaning in their hallucinations, delusions, and other symptoms. Following the prevailing view within the scientific community, Bleuler differentiated between the "physical illness and the symptoms" (Bleuler & Jung, 1908, p. 35), and held that the *cause* of schizophrenia was organic—and unknown—but that psychical "complexes ... determine the greatest part of *the symptomatology of the illness*" (ibid., p. 41). The point is that these symptoms, in Bleuler's view, could not be understood "without having recourse to Freud's discoveries" (Bleuler, 1906/07, p. 27). In the same article, Bleuler tried to show for the first time how "Freudian mechanisms", as he called them, were at work not only in neuroses, dreams, and parapraxes, but also in schizophrenia, even if he underlined that he was "not yet convinced of some details in Freud's theories" (p. 32).[6] Clearly, Bleuler was interested and ready to stomach some strong criticisms, but he was not an uncritical champion of the "Cause".

Freud did not have a particularly high opinion of Bleuler as a scientist, whom he repeatedly admonished for having "too much reverence for words" (*Minutes I*, p. 33), that is, for using terms that explained nothing.[7] His agenda was different and more passionate: to get recognition from established university circles, to get a foothold into the doors of German and Swiss academia and psychiatry that had proved to be firmly locked until then, to remove the "danger" from psychoanalysis "of becoming a Jewish national affair" (F/Abr, p. 39), and to claim and "conquer psychiatry" for psychoanalysis (F/Bleu, p. 100).

What follows is intended to be a contribution to the intense, if short-lived, flirtation between psychoanalysis and academia and psychiatry in Europe. It is also about the reasons for and consequences of the

---

communication from Bleuler before that date, in answer to a query of Freud regarding the admission of a patient to the Burghölzli (F/Bleu).

[6] It should be noted, however, that Bleuler had a somewhat simplified view of Freud's theory, defining those mechanisms as "the tendency to modify the view we take of the world according to our wishes and ambitions" (ibid., p. 22).

[7] To Abraham he wrote: "[Y]our superior's notion of the ego is a rather vague term from surface psychology that does nothing in particular for the understanding of the actual processes, that is to say, does nothing in particular *metapsychologically*. One easily believes, however, that one is saying something meaningful in using it" (F/Abr, p. 12).

fact that their engagement did not end in marriage. It will focus on the peculiar relationship between the two key figures in this affair, and on the interesting role that psychoanalysis proper played in it.

After 1910, in a very short time and in rapid succession, four key figures left or were made to leave the psychoanalytic movement: Alfred Adler, Wilhelm Stekel, Eugen Bleuler, and Carl Gustav Jung; in addition, quite a number of their friends and colleagues left with them. The cases of Adler and Jung are well known and have been described in detail (e.g., for Adler: Bottome, 1939; Falzeder & Handlbauer, 1992; Furtmüller, 1946; Handlbauer, 1984, 1992; Orgler, 1939; Rattner, 1972; Seelmann, 1977; Sperber 1926, 1970; Stepansky, 1983). We know relatively little about Stekel's case (e.g., Kuhn, 1998; Stekel, 1950; Wittels, 1924), but even less about Bleuler's, which has received only scant attention. In 1965, an informative article by Franz Alexander and Sheldon Selesnick was published, which was based on excerpts from the Freud/Bleuler correspondence. In the early 1990s, two short articles by de Ridder and Corveleyn (1992) as well as by Scherbaum (1992) followed. The interest has seemed to grow only recently, such that an anthology about Bleuler's life and work (Hell, Scharfetter, & Möller, 2001) contains a part concerning his relationship to psychoanalysis. Marinelli and Mayer have recently published Bleuler's letters to Freud (2002).

Bleuler's break with the psychoanalytic movement is important because it represents a crucial and until now largely underestimated turning point. Alexander and Selesnick go as far as to say (1965, pp. 1–2)

> that without the dissension which led to Bleuler's resignation, the future isolation of psychoanalysis from the universities and academic institutions never would have occurred, and psychoanalysis would have developed as an integral part of medicine to be taught in medical schools.

The Burghölzli was founded in 1870, in accordance with the plans of Wilhelm Griesinger (1817–1868) and Heinrich Hoffmann (1809–1894, author of the well known children's book, *Der Struwwelpeter* (Shock-headed Peter)). Following Bernhard Aloys von Gudden,[8]

---

[8] He allegedly drowned when he tried to rescue his patient, King Ludwig II of Bavaria.

Gustav Huguenin, Eduard Hitzig, and August Forel, Eugen Bleuler was its fifth director, from 1898 to 1927. He came from a rural background, had a distinctly 'down-to-earth' and 'hands-on' attitude, as well as a farmer's work ethic (Hell, Scharfetter, & Möller, 2001, p. 20). In fact, one of the reasons why he was chosen was that he could speak the local dialect with the patients, which his predecessors could not. As was the case with other great humanitarian psychiatrists of his time (e.g., the Binswangers in Kreuzlingen; cf. Herzog, 1995), the patients had access to him and his family. "[I]t was really a family affair" (interview Manfred Bleuler, CL). The same was expected of the staff, who lived on the grounds of the clinic and had to ask for permission to leave. One of his last students remembered Bleuler as one whom

> we really adored ... deeply. His lectures and the way in which he presented cases was absolutely unforgettable. Extremely good, first class. Probably the best teacher we had in medical school, tremendously conscientious and very sincere, and deeply interested in these problems.
> INT: ... and in patients?
> CAM: Yes, and in patients.
> (Interview Carl A. Meier, CL)

Contrary to popular belief it was Bleuler, not Jung, who introduced psychoanalysis at his clinic. He quickly recruited a staff open to dynamic psychiatry in general, and to this new discipline in particular. "It was me, after all, who called Jung's attention to [psychoanalysis]", as Bleuler himself later pointed out to Freud (F/Bleu, p. 189).

Bleuler had handpicked Jung to join the staff, and had offered him a position as an assistant physician even before the latter had finished his studies (15 July 1900, ETH). At the Burghölzli, Jung conducted his well known experiments on word associations, a brilliant combination of two cutting-edge approaches of the time, which he used for his *Habilitation* (the thesis necessary to apply for tenure). In his report, Bleuler particularly stressed, and endorsed, Jung's finding that the reaction time was influenced by strong affects which "need not be conscious", thus allowing for a "unique insight into unconscious psychical processes". Bleuler added that Jung's interpretations had proven valid "in a great number of cases" and that his method had given "insights into the genesis of hysterical and particularly of catatonic symptoms, insights one could not even have thought of before" (5 January 1905, ETH). This went beyond the usual support for a young collaborator—it is evidence that Bleuler had approved of the notion of unconscious affects and their role in symptom formation, and that he was prepared to defend it against his colleagues on the faculty.

The Burghölzli quickly attracted a great number of young physicians and psychiatrists as interns or members of staff. Bleuler succeeded in helping the new Zurich psychiatric school of thought, with its focus on a psychodynamic and psychoanalytic perspective, attain a "worldwide reputation" (Graf-Nold, 2001, p. 78). The only clinic and name rivaling Bleuler's and that of the Burghölzli was that of Kraepelin in Munich. Carl G. Jung and Adolf Meyer (of Swiss extraction, one of the most influential American psychiatrists in the twentieth century) made fun of Kraepelin from the "camp of dogmatic diagnosticians" (November 1907, JH). "[T]he schematism is now being dearly paid for. ... We shall live to see that Kraepelin, the onetime revolutionary, will become, together with his school, the *caput mortuum* of psychiatry. Pope he is already" (ibid.).

In short, the Burghölzli was *the* place to go for any young, ambitious, open-minded psychiatrist. What is more, Zurich became the main recruiting centre for the nascent psychoanalytic movement. As Frederick Peterson wrote to Abraham A. Brill: "Why don't you go to Zurich—to Bleuler and Jung? They are doing that Freud stuff over there. I think you would like it" (in Lewin & Ross, 1960, p. 27). "Frederick Peterson's advice to Brill in 1907, to leave Paris and study with Jung in Zurich", as Sanford Gifford has pointed out (1978, p. 330), "was a turning point in Brill's career and in the future history of analysis in New York". The Burghölzli went truly international, with staff members from all over Europe, Russia, and the United States. And, of course, there were the Swiss collaborators such as Ludwig Binswanger, Alfons Maeder, Emil Oberholzer, Franz Riklin, or Jakob Honegger.[9]

Franz Riklin wrote in 1912 (p. 1014): "About ten years ago, after a year-long incubation process, psychoanalysis shifted from Vienna to Switzerland and settled primarily in Zurich". When Karl Abraham

---

[9] *Verzeichnis der seit 1. Juli 1870 im Burghölzli tätig gewesenen Direktoren, Sekundar-, Assistenz- und Volontärärzte* (ETH).

came to the Burghölzli in December 1904, interest in psychoanalysis already existed. The following years saw a rapid increase in this interest. The following events definitely *preceded* this: (i) Jung's "Occult Phenomena" (*1902*),[10] in which your *Interpretation of Dreams* is quoted (p. 102). (ii) Jung's attempt at an analysis of the patient B. St., published in the appendix to the Psychology of Dementia Praecox.[11] (iii) Several of the studies on association had already been published. (iv) A case of hysteria (Spielrein) had been analysed by Jung (*definitely* 1904). I assume that stronger interest probably started in 1903 … (F/Abr, p. 216)

This interest soon gained momentum:

Three times a week there were staff meetings for the whole morning. The physicians were all there together, and the physicians presented their new cases which they had examined before; and then there were long discussions with [sic] the patients of my father and Jung and their assistants, and they discussed things; and the main topic of discussion was the application of Freud's theories to schizophrenia. (Interview Manfred Bleuler, CL)

From 1907 onward there existed a *Freud-Gesellschaft* (Freud Society), an open and informal forum for discussions. "No fewer than twenty doctors appeared at the second meeting of our 'Freud Society' here; some came quite a long distance from hospitals in the country. So there is therefore no lack of interest here", Abraham reported to Freud (F/Abr, p. 10). "We have now founded a Freud Society", Jung wrote to Meyer, "with about 22 members, meetings are every other week with two papers at every meeting. They are exclusively devoted to a discussion of Freudian questions" (JH). "The Freudian Round Table is grand. I wish we had the material for something like that here", Meyer replied (JH).

It must have been an especially lively time when Jung was the "Oberarzt" under Bleuler at the Burghölzli. At that time Bleuler was the first Ordinarius who took Freud seriously. Jung knew how

---

[10] His doctoral dissertation.

[11] Jung, 1907, §§ 198 sqq.

to assemble a lot of colleagues such as Maeder, Pfister, and others. They had the most lively and interesting discussions about Freud's theories. (Interview Kurt Binswanger, CL)

The curiosity also extended to everyday situations, including family members. Abraham's daughter Hilda recounted (1974, p. 31) that

> the doctors' wives would not only listen and share in the discussions, but also relate their own dreams. But gradually, as understanding of unconscious trends and impulses became more clear, the doctors forbade their wives to report their dreams.

The doctors' children did not escape, either. Manfred Bleuler's carefully worded description towards Anna Freud may give a hint of the wounds thus inflicted:

> The relationship between our fathers ... has influenced my development in more than one way, starting with the fact that my parents have somehow observed and treated myself differently under the impact of the new theory than they would have done otherwise— and I certainly noticed that. (Letter of 8 April 1950; LC)

Although we have no information on the Bleulers, we do know that many prominent analysts analysed their children, for example, Karl Abraham, Max Graf, C. G. Jung, Melanie Klein, Ernst Kris, and of course Freud himself (see Chapter Three). In my talks and correspondence with persons who served such roles, quite a few felt that they had been treated like *Versuchskaninchen* or "guinea-pigs". The late Peter Lambda, son of Kata and Lajos Lévy, and a renowned writer and sculptor, planned to write a book on this,[12] but unfortunately he could not realise that plan. Similar views were expressed by the late Peter Heller.

But not only children and wives were analysed. Very soon something else entered the picture, something that should play an increasingly important role in the development and spreading of psychoanalysis:

---

[12]Letters to the author, 21 May 1993, 4 July 1993.—[Addition] He called himself "Lambda" after the Greek letter λ, which his father had used to sign his articles. His Freud bust is now in the Freud Museum in London.

the personal analysis of the future therapist. It was Jung who had positively recommended the analysis of the analyst as a general requisite, a view only later taken over by Freud (1912e, p. 116).[13]

Not that Jung conducted training analyses in the modern sense (I found no evidence of Bleuler ever making didactic analyses)—analyses of colleagues in those days were a matter of days or, at most, weeks, as in the three days Leonhard Seif had with Jung (F/Jun, p. 308), or the 'analysis' between Jung and Sándor Ferenczi. In the spring of 1912, Alfred Winterstein of Vienna was sent to Zurich by Freud to have a look at the kind of practice there, and had a "short training analysis" with C. G. Jung (Reminiscences 1954; LC).

Jung's approach was different from Freud's. He proceeded from his association experiment, for which many colleagues offered themselves as test persons. After the experiment had given some general idea, a short "psychanalysis" (Jung's preferred term) followed, much as David Forsyth described psychoanalysis still in 1913. As Jung wrote to Adolph Meyer on 10 July 1907 (JH):

> I am interested to hear that you too have made association experiments. I think you will have encountered greater difficulties, because the path to the final results is a thorny one. The experiment does not give but general guidelines for the psychanalysis, something like the Fraunhofer lines[14] ... The meaning of some lines is empirically more or less known to us, others (and this is the greater part) are unknown to us. This is where analysis must set in, and, so far, the analysis still depends mostly on the individual routine and the compliance of the test person. I have been working for quite a long time on finding empirical rules for the psychanalysis, which is no easy task. One can go astray with the psychanalysis, but the association experiment is an absolutely reliable signpost.

But Jung was not only a cautious scientist, he was also a bold experimenter. Contemporary critics of Ferenczi's experiments with mutual analysis in the early 1930s (see his *Diary*) could note that we find such

---

[13] Among the first to advocate training analysis was also James J. Putnam, calling it "very important, indeed almost essential" (1913, p. 201).

[14] Named after Joseph von Fraunhofer (1787–1826), German optician and physicist.

experimentation already much earlier, in 1908, between Jung and Otto Gross (F/Jun, p. 153), or between Jung and Jakob Honegger (ibid., p. 289). One wonders whether Trigant Burrow's later practice of such mutual analysis with Clarence Shields in 1918 (Burrow, 1958, pp. 44–45) has some roots in those early days, when he worked at the Burghölzli.[15] When Freud came to a critical point in the one public self-analysis of his we know of, he stopped it (Recollections of Max Graf, Balint Archives).

There exists a revealing and important correspondence between Bleuler and Freud, consisting of about forty letters by Freud and fifty by Bleuler.[16] The Bleuler side is accessible in the Library of Congress. Freud's letters to Bleuler are still inaccessible. In the Library of Congress there is a note by Kurt Eissler, former director of the Sigmund Freud Archives:

> Bleuler's son has refused up to now to give the S[igmund] F[reud] A[rchives] copies of Freud's letters to his father ... It is of interest that [Manfred] Bleuler, when I interviewed him, told me that he hesitates to give copies to the Archives since he fears for Freud's reputation in light of what Freud wrote to his father about Jung. This looks like a nice piece of hypocrisy. (Undated cover remarks to a draft translation of Freud's letter to Bleuler of 17 November 1912)

Manfred Bleuler told Gene F. Nameche: "In the letters Freud complains to my father very, very much about Jung. Very much and with very sharp expressions" (CL). In 1950, Bleuler wrote to Anna Freud, obviously in answer to a request by her, that he would "energetically" deal with the matter of Freud's letters to his father (8 April 1950; LC), but

---

[15] At around the time when Ferenczi experimented with mutual analysis, there was an analogous experiment going on in Zurich, in a *ménage à trois*, involving Jung's heir apparent, his wife, and his mistress and former patient: "[Carl A. Meier:] At times I consulted her [Toni Wolff], and she consulted me; it was a mutual sort of thing. As a matter of fact, we had a group. We did group analysis for about a year: Mrs. Jung, Toni, and myself. [Nameche:] You did? The three of you. How incestuous! [Meier:] It was very funny" (CL).

[16] [Addition] The following was written long before the publication of the Freud/Bleuler correspondence (F/Bleu) in December 2012, before the rediscovery of Freud's letters (the actual numbers of the *surviving* letters are: fifty-six by Bleuler, and only twenty-three by Freud; it seems that whole years of Bleuler's overall correspondence were destroyed or thrown away by his heirs). See Schröter's introduction to F/Bleu.

regardless of how or if he did so at all, he neither gave them back to the Freud family nor made them accessible.

Three main topics run through Bleuler's letters: (1) his reservations against a psychoanalytic "movement"; (2) his reluctance to view psychoanalysis as an entity that has to be taken or left as a whole; he rather insisted on a more scientific and rigorous testing of its component parts. Bleuler wanted to treat psychoanalysis as just one, although very valuable, theory among others, and subject its theoretical constructs as well as its organisational structure to the procedures usual for the scientific community at the time. I feel that Bleuler's and Freud's discussion about these topics is still of great interest, in times when the scientific status of psychoanalysis is under intense scrutiny, and when the politics of psychoanalysis are subject to a critical historical re-evaluation. As to the third subject, we will return to it in a moment.

Already Bleuler's letter to Freud of 9 June 1905, a reaction to the *Three Essays* (1905d) and the book on jokes (1905c), is, in general, in line with Bleuler's attitude: He would have liked the theory of sexuality to be "more detailed" and he

> missed the evidence ... The remark that the later analysis of "neuroses" would give this or that result does not quite suffice to show on what the view is based and, what seems to be just as important, *how it is meant*. Given the complete lack of precise psychological terms in our language, the latter can only be shown by way of examples.

He gave Freud the benefit of the doubt, however: "Up to now you have proved to be right in every respect, and so I assume that you are right here too—but I don't see it yet completely" (F/Bleu, p. 73).

Freud's reaction to this reasonable criticism was equally characteristic, as we can deduce from Bleuler's subsequent assertions: "I am not aware of a fight, as you call it, against the theory. Nor can I find a reason for such a fight in myself. ... Therefore I don't yet know in which respect my resistance against your booklet on sexuality ... would be an emotional resistance" (F/Bleu, p. 77). And again, after having carefully reread Freud's book: "I still believe that my resistance against some deductions is not an emotional one. ... What I miss is the material from which you draw your conclusions" (p. 80). Bleuler simply could not find his resistance: "Where can the resistance lie in me, if it is a resistance" (p. 89)?

Freud was hardly impressed; his conviction of Bleuler's "resistance" persisted. In 1910, Freud still maintained: "I know that you have internal resistance which makes it sometimes difficult for you to analyze your own dreams" (p. 114; and Alexander & Selesnick, 1965, p. 3). Ernest Jones chimed in: "I don't understand how he can fail to grasp what you so clearly discussed in the *Traumdeutung*" (F/Jon, p. 87). And again Freud, in 1912: "I know, however, that the resistances against psychoanalysis are of an emotional nature" (F/Bleu, p. 161). And Freud "predicts in this letter that under these conditions 'friendly personal relations' will not survive between him and Bleuler" (Alexander & Selesnick, 1965, p. 8).[17] Such predictions of Freud's usually came true.

On the one hand, Freud treated Bleuler like a patient, pointing out that the latter's failing to understand or accept his, Freud's, constructions was due to an emotional resistance on the other's part, not to missing explanations on his. On the other hand, Bleuler *offered* himself as a patient. He admitted that he succeeded "only in very rare cases to interpret a dream *of my own* correctly", and even asked Freud "to show [him] the way", by sending him "three or four dreams" for interpretation (F/Bleu, p. 75).[18]

While seducing Freud to analyse his dreams, Bleuler did give Freud the opportunity to step back: "If you find this too exacting an imposition, I would understand you; in that case would you please be so kind as to send back my papers without explanation" (ibid.). "*In any case I ask you to tell me straight away if an instruction by correspondence seems too tiresome or impossible for you*" (p. 79). "Should I pester you with my questions, please tell me so; nobody knows better than I do that in life one has to watch one's time" (p. 96). Freud took the bait, however.

So this is the third crucial aspect that comes into the picture: an analytic relationship, an analysis by correspondence. It was clear from the outset that its outcome would have considerable consequences for Bleuler's views on psychoanalysis, and that his support would depend on its success.[19]

---

[17][Addition] In fact, Freud wrote in a more conciliatory way: "Even if one might honestly believe to be able to maintain the personal relations fully intact, they will still get somewhat rusty if one does not vigorously polish the area of fracture" (F/Bleu, p. 161).

[18]Unfortunately, the dreams are lost.

[19][Addition] For other cases, in which Freud tried to convince someone of his theories by analysing him (sometimes by correspondence), see Chapter Five.

With hindsight, we can see that the circumstances were hardly favourable in Bleuler's case. Test cases with a strong personal involvement are not particularly likely to turn out well. Bleuler's offer had some hidden strings attached. It was in fact simultaneously a veiled threat: "If you don't succeed in my own case, you can't expect me to believe in your theory and method." The year was 1905, and hardly anyone had an idea about the power of transference, particularly negative transference, let alone countertransference.

Unfortunately, there are only a few traces of this 'analysis'; more precisely, we have none of the dreams themselves, only two long series of free associations to dreams, from 14 October 1905 and 5 November 1905 respectively. In addition, Bleuler gave rather detailed background information on his childhood, friendships, sexual development, relationship to his wife and children, etc., and also questioned Freud about some of his bodily symptoms, for instance diarrhoea, and their possible connection with sexuality (F/Bleu, p. 91). I will not discuss the contents of these associations—a 'wild' analysis of associations to missing dreams does not seem particularly fruitful.

My point is rather that the fact of an analysis—and of its failure—was of paramount importance for the relationship between Freud and Bleuler and for Bleuler's scientific assessment of psychoanalysis. Notwithstanding his call for a thorough testing and evaluation of psychoanalysis, Bleuler saw in it "neither a science nor a craft; it cannot be taught in the ordinary way. It is an art" (p. 91). Confessing his own "clumsiness" (p. 75) in these matters, Bleuler, hardly a year younger than Freud, considered Freud to be the "Master" (ibid.) and himself the "pupil" (Schüler) (pp. 79, 103). He turned to Freud to tell him if his way of self-analysis was hopeless or if he erred elsewhere, asking him to initiate him into Freud's views "also in practice" (p. 79).

The counterpart to this deferential and nearly submissive tone is also there: an obstinate refusal to make any concessions in theory without convincing proof. The best proof would have been that the method worked with himself which, alas, it did not.

> Perhaps dreams that have been interpreted are dreams of persons of a certain character, to whom the thing can be applied. One fails with others, me included. Isn't it stupid that I, with my little experience, have doubts. But then it is also stupid that I can only very rarely interpret a dream of my own. (F/Bleu, p. 89)

In this context, it is interesting to recall William James's statement, who obviously had also tried out Freud's recommendation that anyone could analyse his or her dreams, and thus also confirm Freud's theory from personal experience: "I can make nothing *in my own case* with his dream theories" (in LeClair, 1966, p. 224; my ital.). Freud largely fostered this kind of negative reaction himself (that he soon came to regard as an offspring of resistance) by making exaggerated claims as to the simplicity and self-evidence of his healing-cum-research method.

But if Bleuler's experience with psychoanalysis was scant, so was everybody else's. It speaks for the power of Freud's belief in the correctness of his views and in the efficiency of his method, as well as for Bleuler's personal and intellectual honesty and his courage to disclose himself so completely before the other, that they were willing to take the risk of testing psychoanalysis *in vivo* on themselves. But was there any other way? Even if Freud still thought of psychoanalysis as a quasi-chemical, laboratory-like psychical analysis, implying that any sufficiently instructed person could perform it on any other person, regardless of their relationship, or, for that matter, on himself or herself; even if he was of the opinion, still in 1914, that a self-analysis with the help of dreams would be possible and would "suffice for anyone who is a good dreamer and not too abnormal" (1914d, p. 20); even if he was of the opinion that each analyst should be able to conduct such a self-analysis (1910d, p. 145)—he had never laid down just how exactly this could be done, and his book on dreams contained not one single full analysis of a dream. As a matter of fact, no one really knew what psychoanalysis was all about. "There will always be the difficulty of convincing other people of the correctness of your ideas. As it is, others don't have your eye and so are not able to make a judgement of their own" (F/Bleu, p. 91). Bleuler also spoke for himself. Eventually, he would make his own judgement.

The conflict between the Burghölzli staff and Freud came to the fore at the first international meeting of psychoanalysts, in April 1908 in Salzburg/Austria, although it was not Bleuler and Freud who crossed swords, but C. G. Jung and Karl Abraham (see Chapter Thirteen). But although there were first clouds on the horizon, the Salzburg meeting brought about a closer collaboration between Zurich and Vienna. At Salzburg, the first psychoanalytic periodical, the *Jahrbuch für psychoanalytische und psychopathologische Forschungen*, was founded; it was under the joint directorship of Bleuler and Freud, and Jung became its acting editor. "I am very glad to know", Freud also assured Abraham, "that all of you in Zurich are taking this heavy labour out of my hands. Your youth and fresh vigour, and the fact that you can spare yourselves the wrong turnings that I took, all promise the best" (F/Abr, p. 4).

In short, in Zurich "one basically had everything that one could wish for for the next ten years to come" (as also quoted on p. 194). But then, in November 1911, Bleuler left the IPA for good. Thus Abraham's fear came true that "[i]t would ... be very unfortunate if the enemies were able to say that the only clinic supporting us had now left us again" (F/Abr, p. 56).

Already shortly after the Salzburg meeting, Freud wrote to Abraham: "Bleuler I surrender to you; in Salzburg I got an uncanny feeling from him, the situation cannot have been to his liking" (p. 54). And: "It will come to nothing with Bl[euler], his breaking away is imminent, the relations between Bl and J[ung] are strained to breaking-point" (p. 60).

But it was especially after the foundation of the IPA at the Nuremberg Congress in 1910—at which Jung was elected its first president—that the conflict between Freud and Bleuler fully emerged. Having learned that Bleuler intended to leave the newly founded organisation, of which his collaborator Jung had just become president, Freud tried to persuade Bleuler not to do so (F/Bleu, pp. 112–115). Bleuler countered (pp. 122–123):

> I understand perfectly well that the Association was founded ...
> Mais c'est le ton qui fait la musique. The statutes exude an exclusiv-
> ity that does not correspond with my character. ... People want to
> remain among themselves ... But if one wants to have a scientific
> discussion, and if one wants to present oneself to the public as a sci-
> entific society, one must not make dissent impossible beforehand;
> on the contrary, one should welcome it. This is an example of a dif-
> ferent affective opinion.

Freud was hardly impressed by these "remarkably dim" arguments, as he wrote to Ferenczi (F/Fer I, p. 227), or "shadowy and intangible" ones, as he put it to Abraham (F/Abr, p. 120). Nevertheless, Freud was prepared to go to Zurich and try to convince Bleuler to rejoin the IPA (or rather, its Zurich branch society). Owing to the strained relation-ship between Bleuler and Jung, however, he finally avoided coming to Zurich and instead met Bleuler separately in Munich. After that meeting, it seemed for some time that Bleuler had allowed himself to be convinced (ibid., p. 125).

But the conflict between them persisted. "I sometimes write to Bleuler, only he is frozen stiff again" (F/Fer I, p. 265). And, finally, in November 1911, Bleuler left the IPA for good, because Jung had not allowed one of Bleuler's medical assistants to participate in the society's meetings without being a member.

> Both from an intellectual and an affective point of view, an intoler-
> ance that disagreeably resents the presence of an honest man, only
> because he is of a different opinion in a few details that have noth-
> ing to do with science, is in my opinion mistaken. I dare hope that
> after what has happened you will accept my resignation as some-
> thing natural and necessary, and above all that this resignation will
> in no way change our personal relationship. (F/Bleu, p. 150)

Freud was furious: "Bleuler is intolerable. He wrote to me that he has again resigned from the Association. I cursed him for that, and now I am awaiting further reports from the theater of war" (F/Fer I, pp. 316–317).

Bleuler stood firm, for instance in his letter to Freud from 4 December 1911 (F/Bleu, p. 151):

> In my opinion, saying "he who is not with us is against us" or "all
> or nothing" is necessary for religious communities and useful for
> political parties. Thus, I can indeed understand the principle, all
> the same I find that it is harmful for science. *Because there is no objec-
> tive truth* ... Psychoanalysis, as a science, will make its way with or
> without myself, because it contains a great number of truths, and
> because it is led by people like you and Jung. ... [Jung] finds [the
> policy of] closed doors justified, and I find it wrong; moreover, for
> him this is a question of life or death for psychanalysis; so it was his
> duty to force me out. Therefore, I can't be cross with him, but his
> hostile attitude towards me is all the more painful. As a matter of
> fact, nothing can be done about it, I think. One can beg for money,
> but not for sympathy. But if this were ever going to change again,
> I would heartily welcome it.

Bleuler underlined that there was no objective truth, while Freud, the "conquistador", affirmed his conviction that there was one indeed, and, moreover, that he, Freud, was in possession of it. As Marina Leitner

(1998) has shown in detail: If it was true that Freud had discovered the Truth, as he and his followers were convinced he had,[20] and if it was true that Freud "emerged" from his self-analysis "serene and benign ..., free to pursue his work in imperturbable composure" (Jones I, p. 320), free from neurosis and any trace of personal dependence (Jones III, p. 44), any opposing or differing views could only be neurotic, "just resistance" (F/Abr, p. 11).

Again Bleuler, on 1 January 1912 (F/Bleu, pp. 153–154):

> I do not think at all that getting together in an association was something harmful for psychanalysis. On the contrary. The association was very welcome, perhaps even a necessity. If it were a scientific association in the same sense as other ones, nobody could have objected, and it would simply have been useful. But it is the *type* of association that is harmful. Instead of trying to have as many points of contact as possible with the other sciences and scientists, it has shielded itself against outside influences with the help of a thick skin, and it hurts friends and enemies alike ... [In Zurich] one basically had everything that one could wish for for the next ten years to come. This has been destroyed by that type of association and it can no longer be re-established, it has partly even turned into its opposite. Hoche's malicious dictum that psychanalysis is a sect—which at the time was incorrect—has been made true by the psychanalysts themselves. And these are facts, not opinions.

Freud commented dryly on the following day, in an unpublished letter to Pfister: "Bl.[euler] still corresponds with me about his resignation. This is quite nice on his part, but it does not enlighten me at all" (F/Pfi).

Bleuler gave an interesting characterisation of Freud's ideas and theories: "Your concepts can only be described in a genetic way, and they are still in the process of development. Therefore, only those who have the whole history in mind—put down in writing only to a minimal extent—can grasp them" (F/Bleu, p. 190). And, on 5 November 1913 (ibid., p. 203):

---

[20] For instance: "We are in possession of the truth; I am as sure of that as I was fifteen years ago" (F/Fer I, p. 483).

From a scientific point of view, I still do not understand why you insist on the fact that psychanalysis should be accepted as a whole, a complete edifice. I remember having said to you once that you make the impression on me of being an artist, despite your great scientific achievements. From *such* a point of view, one can well understand that you do not wish to have your work of art destroyed. A work of art has a unity that cannot be dissolved into components.

Bleuler distanced himself from the "movement" (F/Bleu, pp. 199, 201):

I already fear that more harm for psychanalysis is coming from its disciples than from its enemies. We have just readmitted a schizophrenic patient for whom a whole fortune had been spent on psychanalysis. I refuse to take responsibility for such things, and it costs me a great deal of effort to allow my name still to be printed on the cover of the *Jahrbuch*. I also do not understand why it is necessary, in Zurich, for a psychanalyst to wear a yellow raincoat etc. … You say that at the moment you are no longer alone. If this is true, I am pleased for you. But, in reality, I fear that your friends cannot reach your heights, and that they could harm you more than your enemies.

Coming back to Jung, we can see how the relationship between Bleuler and Freud was the background against which his own personality and theory further developed during that time. He started out first as Bleuler's collaborator and 'right hand man', then as Freud's disciple, crown prince, and heir apparent. Bleuler and Freud were the last in a line of father figures, from which Jung eventually distanced himself. Bleuler, and above all Freud, were worthy opponents, and we can get a glimpse of the effort it cost Jung to go his own way, when he knew that this would cost him the respect and friendship of Freud.

In this chapter of history, we have met two strong, even stubborn personalities, standing for two possible views of science: on the one hand, the "conquistador" Freud, with only a nominal affiliation with academia and none at all with official psychiatry, leaning towards generalisations and a somewhat fundamentalist policy, leading a movement he himself had created; on the other hand the German Swiss Bleuler, head of a renowned psychiatric clinic, a professor at the university, and a leading figure within psychiatry, creator of the term "ambivalence", cautious, perhaps ambiguous, but seeing very clearly the dangers inherent in quasi-religious organisations. It is hardly surprising that these two tendencies could not collaborate or be reunited. One could well discuss the advantages and disadvantages of their final split.

One could also ask oneself who was right, Bleuler or Freud. For my part, I find myself in the position of the Rabbi in the well known joke: A couple comes to the Rabbi, each of them complaining about the other. The wife presents her point of view. The Rabbi listens attentively and concludes: "You are right." Then, the husband tells his version, quite contrary to that of his wife. Again, the Rabbi listens attentively, concluding: "You are also right." The Rabbi's student, having followed the conversation, is bewildered, and tries to explain to the Rabbi that two mutually exclusive versions cannot possibly both be right. The Rabbi listens carefully, thinks for a long time, and finally says: "You know, you are right, too."

CHAPTER NINE

A perfectly staged "concerted action" against psychoanalysis: the 1913 congress of German psychiatrists

(with John Burnham)

Did Freud's views gain a fair hearing in the scientific community of his time? Freud himself certainly did not believe so. According to him, his early communications were met with "silence". His "writings were not reviewed ... or ... were dismissed with expressions of scornful or pitying superiority" (1914d, pp. 21–23). "Word was given out to abandon me, for a void is forming around me" (F/Fli, p. 185).[1] In a letter of 1904, Freud cited the "expressions of malicious superiority" on the part of "his Viennese colleagues" as the reason that he did not publish any substantial works at that time (Gundlach, 1977, p. 912; also LC). There is also that famous instance at the Nuremberg Congress in 1910, where, according to an eyewitness, he said that he was "perpetually attacked", and, seizing his coat by the lapels, cried out: "They won't even leave me a coat to my back" (Wittels, 1924, p. 140).[2]

---

[1] In the first, abbreviated edition the first part of this sentence was cut (Freud, 1950a, p. 162). This phrasing is discussed in detail by Esterson (2002).

[2] There are various accounts of this incident. All concur that Freud was extremely agitated and warned against the efforts of his (and psychoanalysis') "enemies" (Jones II, p. 69).

There is no doubt that he identified a group of "enemies of analysis" (1914d, p. 49).

Freud's self-portrayal as a lone fighter for truth, who met with the fiercest resistance, was taken over, or even further embellished, by many of his followers and biographers (most notably Jones I–III). More recent studies challenged that image. Sulloway tried to refute the "complex myth that both Freud and his followers have sought to prop-agate—a mythology that pictures Freud as the lonely 'psychoanalytic hero' who, all by himself and against a universally hostile outside world, 'invented' a totally original psychology" (1979, dustjacket). Decker (1977), following up on work by Bry and Rifkin (1962), found that, at least until 1907, Freud's publications and ideas gained a respect-ful hearing in major publications. According to Decker, large numbers of people in the German-speaking world were aware that Freud had introduced some innovative ideas, and there was a broad spectrum of reactions. There were indeed strong criticisms, but they were made per-fectly openly. In sum, psychoanalysis had a fair hearing in Germany before the First World War and was often alluded to, even if unfavoura-bly, in, for example, textbooks: "Freud was by no means totally ignored or rejected" (Decker, 1977, p. 1).

Was the hostility against Freud himself and against psychoanaly-sis, then, never as fierce, unfair, and unrelenting as he claimed? Was there no *organised* opposition at all? Was there never "word given out"? And did thus Freud have a "paranoid streak" (Crews, 1995, p. 108), and imagine conspiracies? Esterson (2002, pp. 123–124) speculates, for instance, that Freud's sense that he was isolated by his colleagues was "the reflection of a mild tendency toward paranoia", possibly growing out of his use of cocaine.

In this paper, we shall have a closer look at one seminal event, a session at the annual meeting of German psychiatrists, specifically dedicated to a discussion of psychoanalysis. This event seems spe-cially suited to serve as an example. This was the official congress of the German Society of Psychiatry. It was the first occasion that such an august and influential body had chosen psychoanalysis as a topic. The two main speakers, Eugen Bleuler and Alfred Hoche, who were to present the pros and cons of psychoanalysis, were influential and representative figures of psychiatry in the German-speaking countries. There is ample documentation of the proceedings: the journal of the Society published a detailed congress report, and the two main papers appeared in extenso separately.

This picture changes, however, if, following Decker (1977), we distinguish between two levels on which the responses proceeded within the scientific psychiatric community in Central Europe. One was the level of formal, published science and scholarship. The second was the informal level: personal relationships and networks within which formal science and medicine operated.

The documentation on the latter is much scarcer, or at least very much less investigated and published, than that concerning psychoanalysis. Recent years have seen a veritable avalanche of publications of previously unpublished primary sources, as well as a loosening of archival restrictions (see Chapter Seven). By contrast, very little documentation has come to light on the networking in psychiatric circles with regard to psychoanalysis. It is by now relatively easy to document the unofficial efforts, often not admirable or pristine, of Freud and others to manoeuvre against significant people whom they believed opposed psychoanalysis, while we know very little about the other side. It may well be that this unbalanced state of research gives a lopsided picture. If we had a comparable wealth of documentation on both conflicting movements, it might be necessary to reconsider the question of how fair was the trial that Freud and psychoanalysis had in the marketplace of ideas.

Our present contribution presents precisely such a document, a letter that confirms the existence of a perfectly staged concerted action against Freud's influence in 1913. It is our contention that historians of psychoanalysis and psychiatry have not realised the significance of this document—perhaps Freud himself did not know about the extent to which German psychiatrists joined forces to counter some of the psychoanalytic thinking that was coming into the field of psychiatry.[3]

German psychiatry and psychoanalysis in 1913

Psychiatrists in Germany at the beginning of the twentieth century found themselves in the midst of conflicting trends, trends that were

---

[3] Some of the letter has been published incidentally in both English (Burnham, 1983, p. 74) and French (Borch-Jacobsen & Shamdasani, 2006, pp. 133–134), but little further account of it has appeared in any language. To the best of our knowledge, Borch-Jacobsen and Shamdasani were the first to give a well-documented account of the Breslau Congress, although their perspective is different from that set forth here.

reflected in the meetings of the *Deutsche Irrenärzte* (cf. Schindler, 1990). They were attempting to establish and maintain professional status and authority. They were attempting to resolve the institutional and intellectual conflict between hospital clinicians and university specialists. And they were attempting to resolve the conflict between a psychiatry based on reductionistic, materialistic pathological anatomy, on the one side, and a rigorous clinical science, on the other (Decker, 1977; Schindler, 1990; Engstrom, 2003; Roelcke, 2005).

Into these crosscurrents came another, introduced by a neurologist, Sigmund Freud. The psychiatrists, who already had troubles enough of their own, found that they could not ignore psychoanalysis. The clinical approach in psychiatry was famously represented by Emil Kraepelin (1856–1926), the best known psychiatrist in the world (and a key figure in our story). The clinical approach could segue into borderland areas claimed by psychoanalysis (Hoff, 1994; Roelcke, 1999; Engstrom, 2003) and was most directly threatened by Freud's ideas. The older pathological anatomy reductionists could be more direct in rejecting and attacking the Freudians. Indeed, the main speaker at the 1913 effort to keep psychoanalysis out of psychiatry, Hoche, was opposed even to Kraepelin's developmental approach to mental illnesses, an approach Kraepelin implicitly shared with Freud. Hoche and others wanted to define disease in terms of presenting signs and symptoms, not to follow the course of an illness in a patient. Moreover, swiftly moving medical developments reinforced the reductionists' viewpoint. The 1913 congress fell between two other congresses, 1912 and 1914, that were dominated by exciting discoveries regarding general paralysis (tertiary syphilis), which for many physicians furnished a decidedly non-psychological, neuropathological paradigm for all mental diseases (Schindler, 1990, pp. 110–115). It was under these circumstances that the German psychiatrists were concerned enough to try to derail the momentum that Freud's ideas had developed within their speciality.

Kraepelin, who was aware of and apparently complicit in the 1913 collusion, at times was drawn into using some of the ideas that Freud also used, such as the idea that thoughts can come from the unconscious (cf. Decker, 2004, pp. 260–263). But Kraepelin himself was so well established that he did not bother to make special attacks on psychoanalysis; his few allusions to Freud's ideas were usually scornful dismissals (ibid.). Kraepelin was a pragmatist little moved by theory, and he was caught up in his own agendas. In general he ignored those he opposed. He was "no diplomat" (Engstrom, 1990, pp. 53–54, 69–71) and, however complicit, not likely to have been an initiator of the move to sideline psychoanalysis. Rather he was the model of an authoritarian, self-assured doctor and professor: "One of my basic traits is strong egotism" (Engstrom, Burgmair, & Weber, 2002, p. 109).

Emil Kraepelin (in front at the left) leading a group of students and colleagues on a botanical walk in a garden in Munich in 1906. Among the group were at least three other colleagues who attended the 1913 Congress: Rehm (behind and next to Kraepelin), Alzheimer (standing figure on the right with a cane), and Gaupp (third from the right, partially hiding behind a tree). Informal networking amongst psychiatrists took place in settings such as this, and the photo is remarkable additionally because the "student" sitting fourth from the left on the bench, and leaning forward, is none other than Smith Ely Jelliffe, the recipient of the letter revealing the "concerted action" of 1913.
Source: Original negative with some documentation in possession of John C. Burnham. The list of names is incomplete and possibly inaccurate.

Before the Breslau congress

There had already been various attacks on psychoanalysis in both psychiatric and neurological circles. In May 1906, Gustav Aschaffenburg[4] spoke out against psychoanalysis at a congress in Baden-Baden, saying that Freud's ideas had now to be confronted publicly because of the attention now being given his work, not only by Loewenfeld and Hellpach, but by Bleuler and Jung in Zurich. Aschaffenburg concluded by calling Freud's method "wrong in most cases, objectionable in many, and—superfluous in all" (1906, p. 1798). Alfred Hoche supported him. In September 1907, at the First International Congress of Psychiatry and Neurology in Amsterdam, Aschaffenburg again attacked psychoanalysis. Freud had been invited to take part, but had refused. In his stead, his then "crown prince", C. G. Jung—Bleuler's junior colleague at the Burghölzli—defended Freud's views (cf. Jones II, pp. 112 sqq.) in the "duel" with Aschaffenburg (see the previous chapter). In 1910, at the meeting of the Hamburg Medical Society on 29 March, Hamburg physician Heinrich Georg Embden (1871–1941) warned against referring patients to institutions and sanatoria in which psychoanalysis was practiced. Wilhelm Weygandt (1870–1939) seconded him by proposing that, at each appropriate opportunity arising within scientific societies, the errors and dangers of the psychoanalytic system be revealed and pointed out (*Hamburger Ärzte-Correspondenz*, 1910; *Neurologisches Centralblatt*, 1910). In October 1910, specialists in *neurology*, led by Hermann Oppenheim,[5] again called for a boycott of clinics where psychoanalysis was practiced (F/Abr, pp. 116–118; F/Jun, pp. 364, 418).

Events in the field of *psychiatry*, however, took a turn somewhat different from that in neurology. In the period just before the 1913 meeting in Breslau, a number of psychiatrists intensified their efforts

---

[4] Aschaffenburg (1866–1944) was working with Kraepelin at Heidelberg during the 1890s. He was directly responsible for publishing on the association processes in mentally ill people, work that contributed to Jung's investigations of word associations (Aschaffenburg, 1896). Aschaffenburg left for the hospital at Halle in 1900, and from 1904 to 1934 he was professor of psychiatry at the University of Köln and head of the mental hospital. He ended up in the United States after 1939.

[5] Hermann Oppenheim (1858–1919), German neurologist, founder and head of a renowned private policlinic in Berlin (1891), 1893 professor. His *Lehrbuch der Nervenkrankheiten* (1894) is considered a classic. His wife Martha, née Oppenheimer, was a cousin of psychoanalyst Karl Abraham's mother.

Kraepelin and students (Munich, Summer 1906). Standing (left to right): Alzheimer, Luttge, Kraepelin, Vostein, Jelliffe, Perusini (?), Busch, Probst, Rehm (?). Siting (left to right): Hermann, Wittenerg, Gaupp (?), Cotton (?), Achucarro, Rohde, Cudden.
Source: Original negative with some documentation in possession of John C. Burnham. The list of names is incomplete and possibly inaccurate.

to denounce psychoanalysis. Hoche sent out a circular letter in which he asked colleagues to report cases to him that were harmed by psychoanalytic treatment, so that he could present them in Breslau. Freud knew about this upcoming discussion of psychoanalysis (F/Bleu, p. 182), but not yet about the circular letter. A copy of it reached Zurich, however, where it was read at the meeting of the "Psychoanalytical Society (Society for Analytical Psychology)" on 28 February 1913. The minutes[6] report that the meeting "decided

---

[6] Minutes of the Zurich Psychoanalytic Society, Archives of the Psychological Club, Zurich. With thanks to Sonu Shamdasani.

to suggest to Prof. Freud to publish the content of the letter in the *Zeitschrift*."

On 7 March 1913, Freud acknowledged receipt of Hoche's circular letter (F/Fer, p. 473), and indeed had it published in the *Zeitschrift*. The circular letter (Hoche, 1913a) read:

> Dear Colleague, I have, together with Bleuler, undertaken to give the presentation on the value of psychoanalysis at the annual meeting of the *Deutscher Verein für Psychiatrie* (in May, in Breslau). Among other things, it would be of great importance to me to come to a reliable judgement on the kind and amount of damages caused by psychoanalytic procedures. Should you be in possession of relevant factual material, I am asking you, therefore, for the kindness of communicating it to me ... To my regret, I see no other way of collecting precisely this important material.

Hoche and Bleuler

Alfred Erich Hoche (1865–1943) was professor of psychiatry at the university and director of the psychiatric clinic in Freiburg im Breisgau, Germany (cf. Müller-Seidel, 1997; Schimmelpenning, 1998). Interestingly, Hoche can be found among the guests of the hotel in which the first psychoanalytic congress in Salzburg was held in 1908 (Jones II, p. 40), although Jones does not say if Hoche—who had already publicly attacked psychoanalysis—attended the meeting itself. In November of the same year, "Jung and Hoche had a set-to at the Congress of South-West German Psychiatrists in Tübingen" (ibid., p. 111). At a psychiatric congress in May 1910, he railed against "A psychic epidemic among physicians", announcing that "psychoanalysis was an evil method born of mystical tendencies and full of dangers for the standing of the medical profession" (Hoche, 1910). He went on to assert that psychoanalysts would be eligible to be certified into a lunatic asylum (Jones II, p. 116).[7]

---

[7] In 1920 he published, together with Karl Binding, a book on the annihilation of "life unworthy of life", which was used by the Nazis as a 'scientific' justification for their extermination program (Binding & Hoche, 1920). Hoche claimed that there were forms of human lives that had lost all value of continuation, among whom he also counted chronic

Alfred Erich Hoche (1865–1943)
Source: *Die Medizin der Gegenwart in Selbstdarstellungen*, ed. L. R. Grote. Leipzig: Verlag von Felix Meiner, 1923. Opposite page 1.

Hoche was an active and articulate figure in German psychiatry, but he was not a major figure in the sense that Kraepelin was. In contrast, the other presenter at Breslau in 1913, Eugen Bleuler, definitely was a major figure (on Bleuler and his relationship with Freud see the previous chapter).

schizophrenics. He estimated the number of "idiots" in Germany and the annual costs caused by them, and called for the annihilation of those "ballast existences".

Eugen Bleuler (1857–1939)
Source: *Zeitschrift für die Gesamte Neurologie und Psychiatrie*, 82 (1923),
frontispiece.

At the meeting in Salzburg in 1908 mentioned above, Bleuler had
agreed to co-edit, together with Freud, the first psychoanalytic journal,
the *Jahrbuch für psychoanalytische und psychopathologische Forschungen*,
in which he published a strong defence of psychoanalysis (Bleuler,
1910). In this 110-page paper, Bleuler frequently criticised Hoche's
anti-psychoanalytic publications. Specifically, he wrote that "providing
evidence of the sectarian character of psychanalysts[8] does not provide

---

[8] Bleuler consistently used the terms "psychanalysis" and "psychanalyst(s)."

evidence against the correctness of their views. *And, secondly, most of our* [sic] *enemies could also be nicely portrayed, in the author's own words, as sectarians"* (p. 91). He compared the opponents of psychoanalysis to those of Kepler, Copernicus, and Semmelweis (p. 8), and to those of Galilei who refused to look through his telescope (p. 13). Mostly, however, Bleuler reviewed the general teachings of Freud and reported that his own experience provided critical support for psychoanalytic ideas. "My personal experience with schizophrenia proves Freud right to such an extent that I was extremely surprised myself" (p. 23). *"As far as I was able to verify, Freud has always proven to be in the right until now, even in matters that initially seemed unlikely or even absurd to me"* (p. 59). Shortly afterwards, he published a rejoinder to Oppenheim's attack on psychoanalysis at the 1910 neurologists' meeting in Berlin mentioned above (Bleuler, 1911).

As much as Freud and the psychoanalysts welcomed Bleuler's support, it was equally cause for alarm among his fellow psychiatrists. One from their own midst, and an opinion leader to boot, threatened to become lost to the psychiatric community and to lend credibility to a movement that they believed would undermine the very foundations of the speciality. This was not a purely academic controversy. Significant numbers of patients were already seeking care from psychoanalysts in private practice, clinics, and sanatoria. Theory was important to physicians dealing with the mentally ill, but losing patients struck at both the prestige and patronage of the speciality.

The congress came at a critical time. Until about 1908, psychoanalysis was more or less confined to private discussion circles, such as the Viennese Wednesday Society or the informal "Freud Society" in Zurich. Within only five years, it had become an ever growing international movement that, largely due to Bleuler's support, reached out into academia and psychiatry. Although by 1913 Bleuler had already left the International Psychoanalytic Association, he still gave psychoanalysis critical support in public. One of the main reasons for his leaving the organisation was indeed the, as he saw it, increasing "sectarian" character of the movement. In psychiatric circles, however, he was still viewed as chiefly responsible for this "sect's" growing influence. His German colleagues had already warned him not to get too deeply involved in psychoanalysis (Alexander & Selesnick, 1965, p. 3). It was obvious that they felt challenged and, it turned out, were prepared to take strong action. They certainly did not want to be "conquered" by psychoanalysis. In Breslau, the stage had been set for

Bleuler to declare himself. It would be decisive which side he would eventually join.

The Breslau congress

The meeting took place on 13–14 May 1913. According to the minutes (*Bericht* etc., 1913, pp. 779–780), there were more than 200 participants, including the *crème de la crème* of German psychiatry: apart from Bleuler and Hoche, among others, Alois Alzheimer (Breslau), Karl Bonhoeffer (Berlin), Oswald Bumke (Freiburg i. Br.), Robert Gaupp (Tübingen),[9] Emil Kraepelin (Munich), Hans Laehr (Schweizerhof), Carl Friedrich Otto Westphal (Bonn), and Wilhelm Weygandt (Hamburg). Psychologist William Stern from Breslau was also present—the only non-psychiatrist attending. From psychoanalytic circles, only young Max Eitingon from Berlin and Arnold Stegmann from Dresden participated.[10]

Bleuler opened the congress (Bleuler, 1913). He stipulated that his paper was only a further development of his 1910 publication, but now with additional critical material (p. 665). He tried to take up, point by point, the various fields covered by psychoanalytic theory and practice and then to show which parts, in his view, withstood closer scrutiny, and which not. He saw Freud as "the discoverer", and himself as "the one who checks and examines his statements, not the one who wants to defend them at all costs" (p. 685). On the one hand, he criticised the general structure and the premises of Freud's theory, which would suffer from "lack of clarity, incompleteness, and contradictions", and use "imprecise" terms (p. 668). He discarded "precisely the essence of the theory in some points", and found "some details insufficiently substantiated" (p. 680).

On the other hand, Bleuler listed an impressive number of such "details" that he regarded as "important contributions to our knowledge" (*Bericht* etc., p. 781): the theory of affects, repression (Bleuler,

---

[9]Gaupp was early friendly to psychoanalysis and in his journal published favourable material on psychoanalysis, although he was ultimately ambivalent or skeptical (Decker, 1977, pp. 119–120, 250, etc.).

[10]Eitingon was not yet a major figure in psychoanalysis, nor was Stegmann (1872–1914), who had incidentally been an analysand of Freud's shortly before (May, 2006, pp. 54–56, 89). Ludwig Binswanger had planned to attend (F/Bin, editorial note p. 116), but his name is not listed among the participants.

1913, p. 669), the concept of the unconscious (p. 670), projection and transference (p. 674), infantile sexuality, the Oedipus complex, sexual aetiology, bisexuality, resistance (pp. 686–687), symbolism (p. 692), displacement, condensation, overdetermination (p. 695), Freud's theories of religion (pp. 696–697) and obsessional neurosis (p. 704), flight into and gain from illness (p. 712), etc. Regarding psychoses and, in particular, schizophrenia, he again stated that "I cannot agree with Freud's basic assumptions" (p. 706), but that many symptoms, the manifestation and the improvement of the illness could be explained by Freud's theory (pp. 706–707).

Regarding the technique and therapeutic value of psychoanalysis, he said that one could "quarrel" (*zanken*) over it but "not yet discuss it scientifically", because there were too few data and observations (*Bericht* etc., p. 784). He repeated, in particular, that in order to understand and evaluate the technique, one would have to try it out and experience it oneself (Bleuler, 1913, p. 715). Schizophrenic patients would offer "Freudian" explanations themselves without any prompting: "A number of dreams of … schizophrenics have spontaneously been interpreted by them completely in Freud's sense. I cannot see how the opponents can come to terms with these facts" (p. 716).

In essence, while Bleuler dismissed much of the general metapsychological superstructure, he actually approved of most of the cornerstones of psychoanalytic theory and therapy. His paper can be seen as a masterful example of legendary Swiss neutrality, or one of ambivalence and indecisiveness. As a matter of fact, however, he doubtlessly made an honest and fair-minded attempt to evaluate psychoanalytic theory and therapy on the basis of the contemporary state of scientific and therapeutic knowledge—a rare exception in the heated atmosphere of those times.

Then came Hoche. His opening words shed some light on the purpose of that meeting, while not revealing it fully (1913b, pp. 1055–1056):

> Our Society is rather late in taking a stand on the question of psychoanalysis, but perhaps not too late. … I have been asked repeatedly during the past months: How come your Society chooses psychoanalysis, which is history anyway, as the topic for discussion? I always have to answer that the question might have been settled for many in the scientific sense, but not at all in the practical

and therapeutic one. ... [T]oday I have to fulfill a mandate of the
Society.

He claimed he had made "a special effort to ... examine, without bias,
any extant material", that is, that he had read all available publications
of followers of psychoanalysis, and to have "analysed my own dreams
according to the principles of Freud's interpretation. The one thing
I decided not to do was to apply myself psychoanalytic procedures,
according to the Freudian sect, on patients" (ibid.).[11]

Hoche criticised the "grotesque importance" of sexuality in Freud's
theory (ibid., p. 1058), the confusion of a possibility, analogy, or idea,
with proof, identity, or insight, the "absolute arbitrariness in interpretations" (p. 1059), the pervading "generalisation" (p. 1060), the "intellectual dishonesty of an out-and-out unscientific method" (p. 1061), etc. He
laid special emphasis on the question of the "burden of proof" (p. 1059),
which was at the heart of the controversy. While Bleuler had underlined
that the critics should test the method before passing judgement, Hoche
insisted that the burden of proof was with the psychoanalysts, not with
their critics.

Regarding psychoanalytic therapy, he cited four cases with unfa-
vourable outcomes. Although he allegedly presented them from the
patients' viewpoint, they were (with one exception) not written up
by the patients themselves, but by colleagues in answer to his circular. Moreover, some of his most devastating criticisms (e.g., "several
cases ... of suicide" and "some especially evil effects"; p. 1070) were not
substantiated, "because I am not at liberty to make use of all the material" (ibid.).

Of particular interest in our context are a couple of references made
with regard to his colleague, Eugen Bleuler. Hoche characterised the
diffusion of psychoanalysis as a "technically perfectly-staged concerted action" (ibid., p. 1060)—an interesting choice of words, given that
Hoche and his colleagues were doing exactly that, as we are trying to
show and are alluding to in the title of this paper. All of the followers

---

[11] Hoche, who had grown up as the pious son of a Protestant clergyman, still in 1923
portrayed psychoanalysis as a quasi-religious sect, the false teachings of which it was his
duty to denounce (Hoche, 1923).

of Freud, therefore, "and this also holds true for Bleuler", would bear "collective responsibility … for the overall theory … When I look at Bleuler's relation to psychoanalysis", Hoche continued, "I can never free myself from the impression: 'I've long been grieved to see you in such company'"[12] (ibid.).

Hoche's summary: The teachings of psychoanalysis are proven neither theoretically nor empirically, nor is its therapeutic effect. The gain for clinical psychiatry equals zero; the impression of the psychoanalytic movement given to sober minds is repugnant, due to the overall unscientific method; psychoanalysis as practiced today is a danger to the nervous system of the patients, and compromising for the medical profession; the only lasting interest in this "episode" would be in the field of cultural history (Bericht etc., p. 784).

The two presenters therefore employed very different kinds of rhetoric. Hoche's appeal was transparently emotional. And then members of the audience, as was the custom, took the floor to react to the two presentations. It was at that point that the careful staging appeared clearly. The tenor of the discussants' remarks was extremely critical of psychoanalysis. William Stern, the psychologist, opened the discussion. He was no doubt specially invited because of his known hostility to psychoanalysis (Stern, 1901). Moreover, he had travelled (most uncomfortably, according to Freud, 2002, p. 290), on the same ship with Freud, Jung, and Ferenczi to the famous Clark University conference in 1909, where Stern was discomfited by the attention lavished on Freud (Rosenzweig, 1992). Stern in his remarks at Breslau railed against the lasting damage allegedly inflicted upon helpless children. Referring to Freud's case history of Little Hans, he said that "healing [sic] a phobia with psychoanalysis is equal to expelling the devil by means of Beelzebub",[13] and he called for "child protection" (Bericht etc., p. 786). Kraepelin very briefly but explicitly rejected psychoanalysis, although, in his view, "decomposition phenomena" were already visible—time would dispense with it. He warned most emphatically against its practice, which, he said, had already done much damage

---

[12] Goethe, Faust, part 1, lines 3469–3470. Margarete is saying these words to Faust, deploring his association with the devil, Mephistopheles.

[13] Another allusion to the devil (Luke 11:15).

(ibid., p. 787). Weygandt called psychoanalysis a "raging epidemic", with an "uncritical obsession to interpret", and an "overestimation of sexuality" (p. 788). According to Hugo Liepmann from Berlin, the Freudians had caused a "disastrous devastation of logical and scientific thinking" (p. 789). Stegmann played the role of the lone defender of psychoanalysis.

At one point, Oskar Kohnstamm (Königstein) interjected with the startling observation (p. 789):

> I was surprised that the papers and discussions did not follow another track. Was it the aim, then, to sit in judgement on Freudism, complete with a lawyer for the defense and a state attorney, or rather, as one would have had to assume from the invitation, to discuss the value of psychoanalysis?

Indeed.

In his reply at the end, Bleuler upheld his position. He pointed out that Hoche based his judgement only on the answers he had received to his circular, that is, that he assessed a method

> whose positive results he does not even want to know. ... How easy would it be, for instance, to prove with such reasoning that each surgeon kills all of his patients. Were I to generalise these ... errors as Herr Hoche generalises the errors of psychanalysts, I would have to conclude that everything he says is wrong. (Ibid., p. 794)

Hoche closed the session by summarising that, taking into account also the "mimetic expressions" in the audience, the result was "a uniform rejection of Freud's theory and of the psychoanalytic movement—with the only exception of Dr. Stegmann." "To Bleuler I offer my condolences." Bleuler would have to realise "that we—not only myself, but surely the majority of those present—consider him responsible, to a great extent, for the flourishing of the psychoanalytic movement"; he would be the "'*Renommierstück' der Sekte*" (figurehead of the sect) (ibid., pp. 795–796).

The immediate aftermath

Eitingon (1913, p. 409) gave a short summary for the psychoanalytic readership in the *Zeitschrift*. While he reported that Hoche spoke in the name of the psychiatric society, Eitingon did not realise the true extent of the collusion: "The scathing hypotheses of Prof. Hoche are apparently to be seen as a resolution of the Society, although ... Bleuler was the other main speaker" (ibid.). Abraham reported to Freud: "Breslau was bad. ... Bleuler behaved most unpleasantly. ... Hoche did get the laugh on his side" (F/Abr, p. 185).

Bleuler himself summarised the events in his letter to Freud: "I was quite dissatisfied with Breslau ... Hoche was intelligent enough to underline a great number of actual errors of psychanalysts, and *his* own mistake was essentially that he presented psychanalysis as if it were composed of nothing but such errors" (F/Bleu, p. 197). And, shortly afterwards (pp. 200–201):

> You reproach me ... for not objecting, with one word, to Hoche's method of sending out a circular. It should suffice what I did say ... Would it have been useful to be rude to boot? ... [G]etting into a fight would at best make sense only if one could achieve an important goal with it and, above all, if one were completely in the right. But that is exactly what I would not have been, because Hoche did say correct things.

Let us add that, curiously enough, later in that year, when psychoanalysts met for their Fourth International Congress in Munich on 7–8 September, "[b]y a malicious stroke of chance ... that evil genius,[14] Hoche, had settled in the very building in which the meetings were held" (Freud, 1914d, p. 45). Again!

Enter W. J. Sweasy Powers

At this point, let us introduce another figure into the narrative: William John Sweasey Powers (1875–1938), an American physician studying in Europe.

---

[14] In the manuscript of his "History of the psychoanalytic movement", Freud had originally called him the "filthy genius" (*der unsaubere Geist*). Upon Abraham's objection that this description might "lead to unpleasant consequences", he then changed it into the hardly more flattering "evil genius" (*der böse Geist*) (F/Abr, p. 220). In his autobiography, Hoche later wrote that he counted it "among my honorific titles that the head of the sect had called me its 'evil genius'" (Hoche, 1923, p. 13).

William John Sweasey Powers (1875–1938)
Source: *Homoeopathic Recorder*, 48 (1931), frontispiece.

Standard directories and an obituary reveal that Powers was born in Sacramento, California, in 1875. He received his medical degree from Cooper Medical College (soon to become the medical school of Stanford

University). He subsequently spent a number of years studying in Germany, chiefly at the University of Berlin, returning to the United States in 1915. In 1920, he was licensed to practice medicine in the state of New York, and he was listed in the medical directory with an office at 10 East 61st Street, New York City, in 1921. By 1927, he had moved his office to 666 Madison Avenue, and it was in that office that he died of a heart attack in 1938. At that time, according to his obituary, "he specialized in the treatment of chronic diseases" ("Dr. W. J. Sweasey Powers", 1938).

At some point, Powers became interested in nervous and mental diseases. In 1912, he published an article out of Theodor Ziehen's service in the Charité Hospital in Berlin (Powers, 1912). The letter that is the object of our present publication is a personal letter that he wrote to Smith Ely Jelliffe, the owner and managing editor of the *Journal of Nervous and Mental Disease*, the journal in which Powers had published his 1912 article. Jelliffe, on his part, was an inveterate traveller to European centres of medical learning and research. He had himself studied with Emil Kraepelin in the summers of 1905 and 1906. Jelliffe was also a pioneer psychoanalyst (Burnham, 1983). Powers' letter in fact was written while he, in turn, was studying with Kraepelin. The occasion of this letter was Jelliffe's offer to publish another article about which Powers must have told him in 1913. Clearly they had been in touch and may well have first met during one of Jelliffe's trips to Europe. Powers, at least through his wife later on, had a continuing interest in Freud and psychoanalysis.

He was married to Lillian Delger Powers (1866–1953) who later, in the 1920s, became an internationally well-connected psychoanalyst. In a letter to Bertram Lewin of 5 March 1934 (LC), she listed her qualifications:

> I have been a member of the International Psychoanalytic Society *more* than *five* years. II. I received my own Training Analysis from Professor Freud himself. III. I spent two years (1924–26) at the Psychoanalytic Institute in Vienna, attending all courses, seminars, etc. and receiving at the end, a Certificate testifying to the character of my work while there, and to the completion of same. IV. While at the Institute I conducted Analysis on six cases and was in "Control Analysis" with Dr. Helene Deutsch, Dr. Herman Nunberg, and Dr. Wilhelm Reich ... V. I also did Supervised Practical Work,

i.e., Control Analysis, with Dr. Ferenczi during his stay in this country—1926–27. VI. I am well versed in (all) the most modern views regarding Theory and Technique ... VII. I have made a special study of Psychoanalytic technique ... VIII. I have successfully conducted an appreciable number of therapeutic analyses.

She might have had another 'tranche' with Freud in the mid-1930s (cf. Freud, 1977d; with thanks to Gerhard Fichtner). In New York, where she practiced, she later corresponded with Jelliffe about local psychoanalytic activities, and by one account continued in practice until she was eighty-eight years old, that is, until the year of her death ("Dr. Lillian D. Powers", 1953).[15]

What is known about W. J. Sweasey Powers' own later career is that he himself was active in a quite different direction. Although in the United States he was always listed as a regular medical practitioner, at some point he became deeply involved in homeopathy. In 1932–1933 he served as first vice-president of the International Hahnemannian Association (a group that had broken off half a century earlier to keep homeopathy orthodox) (*Homoeopathic Recorder*, 1931). In 1931, Powers translated and published an address by Gisevius (1931), whom Powers described as "one of the best known homoeopaths of Berlin, Germany". According to Powers (1931) in a separate comment, the address showed that "true Hahnemannian homoeopathy" was returning "to its original home", namely, Germany. His involvement in homeopathy is probably most parallel to that of Heinrich Meng, the well known psychoanalyst and mental hygienist (cf. Brenner, 1975), much valued by Freud. Meng's early publications appeared in many irregular and homeopathic medical journals, including an article (Meng, 1926) that was translated by W. G. [sic] Sweasey Powers![16] In even the few facts now available,

---

[15] Additional information from the reference team at Marin County Free Library on the basis of obituaries of Delger Trowbridge in the *Daily Independent Journal* of Mendocino, 16 December 1958. [Addition] Incidentally, in the 1930s Powers became the analyst of Freud's godchild, Abraham A. Brill's daughter Gioia (named after Freud; joy = *Freud[e]*), and Brill kept Freud informed about the (not entirely successful) progress of the analysis (Freud/Brill correspondence; LC). Freud remarked that when Powers was his analysand her interests were very much focused on her squirrels (for which she was a noted expert).

[16] Thanks for special assistance in tracing Powers go to Arlene Shaner of the New York Academy of Medicine Library.

W. J. Sweasey Powers appears to have had a consistent belief that good, original thinkers, whether orthodox or not, should be heard— a theme that is more than an overtone in the letter that follows, a letter that is here published in its entirety for the first time.

Powers' revealing letter

Munich, Copernicus Strasse 11
May 25, 1913

Dear Doctor Jelliffe:

I wish to thank you for your kindness in offering to take the "Arbeit", but it seems that Prof. Oestreich did not think it would be wise to publish it in both papers at the same time, but either in one or the other. As I had already prepared it in German, I thought it best to let it go. It will come out in "Zeitschrift für allgemeine Neurologie und Psychiatrie" of this month.[17]

I attended the Congress of "deutschen" psychiatricians, recently held at Breslau. Psycho-analysis from the Freud point of view was discussed the first morning.

Prof. Bleuler of Zurich explained Psycho-analysis, explained that he believed in psychoanalysis itself but was not willing to back psychoanalysis based upon the sexual theories of Freud. Prof. Hoche claimed that there was no scientific foundation for the Freudian psycho-analysis, that it was dangerous, and that it was not ethical for a reputable physician to practise it—he did not use these words but said that no one had the right to take a patient's time and money that was necessary in order to find out if the method will improve the condition or not. He devoted most of his time in turning expressions used in explaining the sexual theories so that they would rouse a laugh, and he had the members of the Congress in continual laughter. Prof. Lieppmann [sic] of Berlin (aphasie) protested against treating the subject so. Prof. Kraepelin did not enter into the discussion but said that he wished to throw the weight

---

[17] Powers, 1913. Richard Oestreich, a pathologist of Berlin, occasionally himself published on malignant neoplasms. The article is listed as coming from the pathological institute of the Königin Augusta Hospital in Berlin, of which institute Oestreich was the director.

of his experience against the Freudian psycho-analysis because he had seen results that were most deplorable. Later in München, he asked me what I thought of the Congress. I told him that I was not much impressed by the argument put up against it. He asked if I did not realise that all of the members and that is to say all of the prominent psychiatricians in Germany were against it. I replied that I had hoped to hear some scientific facts brought against it. He then said that was not the purpose of bringing up the discussion. The purpose was to give Bleuler the opportunity to publicly back-slide from the Freud-school as his name was considered to have had a great influence in keeping the Freud theories alive. The purpose was also to place the German psychiatricians on record as being against the Freud theories. A man from Vienna was the only one who spoke for Freud. Kohnstamm got up to emphasize the fact that psycho-analysis without the Freud theories existed long before Freud was ever heard of and that there was much practical benefit to be obtained in employing uncontaminated psycho-analysis.

Later in the day Prof. Kraepelin introduced a plan for a German research institute for psychiatry—to be a part of the Kaiser Wilhelm Research Institute. The July 1, 1913, plan was accepted, and Kraepelin was instructed to see that it was brought to the notice of the proper authorities.

I am almost ashamed to send you what I have written, if it did not tend to show you my good intentions.

Just at present I am "Hausarzt" on a case for Prof. Kraepelin. A wealthy American is in a "depressive Zustand" and does not want to enter a hospital. So Kraepelin put me on the case with two Nurses—I suppose he asked me because he could get no one else. However, I am glad of the opportunity to learn how he handles a private case and to come into close association with him. I can use my free time for an article that I am writing.

Will we see you in London? I was in hopes you would take that in on your way to Ghent.

I have been enjoying a detailed account of the abilities of the different New York psychiatricians given by my patient and his relatives. You happened not to have been among those described. From their point-of-view, the American alienist, the New Yorker especially, is a pretty "bum lot"—they are all grafters and ignoramuses. They certainly hand out a "hot potatoe". I tried to make

them believe that they had not seen straight, but their experience
had been great and they are dead sure of themselves. I guess it isn't
as bad as they paint it.

Yours very sincerely,
W. J. Sweasey Powers[18]

Conclusion

The Powers letter constitutes evidence of a clandestine, "technically
perfectly-staged concerted action". What does it mean that Hoche,
Kraepelin, and their allies were working behind the scenes to use a public occasion to manipulate Bleuler and other colleagues? Clearly they
were using the appearances of proper recognition and collegiality to
manage an intellectual movement: scientific psychiatry, as practitioners
at the time conceived it.

We already know that the psychoanalysts were also trying to manage
an intellectual movement. The Powers letter shows that Freud and his
allies were not the only ones who were trying to do so by using informal networks and behind-the-scenes manoeuvering. Freud's antagonists were employing the very methods they accused him of using.
And Powers' letter shows that, at least in this case, Freud was not even
imagining the lengths to which his opponents were going.

The full importance of the staging at the 1913 Breslau congress now
becomes apparent. The purpose of the Breslau meeting had never been,
despite superficial appearances, to give psychoanalysis a fair hearing.
It is evident that Kohnstamm, in his contribution to the discussion,
was more right than he knew, and that the staging went even beyond
Eitingon's speculation that Hoche's theses "are apparently to be seen
as a resolution of the Society"—that is, the staging even went beyond
what psychoanalysts feared their "enemies" were up to. According to
information freely obtainable on the formal level, Freud and other psychoanalysts fully realised that there would be a counter-move. What
they did not know was what had been going on privately, namely, to
present the united front of German psychiatrists, who were going on

---

[18] The holograph letter is in Box 16 in the Smith Ely Jelliffe Papers in the Library of
Congress. It is presented in its entirety not only to furnish context but to convey a sense
of the clear-headedness and candour of the writer.

record as being against psychoanalysis, and, in that context, to give a leading psychiatrist, whose (however half-hearted) support for psychoanalysis had alarmed his colleagues, a public opportunity for back-pedalling. Bleuler's role had never been intended to be the lawyer for the defence, but that of the prodigal son, coming back to the fold and confessing his sins.

Epilogue

Bleuler continued to use Freudian formulations in his publications (Müller, 1998, pp. 227–241). Eventually, however, he gradually distanced himself more and more from the psychoanalytic movement, even if he never became an outspoken opponent. This withdrawal was not so much the result of the pressure exercised on him by his colleagues, but of the further development of his own thinking, his objections to the growing exclusivity of the psychoanalytic movement, and, last but not least, the experience of a failed analysis (see Chapter Eight).

As Bleuler drifted away, Freud's hopes of an affiliation with official psychiatry and academia were frustrated—at least in Europe. His separation from the psychoanalytic movement was probably more important for the course it has since taken than those of Adler, Stekel, or even Jung. And while the concerted action at Breslau may not have significantly influenced Bleuler, who had his own agenda, still the united front—formal and informal—of the psychiatrists helped close off some institutional avenues through which Freud's teachings might have passed in the hands of open-minded psychiatrists like Bleuler.

CHAPTER TEN

Freud and Jung, Freudians and Jungians

Introduction

To this day, many decades after their deaths, Freud and Jung are still the two "names that most people first think of in connection with psychology" (Shamdasani, in Jung, 2009, p. 193). This curious, anachronistic fact alone would merit a closer investigation. Moreover, apart from the fact that each of them was an extremely influential psychologist in his own right, the relationship between them, their collaboration for a few years, and their falling out, as Aniela Jaffé wrote in 1968 (p. 99),

> still exerts a strange fascination on people—and not only on psychologists of Freudian or Jungian orientation. ... Their friendship and break, which drew so much attention, was one not only of two great personalities engaged in a scientific and human conflict, not only of the old and the young man, but above all of the Jew and the non-Jew. All this adds special weight to their encounter, and explains the tremendous interest, which the world took and still takes in this relationship. It also explains the emotionality and the heated pro and contra in assessing this relationship.

The publication of their correspondence in 1974 further kindled that interest, and spawned a plethora of articles, even books, on their relationship. "With few exceptions" however, as Sonu Shamdasani noted, "these works have uniformly suffered from the Freudocentric frame in which they have viewed the genesis of complex psychology", that is, that they viewed Jung's theory primarily as "on offshoot from psychoanalysis", thus mislocating "Jung and complex psychology in the intellectual history of the twentieth century" (2003, pp. 12–13). While I completely agree that Jung's encounter with Freud was but one episode in the evolution of his personality and his ideas, that there were many other important influences on Jung, and that from the beginning of his relationship with Freud he had his own agenda, I still find it incontestable that this was a crucial encounter for both of the protagonists. Thus, while keeping Shamdasani's warning in mind, I would like to take a fresh look on that relationship, and in particular investigate how stimulating it was for Freud and Jung, what each of them took over from the other, and then have a look at some of the consequences their break had for the following development of psychoanalysis and analytical or complex psychology.

The impact of Freud and Jung

Freud and Jung have become larger than life. Their names have become something like stimulus words in a global association experiment, quickly drawing a host of reactions and associations. While their theories have all but vanished, except as historical references, from most modern curricula in academic medicine, psychiatry, and psychology (interestingly, the last academic fields, in which they still seem to hold some ground, are literary criticism and theology), their ideas have become diffused into popular culture to this very day. Perhaps precisely the fact that their influence in the natural sciences is on the wane, while their influence in general culture is still very high, is one reason for the ongoing controversies. While 'science' wants to show that Freud and Jung are outdated and essentially unscientific, people continue to be stubbornly interested in, and fascinated by, their views.

Their terms and concepts have become part of our everyday language and have become entries in dictionaries, if often in garbled or misunderstood form. Everybody talks about the unconscious or the subconscious, even about the collective unconscious, about

Freudian slips, about archetypes, repression, the Oedipus complex, about narcissism, libido, introverts and extroverts (sic), about castrating mothers, anal-retentive people and potty training, about the midlife crisis, identification and projection, about id, ego and superego, the father imago, the death instinct, inferiority complexes, regression, and so on and on.[1] The very term psychoanalysis has enjoyed immense success, and for many the name 'psychoanalyst' or 'analyst' has become a synonym for psychiatrist, psychotherapist, or 'shrink' in general, and the figure of the analyst and the couch has become a cartoon stereotype. Everybody seems to know that sometimes a cigar is just a cigar, and men still often wonder what Woman really wants …

It has become commonplace to say that Freud has had an enormous influence on Western culture and society of the twentieth century. "It would be hard to find in the history of ideas, even in the history of religion, someone whose influence was so immediate, so broad and so deep" (Wollheim, 1971, p. 9). "There has been nothing like this since the spread of the potato and of maize, and this diffusion [of psychoanalysis] was even faster and may have deeper implications" (Gellner, 1985, p. 11). Freud has become a "whole climate of opinion," as W. (Wystan) H. Auden called it (in Webster, 1995, p. 10), or, in the words of Harold Bloom (1986), "the central imagination of our age", or even "the greatest modern writer". Practically no field in Western culture has escaped his impact: psychotherapy, psychiatry, medicine, literature, biography, autobiography, literary criticism, film, painting, advertisement, public relations, education and pedagogy, sociology, anthropology, ethnology, politics, religion and theology, jurisdiction, the penal system, probation service, and so on. Also journalism. Let me give you just one example. There was an article in the *New York Times* about an exhibit at the Museum of Sex, "Rubbers: The life, history & struggle of the condom", which ended with the line: "The condom is a declaration of sacrifice in the midst of indulgence. It is evidence of civilization and its discontents" (Rothstein, 2010). Note that the author, Edward Rothstein, did not even feel the need to mention the name of Freud. He could be sure that

---

[1] It is less well known that Freud coined another two terms that have entered our language: obsessional neurosis (May, 1998) and "sexual science" = sexology (*Sexualwissenschaft*) (although it is usually Iwan Bloch who is credited with its coinage; Sigusch, 2008, p. 262).

his readers would understand the allusion (to Freud, 1930a). There is probably only one cultural field, in which Freud's impact is not visible, or rather, audible—music.[2]

Much of what I said about Freud is also true for Jung. For instance

> he played a pivotal role in the formation of the modern concept of schizophrenia ... His views on the continued relevance of myth were the seed bed for the mythic revival. His interest in Eastern thought was the harbinger of the postcolonial Easternization of the West. ... [T]here is a massive counterculture that hails him as a founding figure—and the impact of his work on mainstream twentieth-century Western culture has been far wider than has yet been recognised. (Shamdasani, 2003, p. 2)

Add to this that many of his concepts, from the archetypes to the collective unconscious, from the midlife crisis to his theory of complexes, and of course his typology of introverts and extraverts, have become household names. In the process of being absorbed into everyday language, however, some of these terms and concepts have been garbled or distorted. Jung's etymologically correct expression "extraversion," for instance, has turned into "extroversion", which makes everybody with a minimal knowledge of Latin shudder. What would one think of terms such as extro-curricular, extro-dite, extro-marital, extro-ordinary, for instance?[3] Or, few people realise, when they use the popular expression of the "inferiority complex", that this is not a Freudian term, but a concoction of Adler's concept of the "inferiority feeling" and Jung's theory of emotional "complexes".

Another thing Freud and Jung have in common is that they were and continue to be the targets of heavy attacks. Freud is declared dead in regular intervals, but usually with such vehemence and venom

---

[2] Or rather, instrumental music. Many lyrics for songs, musicals, operas, etc. were undoubtedly also influenced by his ideas.

[3] All authoritative English dictionaries I consulted, in print or online, give "extrovert(ed)" as the standard form (both for American and British English), while listing "extravert(ed)" only as a variant. The same is true for German and French. While it is pointless to deplore the ongoing development of a living language, it is nevertheless quite regrettable that "extroversion" can be found repeatedly even in texts that refer expressly to Jung. He himself stated in 1952 that "extrovert is bad Latin and should not be used" (in McGuire & Hull, 1977, p. 213).

that this makes one doubt the accuracy of the death certificate—as if
the coroners of dead bodies in the closets of science were afraid that
he might rise from the dead again. Although Freud's critics have
tried repeatedly to relegate psychoanalysis "to history's ashcan"
(Crews, 1995, p. 223), his name and theories can still provoke heated
controversies—and this more than seventy years after his death. Rather
than being a sign that he and what he stood for is finally history, such
an anachronistic phenomenon is, if nothing else, a tribute to his ongoing influence.

Jung has been called many names:

> Occultist, Scientist, Prophet, Charlatan, Philosopher, Racist, Guru,
> Anti-Semite, Liberator of Women, Misogynist, Freudian Apostate,
> Gnostic, Post-Modernist, Polygamist, Healer, Poet, Con-Artist, Psy-
> chiatrist and Anti-Psychiatrist ... Mention him to someone, and you
> are likely to receive one of these images. For Jung is someone that
> people—informed or not—have opinions about. The swift reaction
> time indicates that people respond to Jung's life and work as if they
> are sufficiently known. (Shamdasani, 2003, p. 1)

Differences

Two highly controversial, if often misunderstood intellectual giants
of the twentieth century, then, who still exert an enormous influence
in popular culture. Myths also surround the few years of their intense
collaboration, friendship, love even, which ended in a brutal falling-
out. After the break, Freud no longer had one good word to say about
the "brutal, sanctimonious Jung", whose "crooked character did not
compensate [him] for his lopsided theories" (F/Abr, pp. 264, 487). The
former friend, crown prince, and heir-apparent had become an enemy.
A quarter of a century later, in 1938, Freud was approached by Franz
Riklin Jr., a relative of Jung's, who had been "chosen by some exceed-
ingly rich Swiss Jews to go into Austria *at once*, with a very large sum
of money, to do all that he could to persuade leading Jews to leave the
country." When he called on Freud with that intention, all the latter
told him was: "I refuse to be beholden to my enemies" (Hannah, 1976,
pp. 254–255).

As to Jung, he continued to pay lip service to the importance of
Freud, but his dismissal of practically all central tenets of the latter's

theory and practice[4] makes one wonder what he still found so important about him—apart, perhaps, from a general bow toward Freud's role in paving the way to depth psychology in general, and to his, Jung's, psychology in particular. Perhaps most striking is Jung's rejection of Freud's method of investigating psychical phenomena, free association, and consequently his abandoning of "analysing" them. For Jung, the method of free association leads to a "reductive explanation", to a *"reductio in primam figuram"* (Jung, 2008, p. 25), because, as he argues, although free association will uncover a person's complexes, it will not uncover the specific meaning of a particular symptom or a particular dream. In fact, according to Jung, you can free associate to just anything, and will always arrive at the same complex or complexes, namely, those by which you are dominated in general, without ever revealing the *specific* meaning of a *particular* dream or symptom.

The underlying, and crucial, difference between Freud's and Jung's views is that for Freud the presenting dream, for instance, is not a direct expression of an unconscious tendency, not a 'natural' expression, so to speak, but already a distortion, a compromise formation between conflicting tendencies within the psyche, hiding a "latent" meaning behind a "manifest" façade, a meaning around which the free associations revolve like beating around the bush. That bush, the 'true' meaning, can then be uncovered by "analysis". The very term "psycho-analysis" was introduced by Freud in analogy to chemical analysis, to describe his method of breaking down complex phenomena into their basic psychic component parts. Like *chemical* analysis was able to show that organic matter was composed of elements such as carbon, hydrogen, oxygen, etc., *psycho*-analysis would be able to make an analogous analysis of psychical phenomena (a comparison Freud made at least twice: F/Fer I, p. 280; Freud & Bullitt, 1967, p. 37).

For Jung, however, dreams are direct, undistorted emanations from the unconscious that need not, indeed should not, be "analysed". According to Jung, dreams are "impartial, spontaneous products of the unconscious psyche … They are pure nature; they show us the unvarnished, natural truth." They represent "a communication or message from the unconscious, unitary soul of humanity" (Jung, 1933, §§

---

[4] According to Edward Glover, "the most consistent trend of Jungian psychology is its negation of every important part of Freudian theory" (1950, p. 190).

317–318).[5] The reason why they are not directly intelligible is that they speak to us in a peculiar language, that is, they speak in images, in symbols. Thus our task is not to analyse a dream by breaking it down into its component parts and finding an alleged "latent" meaning behind the "manifest" content. According to Jung, the manifest content *is* already the meaning and the message, although couched in an archaic language, which we have to learn in order to understand what the unconscious wants to tell us. What Freud called "symbols" (e.g., the church tower as a phallic symbol), Jung called "signs", in that they were an "analogue or an abbreviated designation for a known thing" (Jung, 1921, § 815). In his view, a "symbol" rather is "the best possible description or formulation of a relatively unknown fact, which is none the less known to exist or is postulated as existing" (§ 814). A living symbol represents "the inexpressible in unsurpassable form" (§ 816). "An expression that stands for a known thing remains a mere sign and is never a symbol" (§ 817).

Apart from using dreams, his method of soliciting emanations and manifestations of the unconscious was that of "active imagination", a method that produces a kind of waking visions or phantasies, which he then subjected to what he called "amplification", which essentially consists in finding "parallels" to those images in "collective" imaginations, such as myths, religious systems and practices, visions, alchemy, yoga, etc. In short, as Freudian Edward Glover put it, Jung did not *analyse* dreams, but *read* them (1950, p. 110).[6] To make a perhaps provocative point, one could argue that the term "Jungian *analyst*" for a psychotherapist working in Jung's tradition is actually a misnomer.

While the ties were cut and they went their own ways, secretly, however, the loss of their friendship and relationship was probably very painful to each of them. When Jungian E. A. Bennet asked Freud "about the rupture with Jung[,] Freud, after a pause, said very quietly, 'Jung was

---

[5] Similarly, he says in *Memories, Dreams, Reflections*: "I was never able to agree with Freud that the dream is a 'façade' behind which its meaning lies hidden … To me dreams are a part of nature, which harbours no intention to deceive, but expresses something as best it can. … Long before I met Freud I regarded the unconscious, and dreams, which are its direct exponents, as natural processes to which no arbitrariness can be attributed" (1962, p. 185).

[6] Jung's most detailed account of his method of dream interpretation can be found in his seminar on children's dreams (Jung, 2008).

a great loss'. No more was said" (Bennet, 1961, p. 58). When Freudian Kurt Eissler asked Jung about the break-up, Jung talked about Freud's neurotic element, and that he would not have been able to overcome it. It would have been that element that prevented Jung from further collaborating with him, which otherwise he would have been crazy not to (LC).

Cross-fertilisation

With hindsight it was probably inevitable that Jung took his distance from Freud—the differences, already clearly visible from the very beginning, but tolerated for some time, proved too great. There is no doubt, however, that, as long as they collaborated, their encounter and also their controversies were extremely stimulating to them. Interestingly, and I find quite surprisingly, however, it seems that Freud took over much more from Jung and let himself be more influenced by the latter than vice versa. Freud's foray into psychiatry, his analysis of the Schreber case (1911c), his occupation with ethno-psychology and the psychology of so-called primitives in *Totem and Taboo* (1912–13a), his introduction of the anal phase in the psycho-sexual development (Freud, 1913i; see Chapter Two), his further development of the libido theory and the introduction of the concept of narcissism, the concept of countertransference, his technical recommendations in general, such as the models of the mirror and the surgeon, or the rule of abstinence—all these were at least partly answers to Jung. His fascination with parapsychology, however ambivalent it was, was certainly also stimulated by his encounter with Jung.

Moreover, it is probably no coincidence that in 1910, at the height of their friendship, Freud gave a particular name to one of his most influential concepts, calling it the "Oedipus complex" (1910h, p. 171), thus honouring a term made popular by Jung, and he published the paper in a journal (the *Jahrbuch*), of which Jung was the managing editor.[7] This is not to say that Freud simply took over ideas from Jung in their original form. George Makari has shown how Freud, as in the

----

[7] A year earlier, in his lectures at Clark University, Freud had already talked about "the *nuclear complex* of every neurosis", referring to the "myth of King Oedipus" (Freud, 1910a, p. 47)—Jung was present in the audience.

cases of Charcot and Breuer, took parts of existing theories, sometimes twisted and changed them, mixed them with his own observations and reflections, and used them to create his own synthesis. "As he had done with Charcot, Freud borrowed from Breuer and then, armed with his mentor's ideas, pivoted to face his teacher" (Makari, 2008, p. 46). One could say that Freud used Jung—and others—as his sounding-board, that—while holding fast to what he viewed as the cornerstones of his theory—he borrowed terms, ideas, and concepts, worked them into his own theory, often in a changed form,[8] that he let himself be led to new fields of research, and that he was willing to reconsider some of his own concepts.

Quite a few of Jung's other notions have also entered the psycho-analytic mainstream. "Imago", for instance, is a term first introduced by him in 1911.[9] Freud, and with him the whole psychoanalytic com-munity to this day, took up this term to describe object representa-tions, and in 1912 Freud even named a newly founded journal *Imago, Journal for the Application of Psychoanalysis to the Humanities*—while avoiding any reference to Jung. (To this day, by the way, there exists the psychoanalytic journal *American Imago*.) Freud also took over the concept of "introversion of the libido", which he called "felicitous" (*treffend*) (1912b, p. 102; trans. mod.).[10]

In some of his formulations, Freud came also near to Jung's notion of a "collective unconscious". Freud wrote him in early 1912 that he considered Jung's "demonstration of unconscious heredity in symbol-ism" one of the "most significant" contributions to psychoanalysis, and one that psychoanalysts "should follow" (F/Jun, p. 480). In 1915, Freud wrote (1915e, p. 195):

> The content of the *Ucs.* may be compared with an aboriginal pop-ulation in the mind. If inherited mental formations exist in the human being—something analogous to instincts in animals—these constitute the nucleus of the *Ucs.* Later there is added to them what

---

[8] An example would be the term "Id/It", borrowed from Nietzsche and Groddeck.

[9] Jung borrowed the term from the title of a novel by the Swiss writer Carl Spitteler (1906), and from the ancient religious idea of *"imagines et lares"* (Jung, 1911/12, German ed., p. 164; also in *Collected Works*, volume 5, § 62 and note 5).

[10] He used the expression nineteen times in his own works, for the last time in 1920 in *Beyond the Pleasure Principle* (1920g, p. 51; cf. Guttman et al., 1983, 1995).

is discarded during childhood development as unserviceable; and this need not differ in its nature from what is inherited.

Two years later, referring to Jung's seminal booklet on *The Psychology of Unconscious Processes* (1917), and although he dismissed Jung's typology—"he seems not to have gone beyond the crude conversion into theory of the fact that he came across myself and Adler"—Freud nevertheless conceded: "We meet in the 'archaic' [*im Urtümlichen*]" (F/Abr, p. 353). With this Freud referred to Jung's assumption that the unconscious contains, "apart from personal reminiscences, the great 'archaic' [*urtümliche*] images—the *absolute or collective* unconscious" (Jung, 1917, pp. 94–95).

Freud continued to believe that "[m]an's archaic heritage forms the nucleus of the unconscious mind" (1919e, pp. 203–204), although he did not go so far as to hypothesise the existence of a separate entity such as a "collective unconscious". The problem occupied him to the end of his life, however. Regarding his own theses about trans-generational effects of the events hypothesised in *Totem and Taboo* (1912–13a) and *Moses and Monotheism* (1939a), he stated that

> [w]e cannot at first sight say in what form this past existed during the time of its eclipse. It is not easy for us to carry over the concepts of individual psychology into group psychology; and I do not think we gain anything by introducing the concept of a "collective" unconscious. The content of the unconscious, indeed, is in any case a collective, universal property of mankind.

He concluded, however, in a manner of thinking not unlike Jung's: "We must finally make up our minds to adopt the hypothesis that the psychical precipitates of the primaeval period became inherited property which, in each fresh generation, called not for acquisition but only for awakening" (1939a, p. 132).[11]

Jung, as well as Eugen Bleuler and other collaborators at the Burghölzli, were also the first to investigate *psychoses* from a psychoanalytic

---

[11] The most detailed discussion of the "archaic heritage" in Freud's writings can also be found in *Moses and Monotheism* (1939a, pp. 99–102). See the excellent overview of Freud's views on this matter given by James Strachey in his editorial note (p. 102).

viewpoint. Psychotic cases were practically absent in the private practice of Freud and his followers in Vienna who, if they were medical doctors at all, mainly worked with so-called "nervous diseases", that is, neuroses, and psychosomatic or functional disorders.[12] Jung's book, *The Psychology of Dementia Praecox* (1907), established his worldwide reputation. Ernest Jones (1909) hailed it as a "sensation" that heralded "a new era in psychiatry". It was translated into English by Abraham A. Brill, who still in 1936—by then a dyed-in-the-wool Freudian—described it as "the cornerstone of modern interpretative psychiatry" (1936, p. ix). Later psychoanalysts working with psychotic patients owe much to the pioneering work of Bleuler and Jung, often without acknowledging it, or even without being aware of the fact.

Other concepts, controversial at the time, have also entered psychoanalytic theory and practice to a certain extent, for example, Jung's method of dream interpretation on the "subjective plane" or "level",[13] his view of the compensatory function of the unconscious,[14] his extension of developmental psychology to cover the whole lifespan, or his stress on the importance of *present* conflicts, and not only of repressed childhood memories, in the psychoanalytic process. Surprisingly, Jung also seems to have been the first to see infantile neuroses as the result of what the parents unconsciously project on to their children,[15] and not mainly as the result of a child's internal conflicts, a view so widespread today that it is worth remembering how revolutionary it was at the time. Jung and the "Zurich School" were also the first to call for the necessity of a training analysis of the future analyst, as acknowledged

---

[12] Prior to the study on Schreber (Freud, 1911c)—to whose case Jung had drawn his attention in the first place—Freud had published only one significant case history of a psychotic patient, in which, however, he had introduced the important concept of "projection" as a defence mechanism (Freud, 1896b, p. 184).

[13] That is, that the "dream images do not reflect the relations between the dreamer and the persons seen in the dream, but are an expression of tendencies within the dreamer" (*Protokolle* etc., 1913-1916; cf. Maeder, 1913, pp. 11, 13).

[14] Jung regarded "the activity of the *unconscious* … as a balancing of the one-sidedness of the general *attitude* … produced by the function of *consciousness*" (Jung, 1921, § 694).

[15] For example: "[T]he psyche of the child must be regarded as a functional appendage of that of the parents. … I am therefore inclined to explain the possible incestuous tendencies of the child rather from the standpoint of the psychology of the parents" (Jung, 1927, §§ 61–62).

by Freud (1912b, p. 116)[16]—a training requisite taken over by practically all dynamically oriented psychotherapeutic schools.

In the light of all this, it is beyond me how Edward Glover could arrive at his judgement: "I have been unable to find that Jung has injected anything into Freud's ideas" (1950, pp. 9–10).

This could rather be said about what Freud injected into Jung's ideas. With the exception of a short period of intense collaboration, during which Jung also sometimes toed the line,[17] from the beginning Jung had his own agenda. His agreement with Freud remained on a rather unspecific, general level, while from their first contact onward he voiced his reservations against specific, but central parts of Freud's theory, above all against the sexual theory. Already in his first extant letter to Freud he maintained that "the genesis of hysteria … is not exclusively sexual", and he added that he took the "same [critical] view of [Freud's] sexual theory" in general. He felt "alarmed by the positivism of [Freud's] presentation", but was cautious—or diplomatic—enough to always add something like: "it is possible that my reservations about your far-reaching views are due to lack of experience" (F/Jun, pp. 4–5, 7). (In his own field, psychiatry, Jung had of course much more experience than Freud, and could well judge how or if Freud's theory of schizophrenia, for example, was in accord with his own experiences and observations.)

True, Jung was fascinated by Freud as a person,[18] by how seriously he took psychical phenomena such as phantasies, dreams, slips, etc., by how closely he listened to his patients and looked at details.[19] Nothing was too unimportant, absurd, or seemingly meaningless not

---

[16] [Addition] Recently, Clark-Lowes has argued, however, that it might have been Wilhelm Stekel, and not Jung, who was the first to recommend "that every doctor who wishes to practise psychoanalysis should be analysed himself" (2010, p. 186).

[17] This is the period about which Abraham Brill wrote that Jung "gave the impression that he was fully convinced of everything (Freudian)", and that one "could not express any doubt about Freud's views without arousing his ire" (in Glover, 1950, p. 45).

[18] For some time at least, Jung's "boundless admiration" for Freud "both as a man and a researcher" even had "something of the character of a 'religious' crush", which he felt as "disgusting and ridiculous because of its undeniable erotic undertone. This abominable feeling comes from the fact that as a boy I was the victim of a sexual assault by a man I once worshipped" (F/Jun, p. 95).

[19] "Freud's greatest achievement probably consisted in taking neurotic patients seriously and entering into their peculiar individual psychology" (Jung, 1962, p. 192).

to be studied and analysed. Jung (and Bleuler) valued what he called "the essential thing, your psychology" (F/Jun, p. 5), in other words, the concept of the unconscious and of how the individual was influenced by it, how he reacted to it by what Bleuler called "Freudian mechanisms" (Bleuler, 1906/07) and what was later termed "defence mechanisms". From the beginning, however, Jung had great reservations against the generalised *theoretical* conclusions Freud drew from his observations.

Jung himself explicitly stated (1934, § 1034):

> I did not start from Freud, but from Eugen Bleuler and Pierre Janet, who were my immediate teachers. When I took up the cudgels for Freud in public, I already had a scientific position that was widely known on account of my association experiments, conducted inde-pendently of Freud, and the theory of complexes based upon them. My collaboration was qualified by an objection in principle to the sexual theory, and it lasted up to the time when Freud identified in principle his sexual theory with his method.[20]

For some time, these differences were ignored or downplayed by both protagonists. With hindsight, we may rather ask ourselves why they had become so close at all in the first place for a relatively long period, or why they had not split much sooner. Freud was certainly blinded by his sympathy, by the invaluable support of Bleuler and Jung, two world-famous, non-Jewish psychiatrists and academics, by his hopes to "conquer ... all psychiatry and the approval of the civilized world" with their help (F/Jun, p. 300), to rescue psychoanalysis "from the dan-ger of becoming a Jewish national affair" (F/Abr, p. 38), and by the great plans he had for Jung as his successor.[21] For a long time he made light of the all too clear signals of dissent that Jung kept sending him: "[D]on't

---

[20] There are some parallels between Jung's criticism and that of the so-called neo-psychoanalysts, such as Harry Stack Sullivan, Erich Fromm, Karen Horney, Clara Thompson, or Frieda Fromm-Reichmann, who, like Jung, acknowledged the importance of these mechanisms, but dismissed the drive theory, criticised what they saw as Freud's incorrect generalisations, and stressed other factors. While they focused on cultural fac-tors, however, Jung's interest was in the collective unconscious.

[21] To Ludwig Binswanger, Freud wrote on 14 March 1911: "When the empire I founded is orphaned, no one else but Jung must inherit the lot. As you see, my politics follow this aim unremittingly" (F/Bin, p. 64). And to Jung: "The choice of one's successor is one of the royal prerogatives. Let us allow our royal science the same privilege" (F/Jun, p. 481).

deviate too far from me when you are really so close to me, for if you do, we may one day be played off against one another" (F/Jun, p. 18).

Freudians and Jungians

In the wake of their founding fathers, both Freudians and Jungians upheld the split, at least officially, although there were a few exceptions to this rule, and in the last decades there have been signs for a rapprochement on various levels.[22] One did not find the (later) works of Jung and his followers on the reading lists for psychoanalytic trainees, or on the shelves of the libraries of their institutes, and vice versa. When Edward Glover suggested to Ernest Jones, for instance, "that every candidate should be instructed in the systems propounded by the then most important psycho-analytical schismatics, Jung, Adler and Rank", Jones "rejected it with the brief comment, 'Why waste their time?'" (Glover, 1950, p. 7). In the literature, the works of the respective opposing camp were usually completely ignored, or, if they were mentioned at all, then only to be dismissed. This tradition partly continues to this day. To give you just one recent example: In her book, *Extraordinary Knowing* (2007), the late psychoanalyst Elizabeth Lloyd Mayer gave a fascinating account and overview of the research on parapsychological phenomena. She also quoted at length Freud's and Ferenczi's forays into the field, but failed completely to refer to Jung's numerous and influential contributions. It seems, in fact, that she was not even aware of them. Such is the power of suppression of the former partner in what was perhaps the most powerful tandem in the history of psychology.

I know much less about the development of the Jungian movement than about the Freudian one. Still, I think it is undeniable that there are some interesting differences. One obvious difference between the

---

[22] Kirsch notes that, on part of the Jungians, there were two exceptions to the prevailing strong anti-Freudian sentiment, namely, the groups in San Francisco and London, "where the early Jungians and Freudians were on collegial terms". Still, even "where good personal relations existed, on the institutional level the Jungians continued to be ignored or criticized by the Freudian establishment and its followers." Today, "in many Jungian centers in Switzerland, Germany, England, and the United States, we see a movement towards *rapprochement* with newer developments in psychoanalysis"—such as in the so-called "developmental school"—although there is also a counter-movement towards an "exclusive reading of Jung and certain close followers", and an emphasis on "classical", "archetypal" Jungian analysis (Kirsch, 2000, pp. 237, 245–246, 252).

two movements lies in the number of their members. In the beginnings, the numbers of Jungians can only be estimated, as there were no official organisation and no membership lists. Estimates vary, however. Thomas Kirsch wrote me: "If I were to guess I would say that there were 30 people who would have qualified as Jungian analysts in the decade of 1910–1920. Maybe up to 50 by 1930, and by 1940 maybe 75. … In 1958 at the time of the first Congress of the IAAP in Zurich there were approximately 125 analysts at the Congress."[23] Sonu Shamdasani commented that one would also have to take into account those whom Michael Fordham called "para Jungians", who were then "disenfranchised", so that "the movement actually shrunk from a wider and more eclectic network."[24]

Still, it seems safe to assume that at any given period the Freudians by far outnumbered the Jungians. The International Psychoanalytic Association (IPA) had about 200 active members in 1920 (not counting associate members), some 400 in 1935, and already 560 in 1938.[25] Today, the current number of IPA members is around 12,000,[26] while "there are approximately 3,000 members of the I[nternational] A[ssociation for] A[nalytical] P[sychology]".[27] Thus, if we take the membership numbers of their two biggest and most prestigious international organisations as an indicator, there are still four times as many psychoanalysts as Jungian analysts. In fact, the discrepancy is considerably greater, since there is a much greater number of psychoanalytic organisations besides the IPA than there is of Jungian organisations outside the IAAP—for the United States alone, there are estimates that about 10,000 persons call themselves psychoanalysts. This prosaic fact has also had considerable consequences for the group dynamics in the various local centres. Evidently, the dynamics in a group of a handful of people in a given city differ from those in a group of fifty or one hundred.

---

[23] Email of 24 March 2010.

[24] Email of 18 June 2010.

[25] These numbers are based on the membership lists in the *Korrespondenzblatt* of the *Internationale Zeitschrift für Psychoanalyse*. For the year 1935, there exists a roster listing the members worldwide (LC). The number 560 for 1938 was mentioned by Ernest Jones in his presidential address at the IPA congress (Jones, 1938).

[26] Anikó Solti, Membership Secretary of the IPA, confirmed in an email of 24 March 2010 that the number as of that date was 12,086.

[27] Email from Hester Solomon, President of the IAAP, of 26 March 2010.

This quantitative factor may also have played a role in another difference. Although of course Freud maintained an influence on the development of psychoanalysis for as long as he lived, both overtly and covertly (through the members of the so-called Secret Committee), the movement rapidly became more and more decentralised. If we take (a bit arbitrarily) the publication of *The Interpretation of Dreams* (Freud, 1900a) as the birth of psychoanalysis proper, it was only some ten years later that the International Psycho-Analytical Association was founded, and only twenty years later that the first regular training institute was established in Berlin, whose basic curriculum and 'tripartite' structure of training (training analysis, seminars, and supervision or so-called control analysis) became the model followed by the rapidly growing number of such institutes around the world. Within only two decades, the psychoanalysts had developed a teaching, training, and accreditation system that functioned more or less independently of Freud.

As George Makari has shown, this led, relatively early and still during Freud's lifetime, to the development of pluralistic psychoanalytic schools of "partial Freudians" (2008, p. 296). Contrary to popular belief, the grip that Freud had on the psychoanalytic movement was comparatively weak. After the early splits involving Alfred Adler, Wilhelm Stekel, Eugen Bleuler, and C. G. Jung, various theoretical and practical modifications were introduced in numerous centres around the world, sometimes even against Freud's express wishes, leading to the existence of local schools, many of which, however, stayed within the IPA.[28] Let us just think of Sándor Ferenczi in Budapest, the Anna Freud/Melanie Klein controversies in London, Franz Alexander in Chicago, Karen Horney and Erich Fromm in New York City, Sándor Radó at Columbia University, Jacques Lacan in Paris, the influence of Otto Rank on the landscape of psychotherapy and social work in the United States, and so on, not to mention later developments, which led the then president of the IPA, Robert Wallerstein, to ask in 1988 if there is not one psychoanalysis, but many (Wallerstein, 1988).

The development of organised analytical psychology remained for a long time very much focused on Jung himself. Local societies,

---

[28] Paul Roazen noted that Freud "set out to found a variety of training centers that were designed to be independent, at least to some degree, of his own personal direction" (1995, p. 259).

such as the medical society of analytical psychologists in London, "adopted the Feudal structure: a Jungian was someone recognised and anointed by Jung" (Shamdasani, 2000). Only relatively late did the training and accreditation system become more independent of Jung. "This shift ... occurred ... with the founding of the SAP in 1945 with its training programme, and also with the formal training programme at the Jung Institute in Zurich."[29] Finally, with the founding of the IAAP in 1955 there existed an international body that oversaw training guidelines and an accreditation system (Kirsch, 2000, p. 17).

Training centres for analytical psychology were each founded by "a person or persons who had analyzed with Jung and/or one of his assistants" (ibid., p. 245). This constitutes another difference to psychoanalytic societies, many of which were actually founded by analysts who had had no personal analysis *lege artis* at all, at least at the time; for example, Karl Abraham in Berlin, Ernest Jones in London, Sándor Ferenczi in Budapest, Abraham Brill in New York, James Jackson Putnam in Boston, or, ironically enough, C. G. Jung in Zurich—not to mention Sigmund Freud in Vienna.

How did Jung disseminate his ideas? Apart from his published works, one way he chose was by public statements and presentations. From Freud we know that he gave but one single public talk in his lifetime (on "Creative writers and day-dreaming" (1908e), in Hugo Heller's salon in Vienna, before an audience of ninety[30]). Of course, Freud often spoke on various occasions, as in his courses and lectures at the university, in talks before the Jewish lodge B'nai B'rith, in the Vienna Psychoanalytic Society, or at the psychoanalytic congresses, but these were not accessible to the general public. Toward the public, Freud was very much withdrawn. He profoundly mistrusted journalists and the media in general, and relied on his own written and printed words. Jung, on the other hand, was quite comfortable in giving interviews for newspapers, journals, radio, and TV, he gave public talks, university lectures,

---

[29] Email of Sonu Shamdasani of 18 June 2010.

[30] And even this talk was not truly public, since only invited guests could attend (Tichy & Zwettler-Otte, 1999, pp. 114–115).—Among the listeners were the German writer, bon-vivant and bohemian Oscar A. H. Schmitz and the famous writer Stefan Zweig, who are said to have gone to a brothel together after Freud's talk ...

held seminars, and enjoyed talking to opinion leaders and politicians. In fact, "Jung could never, or only when he was physically weakened, resist whenever a journalist asked him to give an interview" (Jaffé, 1968, p. 132; my trans.).

Another medium through which Jung taught and explained his ideas was his vast correspondence, a large part of which was occupied with precisely that, creating and maintaining a large network by correspondence. In his letters, Freud often did advise his early followers how to conduct their work. In their clinical practice, practically all of these pioneers experimented and often ran into difficulties with their patients. Many of them wrote to Freud for advice. Psychoanalytic supervision actually begins with Freud's professional correspondence of that period, which is to a considerable extent supervision by mail. But Freud did not, or only very rarely, teach, explain, or expand upon his theoretical concepts in those letters. He rather referred the questioners to his written work. In Jung we find a rather contradictory attitude, however, since on the one hand he openly stated that "it was [his] intention to write in such a way that fools get scared and only true scholars and seekers can enjoy its reading" (letter to Wilfred Lay of 20 April 1946; in Shamdasani, 2000). On the other hand, a large part of his correspondence (particularly in his later years) was occupied with trying to explain himself and his theories, and to correct misconceptions about them.

Another peculiarity of Jung's teaching method were his seminars, usually given to participants of whose attendance he personally had to approve. There is no doubt about the value and significance of these seminars among Jung's work. As McGuire notes, these "lively, erudite, and probably rapid-fire sessions" form "[t]he most considerable body of 'Jung speaking'" (McGuire & Hull, 1977, p. xvii). They are "an important feature of his working methodology" (McGuire, 1982, p. 14).

> The Seminar Notes have a substantive importance in the Jungian canon ... [They] are rich in material that is not to be found, or is only hinted at, in the published writings. For Jung they were germinative: he was often evolving ideas as he talked. ... Altogether, the seminars give us a Jung who was self-confidently relaxed, incautious and undiplomatic, disrespectful of institutions and exalted personages, often humorous, even ribald, extravagantly learned in reference and allusion, attuned always to the most subtle

resonances of the case in hand, and true always to himself and his vocation. (McGuire, in Jung, 1984, pp. xv–xvi)

A further characteristic of the organisation of analytical psychology were the so-called Psychological Clubs, meeting places for analysed people and venues for various talks, originally conceptualised as a kind of experimental ground, where likewise oriented people could experiment with and apply what they had learned in their analyses (cf. Shamdasani, 1998)—a concept that has no counterpart in the psychoanalytic tradition.

However, as Shamdasani argues (2000), the later institutional developments did not organically grow out of these structures, but broke with them, and in fact imposed the psychoanalytic model of the future analyst's training, as developed by the Berlin Psychoanalytic Institute in 1920, "as the template of Jungian trainings worldwide". The first place this happened was in London. Still according to Shamdasani, this then critically changed what the whole discipline was, and ultimately reorientated it toward psychoanalysis and led, together with the adoption of the legend that Jung was a disciple of Freud's, and hence his theory an offshoot of psychoanalysis, to "the colonisation of analytical psychology by psychoanalysis".

Conclusion

Freud and Jung, Freudians and Jungians—I am afraid it has been impossible to give more than a few glimpses of the differences and correspondences, of the often subliminal exchanges between the two men and their respective adherents, and of the further development of both movements. Coming to the field of Jung studies as a Freud scholar, in studying Jung I have been increasingly impressed by how crucially different his theories are from those of Freud. I think that many people who see the Freudian and Jungian systems as just two variants of basically the same orientation, and in analytical psychology a further development of psychoanalysis (be it, in their view, in the 'right' or 'wrong' direction), have been disregarding the fact that Jung had a radically different concept of the unconscious. Because at first glance this seems to be their common ground: both were eminent psychologists of the so-called unconscious, so it seems perfectly sensible to see Jung, the younger of the two, as following in Freud's footsteps, especially if one adopts the idea, or rather legend, that Freud was the 'discoverer' of *the* unconscious.

Yet the most devastating criticism voiced against Jung from the Freudians, from the beginning, was probably not that he did not accept the theory of the sexual etiology of the neuroses or the drive theory in general—in fact, that is a criticism which was also voiced by many later psychoanalysts—but that he, as Ferenczi wrote to Freud already in 1912, "doesn't know the unconscious!" (F/Fer I, p. 415). Or, as Glover stated it (1950, pp. 171, 173):

> Jung cannot understand the difference between conscious and unconscious mental activity ... Jung's spiritual home is in the conscious psychology of the pre-Freudian epoch ... he seeks to get rid of those embarrassing manifestations of unconscious function which call for explanation in terms of individual development by projecting them into an alleged Collective "Unconscious".

That seems to be precisely the question: Did Jung mistakenly explain certain psychical phenomena as manifestations, not of personal unconscious conflicts, but of an impersonal, 'collective' entity, or did Freud mistakenly overlook or downplay the fact that certain experiences, often deeply disturbing and dangerous, cannot be explained by the psychology of the individual, but must be seen as messages from something infinitely greater than the psychology of the individual and his personal development? Was Jung a deeply disturbed person,[31] who escaped a psychosis only by a hair's breadth by turning his personal psychopathology into a pseudo-scientific psychological system, or was he a seer, a prophet even, who finally understood that his profoundly disturbing visions, dreams, and experiences were not the signs of a psychotic disposition, but messages from a trans-individual, collective sphere that even predicted world events? That he escaped a potentially psychotic outcome precisely because he *correctly* saw that he was dealing with something completely different?

---

[31] Even prominent Jungians diagnose him as a *"borderline personality"* (Spillmann & Strubel, 2010, p. 127). [Addition] Recently, Jung scholar Paul Bishop called him a "borderline psychotic" (2014, p. 77).

I confess I see no way of reconciling these two views (not even by drawing a mandala …). So it would be only natural to ask: So, then, who was right? Freud or Jung? Many people like to go for simple alternatives. They like to be all for or all against things. If this is really the case, I am afraid I will now disappoint those by not answering that question.[32] I rather suspect that, as in all matters human, arriving at such an impasse is rather due to a question that makes only two mutually exclusive answers possible. The implicit suggestion in such a question is that either Jung or Freud was right, and the other wrong; in other words, that one of them found out the Truth with a capital T. This is the stuff of religions and revelations, not of science. As Jung once said in an interview, after he had been asked whether he believed in God: "I don't need to believe. I know" (in McGuire & Hull, 1977, p. 428). As to all of us who do not "know" the ultimate truth in the psychological study of the human mind, however, let us be content to continue our studies and be grateful to those great minds who lighted a candle in a sea of darkness.

---

[32] [Addition] I have chosen the concluding phrases as they appeared in the French translation of this article.

PART V

TWO OUTSTANDING FOLLOWERS:
SÁNDOR FERENCZI AND
KARL ABRAHAM

CHAPTER ELEVEN

Dreaming of Freud: Ferenczi, Freud, and an analysis without end

I wonder if you don't also have a secret reason for sharing this analysis of your dream with me, and I think I have really found it. The dream must also have a relation to me.

—Freud, F/Fer I, pp. 122–123

On the day after the death of his idolized and adored father ..., he could not resist the temptation to get hold of a little flask of ether used as a drug to animate the dying father. He locked himself in a secluded place, and lit the ether, by which he could easily have caused a great fire, being perfectly aware of the blasphemous and forbidden nature of his action. He still remembered the nearly audible beating of the heart, provoked by the horrible deed. The reaction was contrition and the vow to preserve the memory of the father by thinking of him every day, at least once, for the rest of his life.

—Ferenczi, 1928[283a], pp. 419–420[1]

---

[1]The article from which this quotation is taken, "Psychoanalyse und Kriminologie", has not yet been translated into English or French. As far as I know, I was the first to draw attention to its significance (Falzeder, 1986).

With these words, Ferenczi described a fragment of the training analysis of an anonymous Dr. X, known for his "particularly irreproachable character", for whom this "reproduction" had a "shocking" effect (ibid.). In fact, however, this is a direct record—the only one surviving, it seems—of his own analysis with Freud. He goes on saying (ibid.):

> In the further course of analysis, the still deeper instinctual basis of this traumatic breakthrough could be securely reconstructed in the events of the oedipal conflict. So it was the undying rivalry with the father that was, in final analysis, the motive for lighting the fire of triumph on his death. Thus we see that ... the very refined, indeed overrighteous character was established as compensation, even overcompensation of the infantile instinctual basis. I don't want to keep it secret any longer that this Dr. X is indeed myself, and that I have no doubt that, under unfavorable circumstances, a blasphemous incendiary easily could have developed behind the character traits I so much treasured. Fate was kind enough to content itself with letting me become a psychoanalyst. How much of this development is successful sublimation, I leave to your decision.

A similar statement is found in Ferenczi's letter to Freud of 22 February 1915, after the first period of analysis: "It was no small thing to tame the murderous, incendiary, and (as we now see) eternally restless devil in me and also to conceal him so deeply from myself that I was able to consider myself a peace-loving man of science" (F/Fer II, p. 50). There is no doubt that this episode is of great relevance for Ferenczi's relationship with Freud, including, of course, the very analysis in which its memory occurred.

Ferenczi had three *tranches* of analysis with Freud during the First World War: the first started on 1 October 1914, and lasted for three and a half weeks; the second was from 14 June to 5 July 1916; and the third and last period was between 29 September and 13 October 1916. The circumstances, the substantial points, and the later repercussions of this analysis have been described by Judith Dupont (1993). The present paper attempts to add a more microscopic view by taking the *via regia* to the unconscious, focusing on one particular dream dreamed shortly before the beginning of the analysis.[2]

---

[2]While we do not know the dreams recounted and interpreted in the analysis, we do have more than a dozen dreams from the period prior, between, and after the fractions of

A bloody operation

After Ferenczi had been considering the idea of an analysis with Freud for a long time, this had become a likely possibility in early September 1914. But Ferenczi did not yet know whether Freud would accept him as an analysand when he sent him, on 8 September, a dream that can be called the initial, or rather *initiating* dream of the analysis, the dream of the occlusive pessary:

> *I stuff an occlusive pessary into my urethra. I am alarmed as I do so lest it might slip into the bladder from which it could only be removed by shedding blood. I try, therefore, to hold it steady in the perineal region from outside and to force it back or to press it outwards along the urethra. ...* Here it struck him [the dreamer] that in a dream fragment preceding this dream *the pessary was stuffed into his rectum.* Supplement: *in the dream I was aware that the elastic thing would spread itself in the bladder and then it would be impossible to get it out again [...]*
>
> [added later:] I remember clearly now that *the pessary was too wide for the rectum and threatened to fall out; for the urethra, however, it was too narrow.* (Ferenczi, 1915[160], pp. 304–305, 308)

The account of this dream was part of a manuscript written for publication in the *Internationale Zeitschrift für ärztliche Psychoanalyse*, in which it was presented as a "patient's" dream, and its interpretation as direct speech between this anonymous patient and his analyst, allegedly Ferenczi himself. In the letter accompanying the manuscript, Ferenczi told Freud (F/Fer II, pp. 17–18):

> I don't need to tell you beforehand that it comes from my self-analysis and that I restructured it only after the fact in the form of a dialogue. You will also recognise yourself in it—in the person of the doctor who doesn't want to analyze me. I have rendered all the essentials word for word as they came to me.

---

analysis that Ferenczi either wrote up for Freud in their correspondence, or published as "patients'" dreams (Ferenczi, 1916[188], 1917[193])—in both cases with his free associations and interpretations. In addition, there is the above quoted memory that surfaced during the analysis proper. This paper could be a step toward reconstructing the analysis of a leading psychoanalytic pioneer from 'within' or, in other words, psychoanalytically.

Ferenczi's paper can be divided into four parts: (1) the dream text, (2) the dreamer's associations about the elements of the dream, interspersed by the analyst's remarks, (3) a summarising interpretation by the analyst, and (4) a dialogue between analyst and analysand about their relationship.

The associations lead from the events of the previous night—Ferenczi's sexual intercourse with his lover Gizella Pálos, who used an occlusive pessary—to thoughts about identifying with the woman, to the stuffing of small objects into his nose and ears as a child, to tapeworms and echinococci, to the danger of venereal infection, to pregnancy, to self-impregnation, to the prolapse of vagina and uterus in Gizella, interfering with the sexual enjoyment of both partners, to childbirth, to the fear and the wish of Gizella becoming pregnant, to thoughts of Gizella's daughter Elma, with whom he might have had children and who was presented to him as a bride the day before, to memories of his own strict mother, whom he might want to show how a child should be treated properly, that is, seriously and affectionately, to infantile autoerotic pleasures from micturition and defecation, to the infantile sexual theory of birth through the rectum, to his difficult relationship with Gizella's brothers, who made him feel like an intruder and a coward, to his envying two boyhood friends for the size of their penises and his fright at the size of his father's penis.

These ideas revolve around sexuality and complicated emotions related to it—gender identity, infantile notions of sexuality, pregnancy, feelings of inferiority, the relationship to the mother, by whom Ferenczi did not feel understood, difficult relationships with men, towards whom Ferenczi feels like an intruder and a coward ... In contemporary perspective, all these ideas and feelings point to roots in early object relations, which have led to an insecurity about one's own body and to difficulties in relating to other people.

The analyst's summarising interpretation of this "bloody operation" (Ferenczi, 1915[160], p. 306) is, however, according to the theory of the 1910s, in the language of libido theory and drive psychology. The analyst reminds the analysand of his being troubled by the disproportion between the "too wide" genitals of his mother and his own little penis, his examination of the "too narrow" genitals of little girls, of the ensuing failure in the choice of an object and of his "regression" to masturbation. Stimulated by the experiences with "both the woman [Gizella] with the too wide and the bride [Elma] with the too narrow vagina" the day before, "in the dream *you make yourself into the pessary child"*, the alleged analyst interprets (ibid., p. 309).

Then a (fictitious) dialogue about transference sets in (ibid., pp. 309–310):

> [Analyst:] Now I must, however, return to the fact that at the beginning of the hour you declared the dream to be "nonsense" ... It is an ascertained rule of dream interpretation ... that mockery and scorn are concealed behind such nonsense dreams.
>
> [Analysand:] My next ideas concern you, doctor, though I cannot just at once see the connection. I remember that yesterday you suggested to me that presently I should not require your services any longer, and that I could now manage quite alone. This, however, really only caused me regret, as I did not yet feel myself so far recovered as to be able to do without your assistance.
>
> Now I understand. You mock at me by showing by the unskilful introduction of the pessary how wrong it is to leave you alone and to consider you capable from now on of being your own doctor. You may be partly right; on the other hand, the repeatedly confirmed transference to me that makes breaking off the analysis difficult for you shows itself in your dislike of my remarks. This tendency lets you under-estimate your own capabilities and exaggerates my importance and assistance. The child that you were making for yourself would therefore also be your own self-analysis.
>
> I have ... repeatedly tried to analyse myself. ... My thoughts flow into the immeasurable, I cannot collect them properly, I find no clue to the tangle. On the contrary I often marvel at the skill with which you can reduce to order what seems so disconnected.
>
> ... It is ... no accident that you demonstrate your incapability just on the genitals and the procreation of children; ... we have often confirmed how despondent you were as a child, dispirited by the imposing size of your father and especially by his wealth of children. For a long time you believed you could achieve nothing to the purpose without his support ... A few of your earlier dreams, too, on analysis, contained clear allusions to a certain degree of femininity in your attitude towards your father. Since then, however, I have taken the place of father for you. You like the part of patient and dread to be thrown back on yourself and to undertake the entire responsibility for your further destiny.

The concluding remarks by the 'analyst' underline how well the 'analysand's' "capacity for dreaming" succeeded in transforming the most unpleasant thoughts into a wish-fulfilment—that is, in confirming Freud's theory.

Who is the analyst?

Ferenczi's article is a masterpiece of ambivalence, meta-discourse, and hidden messages. Ferenczi enacted a number of powerful, partly contradictory tendencies in various sceneries, including the dream itself, its self-analytic interpretation, the writing of an article, sending it to Freud, and choosing a specific time and place for its publication; all this happening before the background of an intense and complicated imbroglio of relationships (mainly between Freud, Ferenczi, Gizella, Elma, and Géza Pálos) and the prospect of an analysis between Freud and Ferenczi in the near future.

The situation can be compared to a *theatre play*. The figures do not exist in real life, but their roles stem from the personal experience of the author. There is a 'message', which the author wishes to convey. There are actors, dialogues, indications of place and time, and there are spectators: the readers of the *Zeitschrift*. Ironically, the crucial information is withheld from these spectators, and reserved for a second, special 'public'—Freud. A further complication arises from the fact that this second public, for whom the play was written in order to seduce him, is staged as the leading role of the play.

What is the underlying rationale of Ferenczi's strategy, and what are his motives? Depending on where the spotlight of the investigation is directed, the shape of the whole structure changes. Who, for example, is the analyst in this piece? It is Freud, isn't it? Or at least Freud as Ferenczi wanted or imagined him to be in the article. Or the Freud to whom Ferenczi sent the paper, enticing him to become his analyst in reality. In fact, the article can itself be seen as a wish-fulfilment, staging the longed-for analysis as *fait accompli*, putting Freud into the place of the analyst. This is also confirmed by Ferenczi's remark to Freud that the latter would recognise himself in the article, in the person of the doctor. But strangely enough, this analyst "does not want to analyse" the patient and is about to *terminate* the analysis—an analysis that, we recall, had not yet begun in reality … Actually, Freud as a real person does not appear at all. Although he is impersonated in the analyst, the reader is to believe that the analyst is Ferenczi himself. And the reader is right, because, after all, what he reads are not Freud's thoughts put into the mouth of Ferenczi, but Ferenczi's own thoughts (using some statements Freud had made to him), meant to describe Freud as analyst, while naming him Ferenczi.

In self-analysis, Ferenczi had split himself into an analysed and an analysing part, while attributing, in his comment to Freud, the first to himself and the second to Freud, and, in the article, the first to an anonymous patient and the second to himself. So, on different levels, Ferenczi can be either an anonymous patient (analysed by Ferenczi, or by Freud), or a patient named Ferenczi (analysed by himself, or by Freud), or an analyst named Ferenczi (analysing himself, or an anonymous patient), or an analyst named Freud (analysing an anonymous patient, or Ferenczi).

All this, again, was put on the stage in self-analysis. The difficulty with self-analysis, as the joke implies, is the countertransference—but also *transference*, as we have to add in this case. Ferenczi's thoughts were preoccupied with Freud; the person who had "taken the place of father" for him (ibid., p. 310) absorbed his thoughts nearly "every day, at least once, for the rest of his life" (Ferenczi, 1928[283a], p. 420)—and also his dreams at night. Ferenczi's dream and dream-analysis are not only a message to Freud, but they also solicit the question: Who is the analyst in Ferenczi's *self-analysis*? Ferenczi's difficulties in analysing himself can be seen as a result of the fact that, at that time, he could hardly express himself and see himself other than *in* Freud's terms and *on* Freud's terms. The analysing part in Ferenczi's self-analysis was more an introjected Freud than Ferenczi's own voice. And even the analysed part, the dream, bears distinct features of Freud. Not only is its very 'language' Freudian, but its whole structure and contents closely resemble a part of one of Freud's own dreams:

> Old Brücke must have set me some task; *strangely enough*, it related to a dissection of the lower part of my own body, my pelvis and legs, which I see before me as though in the dissecting-room, but without noticing their absence in myself and also without a trace of any gruesome feeling. ... The pelvis had been eviscerated, and it was visible now in its superior, now in its inferior, aspect, the two being mixed together. Thick flesh-coloured protuberances ...

could be seen. Something which lay over it and was like crumpled silver-paper had also to be carefully fished out. (Freud, 1900a, p. 452)

Freud interpreted (ibid., pp. 453–454):

> I reflected on the amount of self-discipline it was costing me to offer the public ... my book upon dreams—I should have to give away so much of my own private character in it. ... The task which was imposed on me in the dream of carrying out a dissection *of my own body* was thus my *self-analysis* which was linked up with my giving an account of my dreams. Old Brücke came in here appropriately; even in the first years of my scientific work it happened that I allowed a discovery of mine to lie fallow until an energetic remonstrance on his part drove me into publishing it.

In both Ferenczi's and Freud's dreams, there is an operation, performed by the dreamer on the lower part of his own body, in both cases the associations link this operation with self-analysis, resulting in a publication.[3] We can only speculate, but Ferenczi, who knew every sentence of *The Interpretation of Dreams*, could well have (unconsciously) modelled his dream after Freud's.

Analysis interminable

Ferenczi's extreme preoccupation with Freud might look unusual, but such a preoccupation is common in a particular situation: in psychoanalysis—where, in Freud's words, "all the symptoms of the illness" are given "a new transference meaning", and the "ordinary neurosis" is replaced "by a 'transference-neurosis'" (1914g, p. 154). Ferenczi had evidently developed a full-blown transference neurosis already *before* the analysis.

---

[3]There is, however, an interesting difference. In contrast to Ferenczi's dream, Freud's depicts a literally *split* body, the dissecting (analysing) and the dissected (analysed) parts being separated, and this "without noticing their absence in myself and also without a trace of any gruesome feeling."

Freud's position was difficult for many reasons. He had contributed to this situation by constantly blurring the borders between the professional and the private spheres in his relationship with Ferenczi; he had not yet fully developed the tools to handle this, having conceived the notion of transference-neurosis only a few weeks before he took Ferenczi in analysis; also, he had at least two personal agendas in this analysis: to convince Ferenczi that he should marry Gizella, not Elma, and to not lose Ferenczi as a 'son', a stalwart defender and promoter of the Cause and of himself. But then, Freud *knew* all this. With good reason, he had previously declined to analyse Ferenczi several times, writing, for instance (F/Fer I, pp. 481–482):

> If I could be of use to you, then everything else would take precedence over that. But I know that four or six weeks of analysis would be much too insufficient. For that reason something else comes into consideration, namely, my dearth of inclination to expose one of my indispensable helpers to the danger of personal estrangement brought about by the analysis. I don't yet know how Jones will bear finding out that his wife, as a consequence of the analysis, no longer wants to remain his wife.

With the last sentence, Freud all but predicted Ferenczi's lifelong grudge against him because of Freud's preference for Gizella over Elma as Ferenczi's wife. So why, despite his suspicions, did Freud analyse Ferenczi?

I think what we witness in this case and in other, similar ones, is simply a Freud who is *uncertain*, who sometimes is not able to cope with what he himself had conjured up, who struggles with further developing his own therapeutical instruments, and who, inevitably, makes the kind of mistakes his psychical structure leads him to make. At that time, the number of his patients dwindled, and he might have felt personally challenged and intellectually tempted to analyse such an interesting, brilliant, and complicated person, and to further develop psychoanalytic theory and practice with the help of such a case. He also liked Ferenczi very much, wanted to help him, and tried to convince him of what he, Freud, thought would be best for Ferenczi. Being, "by his own admission, of a narcissistic nature" (*Diary*, p. 62), he "needed Ferenczi to be in a very precise place" (Dupont, 1993, p. 318), and "would gladly have left it to [Ferenczi's] self-analysis to take care of that" (F/Fer III,

p. 386). He felt himself entitled to violate nearly all the rules he had just set up for "beginners" (Blanton, 1971, p. 48) in his technical papers, but he underestimated the effects and overestimated his ability to control the ensuing situation: an analysis that continued to be "at an end", but not "terminated" (F/Fer II, p. 149)—or terminated, but without end. It is not without irony and deeper significance that Freud called the essay, in which he discussed Ferenczi's analysis with him, "Analysis terminable and interminable" (1937c).

According to one's theoretical predilections, there are several ways to portray the outcome. Whether Freud remained, in Lacan's words, "'the subject who is supposed to know' what the analysand does not know" (Roustang, 1976, p. 18), whether the representation of him in Ferenczi remained to be a hardly digested "introject", whether he persisted to be Ferenczi's idealised father imago that could not be subjected to "transmuting internalization" (Kohut, 1971), whether the transference neurosis could not be dissolved,[4] or whether, in Ferenczi's own words, Freud represented a "super-ego *intropression*" (1939[308], p. 279), being "too big for [him], too much of a father" (Ferenczi & Groddeck, 1982/2006, p. 53)—until the end of his life Ferenczi struggled with Freud.

> I was brave (and productive) only as long as I (unconsciously) relied for support on another power … Is the only possibility for my continued existence the renunciation of the largest part of one's own self, in order to carry out the will of that higher power to the end (as though it were my own)? … Is the choice here one between dying and "rearranging myself"—and this at the age of fifty-nine? On the other hand, is it worth it always to live the life (will) of another person—is such a life not almost death? (*Diary*, p. 212)

A bloody operation indeed …

Ferenczi had gone a long way to come back to his central conflicts. But let us not forget that, along this way, he had been able to create theoretical insights out of personal suffering, concepts that have been influencing psychoanalysis up to the present day, making "all analysts into his pupils" (Freud, 1933c, p. 228). His difficulties do not devalue

---

[4]While it is questionable whether a transference neurosis is ever dissolved completely, in Ferenczi's case it seems to have persisted to an unusually large degree.

his ideas, but rather help to explain their background and context of discovery. Psychoanalytic technique, our view and use of transference, countertransference and of nonverbal interactions, object relations theory, self psychology, developmental psychology, theory and treatment of child abuse—these are some of the fields to which Ferenczi made substantial contributions. While we are beginning to acknowledge our debt to their creator, it could be "a lesson in humility for all analysts" (Dupont, 1993, p. 319) to witness their painful origins.

CHAPTER TWELVE

The significance of Ferenczi's clinical contributions for working with psychotic patients

In my work with psychotic and severely traumatised persons I have always felt, though somewhat vaguely, that I stand in Ferenczi's tradition. But what exactly is this tradition? It surely cannot mean to follow Ferenczi in all his experimentations, from the association experiment to hypnosis and suggestion, from "classical" analysis to active therapy, from "neo-catharsis" to that final, desperate experiment, mutual analysis. And in all likelihood it is more than just a general attitude: to be humane, authentic, attentive, respectful of the other, aware of one's own shortcomings, and open to modifications. Although Ferenczi was probably the first among psychoanalysts to recognise and explicitly stress this *sine qua non* of psychotherapy, he was certainly not the last. There is more to "Clinical Ferenczi". What, then, is specific to Ferenczi's practice, which conclusions did he draw from it for a psychoanalytic technique, and how can all this be of significance even today?

The early psychoanalysts showed a peculiar inconsequence towards technique. On the one hand, they called for complete honesty and public discussion in matters of technique when *others* were concerned, on the other hand practically none of them wrote about what they actually did in their *own* practice.[1]

We know that Freud abandoned his project to write a general methodology of psychoanalysis, and we also know that he violated all the very recommendations he had laid down for "beginners" (Blanton, 1971, p. 48) in his own practice. But this he did not publish. In fact, when it came to the really hot topics, he forbade public discussion, as in the cases of thought transference and countertransference.

There was, however, an unwritten law to practice 'correct' analysis, even if nobody knew what that really was. Indeed, the standard argument used against the dissenting crown princes, from C. G. Jung to Otto Rank, and, finally, also Sándor Ferenczi, was that they did not practice this correct analysis, but some other, somehow deviating method, while refusing to reveal it. The insinuation was that only (wrong) changes in technique could be responsible for their (wrong) changes in theory, and there were all kinds of "rumors" about their technique (F/Fer III, p. 207).

In these cases, Freud suddenly called for complete transparency. Regarding Jung: "I cannot allow that a psycho-analytic technique has any right to claim the protection of medical discretion" (Freud, 1914d, p. 64). About Rank: "he has practiced secretiveness ... and wouldn't tell anyone ... what he does in technique" (F/Fer III, p. 175). And he admonished Ferenczi: "What one does in the way of technique one must also represent publicly" (ibid., p. 422).

The field was open for *espionage*. Already in 1912, when Alfred Winterstein went to Zurich, Freud asked him "to keep an eye on some prominent persons of the local group there and to report to him about them" (Winterstein memoirs; LC). Probably to this end, Winterstein had "a short training analysis ... with *Jung*" (ibid.). Freud also used an anonymous patient's report in his "History of the psycho-analytical movement" (Freud, 1914d, pp. 63–64) to criticise Jung's technique (in fact, the report came from Oskar Pfister). Freud questioned Frau Hirschfeld, at times his, Jung's, and Pfister's patient, to get information about Jung's and Pfister's technique, and to promptly criticise them for it.

---

[1] Not only was "technique" something secretive among psychoanalysts themselves, Freud also gave Ferenczi "the advice not to let patients learn about the technique" (*Diary*, p. 185). Cf. Leitner, 2001.

One of Rank's former analysands "was questioned in Berlin by various colleagues ... about the manner of his analysis with [Rank], that is to say, [his] technique" (*Rundbriefe IV*, p. 149), after which Rank refused to refer any more patients to Berlin. Ferenczi also tried to find out about the way Rank practiced: "I have been treating a patient whom Rank analyzed in America, so that I was now able to catch glimpses of his technique. The impression that I received is not very favorable" (F/Fer III, p. 211). A few years later, it was Ferenczi's turn to be criticised on the basis of what one of his patients, Clara Thompson, had allegedly said in a group of other analysands, one of whom then reported to Freud ...

True, it is not possible to give an exhaustive account of what one does, and of what really happens, in one's practice. This might be an illusion anyway, and even a videotape may not faithfully record the *"Dialogues of the Unconscious"*, to use Ferenczi's expression (Ferenczi, 1915[159], p. 109; taken up again in the *Diary*, p. 84). Nor is it possible to lay down unalterable rules of treatment, cut in stone, for each and every situation in psychotherapy. But only reflecting and communicating about our respective practices can help, and has helped in the past, to establish some caveats and general guide-lines for treatment—be it for severely traumatised persons, schizophrenics, depressed people, borderline cases, or neurotics.

If, among the leading early analysts, anybody openly talked about his technique to the extent possible, it was Sándor Ferenczi.[2] And this against Freud's express wish, as Ferenczi noted in his *Clinical Diary*: "Against his will I began to deal openly with questions of technique" (p. 186). Ferenczi was not only honest and self-scrutinising in his private life and in his letters—sometimes even to the point of masochism—he also interspersed his works and congress papers with remarks about his practice (and often about his faults and errors). His papers on so-called active therapy and the subsequent relaxation method or neo-catharsis are well known. But his two most important contributions in this respect are probably *Entwicklungsziele der Psychoanalyse* (rather misleadingly translated as *The Development of Psychoanalysis*), written together with Otto Rank (1924), and his *Diary* of 1932.

---

[2]"More than anybody else, Ferenczi had always done precisely this" (Jeannet-Hasler, 2002, p. 171).

Ferenczi's third chapter of *Entwicklungsziele*, "A historical critical retrospect", is crucial.[3] Its reception at the time suffered from its polemical undercurrent. It was a hardly veiled critique of the Berliners', and especially Karl Abraham's, practice. As Ferenczi himself wrote to his friend Groddeck, it was in the service of the "politics of science", aiming at a "restauration" similar to the one Groddeck had in mind (Ferenczi & Groddeck, 1982/2006, p. 102).

I think the underlying questions to which Ferenczi tried to find an answer were: When can words be misleading? When must the analyst be more than a detached listener to and interpreter of associations? What to do with patients who are unable to analyse themselves in the presence of another person? What can we do when the word as such, when the "talking cure", fails? What can we do when the patient is unable to perceive the analyst's words as such, and when he himself is unable to verbalise, but instead "acts out", "repeats", or uses, in Ferenczi's words, "the language of gesture" (Ferenczi & Rank, 1924, p. 3)? Or, in other words: What to do when simply following the basic rule—free association, evenly hovering attention—brings no therapeutic results? Is there more to psychoanalytic technique than the basic rule?

In grappling with these questions, Ferenczi laid down, together with Otto Rank, the foundations of contemporary dynamic psychotherapy. In my opinion, the revolutionary kernel of their contribution is not what aroused most of the heat at the time: the recommendations of setting a fixed time limit for the cure in every case, and of "attributing *the chief rôle in analytic technique to repetition instead of to remembering*" (ibid., p. 4). It is rather what lies behind these mere technical advices: that psychoanalysis (or psychotherapy) is seen as "*a social process*" (ibid., p. 27; my ital.). Already the year before, Ferenczi had written to Groddeck: "In my opinion, analysis is a social phenomenon" (Ferenczi & Groddeck, 1982/2006, p. 73). This social process is seen as taking place in the present "*analytic situation*" (to which the whole second chapter of *Entwicklungsziele*, contributed by Rank, is dedicated).[4]

Before this background, Ferenczi developed *the first fragmentary methodology*, a "dos and dont's", of psychoanalysis and psychotherapy:

---

[3] Drafted by Ferenczi, then "then jointly revised" (translator's preface, in ibid.).

[4] "[T]he *setting of a date* and the analytic situation, which is *always* to be considered *without exception*, comes from Rank, and not from me" (F/Fer III, p. 121).

- Don't just listen, in "a kind of descriptive analysis".[5] Do concentrate on "the dynamic factor of experience".
- Don't collect associations, as they are merely the "rising bubbles of consciousness". Do look out for the "active affects" under the surface, and try to understand why the patient associates in a particular way.
- Don't adhere to the "fanaticism for interpreting ... in a cut and dried translation according to the dictionary", thus overestimating "isolated details". Do see that "the analytic situation of the patient ... has ... the chief meaning".
- Don't analyse symptoms, do analyse "the whole personality".
- Don't "'analyse out' one complex after the other". Do try to get "insight into deeper layers of mental life ... from the dynamic standpoint, which is the only justifiable one in practice".
- Don't analyse "elements", lured by the desire to acquire "too much knowledge". Do concentrate on "the actual analytic task" and the "actual play of forces".
- Don't "prematurely condense everything under a speculative principle", possibly due to "a dodging of uncomfortable technical difficulties".
- Don't make premature "cultural and phylogenetic analogies", or references to the future or the past. Do bear in mind that "almost all of the past, and everything that the unconscious attempts ... expresses itself in actual reactions in relation to the analyst".
- Don't just inform the patient of your conclusions or reconstruct memories. Don't teach theory. Do let your patients be convinced of the reality of the unconscious by experiences in the "analytic situation, that is, in the present". Give your "chief attention to the present reaction".
- Don't put the blame for failed analyses on the patient's "too great resistance", a too "violent transference", especially a negative one. Do concentrate on the analysis of the negative transference as "the most important task of the therapeutic activity".[6]
- Don't 'de-personalise' the relation between the analyst and the patient. Don't unnaturally eliminate "all human factors in the

---

[5] The following quotes are from Ferenczi & Rank, 1924, pp. 28 sqq.

[6] A view Ferenczi had taken over from Groddeck.

analysis", thus leading "again to a theorizing of the analytic experience".

• Don't indulge in a "narcissistic counter transference", because the "narcissism of the analyst seems suited to create a particularly fruitful source of mistakes". Do help the patient to express his criticisms of the analyst plainly or to abreact them. Do help the patient to overcome his anxiety and sense of guilt by your own self-criticism.

• Don't hold fast "to an over-rigid 'passivity'". Do confront the patient with "the pain of necessary intervention", while avoiding "wild activity". It may sometimes be helpful to take on and, to a certain extent, to really carry out "those roles which the unconscious of the patient and his tendency to flight prescribe".

In Ferenczi's view, "repetition" in psychoanalysis gets a new meaning; instead of being an obstacle to be avoided, it becomes the 'hub' of the therapy itself. Whereas "repetition" was eventually seen by Freud as an expression of the death drive, leading, in the end, to therapeutic resignation and pessimism, for Ferenczi it was *a form of communication*. Instead of being viewed as the patient's fatal resistance to the therapist's wish that he gain insight rather than repeat his follies, "repetition" is the analysand's peculiar way to communicate. A "defence mechanism" thus becomes an "exchange mechanism" (Caruso, 1972, pp. 16–17). It is then "a question of understanding also this form of communication, ... and of explaining it to the patient" (Ferenczi & Rank, 1924, pp. 3–4). Here we find today's stress on the observation and microanalysis of the interaction between patient and therapist, the participant observer, with the accompanying phantasies and desires on both sides. And here we find the importance that countertransference, positive, negative, or narcissistic, inevitably gains.

Some nine years later, Ferenczi would make this point the central one, when he laid down his experiences and reflections in his *Clinical Diary*.[7] It is about the analyst's love and hate of his patients. It is

---

[7] It seems that these were not just notes for personal use, but that Ferenczi wanted to make use of them in a future publication. He already rendered the patients' names anonymous, he inserted cross-references, and we know that some of the material and thoughts found their way into his last congress paper.

THE SIGNIFICANCE OF FERENCZI'S CLINICAL CONTRIBUTIONS

about Ferenczi's conviction that one must love one's patients, because: "Only sympathy heals" (p. 200). But it is also about his realisation, to his "enormous surprise" (p. 99), that he hated and feared some of those very patients. It is the first attempt, long before Winnicott (1949), to analyse hate in the countertransference: "*Antipathy is impotence*" (p. 131; my ital.). And it is about Ferenczi's desperate attempt to overcome this difficulty by confessing his fears and hostility to the patient in a mutual analysis.

As we all know only too well, nothing goes in the work with psychotic and/or brutally traumatised patients, if we do not succeed in establishing a modicum of basic trust in the therapeutic relationship. Ferenczi linked this fact with pathogenesis: The lasting damaging impact of the trauma is not caused by the event itself, terrible as it might have been, but by what happened before and afterwards in the relationship between perpetrator and victim. The seductive atmosphere before the trauma, and the adult's denial and hypocrisy afterwards, lead to the child's introjection of the aggressor's guilt, and a permanently split and severely impoverished emotional life. One of the consequences is that the victim develops an increased, almost uncanny, ability to unconsciously read other people's minds, particularly their hostile and passionate tendencies, but is simultaneously unable to trust his own senses and emotions. It is precisely this configuration, according to Ferenczi, that is re-enacted in what we could call a "mirror/surgeon/abstinence" analysis, which, instead of alleviating the effects of the trauma, reinforces them.

When Ferenczi's analysis with Elizabeth Severn came to a dead end, he concluded that this was due, not to the patient's too great resistance or her "un-analysability", but to "dark forces" at work in the analyst himself, above all narcissism and hate,[8] hidden behind professional hypocrisy. It was therefore crucial for the patient to get a confirmation that she did not just project those "dark forces" on to the analyst. At the time, such an attitude was revolutionary: Ferenczi observed that he had never heard any other colleague talk about these obstacles in the analyst (with the exception of his own pupils, "who have inherited from me my obsession with looking for the fault within myself"; *Diary*, p. 61).

---

[8] Whereas Freud attributed it to Ferenczi's "third puberty" (F/Fer III, p. 418).

It seems that some of Ferenczi's problems were homemade, so to speak. He started those analyses in a "classical" way, then vacillated between abstinence and tenderness, and finally forced himself to give more than he could give. For example, he encouraged Elizabeth Severn to describe her sexual phantasies about him in detail, analysed them "with interest and friendliness" (*Diary*, p. 98); then he doubled the number and extended the length of the sessions (up to three hours), went to her instead of her coming to him, gave her sessions on Sundays, and took her with him in his holidays. Little surprise, then, that this sexually traumatised woman developed fantasies about him really loving her, while simultaneously sensing strong undercurrents of antipathy and hate on Ferenczi's part.

Ferenczi's tragedy was that he had nobody with whom he could talk about all this. His analyst and supervisor—Freud—did not help, on the contrary. The same was true for his colleagues. One also wonders how his wife must have felt when he spent hours on end with his (female) patients, even in their own homes, on Sundays, and during the holidays. He was physically ill, burnt out and tired. At some point, he even arrived at the "self-diagnosis of *schizophrenia*" (*Diary*, p. 160). In the end, the person who had first called for the "hygiene of the analyst", and who had even planned to write a work about it (F/Fer III, p. 234),[9] tried to find, or had to find it, by making his own patients his analysts.

Today, I think we would all agree that mutual analysis in all seriousness cannot work. Ferenczi went too far when, for instance, as a "patient" in mutual analysis, he claimed affection, tenderness, embraces, and kisses—and got them from the pseudo-analyst. The latter, however, with precious humour showed Ferenczi his own dilemma when she asked him: "How can I become an analyst if I am so ready to comply with the wishes of my clients?" (*Diary*, p. 167). He came to see it himself: "Mutual analysis: only a last resort! Proper analysis by a stranger, without any obligation, would be better" (p. 115).

---

[9] We can only speculate why Ferenczi did not realise this plan. Did Freud warn him against it? In any case, the topic occupied Ferenczi from early on. Already in 1910, he had written to Freud: "Already before the establishment of your requirement of 'suppression of countertransference', we all did this instinctively, and this continual suppression *has to* add up to something" (F/Fer I, p. 158).

If today we know something about the general guide-lines, but above all the inherent dangers, in the treatment of extremely disturbed persons, we owe much of this knowledge to Ferenczi's pioneering work. His difficulties show us the great importance of the "hygiene" *of* the analyst, and *between* analysts. And again, they are "a lesson in humility for all analysts" (Dupont, 1993, p. 319).

CHAPTER THIRTEEN

Karl Abraham

(with Ludger M. Hermanns)

Karl Abraham was a central figure of early psychoanalysis. His clinical and theoretical contributions came soon to be considered as classics and influenced the development of psychoanalysis for decades. He followed Jung as president of the IPA and as managing editor of the *Jahrbuch*, the first psychoanalytic periodical. Not only did he contribute significant elaborations of Freud's ideas and carried them further, but he also put forth original and new views, the significance of which has been realised and acknowledged only recently, such as his ideas about the pre-oedipal "bad mother" (May, 1997, 2001), about depression, or the female sexual development—hypotheses that were then taken up and further developed, among others, by his pupil Melanie Klein (cf. Aguayo, 1997; Frank, 1999), but also left their mark in the theories of René Spitz, Bertram Lewin, Robert Fließ, and many other creative psychoanalysts. His formulations were systematic, 'exact', and precise, facilitating their being taught and learnt. "In all his works Abraham excels as a master of close observation and of the art of clinical writing. ... He provided lasting models for analytic description, and created, in our literature, the type of the short case history, perfect in its objectivity, yet also so lively" (Radó, 1926, p. 204)—making him the creator of the psychoanalytic case vignette.

He was interested in bringing psychoanalysis out of its ivory tower, and in actively establishing ties with other disciplines and institutions: sexology, academia, psychiatry, gynaecology, ethnology, comparative linguistics, the fine arts, but also with public opinion or new media, such as the movies. Together with Max Eitingon, Hanns Sachs, and Ernst Simmel he developed and implemented the so-called tripartite psychoanalytical training schedule that exists to this day and has been taken over by practically all psychodynamically oriented psychotherapeutic schools.

He never founded a school of his own, however; on the contrary, among his pupils and analysands we find such prominent and differing persons as, for example, Felix Boehm, Helene Deutsch, James and Edward Glover, Karen Horney, Melanie Klein, Carl Müller-Braunschweig, Sándor Radó, Theodor Reik, Ernst Simmel, or Alix Strachey, all of whom made original and partly highly important contributions to psychoanalysis. Under his leadership the Berlin Psychoanalytic Society developed into a lively institution that was open for new ideas.

His relationship with Freud, as it is mirrored in their correspondence, can be roughly divided into three phases. In the first phase Abraham is clearly the one who learns and receives, who is eager to absorb Freud's suggestions and ideas, and who also applies them to his own speciality, psychiatry. A second phase, beginning around his works on Giovanni Segantini (1911[30]) and on depressive and manic states (1911[26]), followed by articles on scopophilia (1913[43]), the oral phase (1916[52]), and on ejaculatio praecox (1917[54]), shows already his increasing independence and mastery of psychoanalytic theory and practice. He transcends the role of a mere pupil and enters, as a partner, into a dialogue with Freud, who himself values Abraham's opinion, co-opts him into the inner centre of power, the "Committee", and makes him interim president of the IPA after Jung's resignation.

In a third and final phase, Abraham secures an even more influential position, in theoretical as well as institutional and political terms. He presents further works on the psychoanalysis of psychoses, above all depression and mania, and his 'classical' papers on libido development (1924[105]) and character formation (1925[106]). He prevails in the conflicts with Sándor Ferenczi and Otto Rank within the Committee. With the foundation of the Berlin polyclinic, the implementation of the training guidelines, the holding of the International Psychoanalytic

Congress in Berlin, and finally his election as president of the IPA, he is at the height of his powers, a central figure of the psychoanalytic movement. Under his leadership, Berlin becomes the centre of power and training. Abraham feels secure enough to voice dissenting views, even at the risk of bringing him into conflict with Freud, as for example in the question of so-called lay analysis, where he advocates a more restrictive policy than Freud (Schröter, 1996), or in the 'film affair', in which he stands for a more liberal position (see below).

Following Ernest Jones (1926),[1] we can divide Abraham's scientific works into five thematic groups: (1) *The psychology of childhood and infantile sexuality.* His first psychoanalytic papers deal with infantile traumata, stressing "from the beginning that not the trauma itself was decisive, but the child's reaction to it" (ibid., p. 163). He then concentrated on the oral and anal phases of libido development, which he further subdivided and linked to later characterological, neurotic and psychotic disturbances (see especially 1916[52], 1924[105]). (2) *Sexuality*, particularly fetishism (1910[18]), voyeurism (1913[43]), premature ejaculation (1917[54]), and the so-called female castration complex (1920[67]). In various works he dealt with the role of sadistic impulses, phantasies, dreams, and the significance of anal erotism. (3) *Clinical* works, particularly those on the psychology of schizophrenia (1908[11]), on depression and bipolar disorders (1911[26], 1916[52], 1923[91], 1924[105]), and on obsessional neurosis (1911[24], 1912[31], 1912[32]), but also on various other topics such as hysterical dream states (1910[17]), locomotor anxiety and agoraphobia (1913[39], 1913[44]), war neuroses (1918[57]), therapeutic technique (1913[37], 1919[58], 1919[62], 1920[68]), and alcoholism (1908[12]). (4) *General topics*, above all Abraham's contribution to character research (1925[106]), which Jones calls "by far the most important work of a general nature that Abraham contributed to psychoanalysis" (Jones, 1926, p. 173). (5) Works on *applied psychoanalysis*, such as those on *Dreams and Myths* (1909[14]), *Giovanni Segantini* (1911[30]) or "Amenhotep IV" (1912[34]).

---

[1] [Addition] Here quoted in a retranslation of the German version of this text, which had originally appeared in English, because the German—in Anna Freud's translation, revised by Freud himself (F/Jon, p. 598), and certainly with Jones's approval—is sometimes more pointed. In the following quote, for instance, the qualifying statement "not the trauma itself, but" is missing in the English version.

There is no doubt that Abraham's contributions strongly influenced the development of psychoanalytic thinking at the time. Not all of his conclusions and hypotheses stood the test of time, however; some have been disproved, some modified, while some still strike us, even today, as surprisingly modern and stimulating. Contrary to the popular image of Abraham as someone who just further elaborated, refined, and applied Freud's theories, he turns out to be, on a closer look, a quite original thinker whose impact on the intellectual history of psychoanalysis—be it directly, or through his pupils and analysands— has still not been fully appreciated.

The early years

Karl Abraham was born on 3 May 1877, as the second son of an orthodox Jewish family in the North German city of Bremen.[2] His father Nathan (1842–1915) was a merchant, and also acted as teacher of religion in the Jewish community, a role also chosen later by his elder son Max (1874–after 1941). The household was managed by his mother Ida, née Oppenheimer (1847–1929), a distant cousin of her husband, together with a maid. The grandparents and two unmarried aunts lived with the family, and for some time also a celibate uncle. Karl attended primary school and the so-called humanistic *Gymnasium* (a secondary school focussing on classical languages and the humanities), and took lessons in Jewish religion and Hebrew. Despite a strong interest in linguistics[3] he enrolled at the University of

---

[2] The following details on family, youth, and adolescence are taken primarily from the unfinished biography by his daughter Hilda (1974), and the excellent biographical study by Bettina Decke (1997). Biographical summaries, entries in lexica, etc., are generally based on Ernest Jones's obituary that appeared in both the *International Journal of Psycho-Analysis* and the *Internationale Zeitschrift für Psychoanalyse* (1926). Johannes Cremerius' introduction to the two-volumed German collected works of Abraham (in Abraham, 1969) has turned out to be, to a large extent, a plagiarism of Jones (see May, 2007b). In English, the short character study by Dinorah Pines (1987), who was close to the family, could draw on unpublished correspondence and personal communications. As far as Abraham's psychoanalytic career is concerned, the main sources—apart from the F/Abr correspondence—are the circular letters of the Committee (*Rundbriefe I-IV*) and Jones's Freud biography (I-III).

[3] Already as a fifteen-year-old he had written a manuscript entitled "Essays and notes on ethnology and linguistics" (Balkanyi, 1975).

Würzburg in 1895 to study dentistry, but switched to human medicine already after the first semester. His first student friend in Würzburg was Iwan Bloch, who became known later as the 'father' of sexology in Germany (H. Abraham, 1974, p. 22). A distant relative, Arthur Stern, wrote in his memoirs about their time together at the university (Stern, 1968). The financial means for his studies were provided by his childless uncle Adolf.

Karl then left Würzburg for the University of Freiburg, where he developed a special interest in embryology and histology, and collaborated with his young teacher Franz Keibel, with whom he also published a joint paper (1900). He also wrote his dissertation with Keibel, on the developmental history of the budgerigar, and graduated in 1901. It was also on the recommendation of Keibel, who had been appointed professor in Berlin in the meantime, that he got a position at the asylum of Dalldorf, then a suburb of Berlin, where he tried to further pursue his scientific interests, working under the supervision of the head physician, the neuropathologist Wilhelm Liepmann.

In his three years in Berlin (1901–1904), Abraham was also in close contact with students and teachers of sociology and economics. He attended the lectures of the sociologist Georg Simmel, and participated, together with his friends such as Hans Bürgner and Alice Salomon, in the legendary "summer house seminars" of the economist Ignaz Jastrow (cf. Braune, 2003, pp. 97–98). He had made the acquaintance of the attorney and notary Hans Bürgner (1882–1974) already in the latter's student days, and, at joint visits of meetings of the *Sozialwissenschaftliche Studentenverein* (Student Association for the Social Sciences) also met Bürgner's sister, his later wife Hedwig (1878–1969) (H. Abraham, 1974, p. 24) who was the Association's secretary for a time. Other student members included Adele Schreiber, Walter Kaesbach, Ludwig Cohn, and Kurt Alexander. Throughout his life, he stayed in touch with his best friends of that time, apart from Bürgner also Sally Altmann and Elisabeth Gottheiner.[4] Ulrike May unearthed a passionate article of a young and militant Abraham that appeared in the Viennese journal *Zeit* in 1902, in which he vehemently protests against the ban on the *Sozialwissenschaftliche Studentenverein*, imposed by the president

---

[4] The doctoral dissertations of Altmann and Gottheiner, both with friendly dedications to Abraham, are now in the Abraham Archives in Berlin (cf. Hermanns & Dahl, 2007).

of the University of Berlin (May, 1999). He also remained befriended with a former colleague at the asylum in Dalldorf, Max Arndt, who later co-founded a renowned private psychiatric clinic in the south of Berlin (Waldhaus Nikolassee), where his daughter Hilda was to work for some time many years later (H. Abraham, 1974, p. 27).

A few talks on neuropathological and experimental topics before the Berlin Psychiatric Association, which were also published, bear witness to his scientific activities at the time. In general, however, he "found nothing to hold his interest any further" in Dalldorf (ibid.), and was quite dissatisfied with the neuropathological orientation there (Good, 1998, p. 4). "I was a physician at the Berlin mental hospital Dalldorf for more than three years, until I could bear it no longer", he later wrote to Freud (p. 10).[5]

Karl Abraham and the Burghölzli

Abraham had tried long and hard to get a position at the Zurich Psychiatric Clinic, the Burghölzli. Its director, Eugen Bleuler, had to specially underline his qualifications before the health authorities to push his appointment despite the application of a competitor for the post, a Swiss native (Graf-Nold, 2006; Loewenberg, 1995). He reported for duty on 8 December 1904, as second assistant physician under the chief physician, Carl Gustav Jung. "In Zurich I could breathe freely again. No clinic in Germany could have offered me even a fraction of what I have found here" (p. 10). As he later remarked: "When I came to the Burghölzli ..., interest in psychoanalysis already existed", and the "following years saw a rapid increase in this interest" (p. 216). The position in Zurich also enabled him to marry Hedwig Bürgner, on 23 January 1906. On 18 November 1906, their first child, his daughter Hildegard (called Hilda), was born.

From 1907 onward, there existed a "Freud Society" at the clinic, an open discussion forum, where Abraham gave one of the first presentations. In June 1907, Abraham sent Freud his first psychoanalytic paper, written under the influence of Jung and Bleuler, "On the significance of sexual trauma in childhood for the symptomatology of dementia

---

[5] All quotes with simple page references are taken from the English 2002 edition of F/Abr.

praecox" (1907[9]).[6] Freud responded with a long and laudatory letter. He was particularly pleased, he wrote, that Abraham had "tackled the problem at the right end and, moreover, at the point where most people are unwilling to touch it" (p. 4)—namely, "the sexual problem" (F/Jun, p. 79). And this is how their correspondence started.

There followed an exchange about general questions of schizophrenia and hysteria. Another main topic between the two of them was sexual child abuse, about which Abraham wrote his next paper, "The experiencing of sexual traumas as a form of sexual activity" (1907[10]).[7] Even if Freud, after abandoning the so-called seduction theory, no longer considered sexual traumas to be the specific aetiology of neurosis, he never doubted their frequent occurrence and found it "really salutary that work on these sexual traumas should be undertaken by someone who, unlike me, has not been made uncertain by the first great error. For you, as for me, the compelling thing is that these traumas become the *form-giving factor* in the symptomatology of neurosis" (p. 2).

Despite repeated attempts, and positive recommendations of Bleuler, Abraham's attempts at securing a higher position in a Swiss clinic were unsuccessful, and so he decided in the autumn of 1907, with a heavy heart, to leave his beloved Switzerland and return to Berlin, where he planned to settle as a specialist for nervous and psychic diseases. Freud wished him well for "being forced into open life '*au grand air*'", and promised to refer patients to him should the occasion arise. "[T]hat as a Jew you will encounter more difficulties will have the effect, as it has with all of us, of bringing out all your productive capabilities" (p. 9). Still in the same year, Abraham paid Freud his first visit in Vienna (being the fourth visitor from Zurich after Eitingon in January 1907, and Jung and Ludwig Binswanger in March 1907), and participated in a meeting of the Wednesday Society and the "Discussion on sexual traumata and sexual enlightenment" (*Minutes I*, pp. 270–275; Abraham's own contribution on p. 272).

---

[6] "Dementia praecox" was the commonly used term for what was later called "schizophrenia", a term coined by Bleuler.

[7] A special issue of the *Jahrbuch der Psychoanalyse* (2006, vol. 52) was dedicated to a discussion of this article, with contributions from Good, Graf-Nold, May, and de Masi.

The Salzburg meeting

At the first international meeting of psychoanalysts, on 27 April 1908, in the (still existing) Hôtel Bristol in Salzburg, an open conflict erupted between Abraham and Jung. It is worth taking a closer look at it and its background, since this episode already shows certain characteristic traits of Abraham, and also of Freud, which would repeatedly play a role in future conflicts. The crisis usually began with Abraham criticising one of his colleagues (Jung, Rank, or Ferenczi), colleagues who were particularly close to Freud because of their original thinking and stimulating collaboration, and who, at one time or another, were destined to rise from the status of 'crown prince' to become Freud's successor. In the case of Jung, and to some extent also in that of Rank, Freud eventually acknowledged, albeit reluctantly, that Abraham's warnings had been justified (cf. Cremerius, 1997).

The relation between Abraham and Jung was strained from the beginning. When Freud asked Jung in the summer of 1907: "What is he like?", it took Jung more than a month to respond: "There are no objections to A. Only, he isn't quite my type"[8] (F/Jun, pp. 75, 78). For the time being, Freud did not question Jung's assessment, but still pointed out two aspects that would Freud bring him closer to Abraham, and alienate him from Jung: "I was predisposed in Abraham's favour by the fact that he attacks the sexual problem head on", and: "By the way, is he a descendant of his eponym?"—that is, a Jew (ibid., pp. 79–80). After Abraham's visit in December 1907, Freud reported to Jung that Abraham was "[m]ore congenial than your account of him, but there is something inhibited about him, no dash. At the crucial moment he can't find the right word" (ibid., p. 105). Still, he found him "very nice", and added that he understood the source of his inhibitions "only too well: the fact of being a Jew and concern over his future" (ibid., p. 109).

Not surprisingly, both Abraham and Jung chose to talk about schizophrenia in Salzburg, the central area of research at the Burghölzli (Abraham, 1908[11]; Jung, 1910b). Abraham's "main idea" was, in Jones's words (1926, p. 166),

> that disturbances of the ego functions could be purely secondary
> to disturbances in the sphere of the libido, in which event it might

---

[8] A more literal translation would read: "No objections can be brought forward against A. It's only that I find him rather unlikeable."

be possible to apply Freud's libido theory to the elucidation of dementia præcox. ... In it the libido is withdrawn from objects—the opposite of hysteria, where there is an exaggerated object cathexis—and applied to the self. To this he traced the delusions of persecution and megalomania.

While Abraham took pains to firmly ground the aetiology of schizophrenia in Freud's libido theory, Jung's paper attempted to give an answer to the tricky question of whether it was ultimately caused by psychical or physiological causes. He pointed out the similarities with states of poisoning or intoxication, particularly with reference to the accompanying *abaissement du niveau mental* (lowering of the mental level; a term of Jung's teacher Pierre Janet), and consequently suggested that a hitherto unknown "toxin" could be an aetiological factor in schizophrenia. Contrary to cases of intoxication or brain diseases, however, in schizophrenia this *abaissement* was not generalised, but affected primarily "complex"-related areas, so that the symptoms could also be influenced by psychic or environmental factors. Ultimately, Jung left open the question which of these two factors—the psychical or physiological—he considered the primary one.

What is also remarkable in both Abraham's and Jung's presentations, is what they do *not* mention. Jung did not pay more than lip service to Freud, and above all did not draw the obvious conclusion that his and Freud's (and therefore also Abraham's) positions would be easily reconcilable if the "toxin" in question were somehow connected to the "libido". Abraham for his part did not mention at all the pioneering works in this area by Jung and Bleuler, his direct superiors, to whom he owed a psychological understanding of psychoses in the first place. Jung was furious and accused Abraham of plagiarism (F/ Jun, p. 149). This is rather puzzling, since the latter's talk was precisely *not* espousing the position taken by Jung and Bleuler but, for the first time in public, presented *Freud's* competing theory on the aetiology of schizophrenia. In addition, Abraham seems to have heard about Freud's ideas for the first time from Jung, with whom Freud had shared them (the ideas) already in early 1907: "I threw out the suggestion",[9] wrote

---

[9] *Ich gab die Anregung frei*, literally: I released the suggestion; that is, everybody would be at liberty to make use of it.

Freud to Jung, *"he heard it from you* and corresponded with me about it as well" (ibid., p. 150; my ital.). So if Abraham plagiarised anybody at all, it was Freud, not Jung. But Freud had expressly waived his priority and assured Abraham that he could use his "suggestion".

Moreover, Freud had actively approved of Abraham's paper and reassured him that it would not bring him into conflict with Jung. "Actually I became involved in the conflict quite innocently", Abraham therefore defended himself. "In December I asked you whether there was any risk of my colliding with Jung on this subject, as you had communicated your ideas to him as well. You dispelled my doubts at the time" (p. 40). Thus, Freud had contributed himself to the conflict for which he then blamed Abraham and Jung (cf. Cremerius, 1997). After Salzburg he interpreted it as a priority dispute between *these two*, a dispute about the question who first solved the riddle of schizophrenia with the help of psychoanalysis. At the same time, he made it crystal clear that the priority was actually his: "I gave the same suggestion to each of you" (p. 53). It seems, however, that he would have preferred his then favourite pupil Jung, and not Abraham, to present it publicly. And indeed he criticised Abraham to have *made* use of the idea, and Jung for *not* doing so. To Jung: "I only regret that you didn't appropriate it [the suggestion]" (F/Jun, p. 150). To Abraham: "it would have shown greater delicacy of feeling not to have made use of it" (p. 53). In the same letter, however, he praised not only "the resolute tone and clarity of Abraham's writings, but also their beauty. May I say that it is consanguineous Jewish traits that attract me to them?[10] We understand each other, don't we?" (ibid.).

The beginnings in Berlin

In Berlin, Abraham moved to his first apartment and office on *Schöneberger Ufer* near the centre, and immediately sprang into action. In the beginning, he made use of his contacts with Hermann Oppenheim, a relative of his wife, and head of a private psychiatric

---

[10] In the early, abbreviated editions of this correspondence (1965), both in German and English, the meaning of this phrase was garbled due to a reading error (*Ihnen* = you, instead of *ihnen* = their): "May I say that it is consanguineous Jewish traits that attract me to *you?*" (Freud & Abraham, 1965, p. 46).

polyclinic. Although Oppenheim vehemently attacked psychoanalysis in public, he did refer patients to Abraham. He was also supported by Magnus Hirschfeld, the founder and long-term chairman of the *Wissenschaftlich-Humanitäres Komitee* (Scientific-Humanitarian Committee), an organisation fighting for the social recognition and decriminalisation of homosexuality. Hirschfeld sent patients to Abraham, got him a side job as a court-appointed psychiatric expert, and published an article of Abraham's (1908[12]) in his *Zeitschrift für Sexualwissenschaft* (Journal of Sexology). Abraham also made an effort to gather a group of physicians around him who were interested in psychoanalysis. The first meeting of this group took place on 27 August 1908, with Hirschfeld, Bloch, Otto Juliusburger, and Heinrich Koerber, who were soon joined by others such as Max Eitingon, who also moved from Zurich to Berlin in late 1909 (see Hermanns, 1997). From early on, he gave talks on psychoanalysis before various organisations, such as the Berlin Society for Psychiatry and Nervous Diseases, or the Psychological Society chaired by Albert Moll (see Jones II, p. 114).

During that time he also wrote his first book, *Dreams and Myths* (1909[14]), in which Freud took a special interest, not least because it was published in a series edited by himself, the *Schriften zur angewandten Seelenkunde* (Works on Applied Psychology). It is interesting to see how Freud commented upon Abraham's style. The latter has often been described as clear, precise, but somewhat dry und uninspired, a feature also witnessed by his letters to Freud. In Freud's words, Jung had "made him out to be something of an 'uninspired plodder'" (F/Jun, p. 79; an allusion to *Faust I*, 521). Even if we subtract Jung's obvious animosity, there may be a kernel of truth in this.[11] In any case, when

---

[11] Although Anna Freud demanded that this remark be omitted *"under all circumstances"* in the published letters (in Shamdasani, 1997, p. 362), their editor William McGuire kept it in. The original German, *trockener Schleicher*, is even stronger; it "includes the notion of insincerity and something 'creepy-crawly' with sinister purposes" (ibid., p. 364). It has to be noted, however, that this was not the expression Jung used, but Freud's association to Jung's description. [Addition] In a recent biography of Abraham, the German psychoanalyst Karin Zienert-Eilts takes to task the Abraham scholarship of the past decades, explicitly and repeatedly referring also to my own scholarship in general, and the above formulation in particular, for "simply" and "uncritically" "taking over" this characterisation as "correct", which would amount to a "continuation of the one-dimensional and idealised image of Freud and Jung", and would have "underhandedly continued the tradition of a hostile disparagement of Abraham" (2013, pp. 12, 287). I must leave it to my readers to judge if this qualification applies.

Freud suggested to Abraham to change "the sober scientific form ... to the style of a lecture or essay" (p. 36), Abraham objected: "actually there is a great deal in it that must first rest on a scientific basis before it is ready to be dealt with in an essay" (p. 43).

Partly as a reaction to the reception he received at his talks in medical circles—where he often met with vehement opposition—and following Freud's advice, Abraham sought to establish direct contact with interested physicians and began, in March 1910, to give a course on Freud's theory of neuroses. His publications show his growing mastery of psychoanalytic theory. On the occasion of the publication of his paper on "Hysterical dream-states" (1910[17]), Freud congratulated him "heartily on all the contributions you render to the cause of psychoanalysis. I do not know of anything to place beside them for clarity, inner solidity, and power of evidence" (p. 115). In the same letter he also addressed him, for the first time, as "Dear Friend". Clearly, Freud valued Abraham highly for his faithful loyalty, his scientific contributions, and his efforts on behalf of the psychoanalytic movement, even if he never developed that kind of warmth, love even, that for years he showed toward Jung, Rank, or Ferenczi. Abraham for his part measured up to Freud's expectations, and kept him constantly informed about his "numerous germs of works" (p. 141), the progress in the circle around him, the consolidation of his practice—and about his family life: on 27 August 1910, his son Gerd was born (p. 117).

After the foundation of the IPA at the second psychoanalytic congress in Nuremberg, the Berlin Society was constituted on the last day of the congress (31 March 1910) as its first branch society. Abraham was to remain its president until his death in 1925. He then helped to organise the third IPA Congress in Weimar (1911), after the end of which he spent some time with Freud in private. He also tried to present Freud at each of his, Freud's, birthdays with a publication as a 'present'. On 1 December 1912, he wrote for the first time about his plans for a *Habilitation*,[12] for which Freud wrote him a letter of recommendation. These plans came to nothing, however.

---

[12] [Addition] The *Habilitation* has no exact equivalent in English-speaking countries. It was and is the highest academic qualification a scholar can achieve in Germany (and Austria), and the prerequisite for applying for full professorship. It requires the submission and approval of a professorial post-doc thesis, and the passing of a habilitation examination.

After a somewhat rocky start, Abraham's practice began to thrive, and in 1912 he conducted already ten analyses per day (p. 159), including such gifted and talented puils as Karen Horney or Carl Müller-Braunschweig. Moreover, he aroused the interest of artists, writers, and pedagogues. Celebrities such as Lou Andreas-Salomé[13] or Helene Stöcker[14] were guests at meetings of the Berlin Psychoanalytic Society; the latter even became a member for a few years. Several university teachers at the Berlin medical clinic, the renowned Charité, showed interest. His psychotherapeutic technique was quite unconventional seen from today's standards, by the way. We know from the recently published diaries of his analysand, the writer and bonvivant Oscar A. H. Schmitz (2006, 2007a, 2007b; Martynkewicz, 2007), that Abraham let him use his private library for his studies, after the analysis had to be suddenly terminated because of the outbreak of war (Martynkewicz, personal communication). Or, almost like a family doctor, when he heard that his analysand Alix Strachey (for whom he was "far & away the best analyst") suffered from severe tonsillitis, he first called her on the phone, then paid her a visit at her home, examined her throat, and sent for the noted laryngologist Wilhelm Fliess—Freud's estranged former friend (Meisel & Kendrick, 1985, pp. 240, 242, 252).

The Committee

In 1911 and 1912, Jung—still president of the IPA—published the two parts of his seminal work, *Transformations and Symbols of the Libido*. From the very beginning, he had voiced reservations against some cornerstones of Freud's theory, particularly against the so-called sexual theory, although both downplayed the crucial differences for some time. Many psychoanalytic colleagues were alarmed by his new definition of the libido as a non-specific psychic energy (roughly comparable to Bergson's *élan vital*), or by his view that the Oedipus complex might be a pathological, sexualised form of development. His personal relationship with Freud, too, became strained. When he gave a series of lectures

---

[13] Today mostly known for her friendships with Nietzsche, Rilke, and Freud, but at the time a bestselling author in her own right.

[14] A prominent feminist, sexual reformer, and pacifist.

at Fordham University (New York City) in 1912, he seized the occasion to present and substantiate his differing views in detail (Jung, 1913).

In view of Jung's threatening defection from the alleged essentials of psychoanalysis, a secret "Committee" was formed among Freud's most trusted disciples, with the task of watching over the 'correct' development of psychoanalytic theory and technique, and of co-ordinating the politics of the movement.[15] The original members were, apart from Freud, Ferenczi, Jones, Rank, and Sachs, soon joined by Abraham (Schröter, 1995b, p. 522). A first meeting took place in Vienna on 25 May 1913. At the Fourth International Psychoanalytic Congress in Munich in September later that year, the conflict with Jung came out in the open, when he stood for re-election as president, and twenty-two of fifty-two members abstained from voting (F/Jun, p. 611). One and a half months later Jung resigned from his role as managing editor of the *Jahrbuch*, and in April 1914 as president of the IPA.

Just as Jung's star was fading in the psychoanalytic movement, Abraham's star began to rise. Freud offered Abraham to take over the two most important roles of Jung: the managing editorship of the *Jahrbuch* (p. 203) and the presidency of the IPA—for the time being as interim president until the next congress, but holding out the prospect of a much greater honour: "[I]t is my personal wish to see you as our definite President. I know what to expect of your energy, correctness, and devotion to duty, in most agreeable contrast to your predecessor" (p. 239).

To expedite, or even force, Jung's resignation, the members of the Committe started a concerted literary action against him, in three waves. To begin with, Ferenczi published a polemical review of *Transformations and Symbols* (Ferenczi, 1913[124]), then appeared a "salvo" of critical contributions in the *Zeitschrift* (F/Fer I, p. 550), and finally the finishing stroke: the "bomb" (ibid.)—Freud's *On the History of the Psycho-Analytic Movement* (1914d). Abraham's contribution to that "salvo" was his critique of Jung's Fordham Lectures (1914[47]), the most scorching and polemical work he ever wrote. Freud congratulated him on it with the words: "[I]t would deserve a civic crown[16] if such distinctions existed

---

[15] See Grosskurth, 1991; Jones II; Schröter, 1995b; Wittenberger, 1995; *Rundbriefe I-IV*.

[16] The civic crown (*corona civica*) was a military award for a Roman who saved the life of a fellow citizen in battle, and showed exceptional courage against the enemy.

in science! It is, in short, excellent, cold steal, clean, clear, and sharp. Moreover, God knows that it is all true" (p. 211).

On 10 July 1914, the Zurich branch society left the IPA, and Freud wrote triumphantly to Abraham (p. 264):

> So we are at last rid of them, the brutal, sanctimonious Jung and his parrots! I feel impelled now to thank you for the vast amount of trouble, for the exceptional, goal-oriented activity, with which you supported me and with which you steered our common cause. All my life I have been searching for friends who would not exploit and then betray me, and now, not far from its natural end, I hope I have found them.

Only shortly before this, however, a quite different "bomb" had gone off: the assassination in Sarajevo, following which Austria-Hungary declared war on Serbia on 28 July 1914. The outbreak of the First World War threw all further plans, be they personal, scientific, or organisational, into disarray.

The First World War and the discussion about depression

Abraham was one of only very few followers with whom Freud could correspond by letter without major problems during the war. Abraham had volunteered for hospital duty, and first served in Berlin, and then from March 1915 onward in Allenstein, where his family joined him in June 1916.[17] In November 1915 he could open a small psychiatric unit, but primarily worked in the operating room, "not only an assistant or dresser, but an operating surgeon, too. The psychoanalyst in me stands amazed while I operate … But war is war" (p. 314). Very probably the years in East Prussia, with its severe winters and his constant overload of work, exacerbated Abraham's bronchial affliction (p. 356). Although after some time he got a collaborator in his fellow analyst Hans Liebermann from Berlin, the latter fell ill himself, and Abraham had to look after up to ninety patients on his own (p. 338). Psychotherapist

---

[17] Allenstein/Olsztyn, then a small garrison town in East Prussia, today in Poland, about 110 miles north of Warsaw.

J. H. Schultz was stationed for some time in Allenstein as an army neurologist, and remembers Abraham in his memoirs (1964, p. 78):

> Carl Abraham, doctor for nervous diseases, a slim, dark-haired, patrician Sephardi, with a fine profile full of character. His whole demeanour was essentially determined by the fact that he had spent his childhood and adolescence in the Hanseatic city of Bremen, and had soaked up its atmosphere.

Schultz mentions approvingly his "subdued manners", his "fine humour", and his "pleasure in wordplays". His nickname with the patients was "Doctor Storyteller", because of the way in which he tried to bring complex psychic constellations to light.

On the rare occasions when he could take a leave of absence, he visited his family, who was still in Berlin, or his mother in Bremen. Surprisingly, he also found the time to work scientifically and to conduct a few analyses, among them his first child analysis (p. 381). In early 1915 he began writing his important article on the oral phase (1916[52]), and finished it at the end of the year, dedicating it to Freud for the latter's sixtieth birthday on 6 May 1916. "The paper with which you presented me", Freud thanked him, "is as excellent as—everything that you have been doing in recent years, distinguished by its many-sidedness, depth, correctness, and, incidentally, it is in full agreement with the truth as it is known to me" (p. 327).

Freud's analytical practice suffered considerably during the first years of the war. In this situation he conceived the plan to write a comprehensive work on psychoanalytic theory. A first allusion to this can be found in his letter to Abraham of 25 November 1914 (p. 285); a month later he confirms: "I might finish a theory of neuroses" (p. 291). We know, however, that he eventually abandoned this plan and instead published only a small series of "metapsychological" papers (p. 361).

One of these papers, "Mourning and melancholia" (Freud, 1916–17g), dealt with a topic that had already earlier aroused Abraham's interest: depression. "Abraham is the first of Freud's followers who found a promising way of approaching depression, and this *before* Freud" (May, 1997, p. 106). His first pertinent contributions are found in his monograph on Giovanni Segantini (1911[30]) and in his article on bipolar states (1911[26]). Ulrike May has shown that Abraham was the first to introduce "the figure of the bad mother ... as the prototype of a specific relationship between son and mother" (May, 1997, p. 107), thus discovering, as it were, the "pre-oedipal mother", a concept that would gain central importance in the theories of his analysand and pupil Melanie Klein. In his view, Segantini's "mother complex" played a dominating role, with him having not only feelings of strong love, but also of strong hate towards his mother. This was due, on the one hand, to a constitutional sadism, and, on the other, to the feeling of not being loved enough. This view brought Abraham into a latent conflict with Freud, who had stressed the boy's overall positive feelings for the mother and the negative ones for the father, who was hated by the boy as a rival, however, but not "constitutionally". In their correspondence Freud complimented Abraham on his "fine and beautiful" book (p. 129), but did not comment on Abraham's central hypothesis.

Immediately after the book, Abraham wrote another paper "on the psychosexual basis of agitated and depressive states" (p. 137), which he then presented before the following psychoanalytic congress in Weimar (1911[26]). He stressed again the great role played by "an insatiable sadism" (ibid., p. 146) in depression: "In every one of these cases it could be discovered that the disease proceeded from an attitude of hate which was paralysing the patient's capacity to love" (ibid., p. 143). The core of depression would be the patient's own incapacity for love, which is then projected outward: "People do not love me, they hate me ... because of my inborn defects. Therefore I am unhappy and depressed" (ibid., p. 145). The suppressed, but continuing feelings of hatred and revenge would manifest themselves in delusional ideas of guilt, the repressed perception of the incapacity for love in delusions of impoverishment. Freud wrote that although he valued Abraham's paper "so highly", he still found "that the formula is not assured and the elements not yet convincingly linked" (p. 154). He himself, however, would not know anything better either.

In contrast to Freud's conviction that psychoses could not be treated by psychotherapeutic means, Abraham held that psychoanalysis seemed to him "to be the only rational therapy to apply to the manic-depressive psychoses", and that it would "lead psychiatry out of the *impasse* of therapeutic nihilism" (1911[26], pp. 154, 156). Quite likely, Abraham had also a very personal reason to be interested in this topic, writing that "I succeeded in attaining a greater psychic *rapport* with the patients than I had ever previously achieved" (ibid., p. 154). Already about his Segantini book he had told Freud that this was "a piece of work with some personal complexes behind it" (p. 126; cf. Mächtlinger, 1997).

Freud had sent a first draft of "Mourning and melancholia" to Ferenczi, who in turn sent it on to Abraham (cf. F/Fer II, pp. 47–49, with note 1). The ensuing discussion of their respective views was characterised by long pauses—each of them took at least a month to reply to the points raised by the other. In the draft (as well as in the later publication), Freud had not mentioned Abraham's central hypothesis at all. Abraham tried to bring himself back into play in a diplomatic way: "The basic points of your exposition ... should definitely stand. I think sadism and oral eroticism should be added" (p. 305; cf. Abraham, 1916[52]). Freud's reply, although worded in a friendly manner, was tantamount to a square rejection of Abraham's position: "you do not bring out sufficiently the essential feature of [Freud's] assumption", and "you overlook the real explanation" (pp. 308–309). Abraham countered that he was "not yet convinced" of Freud's postulate "that reproaches that are actually directed against another person are transposed to one's own ego. I do not remember your bringing detailed proof in your paper" (p. 311). Finally, again after a latency period of a month, Freud ended the discussion: "I should gladly tell you more about melancholia, but could do it *properly* only if we met and talked" (p. 313). It had taken them nearly half a year to reach that conclusion ...

A postscriptum to this discussion—which was never concluded satisfacorily—can be found in Abraham's *Short Study of the Development of the Libido*, published in 1924, in which he presents "a differentiated, aetiological theory of depression" (May, 1997, p. 120). There he writes (1924[105], pp. 437–438):

> I find myself obliged to contribute an experience out of my own life. When Freud published his "Mourning and Melancholia" ... I noticed that I felt a quite unaccustomed difficulty in following his train of thought. I was aware of an inclination to reject the idea of an introjection of the loved object. ... Towards the end of the previous year [1915] my father had died. During the period of mourning which I went through certain things occurred which I was not at the time able to recognise as the consequence of a process of introjection. ... It thus appears that my principal motive in being averse to Freud's theory of the pathological process of melancholia at first

was my own tendency to employ the same mechanism during mourning.

Nevertheless he still upheld, although sometimes in rather convoluted language, that the sadistic impulses of boys who later became depressed were directed primarily toward the mother, not the father, and that in general "the whole psychological process centres *in the main* round the mother" (ibid., p. 461).

In this context it is interesting to see that Abraham never wrote Freud about the death of his father—although he did inform him about the death of his father-in-law (p. 163). After he had had "most alarming news about his father's state of health" (p. 314), he never mentioned him again[18] (cf. Shengold, 1972).

End of war and post-war period

Near the end of the First World War, the Fifth International Psycho-analytic Congress was held in Budapest, on 28–29 September 1918. It was, quite fittingly, dedicated to a discussion of so-called war neuro-ses. Freud gave a talk on "Lines of advance in psycho-analytic therapy" (1919a), and Abraham participated in a panel on war neuroses. Ferenczi was elected president, and Anton von Freund, a rich Hungarian phi-lanthropist, owner of a beer brewery and a budding analyst, secretary of the IPA. Von Freund had donated a huge sum for the advancement of the psychoanalytic movement, and Freud hoped that with its help a polyclinic and a training institute could be founded in Budapest, which city promised to become the "headquarters [*Zentrale*][19] of our movement" (p. 382).

At the Budapest Congress two claims were made that mark a turn in the history of psychoanalysis. First, Freud claimed (1919a, p. 167)

---

[18] At least in the extant letters. But even if a letter or a telegram were missing, it is quite inconceivable that Freud would not have answered with a letter of condolence.

[19] The word *Zentrale* probably alludes to the statutes of the IPA that state: "The Central Office [*Zentrale*] consists of a President and a Secretary" (in F/Jun, p. 569). In a more gen-eral sense, however, Budapest also promised to become—with Ferenczi's presidency, von Freund's money, and the planned infrastructure—the central city of the psychoanalytic movement.

that at some time or other the conscience of society will awake and remind it that the poor man should have just as much right to assistance for his mind as he now has to the life-saving help offered by surgery ... When this happens, institutions or out-patient clinics will be started, to which analytically-trained physicians will be appointed ... Such treatments will be free.

And second, Hermann Nunberg demanded, for the first time in public, that in future nobody should be allowed to learn and practice psychoanalysis who had not undergone an analysis himself. Both predictions came true—not in Budapest, however, but in Berlin.

In the political and economical turmoil of the post-war period that ravaged Hungary, all plans for Budapest came to naught. Von Freund died of cancer; the sum he had donated was for the most part frozen by the authorities, and decimated by the galloping inflation to boot. In this situation, Max Eitingon, himself a member of a very rich family of fur traders, stepped into the breach. In 1920, he funded an outpatient clinic in Berlin, which was headed by himself, Abraham, and Ernst Simmel. For this, he was rewarded by becoming a new member of the inner circle, the Committee.

This first psychoanalytic outpatient clinic in Berlin not only served as a treatment centre for the poor, but simultaneously as a training centre for psychoanalytic candidates, also the first of its kind. The Berlin Institute became the model for practically all the following ones, such as Helene Deutsch's in Vienna, or Sándor Radó's in New York.[20]

In the meantime, Abraham had returned to Berlin. He had been discharged from the army on 14 December 1918, and had found preliminary quarters in Grunewald, a suburb of Berlin and elegant residential area, from where he moved to another apartment in the same area in October 1919, making it his permanent residence and office. Patients soon found their way to the periphery (cf. Abraham, 1924[unnumbered]; Sonnenstuhl, 2006), and his practice was soon thriving again. In 1921, his collected psychoanalytic essays were published by the recently founded *Internationaler psychoanalytischer Verlag* (1921[75]).

---

[20] The role model function and crucial impact of the Berlin Clinic and Institute, particularly in England, the United States, and Palestine/Israel, was the topic of three symposia at the International Psychoanalytic Congress 2007 in Berlin, documented in a special issue of the *Jahrbuch der Psychoanalyse* (2008, vol. 57).

Besides his practice and his teaching at the Institute, Abraham pursued above all two projects dear to his heart: He wanted to bring the next psychoanalytic congress to Berlin, and he tried to obtain a professorship for psychoanalysis at the university. Both plans fell through. Freud, Jones, and Rank were unanimous in showing Abraham that it was quite unrealistic, so shortly after the end of the war, "to get the British and Americans to come to Berlin … Hostile prejudice is indeed stronger than you suppose" (p. 409). With regard to his professorship, Abraham did submit a *Denkschrift* (exposé) to the ministry, and had several talks with influential persons and decision makers, among others with the professor of psychiatry, Karl Bonhoeffer (p. 425). His application was turned down, however, based on negative reports from the medical faculty and the Ministry of Culture (cf. Kaderas, 1998; with reprints of the *Denkschrift* and the reports).

The Sixth International Psychoanalytic Congress took place in The Hague, on 8–11 September 1920. Avoiding the sensitive language problem after the war, Abraham opened it with "a speech in Latin that had to be brought up to date for the occasion" (Jones, 1926, p. 156),[21] and then talked about the female castration complex (1920[67]). In The Hague, the members of the Committee agreed to stay in contact through regular circular letters (*Rundbriefe I-IV*). The Dutch had collected money to cover the travel expenses of the participants from abroad, most of whom were impoverished after the war. Freud gave the surplus of his share to Abraham who could thus fulfill an ardent wish of his children for bicycles.

In 1922, Abraham finally succeeded in bringing the seventh International Psychoanalytic Congress to Berlin (25–27 September). This was the last congress at which Freud was present. He gave a talk on "Something about the unconscious" (1922f; not in S.E.), a summary of the first part of *The Ego and the Id* (1923b), which appeared shortly thereafter. Abraham talked about bipolar states (1922[81]), a prelude to his chef d'oeuvre on the developmental history of the libido (cf. Schröter, 2007).

---

[21] [Addition] It is noteworthy, not only that he could do so on such short notice, but also that he could expect his listeners to understand him. This could be the last occasion in history when Latin was used as a lingua franca in general, international scientific circles …

The Committee dissolves

First signs of severe tensions among the Committe members became visible already in 1921, and they continued to increase.[22] They quarrelled about seemingly minor matters: delays in the submission of manuscripts, how other members were quoted or not quoted in publications, accusations of sloppiness or overeagerness, questions of authority in matters of analytic publishing, etc. The background of all this were more serious things, however: fights for a position of trust with Freud and the role of the crown prince, a struggle for the (informal) hierarchy within the group, all this before the background of a professional, cultural, and scientific environment that was experienced as hostile, growing anti-Semitism, but also diverging scientific and therapeutic differences among themselves. Over time, alliances developed, above all between Otto Rank and Sándor Ferenczi on the one side, and Ernest Jones and Karl Abraham on the other, while the rest remained less outspoken (or hedged their bets) for some time.

For a long time, Freud openly supported the position of Rank and Ferenczi. On 26 November 1922, he sent a circular letter, in which he not only defended Rank, but also gave the interpretation that Jones's hostile stance against Rank was in reality meant for himself, Freud, and only deflected towards Rank, and that Jones should complete the analysis he had had about a decade earlier with, of all persons, Ferenczi (*Rundbriefe III*, pp. 231–235).

In August 1923 the Committee members met in San Cristoforo in South Tyrol. At this meeting, the long pent-up tension erupted. Freud, who spent his holidays in a neighbouring village, did not participate. He had not felt well for some time, and his doctor Felix Deutsch had already diagnosed cancer, without telling Freud this, however. But Rank knew of it, and this may also help to explain why he was so thin-skinned and reacted so violently to a critical remark about him Jones had made to Brill, and of which he had heard via Ferenczi (probably 'embellished' by Brill himself).[23] He accused Jones of anti-Semitism and

---

[22] See, for example, Grosskurth, 1991; Wittenberger, 1995; Lieberman, 1985; Leitner, 1998; and the *Rundbriefe*.

[23] About this affair Jones wrote to his wife, Katharine Jokl: "The chief news is that Freud has a real cancer slowly growing ... He doesn't know it and it is a most deadly secret. ... [I] expect Ferenczi will hardly speak to me for Brill has just been there and told him I had

demanded his explusion from the Committee. Only Abraham defended Jones, who later admitted to him (12 November 1924; LC) that he had not had the courage to defend (even the correctly quoted part of) his "famous remark" in San Cristoforo. With Freud's illness the question of his succession had become acute. Everybody, Freud included, thought that his days were strictly limited, and nobody suspected that he would survive even two of his possible successors.

Not only personal interests were at stake, however. Two books appeared at the end of 1923 (although they bore the imprint of 1924) that set in motion a deep conflict about scientific and therapeutic questions: the joint book by Ferenczi and Rank, *The Development of Psychoanalysis* (1924), originally intended to be submitted for the prize offered by Freud for the best work on "The relation between analytic technique and analytic theory" (Freud, 1922d); and Rank's book, *The Trauma of Birth* (1924). Rank claimed to have found, in the trauma of birth, "the ultimate source of the psychical unconscious in the psychophysical sphere" (ibid., p. 21). Analysis would consist in bringing to a close the coping with the birth trauma that had been mastered only incompletely (ibid., p. 26). The transference libido to be dissipated in both sexes would be the maternal one (ibid., p. 28). With this, Rank questioned a number of fundamental psychoanalytic concepts, or at the least sought to see them in a new perspective: the importance of the Oedipus complex as the nucleus of neurosis, that of the role of the father in the aetiology of neuroses, and of castration anxiety, or the notion of so-called primary narcissism.

Although Rank had not told Abraham, Eitingon, Jones, and Sachs of his new ideas, both Freud and Ferenczi knew of them (contrary to Jones III, p. 77). At first, both were positively impressed. Rank's "finding is great indeed", Freud wrote to Ferenczi (F/Fer III, p. 106). When the book was out, however, Abraham voiced severe reservations: "Results of whatever kind obtained in a legitimate analytic manner would never give me cause for such grave doubts." But here he would "see signs of a disastrous development concerning vital matters of Ψα." And he added that this would "force [him], to [his] deepest sorrow ... to take on the role of the one who issues a warning" (p. 483). He saw "in the

said Rank was a swindling Jew (stark übertrieben [*greatly exaggerated*])" (in Brome, 1982, p. 139).

Entwicklungsziele as well as in the *Trauma der Geburt* manifestations of a scientific regression that correspond, down to the smallest detail, with the symptoms of Jung's renunciation of Ψα ... a turning away from what we have up to now called ψα method" (p. 485).²⁴

Freud was not pleased. Regardless of how justified Abraham's reaction might have been, he wrote him, "quite apart from that, the way you set about things was certainly not friendly [*freundschaftlich*]" (p. 491).²⁵ Abraham found this accusation "extremely painful and ... strange". It would have been he who had saved the Committee from falling apart, and now, after having "plainly put before [Freud] the existing dangers to Ψα", the "[d]isquiet stemming from very certain sources is readily directed against the man who honestly indicates these sources" (pp. 493–494). Rank was so incensed by what he viewed as Abraham's denunciation, however, that he declared, with Freud's consent, the Committee dissolved (*Rundbriefe IV*, p. 194).

The Eighth International Psychoanalytic Congress in Salzburg, on 21–23 April 1924, took place without Freud. Although Abraham, Ferenczi, Jones, and Sachs talked things over and could re-establish some kind of working relationship, "Rank ... proved quite inacessible" (Jones III, p. 67), and the tensions remained. Ferenczi himself proposed Abraham's election to the presidency (ibid.), who chose Eitingon as his secretary. Freud declared that he was growing closer and closer to Abraham's standpoint, even though in the personal aspect he still would not be able take his side (p. 500). And only a few days later he was convinced that Rank's theory of the birth trauma would "fall flat" (in English in the original), and he called Abraham his "rocher de bronce" (pp. 501–502).

Rank left Austria to spend half a year in New York City. From there he wrote to Freud, full of his success: "When people saw that their work gets easier and they achieve better results [both in their own

---

²⁴ Abraham's copy of Rank's book (Abraham archives, Berlin) is full of question and exclamation marks, and margin remarks such as "completely wrong", "arbitrary", "illogical", or "negligent".

²⁵ Ferenczi—who knew of Abraham's letter from Rank, who himself had been informed by Freud—even wrote to Freud that Abraham's "boundless ambition and jealousy ... could blind him in such a way that he ... could slander the ... [two books] as manifestations of a secession [*Abfallserscheinungen*]" (F/Fer III, p. 127; trans. mod.; the English translation misunderstood *Abfallserscheinungen* as "garbage publications").

analysis and with their patients][26] with the modifications I introduced, they praised me as a savior" (F/Ran, p. 209). He criticised Freud for "bring[ing] in personal relations between you and me where they don't belong", and suspected that Freud was "influenced by certain rabble-rousers", among them Abraham to whom he imputed "profound ignorance" (ibid., p. 210). It became clear that Rank was about to distance himself from the common cause, and to resign from his crucial managerial and editorial positions. When Freud sent a copy of Rank's letter to Eitingon, he added: "Naturally, Abraham must not be told about its content. The statements are too nasty" (F/Eit, p. 355). To discuss Rank's replacement in his manifold functions, Freud summoned a meeting in Vienna in November, with the result that Adolf Storfer became Rank's successor as head of the *Psychoanalytischer Verlag*, and Sándor Radó managing editor of the *Zeitschrift* (under Eitingon's supervision). The members of the Committee resumed their correspondence by circular letters on 15 December 1924—without Rank, but including a new member, Freud's daughter Anna.

Success—illness—death

While the Rank crisis came to a head, Abraham intensified his activities in scientific, therapeutic, and organisational matters. He initiated the first meeting of German analysts, in October 1924 in Würzburg. Shortly afterwards, his seminal book on character formation came out (Abraham, 1925[106]). In a letter, he confronted Freud with the question (p. 527)

> whether in early infancy there may be an early *vaginal* blossoming of the female libido, which is destined to be repressed and which is subsequently followed by clitoral primacy as the expression of the phallic phase. ... If the assumption is correct, it would have one advantage for us: we would be better able to understand the *female Oedipus complex* as the result of an early vaginal reaction to the father's penis ... and the change of the leading zone in puberty would then be a resumption of the original state of affairs.

---

[26] Words in brackets missing in the F/Ran edition.

Although Freud conceded: "I do not know anything about it", he still adhered to his "prejudice" that "the vaginal share would more be likely to be replaced by anal expressions" (p. 528). When Abraham repeated his views, Freud answered that he would be "quite eager to learn", that he had "no preconceived ideas", and would "look forward to your novelties in the matter" (p. 532). This was the last time the topic was mentioned, however, and the differing views—like those on the aetiology of depression—were discussed no further. Although Abraham had claimed that his conception could be fitted into the existing theory and would be only a small addition to it (p. 527), it can have hardly escaped him that it would, if followed through, collapse Freud's entire theory of the female castration complex and penis envy (cf. Kovel, 1974). As a matter of fact, his pupils Josine Müller and Karen Horney who further pursued this line of theorising met with Freud's disapproval.

Abraham was at the zenith of his psychoanalytic career. As president of the IPA he was mainly responsible for the organisation of the next International Psychoanalytic Congress, on 3–5 September 1925, in Bad Homburg/Germany. He was re-elected, and Eitingon became the chairman of a newly founded International Committee on training matters, thus further strengthening the central role of Berlin in the psychoanalytic movement. Abraham did not give a paper of his own at Bad Homburg, but was fully occupied by his presidential duties and the chairmanship of the congress, informal talks, etc. He felt all the more exhausted in that he had already been suffering from a lung affliction for a few months, a condition that had not improved despite a recreational holiday in the Swiss Alps.

In May 1925 he had been lecturing in Holland. Back in Berlin, he informed Freud that he had "brought back a feverish bronchial catarrh, which appears persistent" (p. 543). According to Hilda Abraham and Ernst Freud, editors of the first edition of the Freud/Abraham letters,

> [t]his apparent bronchitis was the first manifestation of Abraham's fatal illness. It in fact started with an injury to the pharynx from a fishbone and was followed by septic broncho-pneumonia, lung abscess and terminal suphrenic abscess. The illness took the typical course of septicaemia, prior to the introduction of antibiotics, with swinging temperatures, remissions and euphoria. Abraham's

previous emphysema had doubtless made him susceptible to such infection. (Freud & Abraham, 1965, p. 382)

Jones offered a different opinion in his Freud biography: "In the light of later medical knowledge we are agreed that the undiagnosed complaint must have been a cancer of the lung" (III, p. 116). Hilda Abraham held fast to her view, however, also basing it on the medical opinion of Felix Deutsch: "The septic process would also account for my father's euphoric mood during the later period of his illness.—To those who thought his death so unnecessary the idea of lung-cancer seemed more inevitable and therefore more acceptable."[27]

In the same letter, in which he first mentioned his illness, Abraham raised also an issue that was to cloud his relationship with Freud in the few months that remained him. A film company had approached him, he wrote to Freud, with the intention of producing a "popular scientific ψα film", preferably "with your [Freud's] authorization and with the collaboration and supervision of your recognised scholars" (p. 543). Freud confessed that he did "not feel comfortable about the magnificent project", and he refused to authorise it (p. 547). Shortly afterwards, Siegfried Bernfeld and Storfer in Vienna planned to realise a competing film project, which did not sit well with the Berliners. To Ferenczi Freud wrote: "Stupid things are happening in matters of film. ... filmmaking can be avoided as little as—so it seems—bobbed hair,[28] but I myself won't get mine cut, and don't intend to be brought into personal connection with any film" (F/Fer III, p. 222).

This 'film affair' is well documented in the Freud/Abraham letters and has been variously treated in the literature (e.g., Fallend & Reichmayr, 1992; Ries, 1995, 1997; Sierek & Eppensteiner, 2000). In any case, Abraham further supported the project, together with Sachs. This, and Abraham's criticism of his Viennese competitors, left Freud "with an unpleasant aftertaste" (p. 561), and he accused Abraham of "brusqueness" (*Schroffheit*) (*Rundbriefe IV*, p. 287). In a long letter, the last he was to write to Freud (pp. 564–566), Abraham tried to justify himself. The correspondence ends with Freud's allegation that

---

[27] Letter to Martin Grotjahn, 10 February 1962; BA Koblenz B 399, Nachlaß Martin Grotjahn, Archiv zur Geschichte der Psychoanalyse e.V.

[28] Original: *Bubikopf*, a pageboy haircut, popular in the 1920s.

Abraham would not have told the truth about Storfer, and that he should question his insistence on being right (p. 567):

> You were certainly right about Jung, and not quite so right about Rank. ... It is still possible that you may be even less right in the matter with which we are concerned now. It does not have to be the case that you are always right. But should you turn out to be right this time too, nothing would prevent me from once again admitting it. With that, let us close the argument about something that you yourself describe as a bagatelle. ... What matters more to me is to hear whether you intend to stay in Berlin or spend the winter in a milder climate. I am not quite sure in my mind what to wish for you, but in any case let the outcome be that you cause us no more worry.

The worries were more than justified. A few weeks later, Felix Deutsch was sent to Berlin. When he and Hedwig Abraham hurried to see Abraham on his sickbed on Christmas Day of 1925, he had already died (Pines, 1987). "We bury with him—*integer vitae scelerisque purus*",[29] Freud wrote in his obituary, "one of the firmest hopes of our science, young as it is and still so bitterly assailed, and a part of its future that is now, perhaps, unrealizable" (1926b, p. 277).

---

[29] He that is unstained in life and pure from guilt (Horace, *Odes*, I, xxii, 1).

CHAPTER FOURTEEN

Karl Abraham and Sándor Ferenczi

T here is no doubt that Abraham and Ferenczi were 'heavyweights' among Freud's early followers, through both their scientific contributions and their institutional roles and influence. Of those who remained within the psychoanalytic movement, they were, in their time, the two most important and influential theoreticians and practitioners after Freud. (In political, propagandistic, and organisational matters Ernest Jones prevailed, due not only to his indisputable talent for them, but also to the early death of his two rivals.) My early teacher Igor Caruso once told me that in re-reading the works of Abraham and Ferenczi (in their newly published Collected Works in the early 1970s) he was surprised to find so many ideas that were usually attributed to much later developments in theory. The late 1980s and the 1990s then saw a kind of Ferenczi renaissance, and there are signs that interest in Abraham and his work, too, is now growing again.

There is also no doubt, however, that they were quite different personalities, and antagonists in many theoretical, technical, and organisational questions. In what follows I will try to throw some light on their character, their relationship, and the various areas in which their paths crossed, sometimes to be united, sometimes to be separated again.

In juxtaposing their characters, there is naturally always the danger of exaggerating the differences between the two men, or even of making caricatures out of them, which do not do justice to the persons of flesh and blood with all their facets and also inner contradictions. With that caveat in mind, let me say that they represent two fundamentally different types—Abraham *rather* the thorough, even dry type, sober-minded, conservative, a teamplayer and exemplary family man who regularly spent his free time and his vacations with his family (rather an exception among early analysts—Eitingon, Ferenczi, Jones, and Sachs, for instance, were infamous for their affairs). According to Jones, "Abraham was certainly the most normal member" of the Committee (II, p. 159). He was the systematic theoretician who presented important elaborations, refinements, and further developments of Freud's ideas. He systematised for instance Freud's rather cautious and partly contradictory statements on the early development of so-called object love (cf. Balint, 1968; Falzeder, 1986) and of the psychosexual phases in a schema that he compared "to a time-table of express trains" (Abraham, 1924[105], pp. 495–496). Striving for classification and precision, he sought to facilitate the learning and teaching of psychoanalysis, and "impressed his colleagues with his rigour, his earnestness, his precision in scientific matters, [and] his unrelenting work" (Haynal & Falzeder, 2002, p. xix). When Jung painted a less than flattering picture of him, Freud answered this made him look like an "uninspired plodder" (F/Jun, p. 79; cf. the previous chapter). He was an excellent organiser, however, and a skilful and mediating president of the Berlin Society. Michael Balint, who underwent his first training analysis there, called him

> the very best president I ever met in my life. … Again, he had his limitations. He didn't like fantasy very much. He didn't have much fantasy himself, but he was very much down to earth, excellent clinician, perfect clinician, and really a fair man. (Balint, 1965; in Falzeder, 1987, p. 85)

Ferenczi, on the other hand, was *rather* the "sloppy one", as Freud once said of him, someone of whom one "could not expect the correct execution of some routine work" (F/Eit I, p. 364). He was an original thinker, often hotheaded, who tended to present with great enthusiasm some new and unusal concepts, only to retract or tone down his statements later, someone who sparkled with ideas and experimented with all kinds of things. In his private life he was a "bobo", or bourgeois bohémien, a bachelor who lived in the hotel where he met with avant-garde writers, painters, journalists, and politicians; a womaniser with a number of affairs and adventures. As a student at the university, he once slept with the lover of his roommate, deceiving "her by wearing my friend's *cap*". ("Later it went", as he added not without pride, "without such pretense"; F/Fer II, p. 117.)

He was a gifted entertainer and, to quote again Jones, "the most brilliant member" of the Committee. "He was above all an inspiring lecturer and teacher." His talks were the highlights of the psychoanalytic congresses, and "he was the very life of every Congress. When it was his turn to deliver an address the hall was always thronged, and he never disappointed his audience" (II, pp. 157–158). He wrote a great number of shorter communications and observations, but never a systematic textbook. In the Hungarian Society he was the charismatic, sometimes also authoritarian alpha dog. Even his friend Anton von Freund noticed that he could sometimes "show intolerance toward others, even if he himself was certainly not aware of this" (letter to Freud, 15 March 1919; FML). His 'favourite enemy' Ernest Jones ascribed "a masterful or even domineering attitude" to him (II, p. 158).

Abraham's and Ferenczi's backgrounds were quite different. Abraham grew up as the second son of a small, orthodox Jewish family in Bremen in northern Germany. His father was a merchant and teacher of religion in his Jewish community. The parents were "the centre of a truly patriarchal and very harmonious family life". Although only Karl's brother Max suffered from asthma, "both boys were forbidden any kind of physical exercise apart from walks with their parents on Saturday or Sunday" (H. Abraham, 1974, pp. 19–20). For Karl, it was very bitter to be "guarded against every draught of air, watched with constant concern, and kept away from any games with other boys and from any sports", as his widow wrote later (in F/Abr, p. 861). It is probably no coincidence that later on he became an avid hiker and mountaineer, who was very proud of having made, "besides numerous high mountain tours, also a first ascent in the Alps" (ibid., and note p. 864). It is also interesting (and a bit macabre) that it was an affection of the lungs that led to his death.

Ferenczi was one of twelve children, growing up in the living quarters above his parents' book and print shop. Their house was

> a meeting place of artists and intellectuals from Hungary and abroad. People had animated discussions all the time, and played music. ... It was an open, hospitable home with an intellectually stimulating atmosphere, full of cheerfulness ... The kids were free to invite their friends and leave whenever they wanted. (Dupont, 1982, p. 21)

So when Abraham could complain about a lack of moving space and a severely restricted social life, Ferenczi missed tender care and loving attention.

In their theoretical orientations one could—again at the risk of over-simplifiying their differences—call Abraham a representative of 'classical' drive theory or, to use John Rickman's expression (1951), of "one-person psychology", whereas Ferenczi was a pioneer of so-called object-relations theory or "two-person psychology". In their therapeutical practice Ferenczi experimented with a number of, sometimes rather extreme, modifications, from the so-called active technique to "neocatharsis" and even mutual analysis, while Abraham remained more or less committed to the "classical technique".

In Ferenczi's case histories and vignettes we learn much about his own feelings, his countertransference, and the *dynamics* in the relationship between analyst and analysand. He let himself get engaged in "dramatic dialogues" with his patients, as the following example demonstrates (1931[292], p. 129):

> [A] patient ..., after overcoming strong resistances ... [resolves] to revive in his mind incidents from his earliest childhood. Thanks to the light analysis had already thrown on his early life, I was aware that ... he was identifying me with his grandfather. Suddenly ... he threw his arms round my neck and whispered in my ear: "I say, Grandpapa, I am afraid I am going to have a baby!" Thereupon I had what seems to me a happy inspiration: I said nothing to him for the moment about transference, etc., but retorted, in a similar whisper: "Well, but what makes you think so?"

We will look in vain for such scenes in Abraham's writings. His

> way of thinking and describing is based on the *nosographic* tradition in psychiatry and medicine. He gives us much information

about the behaviour of the patient and about his or her "complexes" but little about what today we would consider specifically "psychoanalytic"—how the analyst experiences the patient and how the interplay of images and phantasies of one about the other develops. (Haynal & Falzeder, 2002, p. xxviii)

Their relationship to Freud, too, was quite different, as is clearly witnessed by their respective correspondences with him. I agree with Jones that Freud's letters "to Ferenczi were by far the most personal", whereas the "correspondence with Abraham was totally different. The tone was throughout warm, but far less personal" (II, pp. 155–156). Without doubt, Ferenczi was much closer to Freud; for many years they went on vacation together, and Ferenczi was the only person Freud invited to accompany him on his trip to America (Jung had received a separate invitation as a speaker). Ferenczi for his part was absolutely loyal to Freud for a long time, and was rewarded by the Master in the form of special sympathy and recognition. Freud even toyed with the idea that Ferenczi could marry his daughter Mathilde.

On the other hand, from early on there were also conflicts, as in their joint trip to Sicily in 1910, in the imbroglio around Ferenczi's love triangle with Gizella and Elma Pálos, in Ferenczi's three short analyses in 1914 and 1916, in the conflicts within the Committee in the 1920s, and finally on the occasion of Ferenczi's radical technical experiments and the theoretical conclusions he drew from those experiences. Ferenczi vacillated between unconditional loyalty and secret—or sometimes even open—rebellion, and the conflict threatened to break him. Towards the end of his life Ferenczi even felt that Freud had never truly and fully understood him, but had used him instead (cf. Falzeder, 2010), and asked himself: "is it worth it always to live the life (will) of another person—is such a life not almost death?" (*Diary*, p. 257).

The relationship between Freud and Abraham never had such a dramatic quality to it. Even if their correspondence was clouded towards the end by the so-called film affair, there was never the shadow of a doubt in Freud's mind about Abraham's loyalty and commitment to Freud and the Cause, and there was never such a fundamental disagreement between them as between Freud and Ferenczi.

Let me repeat, however, that in highlighting their differences I have somewhat exaggerated them. Time and again we also find other examples that contradict such a one-sided picture. The rebellious Ferenczi could be, as I have already hinted at, also quite authoritarian and orthodox. The best known instance is probably his draft of the statutes for the foundational congress of the IPA (which was fully co-ordinated with Freud, and which had decidedly authoritarian features); or when he wrote to Freud that he did "not think that the ψα worldview leads to democratic egalitarianism" and that "the *intellectual elite of humanity* should maintain its hegemony" (F/Fer I, p. 130). The sober-minded and conservative Abraham, on the other hand, could for instance write a flaming protest against the ban on the Student Association for the Social Sciences by the president of Berlin University (May, 1999). Although he was often praised for his even temper, he had "a tendency to occasional explosive outbursts of temper". His mother "used to say that he was like a powder-keg, and she may well have set a spark to it at times" (H. Abraham, 1974, p. 20).

In their analytic practice, Ferenczi's so-called active technique reinforced the hierarchy between analyst and analysand by giving the latter explicit orders—although he later said he went too far, and experimented with the opposite method of extreme indulgence—while Abraham, on the other hand, was not always the 'classical', abstinent analyst he might appear to have been. So for instance he let his analysand Oscar A. H. Schmitz use his personal library, when he had to report for duty in 1914 and had to discontinue the analysis (Martynkewicz, 2007; Schmitz, 2007b). Or he visited his analysand Alix Strachey when she was bedridden because of tonsillitis (see page 279). Another analysand of his, Helene Deutsch, contradicts Balint's opinion quoted above when she calls him a "warm-hearted personality" with a "fertile imagination", which he would have hidden, however, "behind a sober façade" (1973, p. 129).

In addition, the two men also had a great deal in common, a fact that perhaps tends to be overlooked in view of their obvious differences. First of all, for both of them psychoanalysis was at the centre of their professional, even private lives. They were both (non-practising) Jews, belonged roughly to the same generation (Ferenczi was born in 1873, Abraham in 1877), and underwent a similar education and training in neurology and psychiatry so that, unlike many of Freud's Viennese followers, for example, they were well acquainted with psychiatric cases. After the break with Jung and Bleuler they were, together with Paul Federn and István Hollós, among the few analysts who studied the etiology and treatment of psychotic or borderline states, Abraham mainly mania and depression, Ferenczi borderline and schizoid disorders. Both also tried to secure a position at the university; for a short time, Ferenczi became the world's first professor of psychoanalysis during the Hungarian Council Republic (for which he was banned from the Budapest Medical Association after the counter-revolution), while Abraham's attempts failed altogether due to the political and academic resistances in Berlin.

They were also among the very first to settle in private psycho-analytic practice, although in the beginning they had to take on also other jobs to make ends meet, for instance, as forensic experts at court. They were pioneers in two important capitals of continental Europe, who analysed, taught, trained, and influenced a whole gen-eration of analysts. There were only very few analysts (apart from Freud himself, of course, or his daughter Anna) who exerted a com-parable amount of influence. It is important to note that neither of them used this influence to found a 'school' of their own, but that they rather encouraged their students to creatively develop their own thoughts.

A case in point is an analysand of both of them: Melanie Klein. As is well known, she later developed a theory that postulated a very early and very differentiated fantasy life of the infant, and worked—in con-trast to the more 'pedagogical' approach of Anna Freud—with direct, 'deep' interpretations of the child's behaviour as an expression of those unconscious fantasies. Perhaps somewhat oversimplifying one could say that her theory describes how *relationships* are experienced on the matrix of an *instinctual* constitution, how deep-seated unconscious fan-tasies about them arise (e.g., about persecution, envy, or reparation), and how mechanisms are developed to deal with them (e.g., splitting or projective identification). Her main focus, however, was always on the *intrapsychic* representations and processes and not, as in her contempo-raries John Bowlby, Donald W. Winnicott, or Michael Balint, on the *real* interactions. Again at the risk of oversimplification, one could describe her theory as a one-person psychology about two-person relationships, having thus creatively and originally further developed the legacy of *both* her teachers.

As far as Abraham's and Ferenczi's relationship to one another is concerned, it was defined above all by their respective relation to Freud and their positions within the Committee. To quote again Ernest Jones (II, p. 159), Abraham

> was—I will not say exactly the most reserved—but the least expansive of us. He had none of Ferenczi's sparkle and engaging manner. One would scarcely use the word "charm" in describing him; in fact Freud used sometimes to tell me he found him "too Prussian". ... Intellectually independent, he was also emotionally self-contained, and appeared to have no need for any specially warm friendship.

The closest relationship with an analyst he developed was probably the one with Ernest Jones, who in many respects had a similarly pragmatic way of thinking.

Today the attention on their relationship is mostly focused on their conflicts in the 1920s. The joint book by Ferenczi and Rank, *The Development of Psychoanalysis* (1924), was actually in the service of the "politics of science" (Ferenczi & Groddeck, 1982/2006, p. 102)—and especially aimed against the kind of therapeutic technique as it was practiced in Berlin, that is, a veiled attack at Abraham. Two factions developed within the Committee, the main representatives being Ferenczi and Rank on the one side, and Abraham and Jones on the other. Freud at first supported the former, but then distanced himself more and more and eventually changed sides altogether, with the result that Rank left the psychoanalytic movement for good, and Ferenczi's position within it became problematic and marginalised. After the break with Rank, however, Abraham and Ferenczi made efforts to reconcile—efforts that were brutally interrupted by Abraham's untimely death shortly afterwards.

Looking up the indices of their works, we find that Abraham mentioned Ferenczi only twenty-four times, while Ferenczi quoted Abraham even less frequently (nine times). It seems that these two psychoanalytic opinion leaders worked rather independently of one another and pursued their own lines of work, referring to the other's work only occasionally and often probably for tactical reasons or out of politeness.

To conclude, I think it is fair to say that theirs was less a *personal* relationship—it can be doubted whether they would have found each other and collaborated in a different setting—but rather that it was characterised by the roles and positions they assumed in a movement to which both subscribed, by the theoretical and therapeutic-technical stance they took, and their respective relationship with Freud.

When Karl Abraham, president of both the IPA and the Berlin Society, unexpectedly died at Christmas 1925, it became necessary, for the fourth time in the still quite short history of the psychoanalytic movement, to appoint an interim president by circumventing the statutes which stipulated that the president be elected by the members at the congress (1914 from Jung to Abraham, 1919 from Ferenczi to Freud, and from Freud to Jones; see Falzeder, in prep.). Michael Schröter notes that originally Ferenczi "should have filled the gap, above all, as president of the IPA, and it was even seriously considered that he could move to Berlin and replace Abraham as president of the Berlin Society and main lecturer at the Institute" (Schröter, in F/Eit I, p. 18). In his obituary of Abraham, Freud writes that "he won so pre-eminent a place that only one other name could be set beside his" (Freud, 1926b, p. 277). There is no doubt whom he had in mind.

This did not come about (Eitingon was appointed interim president and confirmed at the next congress), and it would be idle to speculate on the possible consequences of Ferenczi's becoming Abraham's direct successor. Idle to speculate, too, what would have happened if both of them had been able to fully continue their creative work—Ferenczi died only a few years later, himself only sixty years old—and also if they had succeeded in fleeing in the 1930s, and where to, and what influence they might have exerted there. As the saying goes, "history is just one thing happening after the other"; it is what it is. They were two brilliant psychoanalysts, each in his own way, and their works still deserve to be read. Let us simply be grateful to have, in the history of psychoanalysis, two such gifted, creative, and inspirational personalities, each in his own way.

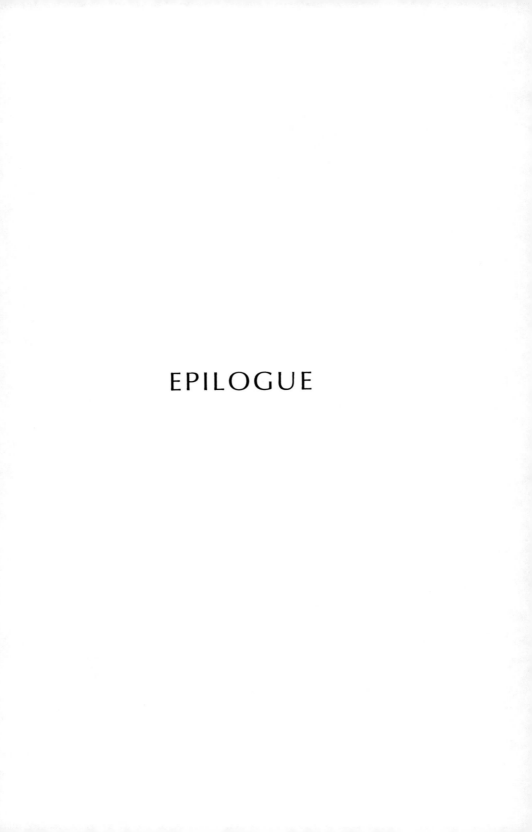

EPILOGUE

"A fat wad of dirty pieces of paper": Freud on America, Freud in America, Freud and America

Introduction: Freud's antipathies

It has been said that Sigmund Freud was a great hater. His follower Isidor Sadger (2005, p. 78), for instance, wrote in his memoirs that he "had always been a ferocious hater. He could always hate much more powerfully than he could love." Another follower, Alfred Winterstein, even let Freud know in the daily newspaper to which he, Freud, subscribed, that Freud was, "as the English say, a good hater" (Winterstein, 1924). According to the late Paul Roazen (1968, p. 313), he "was among the world's great haters", someone "who never forgave [his] opponents."

And indeed, there are a great many persons, things, fashions, attitudes, and beliefs that Sigmund Freud seems to have hated. Among the persons he hated most were those who had once been his followers, or likely candidates to be persuaded to join his Cause, but who then defected. Even if the troop he commanded was a "wild horde" (Ferenczi & Groddeck, 1982/2006, p. 59), for him authority and loyalty were as important as in a regular army. Freud could bear such an unforgiving grudge against those who had left him and psychoanalysis that he wouldn't hear their names uttered in his house. For example, his sister-in-law Minna Bernays told psychoanalyst Else Pappenheim, a friend of hers, that the name of Adler was not to be mentioned in Freud's presence after the break.[1] In 1931 he drew up a "hate list"— "Not many, seven or eight names in all" (F/Eit, p. 747)—but we do not know whose names were on that list.

He was also opposed to many modern trends or innovations of his time, from modern art and music to filmmaking or fashion fads such as the so-called *Bubikopf*, a kind of pageboy haircut popular in the 1920s (F/ Fer III, p. 222). He "hated the telephone and avoided its use whenever possible".[2] He "hated bicycles", that is, until motor-cycles appeared, which then won his detestation (M. Freud, 1957, p. 106). There is also a widespread belief that Freud hated philosophy, music, and Vienna. Not to mention Christianity.[3] And finally, there seems to be a consensus that Freud hated America.

Some of these popular beliefs have been put into perspective. We know that as a student Freud was eminently preoccupied with philosophical problems,[4] but neither did he completely lose this inter-est in his later years, as he so often alleged. Why else would he have had Rank send him Schopenhauer's works to Badgastein during his

---

[1] Pappenheim later told Bernhard Handlbauer this in an interview and also confirmed it in writing (Pappenheim, 2004, p. 39).

[2] According to his son, for Freud "conversation had to be a very personal thing. He looked one straight in the eye, and he could read one's thoughts. ... Father, aware of his power when looking at a person, felt he had lost it when looking at a dead telephone mouthpiece" (ibid.; cf. Berthelsen, 1987, p. 28).

[3] "Freud hated Christianity, he hated all that it stood for" (Isbister, 1985, p. 179).

[4] For example, in his encounter with the ideas of Schopenhauer and Nietzsche in the *Leseverein der deutschen Studenten Wiens*, a Germanophile literary and philosophical circle, of which he was a member between 1872 and 1878 (Brauns & Schöpf, 1989); and also through his encounter with Franz Brentano (1838–1917), then professor of philosophy in Vienna. For four semesters, he had enrolled in the courses of "this splendid man, scholar and philosopher", and even attended other courses given by him without enrolling in them. Brentano also recommended that Freud and his friend Paneth study Kant, and Freud's library indeed contains a copy of *The Critique of Pure Reason* with many notes in his hand (F/Sil, 5 November 1874; Davies & Fichtner, 2006). To Flieβ he wrote that he "most secretly nourish[ed] the hope of arriving ... at my original goal of philosophy. For that is what I wanted originally"; and: "As a young man I knew no longing other than for philosophical knowledge, and now I am about to fulfil it as I move from medicine to psychology" (F/Fli, pp. 159, 180).

vacation (F/AF, p. 232)?[5] Why else, to name but one other example, had he quit reading Nietzsche because of "an *excess* of interest" (*Minutes II*, p. 359; my ital.)?[6]

While the legend of Freud's philosophical ignorance has since been variously treated, and at least partly refuted, in the scholarly literature (e.g., Haynal, 1994), the beliefs in his alleged disdain for music and Vienna respectively still seem mostly to hold their ground. This is not the place to go into detail, but let me just mention that in the letters he sent home to his family from his various travels he reported no fewer than five visits to the opera house (Freud, 2002). His analysand John M. Dorsey recalled that during a session Freud was "leaning over the couch to sing [sic!] one or two strains to me from Mozart's *Don Giovanni*" (Dorsey, 1976, p. 51). Towards one female patient, who recited a long list of men from various countries (Luxemburg, Norway, Sweden, Holland, …) whom she had found attractive, he dryly remarked: "This is exactly like Leporello's aria in Don Giovanni", not without adding the name under which this aria is known among music connoisseurs—"the catalogue aria, it's called" (Koellreuter, 2009, p. 64). There's even an apocryphal anecdote that, when once challenged because of the obvious discrepancy between his proclaimed dislike of music and his love of Mozart, particularly his operas, he is said to have said: "Ah, but Mozart is something else." The often quoted anecdote that Freud had insisted that the piano, which had been rented for his sister Anna, be removed because her practicing broke his concentration during his studies (e.g., Freud-Bernays, 2004, p. 14), might rather be due to the quite understandable irritation by endless, and far from faultless repetitions of the same pieces—something everybody can identify with whose neighbour's child practiced *Für Elise* for the umpteenth

---

[5] This was in preparation for *Beyond the Pleasure Principle* (1920g). Incidentally, Freud quoted Schopenhauer twenty-six times in his works, constantly underlining that he considered him a great thinker. Cf. Guttman et al., 1983, 1995.

[6] The fact that Otto Rank gave him, as a birthday present for his seventieth birthday and as a parting gift, the recently published complete works of Nietzsche, twenty-three volumes bound in white leather (Roazen, 1971, p. 412), is of course not in itself a proof of Freud's interest. However, it "is significant that Freud, who could bring only part of his library out of Vienna, chose to include Rank's gift"—and probably not just out of affection for Rank (Lieberman, 1985, pp. 436–437).

time—than the action of a serious music hater.[7] After all, during those studies schoolboy Sigi was used to humming Viennese folk songs himself in his own room: "There's one thing, dear Lord, I'm asking for, though, send me a fiver, I'm needing some dough" (Freud-Bernays, 2004, p. 221).

I am not claiming that Freud was a music *lover*, however. He much preferred dramas or texts set to music, such as in operas or songs (he adored Yvette Guilbert, for instance),[8] over music without words, such as symphonies, etc., and his taste was quite conventional (*Don Giovanni, Carmen*). His claim of not liking music should also, in my opinion, be seen against the background of the average bourgeois academic in contemporary Vienna, for whom the *Staatsoper* was often like a second living room, who played an instrument himself, and whose children all had to learn to play one. Before the rise of the gramophone and the radio, piano arrangements for two and four hands played the major role in distributing classical and popular music, and the households of the Vienna middle classes resounded with the music played on their upright pianos. Freud certainly did not comply with this standard, but this does not make him a music hater.

As to his attitude toward Vienna, his son Martin (1957, p. 48) has put this into common-sense, and I find quite cogent, perspective:

> I am not convinced that Sigmund Freud's often-expressed dislike of Vienna was either deep-seated or real. It is not difficult for a London man, or a New York man, both devoted to their respective home cities, to say, "How I hate London; how I loathe New York".

Viennese in particular are famous for railing against their home city, in a grumpily devoted and almost tender way. But you should see them race to Vienna's defence if someone from out of town should dare and do the same. From his exile in London, Freud wrote to Eitingon: "The

---

[7] In fact, in his own later household there seems to have been a piano: in a letter to his daughter Mathilde of 19 March 1908 he writes of "the piano in our apartment" (F/Kinder, p. 47).

[8] In 1927, Freud attended all three performances of Guilbert in Vienna, on a seat in the first row reserved for him by the singer herself, and "utterly enjoyed it" (F/Eit, p. 566). He also went to performances in 1929, 1930, and 1931, and recorded this in his diary (Freud, 1992i, pp. 47, 62, 87, 114).

triumphant feeling of liberation is too much mixed with the work of mourning since, after all, one still loved the prison very much from which one was released" (F/Eit, p. 903).[9]

Freud's hatred of America and the Americans was so often expressed, and is so well documented, however, that there seems to be no doubt about his feelings. On the other hand, we do find occasional statements of Freud's, in which he had positive things to say about America, or even expressed his admiration. Various historians and scholars have tried to explain Freud's alleged hatred of America, without taking into account the other side of his ambivalence. What we lack until now, in my opinion, is a satisfactory explanation of Freud's obviously more complex relationship to the United States and its citizens.

In what follows I will first give some choice examples of negative things Freud had to say and write about America, then give a few examples of positive remarks, discuss some of the peculiarities of Freud's attitude, and finally have a look at his possible motives, including one that was first mentioned by Ferenczi (see below) but is rarely mentioned in the literature in this context. In assessing the impact of Freud on America, it might help to try and understand Freud's own changing attitudes toward the culture, into which he tried to introduce his ideas.

Freud's negative attitude toward America

To begin with, let me quote three eminent Freud scholars. Ernest Jones called Freud's attitude toward America a "prejudice", and "so obviously unfair on the subject" that it "actually had nothing to do with America itself" (III, p. 59). Peter Gay, who gave a long (though not exhaustive) compilation of Freud's invectives against America and the Americans in his Freud biography, wrote: "Whatever guise the American assumed, saint or moneygrubber, Freud was ready to write him off as a most unattractive specimen in the human zoo." He slashed "away at Americans wholesale, quite indiscriminately, with imaginative

---

[9] Also quoted by Jones, who writes about Freud's "deep love" of that city, which "was kept so hidden" (II, p. 230). Bruno Bettelheim suggests that "Freud's supposed 'hatred' of Vienna was probably the expression of a deep early love that became frustrated by anti-Semitism in the early twentieth century, a frustration the more keenly felt as the earlier love was never given up" (Bettelheim, 1990, p. 46).

ferocity" (Gay, 1987, pp. 562–570, quotations from pp. 562, 567).[10] Patrick Mahony (2004, p. 35):

> Whereas Freud changed his mind on many topics, he never altered his vehement anti-Americanism which came from the depths of his being. No matter what genre Freud wrote in—scientific treatise, dialogue, history, biography, autobiography, letters, case-history narratives, you name it—America came to his mind as a ready example of what was bad. And no matter what subject Freud discussed—dreams, clinical theory, psychoanalytic treatment, history, or social issues—America emerged as an immediate association of what was bad.[11]

It is true that Freud hardly missed an occasion to express his derision, ridicule, or scorn concerning the Americans. Here are a few examples.

- In 1915, with regard to his love of and addiction to tobacco: "I actually know of no other apology for Columbus's atrocity"—namely, to have discovered America (F/Fer II, p. 58).
- In 1923, he chided Brill for having "submitted far too much to the two big vices of America, the greed for money and the respect of public opinion" (LC).
- In 1924: The only reasonable way to bear a "stay among these uncivilized beings", he wrote to Rank, would be "selling your services as dearly as possible" (F/Ran, p. 202).[12]
- In 1925: "The Americans transfer the democratic principle from politics into science. Everybody must become president once, no one must remain president; none may excel before the others, and thus all of them neither learn nor achieve anything" (in Gay, 1987, p. 566).

---

[10]Gay's use of the words "human zoo" is quite in line with Freud's general misanthropy for mankind in general, and, occasionally, patients in particular. To Eitingon, Freud wrote, for example: "My zoo now comprises two Americans and an Englishman, a second specimen of the latter kind is announced for the beginning of April. The supplier is Jones" (F/Eit, p. 191).

[11]Here quoted from the author's own, unpublished English version of this paper, as delivered at the Austen Riggs Center, 13 November 2003. With thanks to Pat Mahony for providing that paper.

[12]And again, in 1928: "These savages have little interest in scholarship that cannot be immediately put into practice" (to Wittels; LC).

- In 1925: "I recently offended an American with the suggestion that the Statue of Liberty in New York harbor should be replaced by a monkey holding up a Bible. I.e., I tried [to offend him]; he didn't seem to understand me at all" (F/Fer III, p. 227).[13]
- In 1927, he gave the following reasons for the Americans' opposition to so-called lay analysis: "The analysts' lack of authority, the inability of the American public to make sound judgements, and the low standard of public morals in God's own country, looking the other way, particularly where matters of earning money are concerned— the counterpart to American sanctimoniousness and moral hypocrisy. (I do not invent these things *ad hoc*; they are admitted and fought by quite a number of courageous American intellectuals)" (to Brill; LC).
- In 1929, with regard to a planned source book of Freud's psychoanalytic writings for American audiences: "Basically, the whole matter is quite distasteful to me as being so very American. You may rest assured that once such a 'source-book' is available, no American will ever consult an original text" (F/Jon, p. 657; trans. mod.).
- In 1929: "... the American pattern of replacing quality with quantity" (to Frankwood Williams; in Gay, 1987, pp. 566–567).
- In, 1930: America is "Dollaria" (F/Pfi, p. 135).[14]
- In 1930, and in print: Americans "make a hotch-potch out of psycho-analysis and other elements and quote this procedure as evidence of their *broad-mindedness*, whereas it only proves their *lack of judgement*" (Freud, 1930c, pp. 254–255).[15]

---

[13]This was probably an allusion to the notorious Scopes or "Monkey" Trial in Tennessee earlier in the same year (1925), testing whether the state could forbid the teaching of Darwinism. The trial was widely publicised, and Freud could well have learned of it from the press or his Anglo-Saxon followers.—With thanks to the gentleman (whose name I unfortunately do not remember) who drew my attention to this possibility after I had presented this paper at the New York Academy of Medicine.

[14]This contemptuous term for the United States was evidently common among Central European intellectuals. As early as 1921, Albert Einstein, writing about an upcoming trip to America, expected a correspondent, Fritz Haber, to be familiar with a reference to "Dollaria" (in Kormos Buchwald, 2009, p. 127). Reference through the great courtesy of Professor Diana Kormos Buchwald.

[15]To Wittels he wrote in a similar vein in 1928: "The worst thing about the American bustle is their so-called broadmindedness, with which they feel superior to us narrow-minded Europeans, while in reality this is merely a cover-up of their complete lack of judgement" (LC).

- 1937: "There is going through my head an advertisement which I think is the most daring and felicitous piece of American publicity: 'Why live, if you can be buried for ten dollars?'" (to Marie Bonaparte; in Jones III, p. 465; trans. mod.).

In short, America is "Dollaria", "ruled" not by authority, but "by the dollar" (F/Fli, p. 457), it is an "Anti-Paradise" (F/AZ, p. 170), that "[d]amned country!" (F/Fer III, p. 320). "Yes, America is gigantic, but a gigantic mistake" (Jones, 1959, p. 191).

American men are savages, they are stupid, ignorant, shallow, uncultivated, egoistic,[16] sanctimonious, hypocritical, prudish, money-grubbing, anal,[17] dishonest,[18] arrogant, inferior, falsely democratic,[19] stiff, spiritless, loud, anti-Semitic,[20] and dominated by their women whom they do not know how to put in their right place.

In America there is a "petticoat government" (*Frauenherrschaft*) (Freud, 1927c, p. 49). American women "make fools" of their men, they "are an anti-cultural phenomenon [*eine kulturwidrige Erscheinung*]. ... In Europe, things are different: men take the lead and that is as it should be" (Wortis, 1954, p. 98). "[I]n America the father ideal appears to be downgraded, so that the American girl cannot muster the illusion that is necessary for marriage" (*Minutes III*, p. 14). To Blumgart he wrote: "None of you [Americans] has ever found the right attitude toward your women."[21]

---

[16]"Unfortunately I trust the Americans least to have a sense of solidarity, an ability to organise, and an inclination to mitigate competition out of consideration for the common cause" (to Irmarita Putnam, probably 1932; LC).

[17]"Nowhere is one so overwhelmed by the senselessness of human striving as there, where one no longer recognises as a life-purpose even the enthusiastic gratification of natural animal needs. It is a deranged, anal, Adlerish mess" (F/Ran, p. 202). The Americans have "no time for the libido" (F/Jun, p. 256).

[18]Jelliffe was "one of the worst American businessmen, translate: crooks, Columbus has discovered" (F/Abr, p. 162).

[19]In answer to an American Jew's criticism of analysis, Freud wrote: "I had overlooked what the effect must be of a conjuncture of American-democratic outlook and Jewish-Chutzpah" (in Jones III, p. 451).

[20]He wrote of the "redskins": "American anti-Semitism, gigantic in its latency" (F/Eit, p. 801). To Wortis he said: "Every country has the Jews it deserves", and "America certainly hasn't encouraged the best kind of social conduct" (Wortis, 1954, p. 145).

[21]A. A. Brill Library, New York Psychoanalytic Institute.

Does all this reflect pure, unambivalent, and unadulterated hatred? Was Freud really such a simple man? Is a prejudice sometimes simply a prejudice? Or is "[t]he fellow ... actually somewhat more complicated" (Freud, 1960a, p. 402)? Could this be a case of 'The Professor doth protest too much, methinks'?

Peculiarities of Freud's attitude toward America

On a closer look, three things about Freud's America bashing are somewhat peculiar and stand out. First, that he greatly stepped up his attacks after his trip to the United States. Before, his anti-American utterances were not significantly different from those of the average central European bourgeois academic of his time.[22] Michael Molnar writes that

> Freud's persistent and ungracious denigration of America [had] many of the hallmarks of a commonplace European prejudice of the times. ... The United States was projected as a monstrous twin and parody of Europe. A conquistador approach towards them was justified, they, the apparent exploiters, are themselves only fit to be exploited.[23]

After his visit, however, Freud's scorn was spiked with even more vitriol than was usual in central European circles.

Second, even if one is thus forced to conclude that it was precisely his experiences during that trip that made him form such an unforgiving opinion (and he himself *later* stated numerous times that this was so), the letters he sent to his family *from* America sound much more positive. They sound like what one would expect from someone travelling for the first time to a foreign country and culture: there were things that impressed him, positively or negatively, things he liked and didn't like, conveniences he enjoyed or missed. Quite understandably, he also had difficulties in adjusting to the unfamiliar food and in understanding the American accent.[24]

---

[22] Although it should be noted that we have significantly less documentation in general on the years before he began to correspond regularly with his major followers (that is, up until about 1907 or 1908).

[23] Unpublished manuscript, undated.

[24] He was not the only one; immigrants from the German-speaking countries often struggled with the language. Even though they read English, they often understood and spoke

There are actually a number of quite positive remarks:[25] "One quickly gets accustomed to the city [New York]", for instance, or even: "One also understands the moneymaking [!], seeing what one can get for money, and what can be done with it." When he wrote that he "marvel[ed] at the famous sky-scrapers", and added: "I will not let myself be impressed, and I insist on having seen so much more beautiful things, albeit nothing greater and wilder", this sounds like a conscious effort to distance himself from the great impression these things did make upon him, to sober up, so to speak, from the intoxicating impact of New York City. He even wrote: "Within two weeks one would feel at home, and wouldn't want to leave." One wouldn't want to leave! Why write this about a country that he allegedly hated so much? Why don't we take this statement as seriously as the one he wrote on board the ship on his way back: "America was a crazy machine; I am very glad that I am out of it, and even more so that I don't have to live there ... East, West—Home best. I won't object to be again sitting in our little quarters in the ninth district [of Vienna]"? In fact, this sounds like a textbook example of ambivalence: "One wouldn't want to leave" versus "I'm glad to be out of it". And finally, his lectures at Clark University were all as successful as he could reasonably have hoped for. All in all, judging from these letters one cannot but get the impression that he seems to have thoroughly enjoyed himself. Perhaps too much so, for his own taste. He nearly seems to have been swept away by all those powerful impressions, only sobering up once he was out of the crazy machine again, and then blaming the whole country for his own loss of self-control.

Sure, there are some remarks in which he made fun of America and the Americans. He complained about the scarcity of public toilets, for instance: "They escort you along miles of corridors and ultimately you are taken to the very basement where a marble palace awaits you, only

---

the language poorly. Martin Grotjahn tells the amusing story of Otto Fenichel's visit to the Menninger Clinic in Topeka. Having been asked to give a lecture, he "wanted to talk about something he called 'penis envoy'. That did not sound right to us and I tentatively suggested to use the words 'penis ivy'". Another emigré did suggest "penis envy", but this was "rejected as too unlikely" by Fenichel and Grotjahn. So Fenichel "rushed with great enthusiasm into the matter, respected by all and understood by none. 'Penis envoy' finally brought the house down" (Grotjahn, 1987, pp. 148–149).

[25]The following quotes are from his travel diary and letters sent to his family (all in Freud, 2002, pp. 273–318). Some passages from these documents were already quoted by Rosenzweig (1992), occasionally in a questionable or wrong translation.

just in time" (Jones II, p. 60). As to his difficulties in understanding the American accent, there was that episode when "one American asked another to repeat a remark he had not quite caught", upon which "Freud turned to Jung with the acid comment: 'These people cannot even understand each other'" (ibid.). When he visited the Canadian side of the Niagara Falls, he commented: "There the people at once speak clearer English" (Freud, 2002, p. 307). To Max Schur he once remarked: "This race is destined to extinction. They can no longer open their mouths to speak; soon they won't be able to do so to eat" (in Gay, 1987, p. 567).

The tone of these remarks, however, rather strikes me as nearly playful, a bit tongue-in-cheek, as if writing with a wink to his wife and children from a highly cultured gentleman's expedition to a savage and primitive, yet strangely successful tribe—so if there is an admixture of condescension in these remarks, there is nothing to foreshadow his later unrelenting malice. So what did really happen that, in his later memory, made America such a horrible place?

Freud himself always blamed his first-hand and 'first-bowel' experience of America for his disdain of it, and also for the whole "medley of ... [his] transatlantic complaints—destroyed health in general, chronic indigestion, intestinal disorders, prostatitis, appendicitis, writer's cramp, and bad handwriting [!]".[26] And this, Mahony continues, although the medical records left by his personal physician do not confirm such a prostate condition, and he had had attacks of writer's cramp as far back as in the 1880s (Mahony, 2004, pp. 37–38). We know that he had digestive troubles all his adult life; in fact, in a letter to his daughter Mathilde written shortly *before* the departure to America, he already complained about his "rebellious stomach" (F/Kinder, p. 70). Other countries, too, caused such troubles in him. After returning from the International Psychoanalytic Congress in The Hague in 1920, he wrote to his son Ernst that he had "brought back a ruined stomach" (ibid., p. 308)—but this certainly did not make him hate Holland. As to his handwriting, if this was not actually meant as a joke entirely, which I doubt, there are certainly no signs that it "deteriorated" after the journey.

---

[26] After the trip, Freud wrote to Ernest Jones (in English): "My handwriting has deteriorated so very much since the American trip" (F/Jon, p. 42).

The third peculiarity about Freud's attitude toward America is the intriguing fact that the things he hated and criticised most (the materialistic worldview, the greed for money, the rule of the dollar) struck a not unambivalent chord in himself. After all, money was "laughing gas" to him. "I know from my youth that once the wild horses of the pampas have been lassoed, they retain a certain anxiousness for life. Thus I came to know the helplessness of poverty and continually fear it" (F/Fli, p. 374). Before this background, it is interesting to see what Freud had to say about money in his notes during the trip: "From time to time I take out the portefeuille and look at the three big banknotes and the small pile of dirty-green 5-dollar notes that I changed, poor images of the mightiest God—to bring me back again to reality." "In my billfold there reigns polytheism: [Austrian] Crowns, [German] Marks, and now the mightiest God, the Dollar." The quote in the title of this article is taken from the following: "F[erenczi] has a fat wad of dirty pieces of paper with him, black on one side, green on the other, bearing a picture in the middle of something like a buffalo or of other animals. These are dollar notes with a denomination of 10 or 50" (all in Freud, 2002). It is interesting that Freud also counted the other currencies among the "Gods", although in his opinion none was as powerful as the new God, the dollar.

Freud *was* ambitious, he *wanted* to become independent, rich, and famous, despite his loud protestations to the contrary. At the beginning of his medical career, he had even had "the intention of going to America, when the three months for which [he] had made sufficient provision failed to begin very auspiciously" (F/Fer II, p. 348).[27] But why to America, of all places, if he really hated it so much? Why not to his beloved England, for example, where he also had relatives who could have helped him? Or to Germany? He implies it himself: because he believed he could make money in the New World, more or easier money, that is, than if he stayed on in the Old World. So why despise a whole nation for allegedly being after something he himself wanted to achieve?

As to his claim not to be ambitious at all, Jung's friend and pupil Edward A. Bennet recounts what Jung had told him (1961, p. 43):

---

[27]Already as a boy, Freud "knew much about America and American authors", his favourite being Mark Twain (Freud-Bernays, 2004, p. 220). When Mark Twain gave a public lecture in Vienna, Freud "greatly enjoyed" listening to it (Jones III, p. 329).

[W]hen their boat was approaching New York with its famous sky-line, Jung saw Freud gazing—as he thought—at the view and spoke to him. He was surprised when Freud said, "Won't they get a surprise when they hear what we have to say to them"—referring to the coming lectures.[28] "How ambitious you are!" exclaimed Jung. "Me?" said Freud. "I'm the most humble of men, and the only man[29] who isn't ambitious." Jung replied: "That's a big thing—to be the only one".

Freud's critique boils down to his allegation that the Americans do not appreciate the *real* values (ethical norms, classical education, honest work, appreciation of the intellectual elite, etc.), but would do nearly anything for the *false* ones in the interest of their God, the dollar,[30] while maintaining a hypocritical, sanctimonious façade—monkeys holding up the Bible, indeed. Even if there might be a kernel of truth in his criticisms,[31] his attitude bears all the hallmarks of a prejudice. In fact, interestingly enough, his main criticism—greed for money—is

---

[28] In another version Freud is said to have said: "Don't they know that we're bringing them the plague?" (e.g., Noll, 1994, p. 47). According to Elisabeth Roudinesco (1993, p. 398), this anecdote goes back to what Jacques Lacan claimed Jung had told him. Lacan had visited Jung in 1954 to ask him about his relationship with Freud. In a seminar given in Vienna the following year, in German (!), Lacan then declared publicly that Jung had allegedly told him about that statement of Freud's. Roudinesco notes that Lacan's word is the only evidence we have that this might actually have happened. Other sources (Jones, Schur, Ellenberger, Brome, Oberndorf, Roazen, Hale, Gay, or the above quoted Bennet) only report that Freud said something like: "They will be quite surprised at what we will have to say to them!" In his interview with Eissler, Jung has the following to say: "When we entered the harbor of New York, we were standing on the bridge, and Freud said to me: 'If they only knew what we are bringing them!' I thought: Well, we will soon see what the Americans will do, won't we?! (laughs)" (LC).

[29] Probably meaning: among the three of them, Freud, Jung, and Ferenczi.

[30] "It is impossible to escape the impression that people commonly use false standards of measurement—that they seek power, success and wealth for themselves and admire them in others, and that they underestimate what is of true value in life." And: "... individuals of the leader type do not acquire the importance that should fall to them in the formation of a group. The present cultural state of America would give us a good opportunity for studying the damage to civilization which is thus to be feared" (Freud, 1930a, pp. 64, 116).

[31] Not even paranoiacs, when "they project outwards on to others what they do not wish to recognise in themselves, ... project it into the blue, so to speak, where there is nothing of the sort already" (Freud, 1922b, p. 226).

one of the most common *anti-Semitic* prejudices.[32] Freud's view was generalised, it did not change in the light of new experiences, and it was singularly aimed at one nation and its inhabitants (or one "race").

As if Freud could not have found such an attitude (and all the other things he accused the Americans of in his sweeping wholesale attack) also much closer to home! It is true, he often enough criticised culture or civilisation in general, and occasionally made a deprecatory aside about other nations, such as Italy, Hungary, Germany, etc., and above all Austria (and its capital, Vienna), but he certainly did not purely hate these countries as such, and no other nation ever gave rise to so much derision in him as America. So were the Americans Freud's scapegoats for something he could not admit in himself?

Freud's attitude toward particular groups of Americans

Freud reserved some special scorn for particular groups of Americans, for instance businessmen, journalists, publishers, and—psychoanalysts. To one Edward Petrikovitch he wrote: "I may assume that you are a compatriot. If you have been living in America for a long time I am surprised that you still believe anything at all written in an American newspaper. ... With one single exception I have ... not seen an interviewer in the last years. Most of all I am wary of Americans or correspondents for American papers" (17 January 1928; LC). Or: "American publishers are a dangerous sort of human beings" (to Helen Downey; LC). His own publishers Boni and Liveright he called "the two swindlers" (F/Ran, p. 208).

A chapter in itself would be his unrelenting criticisms of American psychoanalysts. A long list of these complaints can be found in a postscript to his article on the question of lay analysis. This postscript

---

[32] I am indebted to David Lotto who sent me an unpublished paper of his after my presentation, in which he makes the following point: "Freud's accusations about Americans' alleged preoccupation with making money and using dishonest methods to acquire wealth are uncomfortably close to the traditional anti-Semitic accusations so frequently made about Jews. Thus Freud's passionate prejudice against Americans can be seen as an attempt at overcompensation by adopting values and ways of behaving that serve to refute the stereotypical canard." In his accompanying email message of 7 October 2009, Lotto added: "I do think that combating anti-Semitism was one of the strongest sources that fueled Freud's vitriol toward America. His anger was displaced (although one could argue about how much distortion this involved) from anti-Semites to Americans."

was originally intended for print, but eventually withdrawn from publication by him, obviously out of political and diplomatic considerations. There he writes, for instance, of "the Americans' dread of authority, their tendency to exert their personal independence in the few areas that are not yet occupied by the relentless pressure of public opinion"; he states that "the level of general education and of the intellectual capacity to absorb is by far lower than in Europe, even in persons who went to an American college"; or "that the American has no time. True, time is—money, but one does not really understand why time has to be converted into money in such haste. It would retain its monetary value anyway, even at a slower pace, and one should also suppose that the more time one invested to begin with, the more money would come out of it in the end." "The American super-ego seems to lower its severity against the ego very much in matters of financial interest." And Freud ends his tirade with the following words: "But perhaps my readers will find that I have said enough bad things about this country, to which we have learned to bow in the last decade" (in Grubrich-Simitis, 1993, pp. 226–229).

The most devastating example of Freud's unsuccessful efforts to deal with the psychoanalytic movement and institutions in America is arguably his effort to make Horace Westlake Frink the leader of American psychoanalysis. Frink, a native American, co-founder of the New York Psychoanalytic Society, suffered from a manic-depressive psychosis, homosexual conflicts, and confusional states, and became Freud's patient in 1921. A married father of two children, Frink fell in love with his rich patient Angelika (Angie) Bijur, also married. Bijur went to Vienna in the summer of 1921 and saw Freud several times about a possible marriage with Frink. She reported Freud's position this way: "[H]e advised my getting a divorce because of my own incomplete existence—and because if I threw Dr. F. over now, he would never again try to come back to normality and probably develop into a homosexual, though in a highly disguised way."[33] To Frink Freud wrote that he had requested Mrs. Bijur

---

[33] On the Freud/Frink disaster see especially Edmunds, 1988; Warner, 1994; and Zitrin, 1998. Mahony (2004) has given an overview on the basis of these three sources. The quoted letters and other materials (here quoted after Mahony) are held by the Alan M. Chesney Archives at Johns Hopkins University.

not to repeat to foreign people I had advised her to marry you on the threat of a nervous breakdown. It gives them a false idea of the kind of advice that is compatible with analysis and is very likely to be used against analysis. May I still suggest to you that your idea Mrs. B had lost part of her beauty be turned into having part of her money. ... Your complaint that you cannot grasp your homosexuality implies that you are not aware of your phantasy of making me a rich man. If matters turn out all right, let us change this imaginary gift into a real contribution to psychoanalytic funds.

Shortly after both had divorced their partners, Frink underwent a second analysis with Freud, during which he decompensated and suffered from psychotic hallucinatory episodes. He recovered, however; Freud said he felt the analysis to be completed, and Horace and Angie went to Paris and married. Back in America, after some time Frink's condition worsened again. He was hospitalised, recovered, released, made two suicidal attempts, was again hospitalised, and Bijur undertook divorce proceedings.[34]

Freud's efforts to make Frink the leader in American psychoanalysis, despite the latter's personal difficulties and the opposition against him in his home country, together with Freud's boundary violations in the analysis, certainly did not help to improve the already strained transatlantic relations. The Frink episode shows, apart from Freud's misjudgement of people, how his anti-Americanism also clouded his judgement of the institutional and political situation in America. So now we may finally ask, what were actually the reasons for Freud's negative attitude toward America?

---

[34]There were further ramifications of this episode, for example, the scandal that threatened to break out when Bijur's first husband wanted to make this public in the *New York Times*. Dr. Thaddeus Ames, who was the President of the New York Psychoanalytic Society and also the analyst of Angie's (first) husband, sent that projected public letter to Freud, and added: "Mr. Bijur has placed his affairs in the hands of his lawyers who on sufficient provocation are to air in the newspapers all the details and attack Dr. Frink and psychoanalysis. ... I am sorry to trouble you with all these details, but I feel that this episode is more far-reaching than just the Frink-Bijurs. If this becomes public, the members of the New York Psychoanalytic Society are likely to be opposed to Frink if they think that his notoriety will mean fewer patients and less money for them."

Possible reasons for Freud's attitude toward America

There is no doubt that Freud had a complex attitude towards money. He was extremely touchy when it came to borrowing or accepting money from others (for example, from Josef Breuer), in other words, to depend on others and lose his independence. This was particularly so when the money came from people Freud did not like or even considered enemies. When in 1938 he was offered money by Franz Riklin Jr., a relative of Jung's, to enable him to flee, he sent him away with the words: "I refuse to be beholden to my enemies" (Hannah, 1976, pp. 254–255; see Chapter Ten).[35] Significantly, in his later years Americans were among those of his analysands and supporters on whose payments he depended most for his income, and he found it "sad" that he was "materially dependent upon these savages, who are not better-class human beings" (to A. Zweig; in Gay, 1987, pp. 563–564).[36]

Americans were good only for being milked for their money. "What is the use of Americans, if they bring no money? They are not good for anything else" (F/Jon, p. 552). He always begrudged Jung the success the latter had in securing huge sums from American benefactors (the McCormicks, the Mellons, for example) for the promotion of Analytical Psychology (F/Fer II, p. 126):

> Rockefeller's daughter presented Jung with a gift of 360,000 francs for the construction of a casino, analytic institute, etc. So, Swiss ethics have finally made their sought-after contact with American money. I think not without bitterness about the pitiful situation of the members of our Association, our difficulties with the *Verlag*, etc.

"All the popularity in America has not produced for analysis the good-will of *one* of the dollar uncles there" (F/Fer III, p. 78). Let us also not

---

[35] Jung was repeatedly reproached "for not doing more to help Freud leave Austria". He "always replied: '[Freud] would not take help from me under any circumstances.' It is rather ironic that when Freud did go to England …, he had to owe his satisfactory house in London to a Jungian: Dr. E. A. Bennet" (ibid.).

[36] "Unfortunately, I am forced … to sell the rest of my sparse working time dearly. I would have to charge a German 250 Marks per hour, and therefore I prefer Englishmen and Americans who pay the hourly rates usual in their own countries. That is, I do not prefer them, I just have to take them on, rather than others" (to Meng; LC).

forget that it was only after Stanley Hall raised the honorarium that he accepted the invitation to Clark University at all: "America should bring in money, not cost money" (F/Fer I, p. 33).

This brought Freud into a dilemma. One the one hand, as he wrote, "money is a means of unchaining slaves; … one obtains freedom in exchange for money", but on the other hand, as he continued, one also "sacrifices freedom for money" (F/Fli, p. 321). Thus one both obtains and sacrifices freedom for money. Freud seems to have dealt with this dilemma by freely accepting, and actively encouraging, donations from followers (e.g., Anton von Freund or Max Eitingon), but only for "the Cause", and never for himself—with one exception: He 'allowed' a woman, Marie Bonaparte (but by no means Franz Riklin jun., let alone C. G. Jung), to fund his emigration by advancing the so-called *Reichsfluchtsteuer*[37]—but took pains to repay this to her in the following summer after arriving in England (Jones III, p. 223).

In all probability, Freud's anti-Americanism was not caused by one single factor. In addition to the already mentioned factors, various further possible motives can be found. His complicated relationships with relatives who had emigrated to the States (Eli Bernays, for example) probably played a role.[38] He had also pinned high hopes on President Wilson and his so-called Fourteen Points, and was very disappointed when the Treaty of Versailles did not fulfill the promises held out therein.[39] Undoubtedly, his later experiences with the development of psychoanalysis in America, and particularly the Americans' opposition against so-called lay analysis, as well as the, as he saw it, unsatisfactory standard of psychoanalytic training and understanding there were important factors. He also linked the stay—and success—in America of some of his followers with their defection or alleged shortcomings.

---

[37]The *Reichsfluchtsteuer*, the Reich Flight Tax or Fugitive Tax, was created in 1931 to prevent wealthy persons from leaving the country and taking their capital with them, but was then used to despoil emigrating Jews. In 1935/36, forty-five million Reichsmark were collected, 342 million in 1938/39, and 300 million in 1939/40.

[38]Saul Rosenzweig (1992) argues that Freud's animosity was the product of a displaced sibling rivalry with Eli Bernays.—About Eli's son, Edward, the famous 'father' of public relations, Freud wrote: He was "an honest boy when I knew him. I know not how far he has become Americanized" (Gay, 1987, p. 568).

[39]Reverberations of this disappointment probably influenced his judgement in the book he drafted with William C. Bullitt (1967).

He found that they had "succumb[ed] to the American dollar-drug" (F/Ran, p. 135).[40]

Peter Gay writes (1987, pp. 569–570) that "Freud and his adherents were copying, often in so many words, the condescending pronouncements that cultivated Europeans had been uttering for years", and then asks

> why Freud should so uncritically swallow this potent, but by his time musty, mixture of tendentious observation and unmitigated cultural arrogance. What happened was that his conformity and his radicalism oddly worked together to keep his anti-Americanism alive. As a … European bourgeois, he thought about Americans as others thought. … [A]s a radical antibourgeois in his ideal of free sexual relations, he found Americans the very model of sexual hypocrisy.

Patrick Mahony has put forward the hypothesis that Freud displaced the feelings he had for the pre-oedipal mother on to America (2004, p. 39):

> Freud's biographers err in writing he rarely spoke of the pre-oedipal mother. The over-determined fact is that he felt always compelled to speak about her, disguised as America. Her demonic power made him regress into an infantile, paranoid state of aggrievement and petulancy that lasted all his life. He tried to control the oedipal but especially pre-oedipal mother by spatially constricting her in his symbolic geography.

Howard L. Kaye argues (1993, pp. 121–122) that what was at the bottom of Freud's hatred of America was

---

[40]Jung first spoke in detail of his differences with Freud's theories in his lectures at Fordham University in New York (Jung, 1913), boasting toward Freud—much to the latter's displeasure—"that his modifications of psycho-analysis had overcome the resistances of many people who had hitherto refused to have anything to do with it" (Freud, 1914d, p. 58). Freud took badly Rank's success in America, and linked it with the latter's defection. He also had reservations against Ferenczi's prolonged stay in New York, and wrote him after his return: "I find *you* more reserved than you were before America. Damned country!" (F/Fer III, p. 320). When Franz Alexander left Berlin in 1930 to take a position as Visiting Professor of Psychoanalysis at the University of Chicago, Freud's parting words were: "I hope America will leave something intact of the real Alexander" (Alexander, 1960, p. 101; cf. Schmidt, 2008).

the problem of authority. Freud saw in America something that he had not anticipated, a disturbing disregard for scientific, political, and familial authority that he ... attributed to American egalitarianism. ... [T]he American principles of equality and competition ... seemed to Freud to stifle the independence of thought he had hoped to find.

The incident on Riverside Drive

Here I would like to suggest still another possible motive, based upon the observation that Freud's criticisms became so much sharper after the trip. There was one experience he had in America that must have been utterly humiliating to him, and that undoubtedly left a strong impression. As far as I know there is one short reference to this event in Ferenczi's *Clinical Diary*, and two more detailed accounts of it, the latter both going back to C. G. Jung. One is an interview he gave to Saul Rosenzweig in 1951, who then wrote about it in his book on the psychoanalysts' expedition to America (1992). The other is the account Jung gave Kurt Eissler, when the latter interviewed him for the Freud Archives in 1953 (transcript at LC).[41]

Ferenczi—obviously an eyewitness—simply mentions Freud's "hysterical symptom" of "incontinence on Riverside Drive", a "weakness, which he could not hide from us and himself" (*Diary*, p. 184).

Rosenzweig tells the story as follows (1992, pp. 64–65):

> [In the interview, Jung] described one aspect of the American journey in detail. ... [T]here was a visit ... to the Columbia University Psychiatric Clinic ... While looking at the Palisades[42] Freud suffered a personal mishap. He accidentally urinated in his trousers and

---

[41]Jung also alluded to this incident in a talk with E. A. Bennet: "In New York Freud spoke to Jung of personal difficulties—Jung did not talk of these—and asked his help in clearing them up" (1961, p. 42).

[42]Rosenzweig comments that this reference to the Palisades was at first puzzling to him, but he then concluded that the mishap must have happened "on the occasion of the group's visit to Columbia University ... The group were on Riverside Drive ... and could see the distant Palisades on the other side of the Hudson river" (1992, p. 292). Rosenzweig's conclusion that this happened on Riverside Drive is substantiated by Ferenczi's remark quoted above (first published seven years before Rosenzweig's book, but obviously overlooked by the latter).

Jung helped him out of this embarrassment. … Freud entertained a fear of similar accidents during the time of the lectures at Clark University. So Jung offered to help Freud overcome this fear if Freud would consent to some analytic intervention. Freud agreed and Jung began the "treatment".

It was then that the following famous incident occurred: Jung asked Freud to give him some intimate personal details, and Freud refused on the grounds that he could not "risk his authority". It was precisely at that moment, as Jung later said and wrote various times, that Freud lost his authority altogether (e.g., Jung, 1962, p. 182).

In his interview with Eissler, Jung also mentions the Palisades. There was no public toilet in the vicinity and Freud—always according to Jung—was suddenly afraid he wouldn't be able to hold his water, upon which he promptly wet his pants, and they had to get a cab to go back to the hotel. Freud was extremely embarrassed, but also feared that this was a sign of approaching senility, a symptom of a paralysis, to which Jung replied, nonsense, that would simply be a neurotic symptom. But of what?, Freud said. Everybody can see that you are extremely ambitious, Jung retorted, which Freud vehemently denied.[43] Still, he told Jung, that he would be immensely relieved if this were 'only' a neurotic symptom. So Jung offered to analyse him and asked him to tell him some dreams. He analysed them up to the point at which—and here Jung again tells the story quoted above—Freud refused to give him further details of a very intimate nature. When pressed by Eissler, Jung then hinted at family affairs, with a thinly veiled reference to Martha Freud and Minna Bernays. Still, Jung maintained, the little analytic work they had done was enough to make this symptom disappear for the duration of their trip.

One wonders, by the way, if Ferenczi and possibly also Brill and/or Jones were also witnesses to the conversation and 'analysis' between Jung and Freud. At least for Ferenczi, the question of Freud's "authority" certainly played an important role in their relationship. Neither he, nor Brill, nor Jones ever mentioned Jung's attempt to analyse Freud, however.

---

[43]Psychoanalytic theory linked enuresis to excessive (repressed) ambitiousness. On Freud's denial of being ambitious, see also above.

In any case, Ferenczi was the first to raise the possibility that this incident might have something to do with Freud's attitude toward the Americans (*Diary*, p. 184):

> Possibly his contempt for Americans is a reaction to this weakness, which he could not hide from us and himself. "How could I take so much pleasure in the honors the Americans have bestowed on me, when I feel such contempt for the Americans?" Not unimportant is the emotion that impressed even me, a reverent spectator, as somewhat ridiculous, when almost with tears in his eyes he thanked the president of the university for the honorary doctorate.[44]

The idea that Freud's enuretic symptom had something to do with his ambitiousness, with his fervent wish to come to something, inevitably brings to mind the scene he tells in *The Interpretation of Dreams*:

> When I was seven or eight years old … [o]ne evening before going to sleep I disregarded the rules which modesty lays down and obeyed the calls of nature in my parents' bedroom while they were present. In the course of his reprimand, my father let fall the words: "The boy will come to nothing." This must have been a frightful blow to my ambition, for references to this scene are still constantly recurring in my dreams and are always linked with an enumeration of my achievements and successes, as though I wanted to say: "You see, I *have* come to something." (1900a, p. 216; cf. Shengold, 1993)

This weakness, which Freud could not hide from his fellow travellers, certainly had also reverberations in his later relations with them. How could Freud ever forgive Jung for having been witness to this humiliating incidence? Was his desperate attempt to preserve a modicum of authority in the ensuing 'analysis' not a reaction to the fact that in reality he had lost it already for good by wetting his pants like a little child? Jung for his part used this episode to rub Freud's nose in it shortly

---

[44]Kaye finds "Ferenczi's suggestion that Freud's anti-American animus was a defensive reaction against his 'American vanity', inspired by the honors he received during his visit" "unpersuasive" (1993, p. 121), but does not take into account the possible link with the incident on Riverside Drive.

before their final break, asking: *"Who's* got the neurosis?" "I am not in the least neurotic", Jung added, giving further fuel to the flames: "You know, of course, how far a patient gets with self-analysis: *not* out of his neurosis—just like you" (F/Jun, p. 535).

Conclusion

Freud's anti-Americanism seems to revolve around two powerful pairs of opposites: ambition and humiliation, and envy and gratitude. He seems to have been tempted to give in, as it were, to the American way of life. Then he ridiculed and despised what had threatened to seduce him. He strove for money, wealth, fame, and independence, but he did not want to be beholden to those who could make this possible.

America is the country in which Freud's ideas enjoyed their greatest success. One could say that the Americans loved Freud. But he always maintained that they only loved him because they did not, indeed could not, understand him. Therefore, they were only good for bringing in money, and even this they did not do to the extent he hoped, while lavishing money on Jung, whose "Swiss ethics" thus "made their sought-after contact with American money" (F/Fer II, p. 126).

But who were most successful in making money in America? Note the irony in Freud's words when he writes of a visit to the Hammerstein roof gardens in Manhattan and the "vaudeville show on the roof of a skyscraper, *naturally* owned by an Austrian Jew, Hammerstein" (Freud, 2002, p. 305; my ital.). Freudian slip or wrong information—it is quite fitting that Freud called Hammerstein an *Austrian* Jew, even if he was in fact a German one. The implicit conclusion is: In Freud's view, Austrian Jews—like himself—can outdo the Americans anytime—*if they want.* For this, however, they would have to sacrifice their old values on the altar of the "mightiest God", the dollar.[45]

Freud's negative attitude was not only his private quirk, it also had an undeniable influence on the reception and development of psychoanalysis in America. Americans who had to deal with the original source of psychoanalytic ideas had also to deal with a combination of Freud's personal attitudes and the Central European stereotypes and

---

[45] Thus also Freud's occasional disdain for Brill, a poor fellow Jewish boy, who, after the first years of studying and working when he could barely make ends meet, was very successful in New York.

prejudices that so often complicated transatlantic relationships (not only) in the first half of the twentieth century.

So why did Freud hate America? Psychobiographical speculations are always tricky; Freud himself can no longer be asked, and we are always in danger of projecting our own fantasies on to him. Perhaps it is safe to say that Freud's attitude toward America is more complex than simply hateful, that he had a deep-seated ambivalence, of which one side—his love of America, his temptation to give in to the seduction of making money the easy way, by bending the rules a little—was repressed, while the other side, the hatred, metastasised into a gigantic prejudice by way of an anticathexis.

But let us stay humble and cautious. Even if Freud's sweeping wholesale attacks were unjustified in their generalisation, and we therefore may take some gleeful delight in looking for unconscious motives in the father of psychoanalysis, let us not forget that such an attitude in someone else would almost certainly have never elicited such attention and scrutiny. We may perhaps also understand how the same man, who on the one hand was impressed by the reality of the America he encountered, was on the other hand sharing the European prejudices against a different culture and civilisation, which many Europeans perceived and resented as an alien one. It is ironic that nevertheless, and notwithstanding his negative attitude, by coming to America Freud in fact helped to close a cultural gap and contributed to a new view and understanding of human beings—in Europe *and* in the United States.

REFERENCES

Bibliographical note:

Karl Abraham's works are cited according to the complete bibliography established by Johannes Cremerius, on the basis of the bibliography in *Selected Papers of Karl Abraham* (503–510) (London: Hogarth, sixth edition 1965), in: Karl Abraham (1971), *Psychoanalytische Schriften II* (pp. 448–61). Frankfurt am Main: S. Fischer.

Sándor Ferenczi's works are cited according to the complete bibliography established by Michael Balint and Godula Faupel, in: Sándor Ferenczi (1972), *Schriften zur Psychoanalyse II* (pp. 411–447). Frankfurt am Main: S. Fischer.

Sigmund Freud's works are cited according to the complete bibliography in: Meyer-Palmedo, Ingeborg, & Fichtner, Gerhard (1999), *Freud-Bibliographie mit Werkkonkordanz*. Frankfurt am Main: S. Fischer, second revised and expanded edition.

References to Carl Gustav Jung's *Collected Works* are, according to international usage, to paragraph numbers, not to page numbers.

A bibliography of my own works can be found at http://www.psyalpha.net/biografien/ernst-falzeder

* * *

Abraham, Hilda (1974). Karl Abraham. An unfinished biography. *International Review of Psycho-Analysis*, 1: 17–72.

Abraham, Karl (1907[9]). On the significance of sexual trauma in child-hood for the symptomatology of dementia praecox. In: *Clinical Papers and Essays on Psycho-Analysis* (13–20). London: Karnac, 1979 [= *Clinical Papers*].

Abraham, Karl (1907[10]). The experiencing of sexual traumas as a form of sexual activity. In: *Selected Papers of Karl Abraham M.D.* (47–63). London: Karnac, 1988 [= *Selected Papers*].

Abraham, Karl (1908[11]). The psycho-sexual differences between hysteria and dementia praecox. In: *Selected Papers* (64–79).

Abraham, Karl (1908[12]). The psychological relations between sexuality and alcoholism. In: *Selected Papers* (80–89).

Abraham, Karl (1909[14]). *Dreams and Myths: A Study in Folk-Psychology.* In: *Clinical Papers* (153–209).

Abraham, Karl (1910[17]). Hysterical dream-states. In: *Selected Papers* (90–124).

Abraham, Karl (1910[18]). Remarks on the psycho-analysis of a case of foot and corset fetishism. In: *Selected Papers* (125–136).

Abraham, Karl (1911[24]). Psychoanalyse einer Zwangsneurose [Psycho-analysis of an obsessional neurosis]. Lecture before the Berlin Psycho-analytic Society.

Abraham, Karl (1911[26]). Notes on the psycho-analytical investigation and treatment of manic-depressive insanity and allied conditions. In: *Selected Papers* (137–156).

Abraham, Karl (1911[30]). *Giovanni Segantini: A Psycho-Analytical Study.* In: *Clinical Papers* (210–261).

Abraham, Karl (1912[31]). Aus der Analyse eines Falles von Grübelzwang [From the analysis of a case of obsessional brooding]. Lecture before the Berlin Psychoanalytic Society.

Abraham, Karl (1912[32]). A complicated ceremonial found in neurotic women. In: *Selected Papers* (157–163).

Abraham, Karl (1912[34]). Amenhotep IV. Psycho-analytical contributions towards the understanding of his personality and of the monotheistic cult of Aton. In: *Clinical Papers* (262–290).

Abraham, Karl (1913[37]). Should patients write down their dreams? In: *Clinical Papers* (33–35).

Abraham, Karl (1913[39]). On the psychogenesis of agoraphobia in child-hood. In: *Clinical Papers* (42–43).

Abraham, Karl (1913[43]). Restrictions and transformations of scopophilia in psycho-neurotics; with remarks on analogous phenomena in folk-psychology. In: *Selected Papers* (169–234).

Abraham, Karl (1913[44]). A constitutional basis of locomotor anxiety. In: *Selected Papers* (235–243).

Abraham, Karl (1914[47]). Review of C. G. Jung's *Versuch einer Darstellung der psychoanalytischen Theorie* (*Attempt at a Representation of Psycho-Analytical Theory*). In: *Clinical Papers* (101–115).

Abraham, Karl (1916[52]). The first pregenital stage of the libido. In: *Selected Papers* (248–279).

Abraham, Karl (1917[54]). Ejaculatio praecox. In: *Selected Papers* (280–298).

Abraham, Karl (1918[57]). Zur Psychoanalyse der Kriegsneurosen. Beitrag zur Diskussion über Kriegsneurosen. In: *Zur Psychoanalyse der Kriegsneurosen* (31–41). Leipzig: Internationaler Psychoanalytischer Verlag, 1919.

Abraham, Karl (1919[58]). A particular form of neurotic resistance against the psycho-analytic method. In: *Selected Papers* (303–311).

Abraham, Karl (1919[62]). The applicability of psycho-analytic treatment to patients at an advanced age. In: *Selected Papers* (312–317).

Abraham, Karl (1920[67]). Manifestations of the female castration complex. In: *Selected Papers* (338–369).

Abraham, Karl (1920[68]). Technisches zur Traumdeutung [On the technique of dream interpretation]. Lecture before the Berlin Psychoanalytic Society.

Abraham, Karl (1921[75]). *Klinische Beiträge zur Psychoanalyse aus den Jahren 1907–1920.* Leipzig: Internationaler Psychoanalytischer Verlag.

Abraham, Karl (1922[81]). Neue Untersuchungen zur Psychologie der manisch-depressiven Zustände [New investigations into the psychology of manic-depressive states]. *Internationale Zeitschrift für Psychoanalyse, 8*: 492–493.

Abraham, Karl (1923[91]). Ein Beitrag zur Psychologie der Melancholie [A contribution to the psychology of melancholia]. Lecture before the Berlin Psychoanalytic Society.

Abraham, Karl (1924[105]). *A Short Study of the Development of the Libido, Viewed in the Light of Mental Disorders.* In: *Selected Papers* (407–502).

Abraham, Karl (1924[unnumbered]). Das Berliner Psychoanalytische Institut. *Grunewald-Echo, Organ für den Amts- und Gemeindebezirk Grunewald, Bezirksanzeiger für Halensee,* Nr. 14, 30 March 1924: 37.

Abraham, Karl (1925[106]). *Psycho-Analytical Studies on Character-Formation.* In: *Selected Papers* (370–418).

Abraham, Karl (1969). *Psychoanalytische Studien I.* Ed. Johannes Cremerius. Frankfurt am Main: S. Fischer.

Abraham, Karl (1971). *Psychoanalytische Studien II.* Ed. Johannes Cremerius. Frankfurt am Main: S. Fischer.

Abraham, Karl (1976 [1913]). Klein Hilda: Tagträume und ein Symptom bei einem siebenjährigen Mädchen [Little Hilda: Daydreams and a symptom in a seven-year-old girl]. In: Hilda Abraham, *Karl Abraham. Sein Leben für die Psychoanalyse* (173–182). Munich: Kindler.

Abraham, Karl, & Keibel, Franz (1900). Normentafel zur Entwicklungsgeschichte des Huhns. *Normentafeln zur Entwicklungsgeschichte der Wirbeltiere*, Heft 2. Jena: [no publisher named].

Ackermann, Gregor (1989). Unbekannte Freudinterviews. *Luzifer-Amor, Zeitschrift zur Geschichte der Psychoanalyse, 11*: 115–122.

Aguayo, Joseph (1997). Historicising the origins of Kleinian psychoanalysis. Klein's analytic and patronal relationships with Ferenczi, Abraham and Jones, 1914–1927. *International Journal of Psycho-Analysis, 78*: 1165–1182.

Alexander, Franz (1960). *The Western Mind in Tradition.* New York: Random House.

Alexander, Franz, & Selesnick, Sheldon T. (1965). Freud-Bleuler correspondence. *Archives of General Psychiatry, 12*: 1–9.

Andreas-Salomé, Lou (1958). *In der Schule bei Freud, Tagebuch eines Jahres (1912/13)*. Frankfurt am Main: Ullstein, 1983. *The Freud Journal of Lou Andreas-Salomé.* New York: Basic Books, 1964.

Andreas-Salomé, Lou, & Freud, Anna (2001). *"... als käm ich heim zu Vater und Schwester". Briefwechsel 1919–1937.* Two volumes. Eds. Daria R. Rothe and Inge Weber. Göttingen: Wallstein.

Anonyma (1988). *Verführung auf der Couch. Eine Niederschrift.* Freiburg: Kore.

Appignanesi, Lisa, & Forrester, John (1992). *Freud's Women.* London: Weidenfeld & Nicolson.

Arlow, Jacob A. (1972). Some dilemmas in psychoanalytic education. *Journal of the American Psychoanalytic Association, 20*: 556–566.

Aron, Lewis (1992). From Ferenczi to Searles and contemporary relational approaches: Commentary on Mark Blechner's "Working in the countertransference". *Psychoanalytic Dialogues, 2*: 181–190.

Aschaffenburg, Gustav (1896). Experimentelle Studien über Associationen. In: Emil Kraepelin (Ed.), *Psychologische Arbeiten I* (209–299). Leipzig: Wilhelm Engelmann.

Aschaffenburg, Gustav (1906). Die Beziehungen des sexuellen Lebens zur Entstehung von Nerven- und Geisteskrankheiten. *Münchener Medizinische Wochenschrift, 53*: 1793–1798.

Balint, Michael (1933). Character analysis and new beginning. In: *Primary Love and Psychoanalytic Technique.* London: Tavistock, 1965. Reprint London: Karnac, 1985.

Balint, Michael (1948). On the psycho-analytic training system. *International Journal of Psycho-Analysis, 29*: 153–173.

Balint, Michael (1965). *The Reminiscences of Michael Balint.* Interview with Bluma Swerdloff in London, 6–7 August 1965. Psychoanalytic Project of the Oral History Research Office, Columbia University, New York (quoted with kind permission of Enid Balint-Edmonds †). Partly reprinted, in German translation, in: Falzeder (1987).

Balint, Michael (1968). *The Basic Fault: Therapeutic Aspects of Regression.* London: Tavistock.

Balint, Michael (1969). Trauma and object relationship. *International Journal of Psycho-Analysis, 50*: 429–435.

Balint, Michael, & Balint, Alice (1939). On transference and countertransference. *International Journal of Psycho-Analysis, 20*: 223–230.

Balkanyi, Charlotte (1975). The linguistic studies of Karl Abraham. Unpublished manuscript.

Bateman, Anthony, & Holmes, Jeremy (1995). *Introduction to Psychoanalysis: Contemporary Theory and Practice.* Routledge: London.

Bennet, Edward Armstrong (1961). *C. G. Jung.* London: Barrie and Rockliff. Reprint, with a foreword by Sonu Shamdasani, Wilmette, IL: Chiron Publications, 2006.

Bericht über die Jahresversammlung des Deutschen Vereins für Psychiatrie zu Breslau am 13. und 14. Mai 1913 (1913). *Allgemeine Zeitschrift für Psychiatrie und psychisch-gerichtliche Medizin, 70*: 779–796.

Berman, Emanuel (2004). Sandor, Gizella, Elma. A biographical journey. *International Journal of Psycho-Analysis, 85*: 489–520.

Bernfeld, Siegfried (1952). Über die psychoanalytische Ausbildung. *Psyche, Zeitschrift für Psychoanalyse und ihre Anwendungen, 1984, 38*: 437–459.

Bernfeld, Siegfried, & Bernfeld Cassirer, Suzanne (1981). *Bausteine der Freud-Biographik.* Ed. Ilse Grubrich-Simitis. Frankfurt am Main: Suhrkamp.

Berthelsen, Detlef (1987). *Alltag bei Familie Freud: Die Erinnerungen der Paula Fichtl.* Munich: Deutscher Taschenbuchverlag. Second revised edition 1989.

Bertin, Celia (1982). *La dernière Bonaparte.* Paris: Librairie Académique Perrin. *Marie Bonaparte. A Life.* London: Quartet, 1983. *Die letzte Bonaparte, Freuds Prinzessin, Ein Leben.* Freiburg: Kore, 1989.

Bettelheim, Bruno (1983). *Freud and Man's Soul.* New York: Knopf.

Bettelheim, Bruno (1990). *Freud's Vienna and Other Essays.* New York: Alfred A. Knopf.

Bettinger, L. A. (1986). *The Relationship Between Psychoanalysis and Academic Psychiatry 1945–1975.* Senior Thesis, Harvard University, Department of the History of Science.

Betz, Wilhelm (1918). *Psychologie des Denkens.* Leipzig: Barth.

Betz, Wilhelm (1927). *Zur Psychologie der Tiere und Menschen.* Leipzig: Barth.

Binding, Karl, & Hoche, Alfred (1920). *Die Freigabe der Vernichtung lebensunwerten Lebens. Ihr Maß und ihre Form.* Leipzig: Felix Meiner.

Binswanger, Ludwig (1936). Freud und die Verfassung der klinischen Psychiatrie. *Schweizer Archiv für Neurologie und Psychiatrie, 37*: 177–199.

Binswanger, Ludwig (1956). *Erinnerungen an Sigmund Freud*. Bern: Francke.

Bishop, Paul (2014). *Carl Jung*. London: Reaktion Books.

Blanton, Smiley (1971). *Diary of My Analysis with Sigmund Freud*. New York: Hawthorn.

Bleuler, Eugen (1892). Zur Auffassung der subcorticalen Aphasien. *Neurologisches Zentralblatt, 11*: 562–563.

Bleuler, Eugen (1896). Breuer und Freud: "Studien über Hysterie". *Münchener Medizinische Wochenschrift, 45*: 524–525.

Bleuler, Eugen (1904). Löwenfeld: "Die psychischen Zwangserscheinungen". *Münchener Medizinische Wochenschrift, 51*: 718.

Bleuler, Eugen (1906/07). Freud'sche Mechanismen in der Symptomatologie von Psychosen. *Psychiatrisch-Neurologische Wochenschrift, 8*: 316–318, 323–325, 338–340. In: Martin Bleuler (Ed.), *Beiträge zur Schizophrenielehre der Zürcher Psychiatrischen Universitätsklinik Burghölzli (1902–1971): einleitende Übersicht und gekürzter Nachdruck von Veröffentlichungen* (21–34). Darmstadt: Wissenschaftliche Buchgesellschaft.

Bleuler, Eugen (1910). Die Psychanalyse Freuds. Verteidigung und kritische Bemerkungen. *Jahrbuch für psychoanalytische und psychopathologische Forschungen, 2*: 623–730.

Bleuler, Eugen (1911). Freud'sche Theorien in der IV. Jahresversammlung der Gesellschaft deutscher Nervenärzte, Berlin, 6.-8. Oktober 1910. *Zentralblatt für Psychoanalyse, 1*: 424–427.

Bleuler, Eugen (1913). Kritik der Freudschen Theorien. *Allgemeine Zeitschrift für Psychiatrie und psychisch-gerichtliche Medizin, 70*: 665–718.

Bleuler, Eugen, & Jung, Carl Gustav (1908). Komplexe und Krankheitsursachen bei Dementia praecox. *Zentralblatt für Nervenheilkunde und Psychiatrie, 31*: 220–227. In: Martin Bleuler (Ed.), *Beiträge zur Schizophrenielehre der Zürcher Psychiatrischen Universitätsklinik Burghölzli (1902–1971): einleitende Übersicht und gekürzter Nachdruck von Veröffentlichungen* (35–43). Darmstadt: Wissenschaftliche Buchgesellschaft.

Bloom, Harold (1986). Freud, the greatest modern writer. *New York Times Book Review*, 23 March 1986.

Borch-Jacobsen, Mikkel, & Shamdasani, Sonu (2006). *Le dossier Freud: Enquête sur l'histoire de la psychanalyse*. Paris: Les Empêcheurs de penser en rond.

Bos, Jaap, & Groenendijk, Leendert (2007). *The Self-Marginalization of Wilhelm Stekel: Freudian Circles Inside and Out*. With contributions by Johan Sturm and Paul Roazen. New York: Springer.

Bottome, Phyllis (1939). *Alfred Adler: Apostle of Freedom*. London: Faber & Faber.

Bourguignon, André (1977). La correspondence entre Freud et Laforgue. *Nouvelle Revue de Psychanalyse, 15*: 233–314.

Braune, Asja (2003). *Konsequent den unbequemen Weg gegangen. Adele Schreiber (1872–1957), Politikerin, Frauenrechtlerin, Journalistin*. Doctoral Thesis, Humboldt University Berlin.

Brauns, Horst-Peter, & Schöpf, Alfred (1989). Freud und Brentano: Der Medizinstudent und der Philosoph. In: Bernd Nitzschke (Ed.), *Freud und die akademische Psychologie: Beiträge zu einer Kontroverse* (40–79). Munich: Psychologie Verlags Union.

Breger, Louis (2000). *Freud: Darkness in the Midst of Vision*. New York: John Wiley & Sons.

Brenner, Ortwin (1975). *Leben und Werk von Professor Dr. Heinrich Meng*. Mainz: Johannes Gutenberg Universität.

Breuer, Josef, & Freud, Sigmund (1895). *Studies on Hysteria*. S.E. 2.

Brill, Abraham A. (1936). Introduction. In: C. G. Jung, *The Psychology of Dementia Praecox* (vii–ix). New York: Nervous and Mental Disease Publishing Company.

Brill, Abraham A. (1944). *Freud's Contribution to Psychiatry*. London: Chapman & Hall.

Brome, Vincent (1982). *Ernest Jones, Freud's Alter Ego*. London: Caliban.

Brückner, Peter (1975). *Sigmund Freuds Privatlektüre*. Frankfurt am Main: Verlag Neue Kritik.

Bry, Ilse, & Rifkin, Alfred H. (1962). Freud and the history of ideas: primary sources, 1886–1910. In: Jules H. Masserman (Ed.), *Science and Psycho-analysis*, volume 5: *Psychoanalytic Education* (6–36). New York: Grune & Stratton.

Burlingham, Michael J. (1989). *The Last Tiffany: A Biography of Dorothy Tiffany Burlingham*. New York: Atheneum.

Burnham, John (1983). *Jelliffe: American Psychoanalyst and Physician and His Correspondence with Sigmund Freud and C. G. Jung*. Ed. William McGuire. Chicago, IL: University of Chicago Press.

Burnham, John (2006). The "New Freud Studies": a historiographical shift. *The Journal of the Historical Society, 6*: 213–233.

Burrow, Trigant (1958). *A Search for Man's Sanity: Selected Letters of Trigant Burrow*. New York: Oxford University Press.

Byck, Robert (Ed.) (1974). *Cocaine Papers by Sigmund Freud*. New York: Stonehill.

Carotenuto, Aldo (Ed.) (1980). *Diario di una segreta simmetria Sabina Spielrein tra Jung e Freud*. Roma: Ubaldina. *A Secret Symmetry. Sabina Spielrein Between Jung and Freud*. New York: Pantheon, 1982. *Tagebuch einer heimlichen Symmetrie. Sabina Spielrein zwischen Jung und Freud.* Freiburg: Kore, 1986.

Caruso, Igor A. (1972). *Soziale Aspekte der Psychoanalyse.* Reinbek bei Hamburg: Rowohlt.

Caruso, Igor A. (1982). Versorgung und Institution in Psychoanalyse. Erich Pakesch in memoriam. In: Rainer Danzinger, Gert Lyon and Walter Pieringer (Eds.). *Psychoanalyse und Institution* (13–21). Vienna: Verband der wissenschaftlichen Gesellschaften Österreichs.

Charcot, Jean-Martin (1886). *Neue Vorlesungen über die Krankheiten des Nervensystems, insbesondere über Hysterie.* Autorisirte deutsche Ausgabe von Dr. Sigm. Freud. Leipzig: Deuticke.

Charcot, Jean-Martin (1892). *Poliklinische Vorträge. 1. Band. Schuljahr 1887–1888.* Übersetzt von Dr. Sigm. Freud. Leipzig: Deuticke.

Charcot, Jean-Martin (1895). *Poliklinische Vorträge. 2. Band. Schuljahr 1888–1889.* Übersetzt von Dr. Max Kahane. Leipzig: Deuticke.

Chertok, Leon (1983). Psychotherapie und Sexualität. *Psychoanalyse, 4*: 2–20.

Chrzanowski, Gerard (1977). Das psychoanalytische Werk von Karen Horney, Harry Stack Sullivan und Erich Fromm. In: Dieter Eicke (Ed.), *Tiefenpsychologie. Band 3: Die Nachfolger Freuds* (346–380). Weinheim: Beltz, 1982.

Clark, Ronald (1980). *Freud: The Man and the Cause.* New York: Random House.

Clark-Lowes, Francis (2010). *Freud's Apostle: Wilhelm Stekel and the Early History of Psychoanalysis.* Gamlingay: Authors OnLine.

Coles, Robert (1992). *Anna Freud: The Dream of Psychoanalysis.* Reading, MA: Addison-Wesley.

Conci, Marco (2000). *Sullivan rivisitato. La sua rilevanza per la psichiatria, la psicoterapia e la psicoanalisi contemporanee.* Bolsena: Massari Editore. *Sullivan Revisited—Life and Work. Harry Stack Sullivan's Relevance for Contemporary Psychiatry, Psychotherapy and Psychoanalysis.* Trento: Tangram Edizioni Scientifiche, 2010.

Cremerius, Johannes (1983). Die Sprache der Zärtlichkeit und der Leidenschaft. *Psyche, Zeitschrift für Psychoanalyse und ihre Anwendungen, 37*: 988–1015.

Cremerius, Johannes (1987). Der Einfluß der Psychoanalyse auf die deutschsprachige Literatur. *Psyche, Zeitschrift für Psychoanalyse und ihre Anwendungen, 41*: 39–54.

Cremerius, Johannes (1997). Karl Abraham, Freuds Sündenbock und "Führer zur Wahrheitsforschung". *Luzifer-Amor, Zeitschrift zur Geschichte der Psychoanalyse, 10*: 61–80.

Crews, Frederick C. (1995). *The Memory Wars: Freud's Legacy in Dispute.* New York: New York Review of Books.

Davies, J. Keith, & Fichtner, Gerhard (2006). *Freud's Library: A Comprehensive Catalogue/Freuds Bibliothek: Vollständiger Katalog.* London/Tübingen: The Freud Museum/edition diskord.

Decke, Bettina (1997). Karl Abraham: Familie, Kindheit und Jugend in Bremen. *Luzifer-Amor, Zeitschrift zur Geschichte der Psychoanalyse, 10*: 7–63.

Decker, Hannah S. (1977). *Freud in Germany: Revolution and Reaction in Science, 1893–1907.* Guilford, CT: International Universities Press.

Decker, Hannah S. (1991). *Freud, Dora, and Vienna 1900.* New York: The Free Press.

Decker, Hannah S. (2004). The psychiatric works of Emil Kraepelin: A many-faceted story of modern medicine. *Journal of the History of the Neurosciences, 13*: 248–276.

de Mijolla, Alain (1989). Image de Freud au travers de sa correspondance. *Revue Internationale d'Histoire de la Psychanalyse, 2*: 9–50. Images of Freud: from his correspondence. In: Patrick Mahony, Carlo Bonomi and Jan Stensson (Eds.), *Behind the Scenes, Freud in Correspondence* (369–412). Stockholm: Scandinavian University Press, 1997.

de Ridder, Helga, & Corveleyn, Jozef (1992). Eugen Bleuler (1857–1939) und die Psychoanalyse. *Zeitschrift für klinische Psychologie, Psychopathologie und Psychotherapie, 40*: 246–262.

Deutsch, Helene (1926). Occult processes occurring during psychoanalysis. In: Georges Devereux (Ed.), *Psychoanalysis and the Occult* (133–146). New York: International Universities Press, 1953.

Deutsch, Helene (1973). *Confrontations with Myself: An Epilogue.* New York: Norton.

Dolin, Raphael (1963). *James Jackson Putnam: A Study in the Reception of Freudian Psychology.* Senior Thesis, Harvard College.

Donn, Linda (1988). *Freud and Jung: Years of Friendship, Years of Loss.* New York, Collier, 1990.

Doolittle, Hilda ("H. D.") (1956). *Tribute to Freud. With Unpublished Letters by Freud to the Author.* New York: Pantheon. Reprint New York: New Directions Publishing Corporation, 1984.

Dorsey, John M. (1976). *An American Psychiatrist in Vienna, 1935–1937, and His Sigmund Freud.* Detroit, MI: Center for Health Education.

"Dr. Lillian D. Powers" (1953). *New York Times,* 13 January 1953.

"Dr. W. J. Sweasey Powers" (1938). *New York Times,* 13 December 1938.

Dupont, Judith (1982). Les sources des inventions. In: Ferenczi & Groddeck (1982) (11–37).

Dupont, Judith (1993). L'analyse de Ferenczi par Freud vue à travers leur correspondance. *Le Coq-Héron*, number 127: 51–56. Freud's analysis of Ferenczi as revealed by their correspondence. *International Journal of Psycho-Analysis*, 1994, 75: 301–320.

Eagle, Morris N. (1984). *Recent Developments in Psychoanalysis: A Critical Evaluation*. Cambridge: Harvard University Press, 1987.

Eckstein, Emma (1904). *Die Sexualfrage in der Erziehung des Kindes*. Leipzig: Modernes Verlagsbureau.

Edmunds, Lavinia (1988). His master's choice. *Johns Hopkins Magazine*, 40: 40–49.

Eissler, Kurt (1966). *Sigmund Freud und die Wiener Universität: Über die Pseudo-Wissenschaftlichkeit der jüngsten Wiener Freud-Biographik*. Bern: Hans Huber.

Eissler, Kurt (1979). *Freud und Wagner-Jauregg vor der Kommission zur Erhebung militärischer Pflichtverletzungen*. Vienna: Löcker.

Eissler, Kurt (1995). Ärztliche Schweigepflicht und wissenschaftliche Forschung. Bemerkungen zur Glosse Gerhard Fichtners. *Psyche, Zeitschrift für Psychoanalyse und ihre Anwendungen*, 49: 182–183.

Eitingon, Max (1913). Jahresversammlung des Deutschen Vereines für Psychiatrie zu Breslau 1913. *Internationale Zeitschrift für ärztliche Psychoanalyse*, 1: 409–414.

Eitingon, Max (1937). Plenarversammlung der Internationalen Unterrichtskommission, Eröffnungsansprache des Vorsitzenden Dr. Eitingon. *Internationale Zeitschrift für Psychoanalyse*, 23: 196–203.

Ellenberger, Henri (1970). *The Discovery of the Unconscious: The History and Evolution of Dynamic Psychiatry*. New York: Basic Books.

Elms, Alan C. (2001). Apocryphal Freud: Sigmund Freud's most famous "quotations" and their actual sources. *The Annual of Psychoanalysis*, 29: 83–104.

Engelmann, Edmund (1976). *Berggasse 19: Sigmund Freud's Home and Offices, Vienna 1938*. New York: Basic Books.

Engstrom, Eric J. (1990). *Emil Kraepelin: Leben und Werk des Psychiaters im Spannungsfeld zwischen positivistischer Wissenschaft und Irrationalität*. MA Thesis, University of Munich.

Engstrom, Eric J. (2003). *Clinical Psychiatry in Imperial Germany: A History of Psychiatric Practice*. Ithaca, NY: Cornell University Press.

Engstrom, Eric J., Burgmair, Wolfgang, & Weber, Matthias M. (2002). Emil Kraepelin's "self-assessment": Clinical autography in historical context. *History of Psychiatry*, 13: 89–119.

Esterson, Allen (2002). The myth of Freud's ostracism by the medical community in 1896–1905. *History of Psychology*, 5: 115–134.

Fallend, Karl (1991). Ein unbekanntes Protokoll der Psychoanalyse. *Werkblatt, Zeitschrift für Psychoanalyse und Gesellschaftskritik, 8*(26): 99–108.

Fallend, Karl, & Reichmayr, Johannes (Eds.) (1992). *Siegfried Bernfeld oder die Grenzen der Psychoanalyse. Materialien zu Leben und Werk.* Basel: Stroemfeld/Nexus.

Falzeder, Ernst (1986). *Die "Sprachverwirrung" und die "Grundstörung". Die Untersuchungen Sándor Ferenczis und Michael Balints über Entstehung und Auswirkungen früher Objektbeziehungen.* Salzburg: Salzburger Sozialisationsstudien.

Falzeder, Ernst (1987). Michael Balint im Gespräch. *Werkblatt, Zeitschrift für Psychoanalyse und Gesellschaftskritik, 4*: 81–94.

Falzeder, Ernst (2010). Sándor Ferenczi between orthodoxy and dissidence. *American Imago, 66*: 395–404.

Falzeder, Ernst (in prep.). Freud's role in choosing the presidents of the International Psychoanalytical Association.

Falzeder, Ernst, & Graf-Nold, Angela (2010). Gustav Eim (1849–1897), ein Patient aus Freuds früher Praxis. Mit zwei unveröffentlichten Freud-Briefen. *Luzifer-Amor, Zeitschrift zur Geschichte der Psychoanalyse, 23*: 8–15.

Falzeder, Ernst, & Handlbauer, Bernhard (1992). Freud, Adler et d'autres psychanalystes. Des débuts de la psychanalyse organisée à la fondation de l'Association Psychanalytique Internationale. *Psychothérapies, 12*: 219–232.

Federn, Ernst (Ed.) (1971). Fünfunddreißig Jahre mit Freud. *Psyche, Zeitschrift für Psychoanalyse und ihre Anwendungen, 25*: 721–737.

Ferenczi, Sándor (1913[124]). C. G. Jung, "Wandlungen und Symbole der Libido". *Internationale Zeitschrift für ärztliche Psychoanalyse, 1*: 391–403.

Ferenczi, Sándor (1915[159]). Psychogenic anomalies of voice production. In: *Further Contributions to the Theory and Technique of Psycho-Analysis* (105–109). London: Hogarth, 1926. Reprint London: Karnac, 1994 [= *Further C.*].

Ferenczi, Sándor (1915[160]). The dream of the occlusive pessary. In: *Further C.* (304–311).

Ferenczi, Sándor (1915[181]). Kollarits, Dr. J., "Contribution à l'étude des rêves". *Internationale Zeitschrift für ärztliche Psychoanalyse, 1*: 391–403. In: *Bausteine IV* (78–85).

Ferenczi, Sándor (1916[188]). Significant variants of the shoe as a vagina symbol. In: *Further C.* (358).

Ferenczi, Sándor (1917[193]). Pollution without dream orgasm and dream orgasm without pollution. In: *Further C.* (297–304).

Ferenczi, Sándor (1923[259]). A psychoanalysis a gyakorló orvos szolgálatában [Psychoanalysis in the service of the practicing physician]. *Gyógyászat*, Nr. 23–24.

Ferenczi, Sándor (1924[268]). *Thalassa: A Theory of Genitality.* Albany, NY: Psychoanalytic Quarterly, 1938.

Ferenczi, Sándor (1928[282]). The problem of termination of the analysis. In: *Final Contributions to the Problems and Methods of Psycho-Analysis* (77–86). London: Hogarth, 1955. Reprint London: Karnac, 1994 [= *Final C.*].

Ferenczi, Sándor (1928[283]). The elasticity of psycho-analytic technique. In: *Final C.* (87–101).

Ferenczi, Sándor (1928[283a]). Psychoanalyse und Kriminologie. In: *Bausteine III* (399–421).

Ferenczi, Sándor (1931[292]). Child analysis in the analysis of adults. In: *Final C.* (126–142).

Ferenczi, Sándor (1933[294]). Confusion of tongues between adults and the child. In: *Final C.* (143–155).

Ferenczi, Sándor (1939[308]). Notes and fragments. In: *Final C.* (216–279).

Ferenczi, Sándor, & Groddeck, Georg (1982). *Correspondance (1921–1933).* Ed. Groupe de traduction du Coq-Héron. Paris: Payot. *Briefwechsel 1921–1933.* Frankfurt am Main: Fischer Taschenbuch Verlag, 1986. *The Ferenczi-Groddeck Correspondence 1921–1933.* Ed. Christopher Fortune. London: Open Gate Press, 2002. *Briefwechsel.* Ed. Michael Giefer. Frankfurt am Main: Stroemfeld, 2006.

Ferenczi, Sándor, & Rank, Otto (1924). *Entwicklungsziele der Psychoanalyse. Zur Wechselbeziehung von Theorie und Praxis.* Leipzig: Internationaler Psychoanalytischer Verlag. *The Development of Psychoanalysis.* Trans. Caroline Newton. New York: Dover, 1956.

Ferris, Paul (1997). *Dr. Freud. A Life.* Washington, DC: Counterpoint.

Fichtner, Gerhard (1989). Freuds Briefe als historische Quelle. *Psyche, Zeitschrift für Psychoanalyse und ihre Anwendungen, 43*: 803–829.

Fichtner, Gerhard (1994). Die ärztliche Schweigepflicht, der Analytiker und der Historiker. *Psyche, Zeitschrift für Psychoanalyse und ihre Anwendungen, 48*: 738–745.

Fichtner, Gerhard, & Meyer-Palmedo, Ingeborg (1999). *Freud-Bibliograpghie mit Werkkonkordanz.* Frankfurt am Main: S. Fischer. Second, revised and enlarged edition.

Fischer, Dominique (1977). *Les analysés parlent.* Paris: Stock.

Fließ, Wilhelm (1906). *In eigener Sache. Gegen Otto Weininger und Hermann Swoboda.* Berlin: Emil Goldschmidt.

Forrester, John (1997). *Dispatches from the Freud Wars: Psychoanalysis and Its Passions.* Cambridge, MA: Harvard University Press.

Forsyth, David (1913). Psychoanalysis. *British Medical Journal, 2*: 13–17.

Fortune, Christopher (1994). A difficult ending: Ferenczi, "R.N.", and the experiment in mutual analysis. In: André Haynal and Ernst Falzeder (Eds.), *100 Years of Psychoanalysis: Contributions to the History of Psychoanalysis* (217–223). Geneva: Cahiers Psychiatriques Genevois.

Frank, Claudia (1999). *Melanie Kleins erste Kinderanalysen. Die Entdeckung des Kindes als Objekt sui generis von Heilen und Forschen.* Stuttgart: frommann-holzboog.

Freud, Ernst; Freud, Lucie; & Grubrich-Simitis, Ilse (Eds.) (1976). *Freud. Sein Leben in Bildern und Texten.* Frankfurt am Main: Suhrkamp.

Freud, Martin (1957). *Sigmund Freud—Man and Father.* London: Angus and Robertson.

Freud, Sigmund (1877a). Über den Ursprung der hinteren Nervenwurzeln im Rückenmarke von Ammocoetes (Petromyzon Planeri). *Sitzungsberichte der Akademie der Wissenschaften in Wien* (Mathematisch-Naturwissenschaftliche Klasse), 3. Abteilung, 75: 15–27.

Freud, Sigmund (1891b). *Zur Auffassung der Aphasien.* Leipzig: Deuticke. Reprint Frankfurt am Main: Fischer Taschenbuch Verlag, 1992. Partly reprinted in S.E. 14 (206–215).

Freud, Sigmund (1896b). Further remarks on the neuro-psychoses of defence. S.E. 3 (162–185).

Freud, Sigmund (1896c). The aetiology of hysteria. S.E. 3 (191–221).

Freud, Sigmund (1899a). Screen memories. S.E. 3 (303–322).

Freud, Sigmund (1900a). *The Interpretation of Dreams.* S.E. 4 and 5.

Freud, Sigmund (1901b). *The Psychopathology of Everyday Life.* S.E. 6.

Freud, Sigmund (1905a). On psychotherapy. S.E. 7 (255–268).

Freud, Sigmund (1905c). *Jokes and Their Relation to the Unconscious.* S.E. 8.

Freud, Sigmund (1905d). *Three Essays on the Theory of Sexuality.* S.E. 7 (135–243).

Freud, Sigmund (1905e). Fragment of an analysis of a case of hysteria. S.E. 7 (7–122).

Freud, Sigmund (1908e). Creative writers and day-dreaming. S.E. 9 (143–153).

Freud, Sigmund (1909d). Notes upon a case of obsessional neurosis. S.E. 10 (155–249).

Freud, Sigmund (1909f). Interview: "Prof. Sigmund Freud". *Boston Evening Transcript*, 11 September 1909.

Freud, Sigmund (1910a). *Five Lectures on Psycho-Analysis.* S.E. 11 (7–55).

Freud, Sigmund (1910d). The future prospects of psycho-analytic therapy. S.E. 11 (141–151).

Freud, Sigmund (1910h). A special type of choice of object made by men (Contributions to the psychology of love I). S.E. 11 (165–175).

Freud, Sigmund (1911c). Psycho-analytic notes on an autobiographical account of a case of paranoia (dementia paranoides). S.E. 12 (9–82).

Freud, Sigmund (1912b). The dynamics of transference. S.E. 12 (99–108).

Freud, Sigmund (1912e). Recommendations to physicians practising psycho-analysis. S.E. 12 (111–120).

Freud, Sigmund (1912–13a). *Totem and Taboo*. S.E. 13 (1–161).

Freud, Sigmund (1913a). An evidential dream. S.E. 12 (169–277).

Freud, Sigmund (1913c). On beginning the treatment (Further recommendations on the technique of psycho-analysis I). S.E. 12 (123–144).

Freud, Sigmund (1913g). Two lies told by children. S. E. 12 (305–309).

Freud, Sigmund (1913i). The disposition to obsessional neurosis. S.E. 12 (317–326).

Freud, Sigmund (1914d). On the history of the psycho-analytic movement. S.E. 14 (7–66).

Freud, Sigmund (1914g). Remembering, repeating and working-through (Further recommendations on the technique of psycho-analysis II). S.E. 12 (147–156).

Freud, Sigmund (1915a). Observations on transference-love (Further recommendations on the technique of psycho-analysis III). S.E. 12 (159–171).

Freud, Sigmund (1915e). The unconscious. S.E. 14 (166–204).

Freud, Sigmund (1916–17g). Mourning and melancholia. S.E. 14 (243–258).

Freud, Sigmund (1918b). From the history of an infantile neurosis. S.E. 17 (7–122).

Freud, Sigmund (1919a). Lines of advance in psycho-analytic therapy. S.E. 17 (159–168).

Freud, Sigmund (1919e). A child is being beaten: A contribution to the study of the origin of sexual perversions. S.E. 17 (179–204).

Freud, Sigmund (1920g). *Beyond the Pleasure Principle*. S.E. 18 (7–64).

Freud, Sigmund (1922b). Some neurotic mechanisms in jealousy, paranoia and homosexuality. S.E. 18 (223–232).

Freud, Sigmud (1922d). Prize offer. S.E. 17 (270).

Freud, Sigmund (1922f). Etwas vom Unbewußten. *Internationale Zeitschrift für Psychoanalyse, 8*: 486.

Freud, Sigmund (1923b). *The Ego and and the Id*. S.E. 19 (12–59).

Freud, Sigmund (1923e). The infantile genital organisation (An interpolation into the theory of sexuality). S.E. 19 (141–145).

Freud, Sigmund (1925d). *An Autobiographical Study*. S.E. 20 (7–70).

Freud, Sigmund (1925i). Some additional notes on dream-interpretation as a whole. S.E. 19 (127–138).

Freud, Sigmund (1926b). Abraham †. S.E. 20 (277–278).

Freud, Sigmund (1926d). *Inhibitions, Symptoms and Anxiety.* S.E. 20 (87–172).

Freud, Sigmund (1927c). *The Future of an Illusion.* S.E. 21 (5–56).

Freud, Sigmund (1927h). Interview: "Mean Men Explained by Freud". *London Weekly Dispatch,* 28 July 1927.

Freud, Sigmund (1930a). *Civilization and Its Discontents.* S.E. 21 (64–145).

Freud, Sigmund (1930c). Introduction to the special psychopathology number of *The Medical Review of Reviews.* S.E. 21 (254–255).

Freud, Sigmund (1932d). Summary (in Hungarian) of the first part of Lecture XXX of the *New Introductory Lectures o Psycho-Analysis. Magyar Hirlap,* 25 December 1932.

Freud, Sigmund (1932g). Interview: "Neurosen als Zeitkrankheit. Welche Heilerfolge hat die Psychoanalyse?" *Neue Freie Presse,* 14 August 1932 (morning edition), supplement (21).

Freud, Sigmund (1933a). *New Introductory Lectures on Psycho-Analysis.* S.E. 22 (5–182).

Freud, Sigmund (1933b). Why war? S.E. 22 (203–215).

Freud, Sigmund (1933c). Sándor Ferenczi †. S.E. 22 (227–229).

Freud, Sigmund (1937c). Analysis terminable and interminable. S.E. 23 (216–253).

Freud, Sigmund (1939a). *Moses and Monotheism: Three Essays.* S.E. 23 (7–137).

Freud, Sigmund (1940a). *An Outline of Psycho-Analysis.* S.E. 23 (144–207).

Freud, Sigmund (1940e). Splitting of the ego in the process of defence. S.E. 23 (275–278).

Freud, Sigmund (1941d [1921]). Psycho-analysis and telepathy. S.E. 18 (177–193).

Freud, Sigmund (1950a). *Aus den Anfängen der Psychoanalyse. Briefe an Wilhelm Fließ, Abhandlungen und Notizen aus den Jahren 1887–1902.* Eds. Marie Bonaparte, Anna Freud and Ernst Kris. London: Imago Publishing. *The Origins of Psychoanalysis. Letters to Wilhelm Fliess, Drafts and Notes: 1887–1902.* Eds. Marie Bonaparte, Anna Freud and Ernst Kris. New York: Basic Books, 1954.

Freud, Sigmund (1950c). Entwurf einer Psychologie [revised version of the text reprinted in 1950a]. In: *Gesammelte Werke, Nachtragsband* (387–477).

Freud, Sigmund (1955a). Originalnotizen zu einem Fall von Zwangsneurose. In: *Gesammelte Werke, Nachtragsband* (509–569). Partly reprinted in S.E. 10 (254–255, 259–318).

Freud, Sigmund (1955c). Memorandum on the electrical treatment of war neurotics. S.E. 17 (211–215).

Freud, Sigmund (1956c). Ten letters to Hilda Aldington (H.D.). In: H.D., *Tribute to Freud. With Unpublished Letters by Freud to the Author* (14, 173–180). New York: Pantheon.

Freud, Sigmund (1960a). *Briefe 1873–1939*. Ed. Ernst L. and Lucie Freud. Frankfurt am Main: S. Fischer. *The Letters of Sigmund Freud*. Ed. Ernst L. Freud. New York: Basic Books; reprint 1975.

Freud, Sigmund (1964a). Freud's letters to Ernst Simmel. Eds. Frances Deri and David Brunswick. *Journal of the American Psychoanalytic Association,* 12: 93–109 (the letters 97–109).

Freud, Sigmund (1969a). Some early unpublished letters of Freud. Ed. Ernst L. Freud. *International Journal of Psycho-Analysis, 50*: 419–427.

Freud, Sigmund (1977d). Telegram to Lillian Powers (1934/36). In: JA Stargardt (Marburg), catalogue 612, number 454.

Freud, Sigmund (1985a). *Übersicht der Übertragungsneurosen. Ein bisher unbekanntes Manuskript.* Ed. Ilse Grubrich-Simitis. Frankfurt am Main: S. Fischer. *A Phylogenetic Fantasy. Overview of the Transference Neuroses.* Ed. Ilse Grubrich-Simitis. Trans. Axel and Peter Hoffer. Cambridge, MA: The Belknap Press of Harvard University Press. 1987.

Freud, Sigmund (1992i). *The Diary of Sigmund Freud, 1929–1939: A Chronicle of Events in the Last Decade.* Ed. Michael Molnar. London: Hogarth Press.

Freud, Sigmund (1996g). Letters to Sam (Soloman) Freud and Pauline Hartwig. In: Thomas Roberts (Ed.), *Lettres de famille de Sigmund Freud et des Freud de Manchester 1911–1938.* Paris: Presses Universitaires de France.

Freud, Sigmund (2002). *Unser Herz zeigt nach dem Süden: Reisebriefe 1895–1923.* Ed. Christfried Tögel, with the collaboration of Michael Molnar. Berlin: Aufbau-Verlag.

Freud, Sigmund (2010). *Freud im Kontext. Gesammelte Schriften auf CD-ROM.* Berlin: Infosoftware.

Freud, Sigmund, & Abraham, Karl (1965). *Briefe 1907–1926.* Eds. Hilda C. Abraham and Ernst L. Freud. Frankfurt am Main: S. Fischer; second, revised edition 1980. *A Psycho-Analytic Dialogue. The Letters of Sigmund Freud and Karl Abraham 1907–1926.* Eds. Hilda C. Abraham and Ernst L. Freud. London: The Hogarth Press and The Institute of Psycho-Analysis.

Freud, Sigmund, & Andreas-Salomé, Lou (1966). *Briefwechsel.* Ed. Ernst Pfeiffer. Frankfurt am Main: S. Fischer. *Letters.* Ed. Ernst Pfeiffer. London: The Hogarth Press and The Institute of Psycho-Analysis, 1972.

Freud, Sigmund, & Bullitt, William C. (1967). *Thomas Woodrow Wilson, Twenty-eighth President of the United States: A Psychological Study.* Boston, MA: Houghton Mifflin.

Freud, Sigmund, & Groddeck, Georg (1970). *Briefe über das Es.* Ed. Margaretha Honegger. Munich: Kindler.

Freud, Sigmund, & Pfister, Oskar (1963). *Briefe 1909–1939.* Frankfurt am Main: S. Fischer. *Psychoanalysis and Faith: The Letters of Sigmund Freud and Oskar Pfister*. New York: Basic Books. Both ed. Ernst L. Freud and Heinrich Meng.

Freud, Sophie (2006). *Im Schatten der Familie Freud. Meine Mutter erlebt das 20. Jahrhundert*. Berlin: claassen, Ullstein.

Freud-Bernays, Anna (2004). *Eine Wienerin in New York: Die Erinnerungen der Schwester Sigmund Freuds*. Ed. Christfried Tögel. Berlin: Aufbau-Verlag.

Freud-Marlé, Lilly (2006). *Mein Onkel Sigmund Freud. Erinnerungen an eine große Familie*. Berlin: Aufbau-Verlag.

Fromm, Erich (1959). *Sigmund Freud's Mission: An Analysis of His Personality and Influence*. New York: Harper & Brothers.

Furtmüller, Carl (1946). Alfred Adlers Werdegang. In: *Denken und Handeln, Schriften zur Psychologie 1905–1950. Von den Anfängen der Psychoanalyse zur Anwendung der Individualpsychologie* (233–287). Ed. Lux Furtmüller. Munich: E. Reinhardt.

Gabbard, Glen O. (1995). The early history of boundary violations in psychoanalysis. *Journal of the American Psychoanalytic Association, 43*: 1115–1136.

Gabbard, Glen O., & Lester, Eva B. (1995). *Boundaries and Boundary Violations in Psychoanalysis*. New York: Basic Books.

Gamwell, Lynn, & Wells, Richard (Eds.) (1989). *Sigmund Freud and Art. His Personal Collection of Antiquities*. New York: State University of New York.

Gardiner, Muriel (Ed.) (1971). *The Wolf-Man*. New York: Basic Books.

Gattel, Felix (1898). *Über die sexuellen Ursachen der Neurasthenie und Angstneurose*. Berlin: August Hirschwald.

Gay, Peter (1987). *Freud: A Life for Our Time*. New York: Anchor Books, Doubleday, 1989.

Gedo, John (1984). *Psychoanalysis and Its Discontents*. New York: The Guilford Press.

Gellner, Ernest (1985). *The Psychoanalytic Movement or The Cunning of Unreason*. London: Paladin.

Gicklhorn, Josef, & Gicklhorn, Renée (1960). *Sigmund Freuds akademische Laufbahn im Lichte der Dokumente*. Vienna: Urban & Schwarzenberg.

Gifford, Sanford (1978). Psychoanalysis in Boston: Innocence and experience. Introduction to the panel discussion, 14 April 1973. In: Gifford, George E., Jr. (Ed.), *Psychoanalysis, Psychotherapy and the New England Medical Scene, 1894–1944* (325–345). New York: Science History Publications.

Gifford, Sanford (1997). *The Emmanuel Movement (Boston, 1904–1929). The Origins of Group Treatment and the Assault on Lay Psychotherapy*. Boston: The Francis Countway Library of Medicine (distributed by Harvard University Press).

Gisevius, Friedrich (1931). Concerning the *simillimum*—one way? Trans. W. J. Sweasy Powers. *Homoeopathic Recorder, 46*: 914–919.

Glaser, Ernst (1981). *Im Umfeld des Austromarxismus. Ein Beitrag zur Geistesgeschichte des österreichischen Sozialismus.* Munich: Europa Verlag.

Glover, Edward (1950). *Freud or Jung.* New York: W. W. Norton. Reprint, with a foreword from James William Anderson. Evanston: Northwestern University Press, 1991.

Goldmann, Stefan (1985). Sigmund Freuds Briefe an seine Patientin Anna v. Vest. *Jahrbuch der Psychoanalyse, 17:* 269–295.

Good, Michael I. (1995). Karl Abraham, and the fate of the seduction theory. *Journal of the American Psychoanalytic Association, 43:* 1136–1167.

Good, Michael I. (1998). Karl Abraham (1877–1925). *Newsletter of the Psychoanalytic Society and Institute of New England, East, 11:* 4–5.

Graf, Max (1942). Reminiscences of Professor Sigmund Freud. *Psychoanalytic Quarterly, 11:* 465–476.

Graf-Nold, Angela (2001). The Zurich School of Psychiatry in theory and practice. Sabina Spielrein's treatment at the Burghölzli Clinic in Zurich. *Journal of Analytical Psychology, 46:* 73–104.

Graf-Nold, Angela (2006). 100 Jahre Peinlichkeit—und (k)ein Ende? Karl Abrahams frühe psychoanalytische Veröffentlichungen und die "sexuelle Frage". *Jahrbuch der Psychoanalyse, 52:* 93–135.

Granoff, Wladimir (1975). *Filiations. L'Avenir du Complexe d'Oedipe.* Paris: Éditions du Minuit.

Greenberg, Jay R., & Mitchell, Stephen A. (1983). *Object Relations in Psychoanalytic Theory.* Cambridge, MA: Harvard University Press.

Grinker, Roy (1975). Reminiscences of Dr. Roy Grinker. *Journal of the American Academy of Psychoanalysis, 3:* 211–221.

Grosskurth, Phyllis (1986). *Melanie Klein: Her World and Her Work.* New York: Alfred A. Knopf.

Grosskurth, Phyllis (1991). *The Secret Ring: Freud's Inner Circle and the Politics of Psychoanalysis.* Reading, MA: Addison-Wesley.

Grotjahn, Martin (1967). "A Psycho-Analytic Dialogue: The Letters of Sigmund Freud and Karl Abraham, 1907–1926." *Voices: The Art and Science of Psychotherapy, 3:* 85–89.

Grotjahn, Martin (1976). Freuds Briefwechsel. In: Dieter Eicke (Ed.), *Tiefenpsychologie. Band 1: Sigmund Freud—Leben und Werk* (29–140). Weinheim: Beltz, 1982.

Grotjahn, Martin (1987). *My Favorite Patient: The Memoirs of a Psychoanalyst.* Frankfurt am Main: Peter Lang.

Grotjahn, Martin, & vom Scheidt, Jürgen (1976). Freud im Spiegel seiner Biographen. In: Dieter Eicke (Ed.), *Tiefenpsychologie. Band 1: Sigmund Freud—Leben und Werk* (191–219). Weinheim: Beltz, 1982.

Grubrich-Simitis, Ilse (1993). *Zurück zu Freuds Texten: Stumme Dokumente sprechen machen.* Frankfurt am Main: S. Fischer. *Back to Freud's Texts:*

Making Silent Documents Speak. New Haven, CT: Yale University Press, 1996.

Grunberger, Béla (1974). Von der "Aktiven Technik" zur "Sprachverwirrung". Studie zu Ferenczis Abweichung. *Jahrbuch der Psychoanalyse*, 1979, 2: 100–124.

Gundlach, Horst (1977). Freud schreibt an Hellpach. Ein Beitrag zur Rezeptionsgeschichte der Psychoanalyse in Deutschland. *Psyche, Zeitschrift für Psychoanalyse und ihre Anwendungen*, 31: 908–934.

Guttman, Samuel A., with the collaboration of Stephen M. Parrish and Randall L. Jones (1983). *The Concordance to The Standard Edition of The Complete Psychological Works of Sigmund Freud.* Six volumes. New York: International Universities Press.

Guttman, Samuel A.; Parrish, Stephen M.; Ruffing, John; & Smith, Philip H. Jr. (Eds.) (1995). *Konkordanz zu den Gesammelten Werken von Sigmund Freud.* Waterloo, Ont.: North Waterloo Academic Press.

"H. D."—see Doolittle, Hilda.

Häberlin, Paul, & Binswanger, Ludwig (1997). *Paul Häberlin—Ludwig Binswanger, Briefwechsel 1908–1960: mit Briefen von Sigmund Freud, Carl Gustav Jung, Karl Jaspers, Martin Heidegger, Ludwig Frank und Eugen Bleuler.* Ed. Jeannine Luczak. Basel: Schwabe.

Hale, Nathan G. (1971a). *Freud and the Americans: The Beginnings of Psychoanalysis in the United States, 1876–1917.* New York: Oxford University Press.

Hale, Nathan G. (1971b). *James Jackson Putnam and Psychoanalysis: Letters Between Putnam and Sigmund Freud, Ernest Jones, William James, Sándor Ferenczi, and Morton Prince, 1877–1917.* Cambridge, MA: Harvard University Press.

Hale, Nathan G. (1978). James Jackson Putnam and Boston neurology: 1877–1918. In: George E. Gifford (Ed.), *Psychoanalysis, Psychotherapy, and the New England Medical Scene, 1894–1944* (151–153). New York: Science History Publications.

Hamburger Ärzte-Correspondenz (1910). Nr. 14, 3 April 1910: 160–161.

Hamilton, Victoria (1996). *The Analyst's Preconscious.* Hillsdale, NJ: The Analytic Press.

Handlbauer, Bernhard (1984). *Die Entstehungsgeschichte der Individualpsychologie Alfred Adlers.* Vienna: Geyer-Edition.

Handlbauer, Bernhard (1992). *Die Adler-Freud-Kontroverse.* Frankfurt am Main: Fischer Taschenbuch Verlag. *The Freud-Adler Controversy.* London: Oneworld, 1998.

Hannah, Barbara (1976). *Jung: His Life and Work. A Biographical Memoir.* Boston, MA: Shambhala.

Harmat, Paul (1986). *Freud, Ferenczi und die ungarische Psychoanalyse.* Tübingen: edition diskord.

Haynal, André (1987). *La Technique en Question: Controverses en Psychanalyse.* Paris: Payot. *The Technique at Issue: Controversies in Psychoanalysis from Freud and Ferenczi to Michael Balint.* London: Karnac, 1988.

Haynal, André (1991). *Psychanalyse et Science Face à Face.* Meyzieu: Césura Lyon Édition. *Psychoanalysis and the Sciences. Epistemology—History.* Berkeley, CA: University of California Press, 1993.

Haynal, André (1994). Freud's relation to philosophy and biology as reflected in his letters. In: André Haynal and Ernst Falzeder (Eds.), *100 Years of Psychoanalysis: Contributions to the History of Psychoanalysis* (151–168). Geneva: Cahiers Psychiatriques Genevois.

Haynal, André (1995). Entgegnung auf Gerhard Fichtners "notwendige Stellungnahme" und Anmerkungen zu Michael Schröters Buchbesprechung. *Psyche, Zeitschrift für Psychoanalyse und ihre Anwendungen, 49:* 174–181.

Haynal, André (2008). Begegnungen mit dem Irrationalen. In: Ludger M. Hermanns (Ed.), *Psychoanalyse in Selbstdarstellungen, Band VII* (9–44). Frankfurt am Main: Brandes & Apsel.

Haynal, André, & Falzeder, Ernst (1993). Slaying the dragons of the past or Cooking the hare in the present. A historical view on affects in the psychoanalytic encounter. *Psychoanalytic Inquiry, 13:* 357–371.

Haynal, André, & Falzeder, Ernst (2002). Introduction. In: F/Abr (xix–xxx).

Haynal, André, & Falzeder, Ernst (2011). The Swiss. In: Peter Loewenberg and Nellie L. Thompson (Eds.), *100 Years of the IPA. The Centenary History of the International Psychoanalytical Association 1910–2010. Evolution and Change* (182–195). Broomhills/London: International Psychoanalytical Association/Karnac.

Heimann, Paula (1950). On countertransference. *International Journal of Psycho-Analysis, 31:* 81–84.

Hell, Daniel, Scharfetter, Christian, & Möller, Arnulf (Eds.) (2001). *Eugen Bleuler—Leben und Werk.* Bern: H. Huber.

Heller, Peter (1992a) (Ed.). *Anna Freud's Letters to Eva Rosenfeld.* Madison: International Universities Press.

Heller, Peter (1992b). Reflections on a child analysis with Anna Freud and an adult analysis with Ernst Kris. *Journal of the American Academy of Psychoanalysis, 20:* 49–74.

Hellpach, Willy (1904). *Grundlinien einer Psychologie der Hysterie.* Leipzig: Engelmann.

Hermanns, Ludger M. (1997). Karl Abraham und die Anfänge der Berliner Psychoanalytischen Vereinigung. In: Michael Hubenstorf, Hans-Uwe Lammel, Ragnhild Münch, Sabine Schleiermacher, Heinz-Peter Schmiedebach and Sigrid Stöckel (Eds.), *Abhandlungen zur Geschichte der Medizin und der Naturwissenschaften, Heft 81: Medizingeschichte und Gesellschaftskritik. Festschrift für Gerhard Baader* (174–188). Husum: Matthiesen.

Hermanns, Ludger M., & Dahl, Gerhard (2007). Karl Abraham Archiv. CD zum Internationalen Psychoanalytischen Kongreß. Berlin: Berliner Psychoanalytisches Institut.

Herzog, Max (Ed.) (1995). *Ludwig Binswanger und die Chronik der Klinik "Bellevue" in Kreuzlingen.* Berlin: Quintessenz.

Hirschmüller, Albrecht (1978). Eine bisher unbekannte Krankenge-schichte Sigmund Freuds und Josef Breuers aus der Entstehungszeit der "Studien über Hysterie". *Jahrbuch der Psychoanalyse, 10:* 136–168.

Hirschmüller, Albrecht (1991). *Freuds Begegnung mit der Psychiatrie. Von der Hirnmythologie zur Neurosenlehre.* Tübingen: edition diskord.

Hoche, Alfred (1910). Eine psychische Epidemie unter Ärzten. Versammlung südwestdeutscher Irrenärzte (Baden-Baden), 29 May 1910. *Medizinische Klinik, 6:* 1007–1010.

Hoche, Alfred (1913a). Rundschreiben. *Internationale Zeitschrift für ärztliche Psychoanalyse, 1:* 199.

Hoche, Alfred (1913b). Über den Wert der "Psychoanalyse". *Archiv für Psychiatrie und Nervenkrankheiten, 51:* 1055–1079.

Hoche, Alfred (1923). Alfred Erich Hoche. In: Louis R. Grote (Ed.), *Die Medizin der Gegenwart in Selbstdarstellungen I* (1–24). Leipzig: Felix Meiner.

Hochsinger, Carl (1938). *Die Geschichte des Ersten Öffentlichen Kinder-Kranken-Instituts in Wien während seines 150 jährigen Bestandes 1788–1938.* Vienna: Verlag des Kinder-Kranken-Instituts.

Hoff, Paul (1994). *Emil Kraepelin und die Psychiatrie als klinische Wissenschaft: Ein Betrag zum Selbstverständnis psychiatrischer Forschung.* Berlin: Springer.

Hoffer, Axel (1996). Introduction. In: F/Fer II (xvii–xlvi).

Homoeopathic Recorder (1931). Vol. 48: inside front cover.

Huber, Wolfgang (1986a). Emma Eckstein—eine Frau in den Anfängen der Psychoanalyse, Freuds Patientin und erste Schülerin. *Studien zur Kinderpsychoanalyse, 6:* 67–81.

Huber, Wolfgang (1986b). Emma Ecksteins Feuilleton zur "Traumdeutung". *Jahrbuch der Psychoanalyse, 19:* 90–106.

Hughes, Athol (Ed.) (1992). Letters from Sigmund Freud to Joan Riviere (1921–1939). *International Review of Psycho-Analysis, 19:* 265–284.

Isbister, J. N. (1985). *Freud: An Introduction to His Life and Work.* Cambridge: Polity Press.

Jaffé, Aniela (1968). *Aus Leben und Werkstatt von C. G. Jung. Parapsychologie—Alchemie—Nationalsozialismus—Erinnerungen aus den letzten Jahren.* Zurich: Rascher.

Jeannet-Hasler, Mady (2002). *Thérapie contre théorie? Les enjeux d'un concours.* Paris: Presses Universitaires de France.

Jones, Ernest (1909). Review of *The Psychology of Dementia Praecox* by C. G. Jung. *Dominion Medical Monthly.*

Jones, Ernest (1920). Dr. James Jackson Putnam †. *International Journal of Psycho-Analysis, 1:* 6–16.

Jones, Ernest (1926). Karl Abraham 1877–1925. *Internationale Zeitschrift für Psychoanalyse, 12:* 155–183.

Jones, Ernest (1938). Presidential address. *Internationale Zeitschrift für Psychoanalyse, 24:* 367.

Jones, Ernest (1959). *Free Associations: Memories of a Psycho-Analyst.* London: Hogarth Press.

Jones, Jack (1960). Otto Rank: A forgotten heresy. *Commentary, 30:* 219–229.

Jung, Carl Gustav (1902). *On the Psychology and Pathology of So-Called Occult Phenomena.* CW 1.

Jung, Carl Gustav (1907). *The Psychology of Dementia Praecox.* CW 3.

Jung, Carl Gustav (1910a). Psychic conflicts in a child. CW 17.

Jung, Carl Gustav (1910b). Autoreferat des Kongreßvortrages in Salzburg. *Zentralblatt für Psychoanalyse, 1:* 128.

Jung, Carl Gustav (1911/12). Wandlungen und Symbole der Libido. Beiträge zur Entwicklungsgeschichte des Denkens. *Jahrbuch für psycho-analytische und psychopathologische Forschungen,* 1911, 3: 120–227; 1912, 4: 162–464. In book form: Viena: Deuticke, 1912. Reprint Munich: Deutscher Taschenbuch Verlag, 1991.

Jung, Carl Gustav (1912). New paths in psychology. CW 7.

Jung, Carl Gustav (1913[1912]). *The Theory of Psychoanalysis.* CW 4. *Jung contra Freud. The 1912 New York Lectures on the Theory of Psychoanalysis.* Intr. Sonu Shamdasani. Princeton, NJ: Princeton University Press, 2012.

Jung, Carl Gustav (1917). *Die Psychologie der unbewussten Prozesse. Ein Überblick über die moderne Theorie und Methode der analytischen Psychologie.* Zurich: Rauscher. *The Psychology of the Unconscious Processes, Being a Survey of the Modern Theory of Analytical Psychology.* In: Constance Long (Ed.), *Collected Papers on Analytical Psychology.* London: Ballière, Tindall & Cox.

Jung, Carl Gustav (1921). *Psychological Types or The Psychology of Individuation.* CW 6.

Jung, Carl Gustav (1927). Mind and earth. CW 10.

Jung, Carl Gustav (1933). The meaning of psychology for modern man. CW 10.

Jung, Carl Gustav (1934). Letter to *Neue Zürcher Zeitung.* CW 10, fn. 544.

Jung, Carl Gustav (1962). *Memories, Dreams, Reflections*. Recorded and edited by Aniela Jaffé. New York: Pantheon, 1973.

Jung, Carl Gustav (1984). *Dream Analysis. Notes of the Seminar Given in 1928–1930*. Ed. William McGuire. Princeton, NJ: Princeton University Press.

Jung, Carl Gustav (2008). *Children's Dreams. Notes from the Seminar Given in 1936–1940*. Eds. Lorenz Jung and Maria Meyer-Grass. Trans. Ernst Falzeder. Princeton, NJ: Princeton University Press.

Jung, Carl Gustav (2009). *The Red Book: Liber Novus*. Ed. Sonu Shamdasani. New York: W. W. Norton.

Kaderas, Brigitte (1998). Karl Abrahams Bemühungen um einen Lehrauftrag für Psychoanalyse an der Friedrich-Wilhelms-Universität. Quellenedition der "Denkschrift der Berliner Psychoanalytischen Vereinigung betreffend Einführung des psychoanalytischen Unterrichts an der Berliner Universität" und ihrer Ablehnung. *Jahrbuch für Universitätsgeschichte*, Band 1 (205–232). Stuttgart: Franz Steiner.

Kahane, Max (1892). *Über das Verhalten des Indicans bei der Tuberculose des Kindesalters*. Leipzig: Deuticke.

Kahane, Max (1901a). *Grundriss der inneren Medicin für Studierende und Ärzte*. Leipzig: Deuticke.

Kahane, Max (1901b). *Die Chlorose: Vegetationsstörung der weiblichen Pubertätsperiode*. Berlin: Urban.

Kahane, Max (1902). *Therapie der Erkrankungen des Respirations- und Circulationsapparates*. Vienna: Hölder.

Kahane, Max (1904). *Therapie der Magenkrankheiten*. Vienna: Hölder.

Kahane, Max (1905). *Therapie der Darmkrankheiten*. Vienna: Hölder.

Kahane, Max (Ed.) (1906). *Mittheilungen aus dem Gebiete der physikalischen Therapie, Band 1*. Vienna: Fischer.

Kahane, Max (1908). *Medizinisches Handlexikon für praktische Ärzte*. Berlin: Urban & Schwarzenberg.

Kahane, Max (1910). *Die Arzneitherapie der Gegenwart: die neuesten Arzneimittel und ihre Anwendung in der ärztlichen Praxis*. Berlin: Urban & Schwarzenberg.

Kahane, Max (1912). *Therapie der Nervenkrankheiten. Handbuch der therapeutischen Praxis in Einzeldarstellungen. Unter Mitwirkung hervorragender Fachgenossen herausgegeben von Dr. Max Kahane. 1. Band*. Leipzig: Georg Szelinski.

Kahane, Max (1922). *Grundzüge der Elektrodiagnostik und Elektrotherapie für praktische Ärzte*. Berlin: Urban & Schwarzenberg.

Kahane, Max, & Pietschmann, Franz (1907). *Die gebräuchlichsten neueren Arzneimittel, deren Anwendung und Dosierung, sowie besondere ärztliche Verschreibungen im Wiener Allgemeinen Krankenhause*. Berlin: Urban & Schwarzenberg.

Kahr, Brett (1996). *D. W. Winnicott: A Biographical Portrait*. London: Karnac.

Kardiner, Abram (1977). *My Analysis with Freud: Reminiscences*. New York: W. W. Norton.

Kaufmann, Walter (1980). *Freud, Adler and Jung: Discovering the Mind. Volume 3*. New Brunswick, NJ: Transaction Publishers, expanded edition 1992.

Kaye, Howard L. (1993). Why Freud hated America. *Wilson Quarterly, 17*: 121–122.

Kempf, Edward J. (1949). Bisexual factors in curable schizophrenia. *The Journal of Abnormal and Social Psychology, 44*: 414–419.

Kempf, Edward J. (1974). *Collected Papers*. Eds. Dorothy C. Kempf and John C. Burnham. Bloomington, IN: Indiana University Press.

Kernberg, Otto F. (1996). Thirty methods to destroy the creativity of psychoanalytic candidates. *International Journal of Psycho-Analysis, 77*: 1031–1040.

Kerr, John (1993). *A Most Dangerous Method: The Story of Jung, Freud, and Sabina Spielrein*. New York: Alfred A. Knopf.

Kiell, Norman (Ed.) (1988). *Freud Without Hindsight: Reviews of His Work (1893–1939)*. Guilford, CT: International Universities Press.

King, Pearl, & Steiner, Riccardo (Eds.) (1991). *The Freud-Klein Controversies 1941–1945*. London: Tavistock, 1992.

Kirsch, Thomas B. (2000). *The Jungians: A Comparative and Historical Perspective*. London: Routledge.

Kirschenbaum, Howard, & Henderson, Valerie Land (Eds.) (1989). *Carl Rogers: Dialogues*. Boston: Houghton Mifflin.

Klein, Dennis B. (1981). *Jewish Origins of the Psychoanalytic Movement*. New York: Praeger.

Knorr-Cetina, Karin (1981). *The Manufacture of Knowledge: An Essay on the Constructivist and Contextual Nature of Science*. Oxford: Pergamon Press. *Die Fabrikation von Erkenntnis. Zur Anthropologie der Naturwissenschaft*. Frankfurt am Main: Suhrkamp, 1984.

Koellreuter, Anna (2009). *"Wie benimmt sich der Prof. Freud eigentlich?" Ein neu entdecktes Tagebuch von 1921 historisch und analytisch kommentiert*. Gießen: Psychosozial-Verlag.

Kohon, Gregorio (Ed.) (1986). *The British School of Psychoanalysis: The Independent Tradition*. London: Free Association Books.

Kohut, Heinz (1971). *The Analysis of the Self: A Systematic Approach to the Psychoanalytic Treatment of Narcissistic Personality Disorders*. New York: International University Press.

Kormos Buchwald, Diana (Ed.) (2009). *The Collected Papers of Albert Einstein. Volume 12*. Princeton, NJ: Princeton University Press.

Kovel, Joel (1974). The castration complex reconsidered. In: Jean Strouse (Ed.), *Women & Analysis. Dialogues on Psychoanalytic Views on Femininity* (1333–1346). New York: Grossman.

Kramer, Robert (1995). The birth of client-centered therapy: Carl Rogers, Otto Rank, and "The Beyond". *Journal of Humanistic Psychology, 35*: 54–110.

Kristeva, Julia (1994). Psychoanalysts in times of distress. In: Sonu Shamdasani and Michael Münchow (Eds.), *Speculations After Freud: Psychoanalysis, Philosophy and Culture* (13–26). London: Routledge.

Krutzenbichler, H. Sebastian, & Essers, Hans (1991). *Muß denn Liebe Sünde sein? Über das Begehren des Analytikers*. Freiburg: Kore.

Kuhn, Philip (1998). "A pretty piece of treachery": The strange case of Dr. Stekel and Sigmund Freud. *International Journal of Psycho-Analysis, 81*: 705–731.

LeClair, Robert C. (Ed.) (1966). *The Letters of William James and Théodore Flournoy*. Madison, WI: University of Wisconsin Press.

Lehrman Weiner, Lynne (Ed.) (2005). *Sigmund Freud durch Lehrmans Linse*. Gießen: Psychosozial-Verlag.

Leitner, Marina (1998). *Freud, Rank und die Folgen. Ein Schlüsselkonflikt für die Psychoanalyse*. Vienna: Turia + Kant.

Leitner, Marina (2001). *Ein gut gehütetes Geheimnis. Die Geschichte der psychoanalytischen Behandlungs-Technik von den Anfängen in Wien bis zur Gründung der Berliner Poliklinik im Jahr 1920*. Gießen: Psychosozial-Verlag.

Leupold-Löwenthal, Harald (1986). *Handbuch der Psychoanalyse*. Vienna: Orac.

Lévy-Freund, Kata (1990). Dernières vacances des Freud avant la fin du monde. *Coq-Héron*, Nr. 117 (juillet): 39–44.

Lewin, Bertram, & Ross, Helen (1960). *Psychoanalytic Education in the United States*. New York: W. W. Norton.

Lieberman, E. James (1985). *Acts of Will: The Life and Work of Otto Rank*. New York: Free Press.

Little, Margaret (1951). Countertransference and the patient's response to it. *International Journal of Psycho-Analysis, 32*: 32–40.

Little, Margaret (1990). *Psychotic Anxieties and Containment: A Personal Record of an Analysis with Winnicott*. Northvale, NJ: Jason Aronson.

Lloyd Mayer, Elizabeth (2007). *Extraordinary Knowing: Science, Skepticism, and the Inexplicable Powers of the Human Mind*. New York: Bantam Books.

Lobner, Hans (1992). "Zur Genese des Fetischismus"—Ein wiederentdecter Vortrag Sigmund Freuds (1909). In: Ernst Federn and Gerhard Wittenberger (Eds.), *Aus dem Kreis um Sigmund Freud. Zu den Protokollen der Wiener Psychoanalytischen Vereinigung* (23–33). Frankfurt am Main: Fischer Taschenbuch Verlag.

Loewenberg, Peter J. (1995). The creation of a scientific community: The Burghölzli, 1902–1914. In: *Fantasy and Reality in History* (46–89). New York: Oxford University Press.

Lucado, S. P. (1994). *A Political Science: An Analysis of the Dissemination of Freudian Theory, With Reference to Morton Prince and James Jackson Putnam.* Senior Thesis, Harvard University, Department of the History of Science.

Ludwig, Ernst [Emil Cohn] (1946). *Der entzauberte Freud.* Zurich: C. Posen. *Doctor Freud. An Analysis and a Warning.* New York: Hellman, Williams & Comp., 1947. Reprint Whitefish, MT: Kessinger Publishing, 2006.

Lynn, David B. (1993). Freud's analysis of A.B., a psychotic man, 1925–1930. *Journal of the American Academy of Psychoanalysis, 21*: 63–78.

Lynn, David B. (1997). Sigmund Freud's psychoanalysis of Albert Hirst. *Bulletin of the History of Medicine, 71*: 69–93.

Mächtlinger, Veronica (1997). Karl Abraham und Giovanni Segantini. Ein psychoanalytischer Versuch. *Luzifer-Amor, Zeitschrift zur Geschichte der Psychoanalyse, 10*: 81–97.

Maciejewski, Franz (2006). Späte Sensation im Freud-Jahr. Archivfund bestätigt Affäre zwischen Sigmund Freud und Minna Bernays. *Frankfurter Rundschau*, 28 September 2006.

MacLean, George, & Rappen, Ulrich (1991). *Hermine Hug-Hellmuth.* London: Routledge.

Maddox, Brenda (2006). *Freud's Wizard: The Enigma of Ernest Jones.* London: John Murray.

Maeder, Alphonse (1913). Über das Traumproblem. *Jahrbuch für psychoanalytische und psychopathologische Forschungen, 5*: 647–686. *The Dream Problem.* Trans. Frank Mead Hallock and Smith Ely Jelliffe. New York: Nervous and Mental Disease Publishing Company, 1916.

Maeder, Alphonse (1988 [1912–1913]). Lettres à Sigmund Freud. *Le Bloc-Notes de la psychanalyse, 8*: 219–226.

Mahony, Patrick (1982). *Freud as a Writer.* New Haven, CT: Yale University Press, expanded edition 1987.

Mahony, Patrick (1984). *Cries of the Wolf Man.* New York: International Universities Press.

Mahony, Patrick (1986). *Freud and the Rat Man.* New Haven, CT: Yale University Press.

Mahony, Patrick (1993). Discussion of Ernst Falzeder, "My grand-patient, my chief tormentor". Canadian Psychoanalytic Society, Montréal, 21 October 1993.

Mahony, Patrick (2004). L'écoute analytique: coûte que coûte. 1. À l'écoute de l'autre Freud. In: Louise Grenier and Isabelle Lasvergnas (Eds.), *Penser Freud avec Patrick Mahony* (23–46). Montréal: Éditions Liber.

Makari, George (2008). *Revolution in Mind: The Creation of Psychoanalysis.* New York: HarperCollins.

Mannoni, Octave (1968). *Freud par lui-même.* Paris: Éditions du Seuil.

Marcus, Steven (1984). *Freud and the Culture of Psychoanalysis. Studies in the Transition from Victorian Humanism to Modernity.* New York: W. W. Norton, 1987.

Marinelli, Lydia, & Mayer, Andreas (2002). *Träume nach Freud. Die "Traumdeutung" und die Geschichte der psychoanalytischen Bewegung.* Vienna: Turia + Kant.

Martynkewicz, Wolfgang (2007). Die dunklen Seiten eines Dandys. Der Schriftsteller Oscar A. H. Schmitz in der Analyse bei Karl Abraham. *Jahrbuch der Psychoanalyse, 55*: 113–142.

Masson, Jeffrey M. (1984). *The Assault on Truth: Freud's Suppression of the Seduction Theory.* New York: Penguin, 1985.

May, Ulrike (1997). Die Entdeckung der "bösen Mutter". Ein Beitrag Abrahams zur Theorie der Depression. *Luzifer-Amor, Zeitschrift zur Geschichte der Psychoanalyse, 10*: 98–131.

May, Ulrike (1998). "Obsessional neurosis": A nosographic innovation by Freud. *History of Psychiatry, 9*: 335–353.

May, Ulrike (1999). Ein Zeitungsartikel des jungen Karl Abraham (1902). *Luzifer-Amor, Zeitschrift zur Geschichte der Psychoanalyse, 12*: 154–157.

May, Ulrike (2001). Abraham's discovery of the "bad mother". A contribution to the history of the theory of depression. *International Journal of Psychoanalysis, 82*: 283–305.

May, Ulrike (2006). Freuds Patientenkalender: Siebzehn Analytiker in Analyse bei Freud (1910–1920). *Luzifer-Amor, Zeitschrift zur Geschichte der Psychoanalyse, 19*: 43–97. Freud's patient calendars: 17 analysts in analysis with Freud (1910–1920). *Psychoanalysis and History,* 2007, *9*: 153–200.

May, Ulrike (2007a). Neunzehn Patienten in Analyse bei Freud (1910–1920). Teil I. Zur Dauer von Freuds Analysen; Teil II. Zur Frequenz von Freuds Analysen und weitere Beobachtungen. *Psyche, Zeitschrift für Psychoanalyse und ihre Anwendungen, 61*: 590–625, 686–709. Nineteen patients in analysis with Freud (1910–1920). *American Imago,* 2008, *65*: 41–106.

May, Ulrike (2007b). Über Johannes Cremerius' Einleitung zu den Gesammelten Werken von Karl Abraham. *Luzifer-Amor, Zeitschrift zur Geschichte der Psychoanalyse, 20*: 145–152.

Maylan, Charles E. (1929). *Freuds tragischer Komplex—eine Analyse der Psychoanalyse.* Munich: Ernst Reinhardt.

McGuire, William (1982). *Bollingen: An Adventure in Collecting the Past.* Princeton, NJ: Princeton University Press.

McGuire, William, & Hull, R. F. C. (Eds.) (1977). *C. G. Jung Speaking. Interviews and Encounters.* Princeton, NJ: Princeton University Press.

Meisel, Perry, & Kendrick, Walter (Eds.) (1985). *Bloomsbury/Freud. The Letters of James and Alix Strachey, 1924–1925*. New York: Basic Books.

Menaker, Esther (1982). *Otto Rank: A Rediscovered Legacy*. New York: Columbia University Press.

Meng, Heinrich (1926). Concerning sleep and its disorders in the healthy and the sick and in those poisened with drugs. Trans. Sweasy Powers. *Homoeopathic Recorder, 41*: 97–108.

Mertens, Wolfgang (1981). *Psychoanalyse*. Stuttgart: W. Kohlhammer.

Mertens, Wolfgang (1990a). *Einführung in die psychoanalytische Therapie. Band 1*. Stuttgart: W. Kohlhammer.

Mertens, Wolfgang (1990b). *Einführung in die psychoanalytische Therapie. Band 2*. Stuttgart: W. Kohlhammer.

Mertens, Wolfgang (1991). *Einführung in die psychoanalytische Therapie. Band 3*. Stuttgart: W. Kohlhammer.

Meyer-Palmedo, Ingeborg, & Fichtner, Gerhard (1999). *Freud-Bibliographie mit Werkkonkordanz*. Second improved and enlarged edition. Frankfurt am Main: S. Fischer.

Michaelis, Edgar (1925). *Die Menschheitsproblematik der Freudschen Psychoanalyse—Urbild und Maske*. Leipzig: J. A. Barth.

Mill, John Stuart (1843). *A System of Logic*. In: *Collected Works*, VII, VIII. Toronto: University of Toronto Press, 1973.

Molnar, Michael (2004a). Am historischen Eckfenster, 17.6.1897. *Luzifer-Amor, Zeitschrift zur Geschichte der Psychoanalyse, 17*(33): 104–114.

Molnar, Michael (2004b). Freud & Co. *Luzifer-Amor, Zeitschrift zur Geschichte der Psychoanalyse, 17*(34): 118–131.

Molnar, Michael (2005a). Alien Enemy: Porträt eines Mädchens. *Luzifer-Amor, Zeitschrift zur Geschichte der Psychoanalyse, 18*(35): 152–167.

Molnar, Michael (2005b). "… das Kind soll wissen …" *Luzifer-Amor, Zeitschrift zur Geschichte der Psychoanalyse, 18*(36): 135–148.

Molnar, Michael (2006a). "… jener nach innen gekehrte nachdenkliche Blick …" *Luzifer-Amor, Zeitschrift zur Geschichte der Psychoanalyse, 19*(37): 14–29.

Molnar, Michael (2006b). Trottoir roulant, 1900. *Luzifer-Amor, Zeitschrift zur Geschichte der Psychoanalyse, 19*(38): 32–45.

Monatsschrift für Psychiatrie und Neurologie (1907). *22*: 565.

Mühlleitner, Elke (1992). *Biographisches Lexikon der Psychoanalyse. Die Mitglieder der Psychologischen Mittwoch-Gesellschaft und der Wiener Psychoanalytischen Vereinigung 1902–1938*. Unter Mitarbeit von Johannes Reichmayr. Tübingen: edition diskord.

Mühlleitner, Elke (2001). Psychoanalysis, History of. In: Neil J. Smelser and Paul B. Baltes (Eds.), *International Encyclopedia of the Social and Behavioral Sciences* (12315–12319). Oxford: Elsevier Science.

Müller, Christian (1998). *Wer hat die Geisteskranken von den Ketten befreit?* Bonn: Psychiatrie-Verlag.

Müller-Seidel, Walter (1997). *Alfred Erich Hoche. Lebensgeschichte im Spannungsfeld von Psychiatrie, Strafrecht und Literatur.* Tübingen: Niemeyer.

Neurologisches Centralblatt (1910). *29*: 659–662.

Nin, Anaïs (1996). *The Diary of Anaïs Nin, 1931–1934.* Ed. Gunther Stuhlman. New York: Summit Books.

Noble, Douglas, & Burnham, Donald (1969). *History of The Washington Psychoanalytic Society and The Washington Psychoanalytic Institute.* Washington, DC: privately printed.

Noll, Richard (1994). *The Jung Cult: Origins of a Charismatic Movement.* New York: Free Press, second ed. 1997.

Oberndorf, Clarence (1953). *A History of Psychoanalysis in America.* New York: Grune & Stratton.

Obholzer, Karin (1980). *Gespräche mit dem Wolfsmann. Eine Psychoanalyse und die Folgen.* Reinbek bei Hamburg: Rowohlt. *The Wolf-Man: Conversations with Freud's Patient Sixty Years Later.* New York: Continuum, 1982.

Oppenheim, Hermann (1894). *Lehrbuch der Nervenkrankheiten für Ärzte und Studierende.* Berlin: S. Karger.

Orgler, Herta (1939). *Alfred Adler, the Man and His Work. Triumph Over the Inferiority Complex.* London: C. W. Daniel.

Ornston, Darius G. (Ed.) (1992). *Translating Freud.* New Haven, CT: Yale University Press.

Pappenheim, Else (2004). *Hölderlin, Feuchtersleben, Freud: Beiträge zur Geschichte der Psychoanalyse, der Psychiatrie und der Neurologie.* Ed. Bernhard Handlbauer. Graz: Nausner & Nausner.

Peters, Uwe H. (1977). *Übertragung—Gegenübertragung.* Munich: Kindler.

Pfennig, Richard (1906). *Wilhelm Fliess und seine Nachentdecker, O. Weininger und H. Swoboda.* Berlin: Emil Goldschmidt.

Phillips, Adam (1988). *Winnicott.* London: Fontana.

Pines, Dinora (1987). Karl Abraham: Aspects of the man and his life. In: *Conférences—débats: "Ici la vie continue d'une manière fort surprenante …" Contributions à l'histoire de la psychanalyse en Allemagne* (128–141). Paris: Goethe Institut.

Pohlen, Manfred (2006). *Freuds Analyse. Die Sitzungsprotokolle Ernst Blums.* Reinbek bei Hamburg: Rowohlt.

Pols, Hans (1995). Frankwood E. Williams: Psychiatrist, mental hygienist, fellow-traveler. Paper presented at the History of Psychiatry group at the New York Hospital-Cornell Medical Center, 27 September 1995. Unpublished manuscript.

Pomer, Sydney L. (1966). Max Eitingon, 1881–1943. The organisation of psychoanalytic training. In: Franz Alexander, Samuel Eisenstein and Martin Grotjahn (Eds.), *Psychoanalytic Pioneers* (51–62). New York: Basic Books.

Powers, W. J. Sweasy (1912). Four interesting cases of emotional dream-state from the psychiatrical wards of the Royal Charité Hospital in Berlin. *Journal of Nervous and Mental Disease, 39*: 375–388.

Powers, W. J. Sweasy (1913). Ein Fall von Angioma cavernosum des Gehirns. *Zeitschrift für die gesamte Neurologie und Psychiatrie, 16*: 487–496.

Powers, W. J. Sweasy (1931). Letter published in *Homoeopathic Recorder, 48*: 921.

Protokolle des Psychoanalytischen Vereins (Verein für analytische Psychologie) (1913–1916). I: January 1913–December 1916. Copy in Archives Sonu Shamdasani.

Puner, Helen Walker (1947). *Freud: His Life and His Mind*. New York: Howell, Sosin. Reprint New Brunswick, NJ: Transaction Publishers, 1992.

Putnam, James Jackson (1913). Remarks on a case with Griselda phantasies. In: *Addresses on Psycho-Analysis* (175–193). London: Hogarth Press.

Putnam, James Jackson (1914). On some of the broader issues of the psycho-analytic movement. In: *Addresses on Psycho-Analysis* (194–222). London: Hogarth Press.

Quen, Jacques M. & Carlson, Eric T. (Eds.) (1978). *American Psychoanalysis: Origins and Development*. New York: Brunner & Mazel.

Quinn, Susan (1987). *A Mind of Her Own: The Life of Karen Horney*. New York: Summit Books.

Radó, Sándor (1926). Gedenkrede über Karl Abraham. *Internationale Zeitschrift für Psychoanalyse, 12*: 203–208.

Rank, Otto (1924). *Das Trauma der Geburt und seine Bedeutung für die Psycho-analyse*. Leipzig: Internationaler Psychoanalytischer Verlag. *The Trauma of Birth*. New York: Brunner, 1952.

Rattner, Josef (1972). *Alfred Adler*. Hamburg, Rowohlt.

Rattner, Josef (1990). *Klassiker der Tiefenpsychologie*. Munich: Psychologie Verlags-Union.

Reich, Wilhelm (1952). *Von der Psychoanalyse zur Orgonomie. Das Interview über Sigmund Freud im Auftrag des Freud-Archivs 1952*. Berlin: Edition Freiheit und Glück, second edition 1984. *Reich Speaks of Freud. Wilhelm Reich Discusses His Work and His Relationship with Sigmund Freud*. Eds. Mary Higgins and Chester M. Raphael. New York: Farrar, Straus & Giroux, 1967.

Reich, Wilhelm (1988). *Passion of Youth: An Autobiography, 1897–1922*. New York: Farrar, Straus & Giroux.

Reik, Theodor (1956). *The Search Within—The Inner Experience of a Psychoanalyst*. New York: Grove.

Richards, Angela (1969). Erläuterungen zur Edition. In: Sigmund Freud, *Studienausgabe, Band 1* (26–31). Frankfurt am Main: S. Fischer.

Richebächer, Sabine (2005). *Sabina Spielrein—"Eine fast grausame Liebe zur Wissenschaft"*. Zurich: Dörlemann.

Rickman, John (1951). Number and the human sciences. In: George B. Wilbur and Warner Muensterberger (Eds.), *Psychoanalysis and Culture* (150–155). New York: International Universities Press.

Ries, Paul (1995). Popularise and/or be damned: Psychoanalysis and film at the crossroads in 1925. *International Journal of Psycho-Analysis, 76*: 759–791.

Ries, Paul (1997). Geheimnisse einer Seele: Wessen Film und wessen Psychoanalyse? *Jahrbuch der Psychoanalyse, 39*: 46–80.

Riklin, Franz (1912). Ödipus und die Psychoanalyse. *Wissen und Leben, 6*: 26–46.

Roazen, Paul (1968). *Freud: Political and Social Thought*. New York: Alfred A. Knopf.

Roazen, Paul (1969). *Brother Animal: The Story of Freud and Tausk*. New Brunswick, NJ: Transaction Books, 1990.

Roazen, Paul (1971). *Freud and His Followers*. New York: Alfred A. Knopf. Reprint New York: Da Capo Press, 1992.

Roazen, Paul (1992). Freud's patients. First-person accounts. In: Toby Gelfand and John Kerr (Eds.), *Freud and the History of Psychoanalysis* (289–306). Hillsdale, NJ: The Analytic Press.

Roazen, Paul (1993). *Meeting Freud's Family*. Amherst, MA: University of Massachusetts Press.

Roazen, Paul (1995). *How Freud Worked: First-Hand Accounts of Patients*. Northvale, NJ: Jason Aronson.

Roazen, Paul (2005). *Edoardo Weiss: The House that Freud Built*. New Brunswick, NJ: Transaction Publishers.

Roazen, Paul, & Swerdloff, Bluma (Eds.) (1995). *Heresy: Sándor Radó and the Psychoanalytic Movement*. Northvale, NJ: Jason Aronson.

Robert, Marthe (1964). *La Révolution Psychanalytique. La Vie et l'Oeuvre de Sigmund Freud*. Two volumes. Paris: Payot. *The Psychoanalytic Revolution: Sigmund Freud's Life and Achievement*. Trans. Kenneth Morgan. New York: Harcourt Brace and World, 1966.

Rodrigué, Emilio (1996). *Sigmund Freud. El siglo del psicoanálisis*. Buenos Aires: Editorial Sudamericana. *Freud. Le siècle de la psychanalyse*. Two volumes. Paris: Payot & Rivages, 2000.

Roelcke, Volker (1999). *Krankheit und Kulturkritik: Psychiatrische Gesellschaftsdeutungen im bürgerlichen Zeitalter (1790–1914)*. Frankfurt am Main: Campus.

Roelcke, Volker (2005). Continuities or ruptures? Concepts, institutions and contexts of twentieth-century German psychiatry and mental health care. In: Marijke Gijswijt-Hofstra, Harry Oosterhuis and Joost Vijselaa (Eds.), *Psychiatric Cultures Compared: Psychiatry and Mental Health Care in the Twentieth Century, Comparisons and Approaches* (162–168). Amsterdam: Amsterdam University Press.

Rohrwasser, Michael (2006). *Freuds Lektüren. Von Arthur Conan Doyle bis Arthur Schnitzler.* Gießen: Psychosozial-Verlag.

Romm, May E. (1966). Abraham Arden Brill, 1874–1948. In: Franz Alexander, Samuel Eisenstein and Martin Grotjahn (Eds.), *Psychoanalytic Pioneers* (210–223). New York: Basic Books.

Romm, Sharon (1983). *The Unwelcome Intruder: Freud's Struggle with Cancer.* New York: Praeger.

Rosenzweig, Saul (1992). *Freud, Jung, and Hall the King-Maker: The Historic Expedition to America (1909), with G. Stanley Hall as Host and William James as Guest.* Seattle: Hogrefe and Huber.

Rothstein, Edward (2010). Condoms, unrolled and unabashed. *The New York Times*, 4 February 2010.

Roudinesco, Elisabeth (1982). *La bataille de cent ans. Histoire de la psychanalyse en France. Volume 1, 1885–1939.* Paris: Seuil.

Roudinesco, Elisabeth (1986). *La bataille de cent ans. Histoire de la Psychanalyse en France. Volume 2, 1925–1985.* Paris: Seuil.

Roudinesco, Elisabeth (1993). *Jacques Lacan: Esquisse d'une vie, histoire d'un système de pensée.* Paris: Librairie Arthème Fayard. *Jacques Lacan: Bericht über ein Leben, Geschichte eines Denksystems.* Köln: Kiepenheuer & Witsch, 1996.

Roustang, François (1976). *Un destin si funeste.* Paris: Éditions de Minuit. *Dire Mastery, Discipleship from Freud to Lacan.* Washington, DC: American Psychiatric Press, 1986.

Rudnytsky, Peter (1991). *The Psychoanalytic Vocation: Rank, Winnicott, and the Legacy of Freud.* New Haven, CT: Yale University Press.

Ruitenbeek, Hendrik M. (Ed.) (1973). *Freud As We Knew Him.* Detroit, MI: Wayne State University Press.

Sachs, Hanns (1944). *Freud: Master and Friend.* Cambridge, MA: Harvard University Press.

Sadger, Isidor (2005). *Recollecting Freud.* Ed. Alan Dundes. Madison, WI: University of Wisconsin Press. *Persönliche Erinnerungen an Sigmund Freud.* Eds. Andrea Huppke and Michael Schröter. Tübingen: edition diskord, 2006.

Scharnberg, Max (1993). *The Non-Authentic Nature of Freud's Observations. Vol. 2. Felix Gattel's Early Freudian Cases, and the Astrological Origin of the*

Anal Theory. Uppsala: Acta Universitatis Upsaliensis (distributed by Almqvist & Wiksell, Stockholm).

Schepeler, Eva M. (1993). Jean Piaget's experiences on the couch: Some clues to a mystery. *International Journal of Psycho-Analysis, 74*: 255–273.

Scherbaum, Norbert (1992). Psychiatrie und Psychoanalyse—Eugen Bleulers "Dementia praecox oder Gruppe der Schizophrenien" (1911). *Fortschritte der Neurologie und Psychiatrie, 60*: 289–316.

Schimmelpenning, Gustav W. (1998). Alfred Erich Hoche (1865–1943). In: Hans Schliack and Hanns Hippius (Eds.), *Nervenärzte. Biographien* (21–29). Stuttgart: Thieme.

Schindler, Thomas-Peter (1990). *Psychiatrie im Wilhelminischen Deutschland im Spiegel der Verhandlungen des "Vereins der deutschen Irrenärzte" (ab 1903: "Deutscher Verein für Psychiatrie") von 1891–1914.* Doctoral Thesis, Freie Universität Berlin.

Schmidt, Erika S. (2008). Franz Alexander und die Berliner Tradition in Chicago. *Jahrbuch der Psychoanalyse, 57*: 95–116.

Schmitz, Oscar A. H. (2006). *Das wilde Leben der Boheme. Tagebücher Band 1, 1896–1906.* Ed. Wolfgang Martynkewicz. Berlin: Aufbau-Verlag.

Schmitz, Oscar A. H. (2007a). *Ein Dandy auf Reisen. Tagebücher Band 2, 1907–1912.* Ed. Wolfgang Martynkewicz. Berlin: Aufbau-Verlag.

Schmitz, Oscar A. H. (2007b). *Durch das Land der Dämonen. Tagebücher Band 3, 1912–1918.* Ed. Wolfgang Martynkewicz. Berlin: Aufbau-Verlag.

Schröter, Michael (1995a). Sollen Patientennamen in den Korrespondenzen Freuds verschlüsselt werden? Zehn Thesen zur Diskussion. *Psyche, Zeitschrift für Psychoanalyse und ihre Anwendungen, 49*: 805–809.

Schröter, Michael (1995b). Freuds Komitee 1912–1914. Ein Beitrag zum Verständnis psychoanalytischer Gruppenbildung. *Psyche, Zeitschrift für Psychoanalyse und ihre Anwendungen, 49*: 513–563.

Schröter, Michael (1996). Zur Frühgeschichte der Laienanalyse. Strukturen eines Kernkonflikts der Freud-Schule. *Psyche, Zeitschrift für Psychoanalyse und ihre Anwendungen, 50*: 1127–1175.

Schröter, Michael (2006). Briefe. In: Hans-Martin Lohmann und Joachim Pfeiffer (Eds.), *Freud-Handbuch, Leben—Werk—Wirkung* (220–231). Stuttgart: Metzler.

Schröter, Michael (2007). Volle Kraft voraus: Der 7. Internationale Psychoanalytische Kongreß in Berlin (25.-27. September 1922). *Psyche, Zeitschrift für Psychoanalyse und ihre Anwendungen, 61*: 412–437.

Schröter, Michael, & Hermanns, Ludger M. (1992a). Felix Gattel (1879–1904): Freud's first pupil. Part I. *International Review of Psycho-Analysis, 19*: 91–104.

Schröter, Michael, & Hermanns, Ludger H. (1992b). Felix Gattel (1879–1904): Freud's first pupil. Part II. *International Review of Psycho-Analysis, 19*: 197–208.

Schultz, Johannes Heinrich (1964). *Lebensbilderbuch eines Nervenarztes. Jahrzehnte in Dankbarkeit.* Stuttgart: Georg Thieme.

Schur, Max (1972). *Sigmund Freud: Living and Dying.* New York: International Universities Press.

Schwartz, Lester (1970). Book review: "Reich Speaks of Freud". *Psychoanalytic Quarterly, 39*: 316–317.

Seelmann, Kurt (1977). Adlers Lebenslauf—bis zu seiner Trennung von Freud. In: Dieter Eicke (Ed.), *Tiefenpsychologie. Band 4: Individualpsychologie und Analytische Psychologie* (6–18). Weinheim: Beltz, 1982.

Shamdasani, Sonu (1990). A woman called Frank. *Spring: A Journal of Archetype and Culture, 50*: 26–56.

Shamdasani, Sonu (1997). "Should this remain?" Anna Freud's misgivings concerning the Freud-Jung letters. In: Patrick Mahony, Carlo Bonomi and Jan Stensson (Eds.), *Behind the Scenes, Freud in Correspondence* (357–367). Stockholm: Scandinavian University Press.

Shamdasani, Sonu (1998). *Cult Fictions: C. G. Jung and the Founding of Analytical Psychology.* London: Routledge.

Shamdasani, Sonu (2000). Unpublished notes to a presentation given in San Francisco.

Shamdasani, Sonu (2003). *Jung and the Making of Modern Psychology: The Dream of a Science.* Cambridge: Cambridge University Press.

Shengold, Leonard (1972). A parapraxis of Freud's in relation to Karl Abraham. *American Imago, 29*: 123–159.

Shengold, Leonard (1993). Freud, Fließ und Abraham. *Jahrbuch der Psychoanalyse, 33*: 9–48.

Sierek, Karl, & Eppensteiner, Barbara (Eds.) (2000). *Siegfried Bernfeld. Psychoanalyse—Filmtheorie: der Analytiker im Kino.* Frankfurt am Main: Stroemfeld & Nexus.

Sigmund Freud. Stationen eines Lebens (2001). Katalog zur Ausstellung im Sigmund-Freud-Zentrum des Fachkrankenhauses Uchtspringe. Uchtspringe: Eigenverlag.

Sigusch, Volkmar (2008). *Geschichte der Sexualwissenschaft.* Frankfurt am Main: Campus.

Silver, Ann-Louise S. (1993). Countertransference, Ferenczi, and Washington, DC. *Journal of The American Academy of Psychoanalysis, 21*: 637–654.

Silver, Ann-Louise S. (1995). Introduction to Fromm-Reichmann's "Female Psychosexuality" and "Jewish Food Rituals". *Journal of The American Academy of Psychoanalysis, 23*: 1–6.

Sonnenstuhl, Burckhardt (Ed.) (2006). *Prominente in Berlin-Grunewald und ihre Geschichten*. Berlin-Brandenburg: berlin edition im be-bra Verlag.

Sperber, Manès (1926). *Alfred Adler—der Mensch und seine Lehre. Ein Essay*. Munich: Bergmann.

Sperber, Manès (1970). *Alfred Adler oder Das Elend der Psychologie*. Vienna: Molden.

Spillmann Brigitte, & Strubel, Robert (2010). *C. G. Jung—zerrissen zwischen Mythos und Wirklichkeit. Über die Folgen persönlicher und kollektiver Spaltungen im tiefenpsychologischen Erbe*. Gießen: Psychosozial-Verlag.

Spitteler, Carl (1906). *Imago*. Frankfurt am Main: Suhrkamp, 1979.

Stekel, Wilhelm (1950). *The Autobiography of Wilhelm Stekel: The Life of a Pioneer Psychoanalyst*. Ed. Emil A. Gutheil. New York: Liveright.

Stepansky, Paul E. (1983). *In Freud's Shadow: Adler in Context*. Hillsdale, NJ: International Universities Press.

Stepansky, Paul E. (Ed.) (1988). *The Memoirs of Margaret S. Mahler*. New York: Free Press.

Sterba, Richard (1982). *Reminiscences of a Viennese Psychoanalyst*. Detroit, MI: Wayne State University Press.

Stern, Arthur (1968). *In bewegter Zeit. Erinnerungen und Gedanken eines jüdischen Nervenarztes, Berlin-Jerusalem*. Jerusalem: R. Mass.

Stern, William (1901). Sigmund Freud, "Die Traumdeutung". *Zeitschrift für Psychologie und Physiologie der Sinnesorgane, 25*: 130–133. English translation in Kiell (1988), 142–145.

Stone, Alan (1997). Where will psychoanalysis survive? *Harvard Magazine*, January–February: 35–39.

Stone, Irving (1971). *The Passions of the Mind*. New York: Doubleday.

Sulloway, Frank (1979). *Freud, Biologist of the Mind: Beyond the Psychoanalytic Legend*. New York: Basic Books.

Sulloway, Frank (1994). Freud recycleur: cryptobiologie et pseudoscience. In: Catherine Meyer (Ed.), *Le livre noir de la psychanalyse. Vivre, penser et aller mieux sans Freud* (49–65). Paris: Éditions des Arènes, 2005.

Swales, Peter J. (1982). Freud, Minna Bernays, and the conquest of Rome. New light on the origins of psychoanalysis. *The New American Review, 1*: 1–23.

Swales, Peter J. (1989). Freud, cocaine, and sexual chemistry: the role of cocaine in Freud's conception of the libido. In: Laurence Spurling (Ed.), *Sigmund Freud: Critical Assessments, Volume 1* (273–301). London: Routledge.

Swales, Peter J. (1992). What Jung didn't say. *Harvest—Journal for Jungian Studies, 38*: 30–43.

Swales, Peter J. (1993). Freud, the man, a century later. Did he always carry an umbrella? Unpublished paper given at the congress "100 Years of Psychoanalysis", Geneva, Switzerland.

Swales, Peter J. (1998). In statu nascendi: Freud, Minna Bernays, and the creation of Herr Aliquis. Unpublished paper.

Swales, Peter J. (2000). Freud, death, and sexual pleasure. On the psychical mechanism of Dr. Sigm. Freud. Unpublished paper.

Taft, Jessie (1958). *Otto Rank*. New York: The Julian Press.

Thompson, Clara (1944). Ferenczi's contribution to psychoanalysis. *Psychiatry, 7*: 245–252.

Thompson, Clara (1956). The rôle of the analyst's personality in therapy. *American Journal of Psychotherapy, 10*: 347–359.

Tichy, Marina, & Zwettler-Otte, Sylvia (1999). *Freud in der Presse. Rezeption Sigmund Freuds und der Psychoanalyse in Österreich 1895–1938*. Vienna: Sonderzahl.

Tögel, Christfried (2006). Sigmund Freuds Praxis. Visiten und Ordination—Psychoanalysen—Einnahmen. *Psyche, Zeitschrift für Psychoanalyse und ihre Anwendungen, 60*: 860–880.

Tögel, Christfried, & Schröter, Michael (2002). Sigmund Freud und Hermann Swoboda: Unveröffentlichter Briefwechsel. *Psyche, Zeitschrift für Psychoanalyse und ihre Anwendungen, 56*: 313–337.

Tögel, Christfried, & Schröter, Michael (2004a). Sigmund Freud: Briefe an Maria (Mitzi) Freud und ihre Familie. *Luzifer-Amor, Zeitschrift zur Geschichte der Psychoanalyse, 17*: 51–72.

Tögel, Christfried, & Schröter, Michael (2004b). Jacob Freud mit Familie in Leipzig (1859). Erzählung und Dokumente. *Luzifer-Amor, Zeitschrift zur Geschichte der Psychoanalyse, 17*: 8–32.

van Wayenburg, Gerard Anton Marie (1908). *Compte rendu des travaux du 1er Congrès International de Psychiatrie, de Neurologie, de Psychologie et de l'Assistance des Aliénés, tenu à Amsterdam du 2 à 7 Septembre 1907*. Amsterdam: J. H. de Bussy.

Vasile, Russell (1977). *James Jackson Putnam, from Neurology to Psychoanalysis. A Study of the Reception and Promulgation of Freudian Psychoanalytic Theory in America, 1895–1918*. Oceanside, NY: Dabor Science Publications.

Vermorel, Henri, & Vermorel, Madeleine (1993). *Sigmund Freud et Romain Rolland. Correspondance 1923–1936*. Paris: Presses Universitaires de France.

Wallerstein, Robert S. (1988). One psychoanalysis or many? *International Journal of Psycho-Analysis, 69*: 5–21.

Warner, Silas (1994). Freud's analysis of Horace Frink, M.D.: A previously unexplained therapeutic disaster. *Journal of the American Academy of Psychoanalysis, 22*: 137–152.

Webster, Richard (1995). *Why Freud Was Wrong: Sin, Science, and Psychoanalysis*. New York: Basic Books.

Wieser, Annatina (2001). *Zur frühen Psychoanalyse in Zurich 1900–1914*. Doctoral Thesis, University of Zurich. Online at www.luzifer-amor.de/index.php?id=287

Will, Herbert (1984). *Georg Groddeck. Die Geburt der Psychosomatik*. Munich: Deutscher Taschenbuch Verlag.

Wilmers, Mary-Kay (2009). *The Eitingons: A Twentieth-Century Story*. London: Faber and Faber.

Winnicott, Donald W. (1949). Hate in the countertransference. *International Journal of Psycho-Analysis, 30*: 69–74.

Winterstein, Alfred (1924). Sigmund Freud. *Neue Freie Presse*, 8 February 1924.

Wittels, Fritz (1924). *Sigmund Freud: His Personality, His Teaching, and His School*. London: Allen & Unwin.

Wittenberger, Gerhard (1995). *Das "Geheime Komitee" Sigmund Freuds. Institutionalisierungsprozesse in der "Psychoanalytischen Bewegung" zwischen 1912 und 1927*. Tübingen: edition diskord.

Wollheim, Richard (1971). *Freud*. London: Fontana.

Wortis, Joseph (1954). *Fragments of an Analysis with Freud*. New York: Simon and Schuster. Reprint Northvale, NJ: Jason Aronson, 1994.

Young-Bruehl, Elisabeth (1988). *Anna Freud: A Biography*. New York: Summit Books.

Young-Bruehl, Elisabeth (1994). A history of Freud biographies. In: Mark S. Micale and Roy Porter (Eds.), *Discovering the History of Psychiatry* (157–173). Oxford: Oxford University Press.

Zienert-Eilts, Karin (2013). *Karl Abraham. Eine Biografie im Kontext der psychoanalytischen Bewegung*. Gießen: Psychosozial-Verlag.

Zitrin, Arthur (1998). Freud-Frink-Brill: A puzzling episode in the history of psychoanalysis. *Bulletin of the Association for Psychoanalytic Medicine of the Columbia University Psychoanalytic Center*: 1–19.

Zulliger, Hans (1966). Oskar Pfister, 1873–1956. Psychoanalysis and faith. In: Franz Alexander, Samuel Eisenstein and Martin Grotjahn (Eds.), *Psychoanalytic Pioneers* (169–179). New York: Basic Books.

Zweig, Stefan (1931). *Die Heilung durch den Geist. Mesmer—Mary Baker-Eddy—Freud*. Leipzig: Insel Verlag.

Zweig, Stefan (1987). *Briefwechsel mit Hermann Bahr, Sigmund Freud, Rainer Maria Rilke und Arthur Schnitzler*. Jeffrey B. Berlin, Hans-Ulrich Lindken and Donald A. Prater (Eds.). Frankfurt am Main: Fischer Taschenbuch Verlag.

INDEX

Note: In the case of persons whose names are so often mentioned that an exact indexing would have rendered the information meaningless, a choice of particularly relevant passages has been made. Italicised page numbers refer to whole chapters that deal with a particular person. Not included are bibliographical references, and the series editor's foreword.